T0398892

Advance Praise for *Memory and Narrative Ethics*

"In this timely, deeply felt and powerfully insightful book, Jakob Lothe delves into the ethical obligations of memory and examines the Holocaust's legacy through testimony, narrative fiction, and film. Like Lothe's earlier work, which recorded the narratives of Norwegian Holocaust survivors, the impact on the reader will be lasting."
—**Roger Frie,** author of *Not in My Family: German Memory and Responsibility after the Holocaust*

"This is a thoroughly researched, thoughtfully composed, and elegantly formulated book synthesizing many years of studies on the nexus of narrative, film, and memory. It sheds new light on the fundamental ethical issues that permeate the fabric of remembering, narrative hermeneutics, and history—especially the history of Nazi terror in Europe."
—**Jens Brockmeier,** author of *Beyond the Archive: Memory, Narrative, and the Autobiographical Process*

"Bringing together personal testimony, literature and film, Lothe applies his expertise as a narrative scholar to demonstrate the profound sense in which memory and narrative ethics are 'inescapably intertwined' as he leads us on an interpretive journey, as listeners, readers, and viewers. A morally compelling book, in which the reader directly experiences the 'challenge and pain of bearing witness.'"
—**Molly Andrews,** author of *Narrative Imagination and Everyday Life*

Explorations in Narrative Psychology

Mark Freeman
Series Editor

Books in the Series

Memory and Narrative Ethics

Holocaust Testimony, Fiction, and Film

JAKOB LOTHE

OXFORD
UNIVERSITY PRESS

Oxford University Press is a department of the University of Oxford.
It furthers the University's objective of excellence in research, scholarship,
and education by publishing worldwide. Oxford is a registered trade mark of
Oxford University Press in the UK and in certain other countries.

Published in the United States of America by Oxford University Press
198 Madison Avenue, New York, NY 10016, United States of America.

CIP data is on file at the Library of Congress

ISBN 9780197579503

DOI: 10.1093/9780197579534.001.0001

Printed by Integrated Books International, United States of America

For James Phelan

Contents

List of Figures

Acknowledgments

Work on this book began around 2012. It is linked to, and inspired by, three of my other books: *After Testimony: The Ethics and Aesthetics of Holocaust Narrative for the Future* (co-edited with Susan Rubin Suleiman and James Phelan, 2012), *Narrative Ethics* (co-edited with Jeremy Hawthorn, 2013), and *Time's Witnesses: Women's Voices from the Holocaust* (edited, 2017 [first published in Norwegian in 2013]). The origin of all three volumes was the research project "Narrative Theory and Analysis" that I ran at the Centre for Advanced Study (CAS) in Oslo in 2005–2006. I am indebted to the participants in that project: Susan Rubin Suleiman, James Phelan, Jeremy Hawthorn, the late J. Hillis Miller, Beatrice Sandberg, Daphna Erdinast-Vulcan, Anniken Greve, Anette H. Storeide, and Anne Thelle. I am also grateful to the director of CAS, Willy Østreng, for his inspirational leadership and genuine interest in the project.

Memory and Narrative Ethics also draws on *Etikk i litteratur og film* (Ethics in Literature and Film) (Oslo: Pax, 2016). I would like to thank the publisher, Pax, for supporting this book project, and Heidi Norland and Astrid de Vibe for their encouragement and suggestions.

As indicated above, the book has taken many years to mature. Over the course of these years, I have been privileged to have had the support of and to have been encouraged by scholars in Norway and other countries, including the members of the research group at CAS. I am most grateful to the extremely generous colleagues who read earlier text versions, providing helpful comments and making constructive criticisms: Hanna Meretoja, Jeremy Hawthorn, Leona Toker, Jens Brockmeier, Colin Davis, James Phelan, Arne Johan Vetlesen, Asbjørn Grønstad, Jan Arthur Christophersen, Stine Holte, and Désirée Shyns.

I have also incurred a debt of gratitude to friends and colleagues whose interest in my work and comments on aspects of the book I much appreciate: Helga Arntzen, Mieke Bal, Clare Cain, Audun Engelstad, Irene Engelstad, Lykke Harmony Alara Guanio-Uluru, Anne Marie Hagen, Jan-Olav Henriksen, Thor Holt, Benedikt Jäger, Lene Johannessen, Magnar Kartveit, Randi

Koppen, Irene Levin, Kari Marstein, Randi Cathinka Neverdal, Geir Røsset, Svein Olaf Thorbjørnsen, Øyvind Toft, Geir Ulfsløkk, Janet Walker, and Kathrine Asla Østby.

I am most grateful to Terence Cave and Stuart Sillars: their perceptive observations on the book proposal influenced my approach and prompted me to change the book's structure. So too did the criticisms and suggestions made by the anonymous readers for Oxford University Press. I thank Mark Freeman, the series editor of Explorations in Narrative Psychology, in which the book appears, and Hayley Singer of Oxford University Press, for their interest in the book and their wise advice.

I am indebted to the staffs and facilities of the University of Oslo Library and the Bodleian Library, Oxford. I would like to thank Paul Fiddes for inviting me to Regent's Park College, University of Oxford, where I made progress on the book in 2017–2018. I also thank the Norwegian Non-fiction and Translators Association (NFFO) for a travel grant that made it possible for me to work on the chapters on W. G. Sebald and Jenny Erpenbeck in Berlin in the fall of 2022.

The book could not have been written without the encouragement of my wife, Elin Toft. I am extremely grateful to Elin for her invaluable support.

I dedicate this book to James Phelan. Jim was a member of the research project at CAS, and he played a key role in placing the three books in which the project resulted with The Ohio State University Press: *Joseph Conrad* (2008), *Franz Kafka* (2011), and *After Testimony* (2012). My debts to Jim are both personal and intellectual in nature; moreover, Jim has made, and continues to make, an extraordinary contribution to the study of narrative in many countries around the world.

Some of the ideas and points presented in this book first appeared in earlier publications. Although all this material has been considerably revised and elaborated, I am grateful to the publishers for permission to reprint parts of and develop ideas from the following articles and book chapters:

"The title of W. G. Sebald's novel *Austerlitz*." (2008). In Mats Jansson et al. (Eds.), *Comparative approaches to European and Nordic modernisms* (pp. 109–126). Helsinki: Gaudeamus/Helsinki University Press.
"Forgiveness, history, narrative: W. G. Sebald's *Austerlitz*." (2012). In C. Fricke (Ed.), *The ethics of forgiveness: A collection of essays* (pp. 179–196). New York: Routledge.
"Narrative, memory, and visual image: W. G. Sebald's *Luftkrieg und Literatur* and *Austerlitz*." (2012). In J. Lothe, S. Rubin Suleiman, & J. Phelan (Eds.),

After Testimony: The Ethics and Aesthetics of Holocaust Narrative for the Future (pp. 221–246). Columbus: Ohio State University Press.

"Authority, reliability, and the challenge of reading: Jonathan Littell's *The Kindly Ones*." (2013). In J. Lothe & J. Hawthorn (Eds.), *Narrative ethics* (pp. 103–118). New York: Rodopi.

"Narrative, testimony, fiction: The challenge of not forgetting the Holocaust." (2016). In L. Brozgal & S. Kippur (Eds.), *Being contemporary: French literature, culture, and politics today* (pp. 162–176). Liverpool: Liverpool University Press.

"Introduction." (2017). In J. Lothe (Ed.), *The future of literary studies* (pp. 3–21). Oslo: Novus Press.

"Narrative beginnings and expectations in testimony and fiction: Primo Levi compared to Samuel Steinmann and W. G. Sebald." (2017). In S. Grumsen et al. (Eds.), *Expectations: Reader assumptions and author intentions in narrative discourse* (pp. 98–116). Copenhagen: Medusa.

"Introduction." (2017). In J. Lothe (Ed.), *Time's witnesses: Women's voices from the Holocaust* (pp. 1–23). Edinburgh: Fledgling Press.

"The author's ethical responsibility and the ethics of reading." (2018). *CounterText*, 4(1), 57–77.

"Narrative communication as a rhetorical act: James Phelan's poetics of narrative." (2019). *Poetics Today*, 40(1), 355–365.

"Narrative." (2020). In H. Meretoja & C. Davis (Eds.), *Trauma and literature* (pp. 152–161). London: Routledge.

"Aspects of evil and ethical challenges in Claude Lanzmann's *Shoah*." (2020). In O. Lysaker (Ed.), *Between closeness and evil: A Festschrift for Arne Johan Vetlesen* (pp. 333–356). Oslo: Scandinavian Academic Press.

"Ethics." (2022). In L. Gammelgaard et al. (Eds.), *Fictionality* (pp. 265 –283). Columbus: Ohio State University Press.

I thank the Norwegian News Agency (NTB) for permission to use Georg W. Fossum's photograph of the steamer *Donau* as an illustration on the cover of the book. My thanks are also due to Fledgling Press for permission to use the photographs of Holocaust survivors Maria Gabrielsen, Ella Blumenthal, Edith Notowicz, and Olga Horak from my edited volume *Time's Witnesses: Women's Voices from the Holocaust*.

Introduction

The photograph on the front cover of this book depicts a group of people standing on a quay and looking at a ship that is apparently leaving a harbor. The name of the ship is *Donau*; it is departing from Vippetangen quay in Oslo with 532 Norwegian Jews on board. Arriving in Szezcin in German-occupied Poland three days later, the Norwegian Jews were sent by train to Auschwitz, where nearly all of them were murdered. The photograph, taken by Georg W. Fossum on November 26, 1942, has become an iconic visual representation of the Norwegian Holocaust. Its status, however, has been established relatively—and in one sense surprisingly—recently.

The combination of the photograph's significance and the belated recognition of its importance is illustrative of the questions that I discuss in this book. I therefore begin this introduction by identifying three linked issues prompted by the photograph: memory, narrative, and ethics. To do this, however, I need to point out that virtually all my comments on the photograph presuppose extratextual knowledge, that is, knowledge about the context in which the photo was taken and the way in which it is framed by the German occupation of Norway in 1940–1945 and the Norwegian Holocaust in 1942–1943 (Bruland, 2012). The first aspect concerns memory. As a visual representation of the deportation of 532 Norwegian Jews, Fossum's photograph is a forceful reminder that the European Holocaust also happened in Norway. It also reminds Norwegian citizens, including myself, that although the Norwegian Holocaust was made possible because of the German occupation, the Norwegian State Police played an active role in the process of arresting Norwegian Jews and taking them to Vippetangen quay. Although the photograph is not in itself a memory, for those involved it will have had the power to trigger memories. The photograph is a record of the event and a reminder to those who look at it of the experiences that those deported must have gone through. For the 532 Norwegian Jews aboard the *Donau*, the experience of leaving Vippetangen quay was part of the wider experience of being deported to Auschwitz.

The aspect of memory blends into that of narrative. The photograph's significance is enhanced by the fact that we can see the *Donau* leaving Oslo harbor; the people on the quay, and by implication I as a viewer, are

Memory and Narrative Ethics. Jakob Lothe, Oxford University Press. © Oxford University Press (2025).
DOI: 10.1093/9780197579534.003.0001

witnessing a deportation of Jews. As it documents a historical event, the photograph is part of the archive of the German occupation of Norway and the Norwegian Holocaust. Yet it is more than an archival item since it serves to remind the viewer of how difficult it has been for Norwegians to come to terms with the fact that the Holocaust occurred in Norway too. This is perhaps one reason it took many years before the photograph was made public. When an exhibition on the Holocaust was about to open at Wannsee in Berlin in 1992,[1] it emerged that Norway appeared to be the only European nation not in possession of photographs that documented the deportation of Jews. When the Norwegian newspaper *Aftenposten* published a call for such photographs, Fossum responded that he had a photo negative that might be of interest. This negative, which had been lying unprinted in his apartment in Oslo for 50 years, contained the photograph of the *Donau*. All these years, either Fossum had never mentioned the photograph to anyone or nobody had asked to see it (Belgaux, 2020).

As a visual illustration of narrative memory, the photograph has a distinctly ethical dimension. By documenting the deportation that occurred in Oslo on November 26, 1942, it prompts the viewer to ask questions: Why did this happen? Was there nothing the people on the quay, and by implication all Norwegians, could have done to save these Norwegian Jews before they were arrested by the Norwegian State Police? How can or should I, a Norwegian born after the Second World War, respond to the failure to rescue them? Looking at the people on the quay, must I share the complicity that may be ascribed to them? Fossum's photograph does not just document an event; as a forceful visual image it depicts something fascinating yet impenetrable: a scene or tableau in which a ship is slowly departing while nobody seems aware of what this means or capable of preventing this from happening. Looking at the photograph, I immediately start interpreting it; for me, it is as though the smoke from the tall chimney on the *Donau* prefigures the smoke rising from the crematoria at Auschwitz.

Fossum's photograph of the *Donau* serves as a leitmotif for this book, which explores different narrative presentations of the Holocaust. A premise for the book is that in Holocaust testimony, narrative fiction, and film, memory and narrative ethics are closely, even inescapably linked and therefore need to be considered together rather than separately. I therefore study verbal fiction and film as narratives possessed of and distinguished by a series of constituent elements—formal, semantic, cognitive, affective—that identify and shape ethical issues through a narrative communication consisting of authors/directors, narrators, characters, and readers/viewers. Memory plays a key role in this communication.

On the one hand, memory can color and in part determine what and how human beings narrate; on the other hand—or more precisely, at the same time—narrative gives shape to memory and may tease into consciousness autobiographical knowledge that has been repressed or suspended. If, as my discussion suggests, narrative is a constituent element of memory, ethics is a significant aspect of both narrative and memory. I relate narrative ethics to values (in the plural): rather than providing answers, ethics in Holocaust testimony, narrative fiction, and film tends to assume the form of questions stirred by tensions or conflicts—questions asked, or implied, by the author or director via the different agents of a verbal narrative or a film, and questions asked, or implied, by the reader about the written narrative or by the viewer about the film. Whether explicitly or implicitly formulated, such questions can further readers' and viewers' sense of empathy as well as distance, thus contributing to our understanding of the questions' complexity and perhaps also of the feelings, experiences, and memories of another individual or group of people. In my experience, this kind of "perspective-awareness," to appropriate a helpful concept coined by Hanna Meretoja (2018a, p. 128), can be a humbling experience whose individual significance is paradoxically enhanced, rather than impaired, by the difficulty of explaining it precisely through written or oral language.

Positing that memory is a constituent element of the interplay between formal aspects of narrative and moral values and considering memory as an important feature of narrative psychology and other disciplines such as literary and cultural studies, the book undertakes a series of narrative analyses of verbal and filmic texts in which memory plays a significant role in the presentation of these texts' narrative ethics. Before I give working definitions of the most important concepts I use in these narrative analyses,[2] I specify that all the texts are tied to the series of historical events often referred to as the Holocaust. The narrative texts include four testimonies (by Maria Gabrielsen, Ella Blumenthal, Edith Notowicz, and Olga Horak), two variants of filmic testimony (Claude Lanzmann's *Shoah* and Alain Resnais's *Night and Fog*), a film adaptation (James Ivory's *The Remains of the Day*), a Nazi propaganda film (Leni Riefenstahl's *Triumph of the Will*), and four novels (Jonathan Littell's *The Kindly Ones*, Kazuo Ishiguro's *The Remains of the Day*, W. G. Sebald's *Austerlitz*, and Jenny Erpenbeck's *The End of Days*). The oldest text was released in 1935; the most recent was published in 2012.

Although Riefenstahl's film was made and released before the Second World War, I cannot watch it without thinking of the Holocaust. Strengthening the book's critical coherence, this focus on the Holocaust connects the narrative analyses with a complex and extended set of linked historical events that, combined with and becoming part of human beings' memories, experiences, and knowledge of these events, continues to present challenging ethical issues to those who attempt to engage with them.

The Holocaust

The Holocaust Encyclopedia published by the United States Holocaust Memorial Museum describes the Holocaust as the systematic, state-financed genocide of about six million Jews carried out by Nazi Germany and its allies; it was "an evolving process that took place throughout Europe between 1933 and 1945."[3] While the extermination of the Jews was the Nazis' main aim of the Holocaust, they also hunted down and killed a large number of non-Jews, including several thousand Roma, two million civilian Poles, almost three million Soviet prisoners of war, several thousand homosexuals and Jehovah's Witnesses, many thousand political prisoners of war, and 200,000 handicapped persons. The Nazis deported Jews from large parts of Europe—from Tromsø in northern Norway in the north to the island of Rhodes in the Mediterranean in the southeast, from the British Channel Islands in the west to villages deep inside the Soviet Union in the east. Recent research has revealed that the extent of the system of camps and ghettos was much larger than we were previously aware of. Behind such well-known names as Auschwitz and the Warsaw ghetto there was a network of smaller subcamps and bases—around 44,000 in all—where Jews and others were systematically hunted down, arrested, incarcerated, and murdered (Megaree, 2009–).[4]

My understanding of narrative ethics and memory is a motivating factor for my choice of texts that are variously related to and in different ways respond to the Holocaust. To tell about the Holocaust (in whatever medium) is an ethical act, and so is the act of listening to or looking at somebody who is attempting to talk about his or her Holocaust experience. This act includes, as Chapter 1 illustrates, the act of reading a written, verbal narrative about the experience. The Holocaust is a test case for the way in which different kinds of narratives present and represent a particularly gruesome, in one sense literally unspeakable, series of events in recent European history. It is also a test case for my interpretation of these events. This is the main reason I take a particular interest in the ways in which different strategies of remembering and presenting the Holocaust illustrate narrative's ethical dimension. This interest is strengthened by what I consider a crisis of memory at a time when the last firsthand witnesses of the Holocaust are passing away.

The Holocaust happened in Europe, and as a European I am overwhelmed by the brutality and ethical ramifications of the event. For me, it is therefore unsurprising that the Holocaust has attracted more critical attention than any other genocide. This said, I recognize that, perhaps especially for non-Europeans, my focus on the Holocaust may be perceived as problematic. In *Multidirectional Memory*, Michael Rothberg refers to the literary critic Walter Benn Michaels's observation on "the seemingly incompatible legacies of slavery and the Nazi genocide in the United States" (Rothberg, 2009, p. 1). Noting that Michaels takes up a pressing issue, Rothberg asks, "When memories of slavery and colonialism bump up against memories of the Holocaust in contemporary multicultural societies, must a competition of victims ensue?" (Rothberg, 2009, p. 2). The importance and relevance of this question became clearer to me when I gave a talk at a research center in Kolkata, India, a few years ago. I presented my book *Time's Witnesses: Women's Voices from the Holocaust* (Lothe, 2017a), briefly discussing some of the testimonies in that book (see Chapter 1). After my talk, I noticed that, though polite, some of the listeners' questions and comments were somewhat skeptical about my focus as well as my approach. How did I know what questions to ask the Holocaust survivors? Why did I not compare the Holocaust with other genocides, not least in Asia, about which much less has been written?

Although I found, and continue to find, it difficult to reply to these questions, a partial answer could consist of three linked parts. First, in common with Jonathan C. Friedman, I am inclined to agree with Zygmunt Bauman's view of the Holocaust as "a blistering comment on modernity, unprecedented in terms of the theory and technology of murder, specifically the taxonomic classification of victims, the desire for 'efficient' killing methods, the use of poison gas in gas chambers, and the assembly-line process of the killing centers" (Friedman, 2012, p. 3; cf. Bauman, 2001). Second, seen from my perspective as a Norwegian born after the war, it is beyond belief that the Holocaust could be conceived of, implemented, and executed by the nation that may have meant more for Norway's process toward independence and a modern democracy than any other. Before the Third Reich, Germany was at the center of European culture and civilization, and so is present-day Germany. The University of Oslo, founded as late as 1811 because Norway was a colony under Denmark, received formative impulses from the University of Göttingen and Humboldt University in Berlin. If the Holocaust could occur in Germany, it can happen anywhere. Thus, as Zdenka Fantlová puts it in her testimony in *Time's Witnesses*, "the Holocaust is not just a historical event. It is a warning" (Lothe, 2017a, p. 157). Third, looking again at the photograph of the *Donau* departing from Vippetangen quay, I experience a wish and a need to augment my knowledge of the Holocaust. One reason for this need is my experience of being uncomfortably close to an event from which I want to distance myself. If I were one of the people standing on Vippetangen quay on November 26, 1942, what would I have done? Probably very little. My position as a Norwegian citizen approximates to Rothberg's category of the implicated subject: "An implicated subject is neither a victim nor a perpetrator, but rather a participant in histories and social formations that generate the positions of victim and perpetrator, and yet in which most people do not occupy such clear-cut roles" (2019, p. 1; cf. Rothberg, 2020).[5] My work on this book has made it difficult to conclude that, remote as the Holocaust may seem, I am not such a participant.

While the Holocaust is exceedingly difficult to talk and write about, and while it is also extremely challenging to present by means of a photograph or a film, it is *necessary* to continue to do this. This point applies to the agent who initiates and performs the narrative communication, however inadequate it may be as a presentation of the Holocaust. It also applies to the recipient or receiver of that communication—whether he or she is a listener, a reader, or a viewer. My incomprehension of the Holocaust is one of the reasons why, for me, any attempt to communicate aspects of the Holocaust will involve a measure of interpretation, and this concerns both the agent of the communication (Holocaust survivor, author, narrator, or character) and the listener, reader, or viewer. The interpretation of narrative communication and self-interpretation is a constituent element of the discussions presented in this book.

If there is, as Eli Wiesel argued in the *New York Times* in 1978, a danger of trivializing the Holocaust, there is also a risk of repeating information that readers and viewers already know, or think they know, thus making them less rather than more concerned with the event and memories of the event. Wiesel was a Holocaust survivor, and his skepticism about "semi-fact" and "semi-fiction" is shared by the four Holocaust survivors whose testimonies I discuss in Chapter 1. Yet in spite of their awareness of "the problem of having to insert into a horizon of meaning a set of experiences that seemed to be completely without meaning" (Reiter, 2000, p. 12), these women chose to bear witness by imparting their Holocaust experience—first to me as a listener and then to the reader.

An episode incorporated into Judith Meisel's story in *Time's Witnesses* provides an example of the Holocaust survivor's decision to bear witness:

> One episode in Stutthof made a strong impression on me.[6] Right in front of me was a young woman. Later I found out her name. It was Chavah. She wore a dress; she had to undress, and a little baby fell out, an infant. The Nazi guy picked up the infant, threw it against the asphalt, and killed it.
>
> Chavah was assigned to our group. We were in wooden barracks, three, four, or five to a bunk bed—I was in a three-tiered one. Chavah was next to me. She would not open her fist; she had something in her fist. I told her it was okay at the same time as we all asked: "What do you have in your fist?" It was a tiny baby shoe. When the Nazis found out, they wanted to take it away. When she refused, they put a bullet in her head. (Lothe, 2017a, p. 73)

If at one level Chavah's stubborn resistance, manifested in her refusal to give the Nazis the shoe that metaphorically represents her murdered baby, shows how oppressed she is as a Jewish prisoner in Stutthof, at a different yet related level her silence demonstrates her freedom. This freedom is connected with and underlies her power to resist. One contributing factor to this power is a remarkable courage. The Nazi who throws the baby against the asphalt is not courageous; he just enacts Nazi ideology. But Chavah displays a courage that, while personal, is simultaneously activated and manifested in a perverted form of social interaction. The concentration camp was no community in the normal, civil sense of the word (Miller, 2011). Yet there is an uncanny interaction between Chavah, the Nazi, and the murdered baby. Her refusal to give the Nazis the shoe of her dead child is a powerful response to the evil act of killing it. Her response is an affirmation of life in the face of death. Moreover, Meisel's decision to include the episode in her testimony is also a courageous act since this part of her narrative brings back and reactivates a particularly painful memory.

Narrative

On the first page of my *Narrative in Fiction and Film*, after having noted that "a narrative presents a chain of events which is situated in time and space," I claim that narrative "is fundamental not only to different forms of cultural expression but also to our own patterns of experience and to our insights into our own lives" (Lothe, 2000, p. 3). While I use parts of this working definition of narrative in this book too, I now link "events" more closely to human beings' experiences of those events, and I relate "different forms of cultural expression" and "our patterns of experience" more directly to variants of individual, collective, and cultural memory. I also put more emphasis on narrative ethics. My view of narrative as "fundamental . . . to our own patterns of experience and to our insights into our own lives" implies that I consider narrative not just a powerful mode of communication but also a tool for "existential meaning-making" (Brockmeier, 2015, p. 51). As already indicated, this narrative process of meaning-making includes a communicative aspect: the communication of a message (however vague or confusing) from a sender (author or film director) to a receiver (reader or viewer) and, importantly, the receiver's response to and interpretation of that message. Moreover, a narrative is told or shown by one or more narrators and characters from a given perspective or a combination of perspectives. And, as it is temporally situated, "narration has at its core a dimension of distance" (Freeman, 2010, p. 175; cf. Carr, 1986; Gadamer, 2013). In all the texts analyzed in this book, manipulations and combinations of perspective and distance contribute to yet also complicate narrative communication.[7]

My approach to narrative is aligned with Mieke Bal's definition of a narrative text as "a text in which an agent or subject conveys to an addressee ('tells' the reader, viewer, or listener) a story in a medium, such as language, imagery, sound, buildings, or a combination thereof" (2017, p. 5) and of storytelling as "the presentation in whatever medium of a focalized series of events" (Bal, 2018, p. 37; cf. Bal, 2017). This view of focalized presentation, which is associated with my use of the term "perspective,"[8] is not neutral, and it often has an ethical component. In common with Mark Freeman, David Carr, and Hans-Georg Gadamer, Ernst van Alphen emphasizes the temporal dimension of narrative: "Narrative can be seen as an existential response to the world and to the experience of that world" (2018, p. 68). Since this existential response to and experience of the world occurs in a specific place or places, the spatial or territorial dimension of narrative is also crucial. Human beings' combined experience of time and space is an essential reason why narrative "has functioned as the medium of identity" (p. 68). Referring to Paul Ricoeur (1994), Alphen calls this notion of identity "narrative identity" (Alphen, 2018, p. 68). Although ongoing historical and cultural changes challenge the idea of narrative identity, this challenge does not in itself make the notion less important. Ricoeur's understanding of identity in *Oneself as Another* becomes more, not less, pertinent when seen in the light of challenges to narrative identity, including those identified and discussed in the following chapters. This said, we must be wary of collapsing the concepts of language, including narrative language, and identity into one. Although texts (whether oral, written, or filmic) are essential for the formation and negotiation of self-understanding and identity, "the issue of identity belongs to a picture that is more extended than that of language [as it] also comprises pre- and nonconceptual modes of meaning-making and identity that draw on bodily, intersubjective, and other cultural forms of life" (Brockmeier, 2015, p. 173). These "pre- and nonconceptual modes of meaning-making and identity" constitute an interpretive challenge for anyone attempting to understand narrative presentations of the Holocaust.

The challenges to narrative identity make Hannah Arendt's interlinking of human identity and narrative even more thought-provoking today than when she published *The Human Condition* in 1958. Developing an argument based on premises and observations quite different from Ricoeur's, Arendt claims, "*Who* somebody is or was we can only know by knowing the story of which he is himself the hero—his biography, in other words" (2018, p. 186, original emphasis). I agree with Hanna Meretoja (2018a) that Arendt's idea of narrative identity tends toward or aims for a non-subsumptive dialogic understanding of narrative communication and exploration that does justice to the other's singularity instead of subsuming it under a general explanatory grid. I also concur with Meretoja's accompanying point that this kind of understanding is closely related to (both resulting from and furthering) narrative's ethical dimension. Thus, I connect my working definition of narrative, including the definitions with which it is associated and to which it is indebted, to Meretoja's conceptualization of narrative as "a *culturally mediated practice of sense-making* that involves the activities of *interpreting* and *presenting* someone's experiences in a specific situation to someone from a certain *perspective* or perspectives" (p. 48, original emphasis). Narrative is a way of making sense of the world, and this mediated narrative presentation requires a measure of interpretation. As a listener, reader, or viewer I immediately start interpreting the narrative that I hear, read, or watch. As Jens Brockmeier puts it, "narrative experience is experience interpreted" (2015, p. 114; cf. Brockmeier, 2022, 2023). While I relate Brockmeier's important point to the listener, reader, or viewer, I also link it to the narrative agent that communicates his or her memories, experiences, and interpretations. As I suggest below and argue throughout, narrative has self-interpretive components that influence, though they do not determine, my own interpretation.

My understanding of narrative is associated with, and thus enables me to activate, a range of narrative resources, including, for example, an author's use of one or more narrators and a film director's use of cameras (cf. Lothe, 2000, 2023a). This means that the narrative analyses presented in this book are indebted not only to the narrative theorists already mentioned but also to the interdisciplinary field of study commonly referred to as narrative theory or narratology.[9] Precursors of current narrative studies include Russian formalism of the 1920s and French structuralism of the 1960s and early 1970s, not least Gérard Genette's *Discours du récit* (1972; translated as *Narrative Discourse*, 1980). In Genette's study, as in this book, "narrative discourse" refers to the *presentation* of narrative: the verbal or filmic text that I read or watch, including all its constituent elements. While Genette discusses narrative form from a structuralist perspective, a major representative of current narrative theory, James Phelan, does so from a rhetorical perspective that has also proved helpful.[10] My narrative analyses are also aided by the insights of other narrative theorists. One reason why the work of Mieke Bal has proved important is that, as already indicated, her definitions of text and storytelling refer to and thus include both verbal narrative and film narrative. Moreover, Bal's work has furthered my understanding of the connections between narrative and memory. For example, I am indebted to the distinction she makes between "unreflective habitual memories" and "narrative memories": "Narrative memories, even of unimportant events, differ from routine or habitual memories in that they are affectively colored, surrounded by an emotional aura that, precisely, makes them memorable" (Bal, 1999, p. viii). This description of narrative memories, which I explore in this book, is affiliated with Brockmeier's interlinking of memory and narrative.

Memory

If I am a subject implicated, however indirectly, in the Holocaust, then it becomes even more difficult to answer the question asked by my Kolkata audience as well as by Rothberg (and, more provocatively, by Michaels): Do I, by editing *Time's Witnesses* and writing this book, engage in "a competition of victims"? As my partial answer indicates, I hope not, though I cannot be sure. At any rate, I second Rothberg's criticism of a framework that understands memory, and particularly collective memory, as competitive memory. I also support his alternative notion of collective memory as "*multidirectional*: as subject to ongoing negotiation, cross-referencing, and borrowing; as productive and not privative" (Rothberg, 2009, p. 3, original emphasis). Although I discuss variants of individual memory, I relate the narrative communication of these individual memories to instances of collective memory that, seen from my perspective, are distinctly multidirectional—not least because, as Rothberg suggests, knowledge about the Holocaust can make me more conscious of other instances of violence, racism, and abuse of power. No memory is just individual since, situated in and framed by history and context, it is socially mediated (Erll, 2011; Laanes & Meretoja, 2021; Olick et al., 2011).

Implicit in my introductory comments on narrative and identity is a view of memory that connects memory closely to both. It is exceedingly difficult to come to terms with the concepts of narrative and identity without activating, implicitly or explicitly, aspects of memory. If I cannot conceive of narrative divorced from memory, neither can I think of identity without remembering something of myself before the point or stage of my life where I am now. Narrative representations of experience necessarily involve aspects of memory (Brockmeier, 2015). But what is memory? Rothberg responds to this question by noting, and then commenting on, the minimalist definition given by Richard Terdiman: "[M]emory is the past made present. The notion of a 'making present' has two important corollaries: first, that memory is a contemporary phenomenon, something that, while concerned with the past, happens in the present; and second, that memory is a form of work, working through, labor, or action" (Rothberg, 2009, pp. 3–4; Terdiman, 1993). Variants of these two corollaries are observable in all the texts discussed in this book. In a text such as Lanzmann's film *Shoah*, the past's painful intrusion into the present is perhaps particularly striking. Yet in Ishiguro's novel *The Remains of the Day*, the main character Stevens's memories of his dismissal of the Jewish girls are painful too—even though, in this work of narrative fiction, the references to historical reality, and the Holocaust as an integral part of that reality, are more indirect.

As Astrid Erll notes, "'memory' is a topic that integrates disparate elements like no other" (2011, p. 1). As it describes a complex phenomenon, the concept of memory is complicated, and it is defined in different ways by various scholars in a range of disciplines. And yet, seen from my perspective, memory is also a resource. Although there is something disconcertingly elusive about memory, aspects of memory prove indispensable tools as I attempt to improve my understanding of narrative and identity—and thus of my life. I agree with Ricoeur that we should not only approach memory "on the basis of its deficiencies" but also "approach the description of mnemonic phenomena from the standpoint of the *capacities* (2006, p. 21, original emphasis). As Ricoeur observes, "To put it bluntly, we have nothing better than memory to signify that something has taken place, has occurred, has happened *before* we declare that we remember it" (p. 21, original emphasis). While I accept the neuroscientific view of memory as malleable and repeatedly reconstructed, I am inclined to agree with Aleida Assmann's observation that these premises "cannot do full justice to the complexity of memory" (2015, p. 42). Part of this complexity is suggested by "the aspects involved in the dynamics of memory" (p. 42).

On the one hand, memory, including the memories of the Holocaust survivors whose testimonies I discuss in chapters 1 and 3, may seem "not just fundamentally individual, but quintessentially so, as primal and lonely as pain" (Olick et al., 2011, p. 16). On the other hand, as the editors of *The Collective Memory Reader* also emphasize:

> The new insight of memory studies is thus not merely that memory is omnipresent but that it is at once situated in social frameworks (e.g., family and nation), enabled by changing media technologies (e.g., the Internet and digital recording), confronted with cultural institutions (e.g., memorials and museums), and shaped by political circumstances (e.g., wars and catastrophes). (Olick et al., p. 37)

It does not follow that individual memories are unimportant: there is a sense in which collective memory is a metaphorical extension of individual memory. And yet, if no narrative can be told, written, or shown in a cultural or historical vacuum, the same observation applies to our memories—and particularly to memories of a colossal crime such as the

Holocaust. Although I use the concepts of individual and collective memory, I stress how interdependent they are.

My decision to discuss a selection of texts in which characters, narrators, implied authors, and film directors tell about the Holocaust more or less directly invites, even forces me to link memory, and especially individual memory, to trauma, which I provisionally define as the lasting effect(s) of a deeply distressing or disturbing experience. This working definition includes aspects of trauma in disaster psychiatry (Ursano et al., 2017). It is also indebted to discussions of trauma by literary and cultural critics, including Cathy Caruth (1995, 2016), Ruth Leys (2000), Dominick LaCapra (1996, 1998), Stef Craps (2012), and Hanna Meretoja (2018a, 2021).[11] Caruth is right to stress trauma's "enigmatic core." But I find her explanation of this "core" unpersuasive: "the delay or incompletion in knowing, or even in seeing, an overwhelming occurrence that then remains, in its insistent return, absolutely *true* to the event" (Caruth, 1995, p. 5, original emphasis). Many Holocaust survivors were injured both physically and mentally. Yet it does not follow that traumatic experience is inaccessible; the testimonies I discuss do not indicate that there is a stable or unchanging break between word and world, or between word (or narrative) and wound (Caruth, 1995, 2016; cf. Pederson, 2018). What these narratives suggest, though, is that while narrative—including the decision to narrate, the attempt to narrate, and constituent elements of narration—can enable a Holocaust survivor to come to terms with aspects of his or her traumatic experience, other aspects of that experience, including the way it is remembered, resist narrativization (LaCapra, 1996; Leys, 2000; Lothe, 2020b). One reason for this kind of resistance—though, as Brockmeier (2015) notes, even latent memories include narrative elements—is that the attempt to narrate blends into an act of remembering that activates, or intensifies, painful memories of the traumatic experience. For a Holocaust survivor, this experience includes being deported to the concentration camp, living (or existing) in the camp, and escaping from the camp—where family members may have been murdered. Attempting to use verbal language to tell about, and thus remember, a wound or mark he or she has experienced in the world, a Holocaust survivor may thus be inclined to consider narrative both as a resource and as a challenge involving an element of risk. This combination of narrative as a resource and a risk is noticeable in Judith Meisel's story about Chavah. Importantly, both the possibility of gain and the potential risk of narration change over time.

As these comments suggest, the relationship between trauma and narrative is close but problematic. On the one hand, a person who experiences an event in his or her life as traumatic, and who feels a need to tell others about the experience, may choose to do so, and be able to do so. On the other hand, a different person who experiences the same event may not feel the same need or be able to talk or write about it; while the event may be the same, the experience of it may vary from person to person. While memory of a traumatic event may prompt narration, it may also thwart narration. Moreover, although a person who tries to talk about a traumatic event may find the narrative activity helpful, narration inevitably takes him or her back to the event, thus perhaps making the person remember what he or she wants to forget. Again, Meisel's testimony is an illustrative example. A narrative of trauma cannot be a coherent, clear, and unfissured narrative; rather, it is fragmented and incomplete, requiring, as Alphen observes, a kind of performativity that allows for a non-subsumptive, affect-based ethics (1999; cf. Meretoja, 2018a). Yet traumatic memory can be associated with forms of memory that are less traumatic. This point is related to Erll's critique of trauma theories that, though derived from studies of individuals' traumatic experiences, are used to define societal or cultural trauma: "Denial and repression might well make an individual organism sick, but not necessarily a society" (2011, p. 100). As this statement indicates, there are both differences and affinities between individual memory (which may or may not include elements of trauma) and collective memory (which may also contain aspects of trauma, broadly understood). For Erll, the umbrella term "cultural memory" refers, first, to memory as a metonymy ("cultural" memory) at the level of individual remembering in a sociocultural context and, second, to memory as a metaphor (cultural "memory") at the collective level (p. 99).

One critical advantage of the concept of cultural memory is the integrative power of the concept's constituent elements. To relate this point to the present study, while I focus on individual memories, experiences, and attempts to communicate these memories and experiences through narrative, I am also interested in the connections between these mnemonic variants (all of which can include traumatic elements) and aspects of collective memory, including those produced in media cultures. The term "premediation" is helpful here: "the (usually non-conscious) process by which images and narratives recalled from representations circulating in media culture turn into powerful schemata and preform imagination, experience, memory, storytelling, and action" (Erll, 2019, p. 229). As the temporal distance from the Holocaust increases, and as the last time's witnesses are passing away, premediation is becoming a key aspect of cultural memories of the Holocaust. Erll is right to highlight the ethical challenges associated with, and stirred by, "the hidden power . . . of implicit cultural memory" (p. 230).[12]

Neither individual nor collective nor cultural memories of the Holocaust are static; as complex memorial forms, they change over time. The concepts of "postmemory" and "post memory" are helpful here. Marianne Hirsch understands postmemory as "the relationship that the 'generation after' bears to the personal, collective, and cultural trauma" of those who experienced, and survived, the Holocaust: "To grow up with overwhelming inherited memories . . . is to risk having one's own life stories displaced. . . . It is to be shaped, however indirectly, by traumatic fragments of events that still defy narrative reconstruction and exceed comprehension."[13] In common with Eva Hoffmann (2004) and many other Holocaust scholars, Hirsch belongs to the "generation after": survivors' children. Their perspective on the Holocaust has been and continues to be invaluable. Yet as Assmann suggests, it is now possible also to relate postmemory to "the inclusive community of Holocaust memory from the point of view of all succeeding generations. . . . Moving along the temporal axis from second to third and fourth generation, the condition 'postmemory' is becoming a condition 'post memory'" (2018, p. 213) in which premediation plays an important role. As my book is influenced by and to some extent predicated on this temporal transition, I will return to the interpretive potential and value of these concepts in Chapter 8.

Studying the collective elements of individual memory, Maurice Halbwachs reaches the conclusion that, as Erll puts it, "the recourse to *cadre sociaux*, social frameworks, is an indispensable prerequisite for every act of remembering" (Erll, 2011, p. 15; Halbwachs, 1925, 1992). "Every act" here includes acts of remembering, or attempts to remember, a traumatic event or process. In my discussion of such narrative acts, the narrator's distance from the traumatic experience plays a key role, as does my own temporal and spatial distance from the Holocaust.[14] The Holocaust narratives I discuss in this book support Halbwachs's view of individual memory as a psychological process embedded in social frameworks of memory. This key point of Halbwachs's *Les cadres sociaux de la mémoire* (1925) has become a premise for memory studies.[15]

Inspired by Bergson, Halbwachs has himself inspired and influenced later scholars of memory, including Ricoeur. In *History, Memory, Forgetting*, Ricoeur notes that "it is always in historically limited cultural forms that the capacity to remember (*faire mémoire*) can be apprehended" (2006, p. 392). Halbwachs's work preempts the way in which Ricoeur's connects variants of memory not only to forgetting but also to history and narrative, including ethical aspects of narrative. Two current scholars who also relate memory to narrative in ways that have influenced my approach are Jens Brockmeier and Hanna Meretoja. While Brockmeier's (2015) notion of narrative forms of life suggests that autobiographical memory tends to take on narrative shape, Meretoja has shown that narrative models of sense-making are important cultural forms for mediating memory (2018a; Laanes & Meretoja, 2021). Yet if there is a sense in which individual memory depends on cultural memory, the opposite is also true; the testimonies I discuss in Chapters 1 and 3 are verbal expressions of individual memories that contribute to our cultural memory of the Holocaust. In common with memory and narrative, these two main variants of memory are interdependent.

Moreover, memory and narrative are both closely related to human beings' experience, including the experience of the event of the Holocaust. My understanding of experience is influenced by Walter Benjamin, whose classic essay "Der Erzähler" (The Storyteller) (1936) conceptualizes story-telling in terms of exchanging experiencing. (Compare my discussion of the narrative situations in Sebald's *Austerlitz* in Chapter 6.) This kind of exchange can further narrative self-reflection—not only for the characters in the text but also for the reader or viewer of the verbal narrative or the film narrative. In the Holocaust narratives I interpret, the event (or series of events) presented in the narrative is indistinguishable from the experience, memory, or postmemory of that event. As I will show, human beings' as well as fictional characters' experience and interpretation of the Holocaust vary considerably; this experiential and interpretive variability is generated by the narrative discourse, including the ethical components of that discourse. Moreover, the exchange of experiences is not limited to the characters since it also includes the narrator, the author or director, and the reader or viewer. Although it can signal a border or limit of language, "language is already present in any acquisition of experience, and in it the individual ego comes to belong to a particular linguistic community" (Gadamer, 2013, p. 356). Experience thus possesses an element not only of narrative communication but also of dialogue and learning in an encounter with the text: "understanding belongs to the encounter with the work of art itself, and so this belonging can be illuminated only on the basis of the *mode of being of the work of art itself*" (p. 91, original emphasis). Taking Gadamer's notion of the artwork's "mode of being" as a synonym of the text's narrative discourse, I agree with Meretoja that "such encounters can provide us with richer hermeneutic resources for understanding our experiences, responses, fears and desires" (Meretoja, 2017, p. 140). These encounters are often, as I aim to show, ethical; if narrative proposes to the reader or viewer "a vision of the world that is never ethically neutral" (Ricoeur, 1988, p. 249), neither is my interpretation of that vision.

Narrative Ethics

When Halbwachs protested the arrest of his Jewish wife's father, he performed a courageous act based on and motivated by values opposed to those of Nazi Germany. Since his moral act of protest cost him his life, it constituted a turning point in his autobiographical narrative. It is thus an example of narrative ethics. For the purposes of the present study, "ethics" is understood as the moral values aesthetically presented in narrative nonfiction, narrative fiction, and film. These values may be different in kind and scope, thus often creating tensions related to and expressed through the varying views, actions, and attitudes of the texts' characters, narrators, and implied authors or directors (Hawthorn & Lothe, 2013; Phelan, 2014). Narrative ethics is thus a complex interrelational system.

My understanding of ethics is inspired by Aristotle's notion of *ethos*—a historical person or fictional character's moral qualities (Altes, 2014). These qualities need not be "good"; on the contrary, it is often actions and attitudes considered "bad" or unacceptable (by other persons or by society) that result in ethical considerations and, in society at large, necessitate legal regulations and systems of punishment. I consider ethics to be inseparable from aesthetics, which I relate closely to narrative form and presentation. It follows that, for me, form is inseparable from content. The reciprocity between narrative ethics and narrative aesthetics applies to both written narrative and film, even though the aesthetic techniques of the two media differ. It is this interplay that is crucial and that I examine in this book. Importantly, ethics as I understand the concept also includes the reader's or viewer's ethics, which necessarily influences the acts of reading or viewing.[16]

The book is indebted to the "ethical turn" (Altes, 2008, p. 142; cf. Lothe and Hawthorn, 2013a) in literary studies. Aiming to contribute to narrative ethics, I am, as Phelan (2014) puts it, "specifically concerned with the intersection between various formal aspects of narrative and moral values." Studies by Ricoeur and Alaisdair MacIntyre in the 1980s proved important precursors for the ethical turn.[17] Significant contributions to ethical criticism from around 1990 onward include Wayne C. Booth's *The Company We Keep* (1988) and Martha Nussbaum's *Love's Knowledge* (1992).[18] A distinguishing characteristic of Phelan's (2007, 2017) exploration of narrative ethics is his sustained attempt to develop methods of uncovering the ethical values underlying the specific rhetorical exchanges of a particular narrative. He distinguishes four subfields of narrative ethics: "(1) the ethics of the told; (2) the ethics of the telling; (3) the ethics of writing/producing; and (4) the ethics of reading/reception" (Phelan, 2014). This distinction is helpful, not least because it refers not just to the narrative ethics of verbal fiction but also to that of film. In my narrative analyses, the narrative ethics of the told and of the telling are virtually inseparable. What makes "the ethics of the told" of the texts I interpret unique is the texts' form, which I use synonymously with telling and narrative presentation. My focus is therefore on the three last subfields of narrative ethics that Phelan identifies. I want to add, though, that as the ethics of the telling does not occur in a historical vacuum, there is a sense in which the texts discussed in this book are predicated on the Holocaust as an event that should not, though it can be, misrepresented through narrative. This kind of ethical demand is associated with Phelan's notion of the ethics of the told.

A notable gain of Adam Zachary Newton's contribution is his demonstration, in a series of books from *Narrative Ethics* (1995) onward, that narrative and ethics are inseparable. This point is also made by Leona Toker, who in *Towards the Ethics of Form in Fiction* (2010) argues convincingly that the ethical consequences of reading fiction result from features of its aesthetics. Following the semiotician Louis Hjelmslev, Toker calls these aesthetic features "the form of content" (Toker, 2010, p. 2).[19] Toker's concern with textual detail is shared by J. Hillis Miller, who in *The Ethics of Reading* (1987) argues that "there is a necessary ethical moment in [the] act of reading as such, a moment neither cognitive, nor political, nor social, nor interpersonal, but properly and independently ethical" (p. 1). Ethics, Miller goes on to note, "has a peculiar relation to that form of language we call narrative. . . . Without storytelling there is no theory of ethics" (p. 3).[20]

Approaching narrative ethics from the perspective of narrative hermeneutics (see below), Meretoja too underlines narrative's ethical dimension: a key point argued in *The Ethics of Storytelling* (2018a) is "the ethical significance of storytelling for human existence" (p. 27). For Meretoja, "[s]torytelling is ethically loaded precisely because it is a way of making sense of our being in the world, and narrative fiction is a particular form of such storytelling—one that has specific ethical potential in engaging us through its own literary means" (p. 27). Agreeing with this view, I also second Meretoja's accompanying point: "Narrative ethics challenges abstract, universalizing, top-down, and principlist ethical theories" (p. 26). This is the main reason I put emphasis on narrative analyses, making those analyses the basis for my observations on and the questions prompted by the narratives' ethics. In common with Meretoja, I am inspired by the approaches to ethics—including those developed by Arendt, MacIntyre, Ricoeur, and Charles Taylor—that stress the connections between narrative, identity, and ethics, understanding "morality . . . [as an] interpersonal and dialogical practice" (Meretoja, 2018a, p. 26; cf. Brockmeier & Meretoja, 2014). "Morality" encompasses the moral values that underlie and become visible through not only verbal and filmic narratives but narrative practices overall. After having made a distinction between "*naturalizing narratives,* which hide their own mediating and interpretative role, and *self-reflexive narratives,* which openly present themselves *as narratives,*" Meretoja argues that

> naturalizing and self-reflexive narrative strategies are intimately linked to ethically distinct logics manifested by *subsumptive* and *non-subsumptive* narrative practices: while some (typically naturalizing) narratives seek to subsume the particular under the general, others (typically self-reflexive ones) destabilize such appropriative aspirations and display a non-subsumptive logic by foregrounding the temporal process of encountering the singularity of the narrated experiences. (2018a, p. 12, original emphasis; see also 2018b)

The narratives I discuss illustrate both these variants of narratives and of narrative practices. An example of a naturalizing narrative whose narrative practice is clearly subsumptive is, as I show in Chapter 2, Riefenstahl's film *Triumph of the Will*; an instance of a self-reflexive narrative that engages in a non-subsumptive practice is Erpenbeck's novel *Aller Tage Abend* (discussed in Chapter 7). It does not follow that a naturalizing narrative presents the reader or viewer with just one set of moral values, but certain values—such as those of Nazism in Riefenstahl's film—are typically highlighted and supported at the expense of others. While I find Meretoja's distinction between naturalizing and self-reflexive narrative helpful, and while I also endorse her accompanying differentiation between subsumptive and non-subsumptive narrative practices, my analyses suggest that one and the same Holocaust narrative can display elements of both variants of stories and narrative practices. Part of the reason for this kind of variation can be conflicting ethical signals given by narrative's genre or medium, as well as by the different moral values of its characters and narrators. A related, equally important reason is that while one reader or viewer may experience a Holocaust narrative as naturalizing, and its narrative practice as subsumptive, a different reader or viewer may not. This kind of interpretive variability does not render Meretoja's distinction invalid, however. Rather, it is affiliated with and supports the emphasis she puts on "the dialogical character of narrative identity, (inter)subjectivity, and agency" (Meretoja, 2018a, p. 13) by suggesting that this "dialogical character" includes not just the narrative but also the reader or viewer of that narrative.

Rereading and rewatching the narratives discussed in this book, I find my working definition of narrative ethics repeatedly challenged. When I consider ethics as "the moral values aesthetically presented in narrative nonfiction, narrative fiction, and film," I presume that, though I specify that "these values may be different in kind and scope," at least some form of negotiation or exchange of values is possible among the agents of the narrative communication. Yet in many Holocaust narratives, the values of the characters and narrators are opposed to the extent of rendering meaningful communication impossible. The episode that Judith Meisel incorporates into her testimony illustrates such an unnegotiable opposition of values: the contrast between Chavah's ethics and that of the Nazi who kills her child appears absolute.

Chavah's act of resistance is also a forceful demonstration of the importance of memory. Not just metonymically representing her child, the shoe is also a memory of it. This memory informs her narrative ethics: her stubborn act of keeping the shoe in her clenched fist becomes the fragment of a narrative which illustrates not only her love of her child but also her way of honoring the child's memory. Although this narrative is brutally ended when the Nazi shoots Chavah, Meisel's testimony ensures that, in one sense at least, it continues. In my interpretation of this "episode"—and it is revealing that

Meisel uses this word—the way she relates it is a key component of her narrative ethics. After having stated that the episode made "a strong impression" on her, she just reports what she observed in the camp. It does not follow that Meisel does not interpret what she witnesses. Yet by not elaborating—because she does not want to, or perhaps because she is unable to—she makes her testimony more, not less, convincing. If she cannot forget this episode, neither can I.

The Nazi's evil act of killing Chavah's baby was part of an ethnic war that was one of the strongest driving forces of the Holocaust. The Nazis' hatred of the Jews was predicated on their conception of themselves as being qualitatively "better" than the Jews. It was also related to evil or, more precisely, to evil human acts. In *Evil and Human Agency*, Arne Johan Vetlesen defines evil as "*to intentionally inflict pain and suffering on another human being, against her will, and causing serious and foreseeable harm to her*" (2005, p. 2, original emphasis).[21] In the case of the Holocaust, this was done not only systematically and industrially but also, as in the episode reported by Meisel, individually and spontaneously. All the Holocaust survivors who testify in *Time's Witnesses* were exposed to different forms of evil. A characteristic feature of these women's stories is that the women reacted just as strongly to the hatred and the evil acts perpetrated against others as to those to which they were personally exposed. Meisel's narrative ethics approximates to a set of values that, opposing those of Nazism, supports Chavah's ethics. Conversely, Chavah's moral values may have strengthened Meisel's. She does not comment on the motivation of the Nazi.

An essential dimension of Chavah's ethics is indicated by the word *care*. Meisel's narrative ethics convinces me that, for Chavah, the ethical demand placed on her by her child is absolute. In *The Ethical Demand*, Knud E. Løgstrup argues that as human beings we are confronted with a demand that,

> precisely because it is unspoken, is radical. . . . The radicality of the demand consists, further, in the fact that it asks me to take care of the other person's life not only when to do so strengthens me but also when it is very unpleasant, because it intrudes disturbingly into my own existence. (1997, pp. 44–45)

For Løgstrup, our dependence on the caring attitude and solicitude of other people is the distinctive characteristic that makes us human.[22] The Nazi death camps militated against human caring, and this was one of the reasons why many prisoners felt they gradually became stunted as human beings. The prototype of the fundamental relation of moral solicitude is the relationship between mother and child—especially the newborn child, to whom the mother first gives life and whom she subsequently helps to live by caring.

Løgstrup's notion of care as an integral part of the ethical demand is related to Emmanuel Levinas's idea of the face-to-face encounter with and command of the Other. Although it is unclear who or what this "Other" is, aspects of the Other can be visible in or emerge through a human face: "[T]here arises, awakened before the face of the other, a responsibility for the other to whom I was committed before any committing" (Levinas, 1999, pp. 30–31; cf. Freeman, 2023). Seen from Levinas's phenomenological perspective, human beings and characters who represent human beings in narrative fiction are involved in projects directed toward others and toward the world. This kind of relational project—which assumes the form of intentional orientation in the world, and which thus expresses a desire to achieve or accomplish something—is radically challenged in the face-to-face encounter (Levinas, 1969). The encounter with the Other is not "an empirical event (though it may be enacted in any number of empirical events); it is rather . . . original, essential or fundamental . . . [and] ethical" (Davis, 2007b, p. 48).[23]

In spite of significant differences, Levinas and Løgstrup both emphasize "my responsibility for the Other [which] is prior to and independent both of my own choices, desires and attitudes and of my particular social relationships to the Other" (Fink & MacIntyre, 1997, p. xxxiv). While the Nazi who kills Chavah's child denies the experience of this ethical demand (Løgstrup) or command (Levinas), Chavah responds to it. In my interpretation of this episode from Meisel's testimony, the authenticity of Chavah's response is confirmed by her loss of life. Her silent riposte is also associated with, and in fact underlies, a question asked by John K. Roth: "What should ethics be, and what can it do after the Holocaust?" (2009, p. 31). As his study *Ethics during and after the Holocaust: In the Shadow of Birkenau* demonstrates, the Holocaust changed our understanding of human values. Although I cannot answer Roth's question, I posit that the texts I discuss give partial answers to it. However, these answers stir further questions.

This book is also inspired by the ethical turn in film and image studies. Spurred by the growing interest in ethics in literary and cultural studies, the notion of an "ethical turn" in film studies evolved over the past couple of decades. Important precursors are, as Asbjørn Grønstad notes in *Film and the Ethical Imagination* (2016), Bill Nichols's *Representing Reality* (1991) and Kaja Silverman's *The Threshold of the Visible World* (1996). Grønstad helpfully identifies two strands in the ethical turn of film studies, both of which are relevant to my concerns. First, there is a thematic strand that gravitates toward the Holocaust as an unspeakable crime and a privileged site of memory. I comment on aspects of this strand in my discussions of Riefenstahl's *Triumph of the Will* in Chapter 2 and Lanzmann's *Shoah* in Chapter 3. Second, there is a conceptual strand illustrative of the lasting impact of Levinas. As already indicated, Levinas, dissenting from a normative approach to ethics, emphasizes the concept of alterity and the individual's responsibility for his or her face-to-face encounter with the Other. Levinas's importance for the expanding field of ethically inclined film studies is evident in Lisa Downing and Libby Saxton's *Film and Ethics: Foreclosed Encounters*, a key study that, facilitating a change of emphasis from what ethics *is* to what ethics *does*, demonstrates that "in a society increasingly saturated with images . . . the visual, rather than the written word, becomes a privileged locus of exploration of the ethical" (2010, p. 1). Combined with the insights of film scholars such as Grønstad (2016) and Hagi Kenaan (2013), several of the observations made by Downing and Saxton establish productive reference points for critical dialogue in the chapters that include discussions of films, whether or not these are adaptations of written narrative texts, and whether or not the references are explicit or implied.[24]

Narrative Psychology

The various connections that I explore between memory and narrative ethics align this book with narrative psychology's concern with narrative as a key aspect human experience, memory, and meaning-making. While the history of my own discipline (literary studies) includes structuralism and rhetorical narrative theory, that of narrative psychology is often related to Theodore Sarbin's *Narrative Psychology: The Storied Nature of Human Conduct* (1986) and Jerome Bruner's *Actual Minds, Possible Worlds* (1986) as well as his seminal essay "Life as Narrative" (1987). An important point of contact between the two disciplines' history is, seen from my perspective, that of narrative hermeneutics. As Matti Hyvärinen observes, "While the earlier generation of literary narratologists . . . had always thought of narrative as a primarily *textual* phenomenon, a particular category of fictional and non-fictional texts, the hermeneutical turn radically extends narrative into a special capacity of life" (2017, p. vix, original emphasis). It does not follow that narrative texts should not be carefully analyzed, however. The interpretations I give in the following chapters aim to show that "narratives are forms inherent in our ways of getting knowledge that structure experience about the world and ourselves" (Brockmeier & Harré, 2001, p. 50). Moreover, I hope to demonstrate that these narrative forms, and the knowledge they can generate, often include ethical facets.

In common with the editors of *Life and Narrative*, I am fascinated by Bruner's attempt to describe "the circulation of meaning between experience and the recounting of experience" (Schiff et al., 2017, p. xxxi). To make such an attempt is not to collapse the concepts of experience and narrative into one. Moreover, as Chapters 1 and 3 indicate, not all aspects of experience can or should be narrated. One notable gain of Bruner's contribution turns on the word "circulation," connecting experience to narrative and vice versa. Although some of the arguments against the "Life as Narrative" thesis are strong—not all aspects of a complex human life are necessarily examples of narrative, or even capable of being rendered in narrative form—I concur with Freeman that "ultimately, there is no speaking about 'what happened' wholly apart from narrative" (2017, p. 23). Or, in Bruner's phrase, "We seem to have no other way of describing 'lived time' save in the form of a narrative" (1987, p. 12). The relevance of narrative psychology for my critical concerns is strengthened by the emphasis that the contributors to *Life and Narrative* place on the ethics of narrating life. This form of ethics is closely associated with my understanding of narrative ethics as an ongoing negotiation and exploration of moral values.

In addition to Meretoja's *The Ethics of Storytelling* and the other studies referred to above, Freeman's *Hindsight* (2010) and Brockmeier's *Beyond the Archive* (2015) have proved helpful in establishing a theoretical basis for the narrative analyses presented in this book. The relevance of Freeman's work is enhanced by the way he connects elements of narrative psychology to aspects of narrative, memory, and narrative hermeneutics. In *Hindsight: The Promise and Peril of Looking Backward* (2010), Freeman argues convincingly that there is a close linkage between hindsight, narrative reflection, and self-understanding. For Freeman, hindsight is a synonym of "temporal distance": "the distance in time between whatever events may have transpired in the past and the historian's own position as interpreter and writer in the present" (2015, p. 236; cf. Freeman, 2023). In the following analyses, "the historian's own position" is closely related to, though not necessarily identical with, the positions of the author or film director, the narrator, and the reader or viewer in relation to what is told. Referring to Gadamer, Freeman finds that "temporal distance allows one access to dimensions of meaning and significance that cannot be had amidst the 'fleeting circumstances' of the object's initial appearance" (Freeman, 2015, p. 236; cf. Gadamer, 2013). This understanding of temporal distance is a constituent element of my approach. I am also inspired by his notion of narrative reflection, which in this discussion of Holocaust narratives accommodates ethical questions and ethical reflection.

The most important reason why Brockmeier's work provides a theoretical basis for my discussion is his exploration of narrative as a model for autobiographical processes, including the processes of remembering and forgetting. Combining insights from narrative psychology, the neurosciences, and memory studies with philosophy and narrative studies, Brockmeier investigates, as succinctly indicated by the title of his latest book, *Erzählen als Lebensform* (Narration as a Way of Life) (2022). This title is associated with Brockmeier's "strong narrative thesis": "[T]he intricacies of autobiographical meaning-making are not just represented or expressed by narrative, they only come into being through and in narrative" (2015, p. 119). Although Brockmeier's concept of autobiographical meaning-making applies most directly to the testimonies I discuss in Chapters 1 and 3, I also relate it to the complex processes of meaning-making in the other narratives I consider.[25] Moreover, although Brockmeier does not focus on narrative ethics, the way he expounds his strong narrative thesis suggests that, for him, not only does ethics have a narrative component; it is also a constituent element of narrative discourse.[26]

The strong narrative thesis also underlies my understanding of trauma as an aspect of Holocaust testimony. For Brockmeier, "[w]hat is foregrounded in many trauma stories is not the traumatic event as such but its felt quality, the emotional impact of what it meant to have gone through it" (2015, p. 119). While I agree with this point, and while I also find that "[i]t is hard to see how this sense of what it is like, which is pivotal for an entire spectrum of experiences, would come into a meaningful existence without its narrative shape" (p. 119), my analyses of Holocaust testimonies suggest that there can be a difference between a traumatic experience and the narrative rendering of that experience. An illustrative example is Abraham Bomba's three-minute silence in Lanzmann's *Shoah*: as I argue in Chapter 3, his silence is part of his Holocaust experience, but I am not sure it is part of his Holocaust narrative. And yet, when I try to interpret Bomba's silence it becomes part of that fragmented narrative.

Narrative Hermeneutics

Meretoja, Freeman, and Brockmeier have all contributed to the development of the concept of narrative hermeneutics as a theoretical and philosophical approach to narrative. In this study, narrative hermeneutics is also part of and lays the foundation for my analytical approach. "Hermeneutics" refers to the theory of interpretation, and, combined with the components of narrative that I have already introduced, narrative hermeneutics forms the basis for the interpretations presented in the following chapters. As Meretoja and Freeman note in their introduction to *The Use and Abuse of Stories*, hermeneutic approaches to narrative "go far beyond theorizing the interpretation of written narratives" (2023, p. 4); in this book, hermeneutics also informs my interpretations of film narratives.

My understanding of narrative hermeneutics is affiliated with and builds on the 20th-century tradition of philosophical hermeneutics that emphasizes the interpretive structure of human life: "we exist in the world with others by constantly interpreting and making sense of our experiences" (Meretoja & Freeman, 2023, p. 4). Gadamer's *Wahrheit und Methode* (1960/1975) (*Truth and Method*) (1960/2013) plays a key role in this tradition.[27] Four of Gadamer's concepts have proved particularly important for my interpretations of narrative presentation of the Holocaust: horizon, distance, dialogue, and the question. Gadamer links the concept of "horizon" to that of "situation": "We define the concept of 'situation' by saying that it represents a standpoint that limits the possibility of vision. Hence essential to the concept of situation is the concept of 'horizon.' The horizon is the range of vision that includes everything that can be seen from a particular vantage point" (1960/2013, p. 313, original emphasis). As my horizon is limited to what I can see, to my perspective, there is a lot that I cannot see. However, "[a] person who has no horizon does not see far enough and hence over-values what is nearest to him" (p. 313). Thus, my limited horizon is not just an interpretive limitation; it also represents an interpretive possibility of gaining knowledge of "the relative significance of everything within this horizon, whether it is near or far, great or small" (p. 313). The concept of horizon, which I relate to perspective, is an important aspect of my approach.

When I use "horizon" as a metaphor, I implicitly activate the word's spatial aspect. While this aspect is not unimportant for Gadamer, he highlights the *temporal* dimension of the concept of horizon. He does so by connecting the concept of horizon with that of distance, primarily (though not only) temporal distance. In one sense, my temporal distance from the texts I read and watch is an interpretive challenge—a challenge that increases as the Holocaust is receding into the past. In fact, there are multiple temporal distances involved here: the survivors' distance from the genocide when they tell their stories and afterward, and my distance from my first experience of these stories and from the events they narrate. Yet Gadamer argues that "temporal distance is not something that must be overcome. . . . In fact the important thing is to recognize temporal distance as a positive and productive condition enabling understanding" (2013, p. 308). For Gadamer, "the judgment of contemporary works of art is desperately uncertain for the scholarly consciousness. . . . Only when all their relations to the present time have faded away can their real nature appear" (p. 308). It does not follow that my temporal distance from Holocaust narratives, as well as from the Holocaust as a series of historical events, makes my interpretation convincing. Although temporal distance "lets the true meaning of the object emerge fully . . . [the] discovery of the true meaning of a text or a work of art is never finished; it is in fact an infinite process" (p. 309). Ideally, this interpretive process is dialogical; it involves an exchange, an ongoing conversation, between the reader or viewer and the text. An important constituent element of such a dialogue is the question: "[A]ll suspension of judgments and hence, a fortiori, of prejudices, has the logical structure of a *question*. . . . The essence of the *question* is to open up possibilities and keep them open" (p. 310, original emphasis). In this study of Holocaust narratives, the question often approximates to *ethical* questions stirred by my dialogue with the text. As Meretoja and Colin Davis observe, "there are no ethically neutral narratives, and the ethical dimension of a narrative takes shape in dialogue with the reader or the viewer" (Meretoja & Davis, 2018, p. 7). Responding to questions created by such a dialogue does not necessarily make me a better person. Yet I concur with Meretoja (2018a) that ethical questions can reveal how limited my perspective is, thus perhaps augmenting my understanding of other human beings' perspectives and values.

Approach

My approach builds on and refines that developed in a series of my essays and books, including *Narrative in Fiction and Film*. As this introduction indicates, I aim to integrate key aspects of classical narratology, rhetorical narrative theory, memory studies, narrative psychology, narrative hermeneutics, work on narrative ethics, and ethically inclined film studies. The approach is inspired by Ricoeur's (1994) important point that as critics of texts we need to combine a hermeneutics of suspicion with a hermeneutics of trust or restoration.[28] Rather than using a particular theory of ethics, I seek to identify and discuss significant aspects of the discourse that an author or director has deployed (consciously or intuitively) in the narrative. The aim throughout is to further my understanding—and hopefully my reader's understanding—of how the ethics of the narrative is presented to the reader or viewer, while at the same time highlighting the key role of the ethics that I take with me to the act and experience of reading and viewing. Experience and memory are constituent elements of this ethics, and this applies both to the narrative presentation of the ethics and to the way it is perceived and interpreted. In this study of the ethics of Holocaust narratives, experience, memory, and narrative are closely related, each element blending into the two others while simultaneously being affected by them.

In different ways, cognitive, hermeneutic, and reception-oriented theories of narrative have persuasively argued that it is the reader or viewer who makes the meaning of a verbal narrative or film narrative. This observation is particularly important as regards narrative ethics. Yet as Bal has noted, "in doing so, the reader [or viewer] is in dialogue with the text. It is only once we know how a text is structured that the reader's [or viewer's] share and responsibility for acting within those constraints can be assessed" (2018, p. 52; cf. Bal, 2017). This important point supports the approach in the present book. There is a need for close reading and rereading—and of watching and rewatching—in order to come to terms with the ethics of complex narratives. This need becomes even stronger if we want to explore the ways in which narrative, memory, and experience are interconnected. As my interpretations are based on and made possible by acts of rereading and rewatching the relevant texts, my approach approximates to an ethics of rereading and rewatching Holocaust narratives. Rereading and rewatching the verbal narratives and the film narratives, I inevitably reinterpret them. Influenced by Gadamer and Ricoeur, I tend to think of interpretation as "an endless spiral that would carry the meditation past the same point a number of times, but at different altitudes" (Ricoeur, 1984, p. 72).

The elements of narrative have been conceived, deployed, and combined by the author or director. Yet although it is not unimportant what the author or director attempts to communicate, once the text has been published or released it takes on a life of its own; it speaks for itself as narrative discourse. It is this narrative discourse that I read or watch—and that (in the following chapters) I interpret after having read or watched it at least twice. Thus, when I refer to, say, Ishiguro's *The Remains of the Day*, I am thinking of Ishiguro as *implied* author: my image or idea of the author, including his ethics, based on my interpretation of the novel's narrative discourse (Lothe, 2019). Similarly, when I refer to Lanzmann as the director of *Shoah*, that reference builds on and follows from my interpretation of *Shoah* as a complex narrative discourse. In my analyses, I thus use narrative discourse as a synonym of narrative text as defined by Bal; it is this text I have access to and that forms the basis for my interpretation.

While the analyses are aided by Genette's study of narrative, they are not narrowly or exclusively structuralist. Narrative is contextually situated and historically framed—and the narratives I discuss are all linked, albeit in different ways, to the Holocaust as a particular series of events. Moreover, as already signaled, I relate narrative more closely to variants of memory, experience, and interpretation than does structuralist narratology. My approach is associated with, though not identical to, Phelan's rhetorical view of narrative communication. In *Somebody Telling Somebody Else*, Phelan presents a chart of narrative possibilities that identifies "the two constants in the communication, the somebody who tells and the somebody who listens" (2017, p. 25). In the communication of narratives that I discuss in Chapter 1, the "somebody who tells" is the Holocaust survivor, while I am the "somebody who listens." In Sebald's novel *Austerlitz*, "the somebody who tells" consists of at least four narrative agents: Sebald as implied author, the frame narrator, Austerlitz, and Věra. Concomitantly, the "somebody who listens" includes at least three agents: after having listened to Věra, Austerlitz tells his story to the frame narrator, who relays that story (and fragments of his own) to the reader.[29]

One attractive feature of Phelan's chart of narrative possibilities is that, compared to the narrative communication model that I present in *Narrative in Fiction and Film*, it is less unidirectional: throughout his examination of narrative resources, Phelan pays "attention to narrative progression and to the affective, ethical, and aesthetic effects of author-audience interactions" (2017, p. 65). I connect "author-audience interactions" to the dialogue between the implied author or director (as represented by the narrative discourse) and the reader or viewer. My understanding of this dialogue (or "interactions") is an integral part of my interpretive activity: building on the text's self-interpretive elements, I attempt to come to terms with the ethics of its narrative presentation of the Holocaust. A self-interpretive element or sign is a word or image or a larger textual segment that strikes me as important when I read a verbal narrative or watch a film narrative. On a second reading, its significance—or more precisely, its contribution to my interpretation—is enhanced, though it can also be reduced.[30]

Two further aspects of *Somebody Telling Somebody Else* inform my discussion. First, Phelan rightly emphasizes the key role that characters play in narrative communication. In classical, predominantly structuralist narratology, characters are conspicuously absent from narrative communication. Yet characters not only influence the way a narrative is presented to the reader or viewer; they also contribute to one's interpretation of the narrative. One reason for characters' interpretive contribution is that as a reader or viewer I may react to (support or take exception to) a given character's values, and that reaction may color my interpretation of the narrative's ethics. Second, I endorse the way Phelan relates a narrative's values to various constituent elements of the narrative, including not only the implied author but also the narrator(s), the characters, the listener, and the "audience." The main reason I substitute "reader" and "viewer" for "audience" is that, from the perspective of narrative hermeneutics, I am hesitant to include more than one reader or viewer in my interpretations of the narrative ethics of Holocaust narrative.[31]

Because, as Ricoeur (2006) shows, the process of remembering necessitates an accompanying act of forgetting, the interpretive process involves a selection of textual components at the expense of others. This selection starts immediately: once I ask myself what the text I am reading or watching is about, I start interpreting it. This book highlights, and thus selects and interprets, textual aspects associated with the historical event of the Holocaust. While I discuss the narrative's beginning, middle, and end, I take a particular interest in narrative beginnings, for four reasons. First, reflecting the author's or director's innumerable possibilities of plot formation, character construction, and other aspects of narrative, narrative beginnings involve, and are the result of, a series of choices, priorities, and purposes that are not just aesthetic but also ethical. Second, though it may be possible to identify one beginning of a narrative text, the various agents of narrative communication represent different constituent elements of that beginning (Auerbach, 1947/2003; Insdorf, 2017; Phelan, 2007; Richardson, 2008; Said, 1975). All of these possess an ethical dimension. Beginnings are dynamic and complex, and their significance, including their ethical import, is enhanced by middles and ends (Miller, 1998). Third, if a narrative beginning is aesthetically constitutive, it is also ethically constitutive in ways that interact and cumulatively reinforce each other. The narrative's self-interpretive signs play a key role here. Fourth, responses to and interpretations of the ethics of narrative beginnings are closely associated with, and cannot be separated from, reading or viewing a second (or third or fourth) time. This is what I do as I develop my version of an ethics of rereading.

As I discuss how aspects of memory and narrative ethics are presented in Holocaust testimony, narrative fiction, and film, my approach cannot be wholly identical in each chapter since my chosen texts belong to and exhibit characteristic traits of different genres and media. The narrative analyses include observations on the generic features of the text under consideration; these observations are inseparable from my interpretation of that text. I incorporate observations on testimony into Chapter 1; I consider aspects of documentary film in Chapters 2 and 3; and I discuss elements of narrative fiction and the fiction film in Chapters 4–7.

In this introduction, I comment briefly on one notable difference between testimony and narrative fiction because this generic divergence has consequences for my approach. For Ricoeur, testimony's most distinctive feature emerges from and is illuminated by three words: "I was there" (2006, p. 163). He notes, "What is attested to is indivisibly the reality of the past thing and the presence of the narrator at the place of its occurrence" (p. 163). Emphasizing that it is the witness who first declares himself or herself to be a witness, he specifies that "[a] triple deictic marks this self-designation: the first-person singular, the past tense of the verb, and the mention of there in relation to here" (p. 164). Ricoeur's understanding of this triple deictic influences my interpretations of testimonies in Chapters 1 and 3, and also those of narrative fiction in Chapters 4–7. As "I was there" indicates, the narrator of a testimony claims that what he or she narrates happened in history; it was a historical occurrence.[32] "The largest single difference," notes Inga Clendinnen, "between History and Fiction (at moments like these they require capitalization) is that each establishes quite different relationships between writer and subject, and writer and reader" (2002, p. 170). Contrasting nonfiction with fiction, Clendinnen emphasizes that "when I read a story [e.g., a testimony] which claims to be true[,] I will know very much less about the protagonists. . . . Nonetheless, I engage with them differently because I stand in a moral relationship with these people" (p. 170). This moral relationship affects my interpretation, thus making my approach to (and interpretation of) a testimony different from that to a novel—even though both are narratives.[33] Although characters in a literary narrative or a fiction film are person-like, they are not human beings. As John Frow observes, "'Person' makes explicit the assumption . . . that the category of fictional character depends upon the prior category of human being" (2014, p. 33). Considering the human beings in the testimonies and nonfiction films that I discuss in Chapters 1–3 as persons, I reserve the concept of "character" for the discussions of literary narrative and film narrative in Chapters 4–7. As Jeremy Hawthorn observes:

> Fictions are not true, but they are not lies; they typically describe that which is not real but which is nonetheless not totally unreal; they can include references to real people and events without jeopardizing their fictional status; they are designed to get readers or listeners to respond "as if," but not (normally) to deceive them; even though readers are aware that fictions describe people who do not exist or events which have not happened, they may nonetheless produce real emotions, important reflections, and even altered behaviour in the real world. (2023, p. 2)

Hawthorn's important point about narrative fiction's paradoxical capacity to "produce real emotions, important reflections, and even altered behaviour in the real world" has a bearing on my approach to *Les Bienveillantes*, *The Remains of the Day*, *Austerlitz*, and *Aller Tage Abend*. My interpretations of these novels suggest that "important reflections" can include ethical reflections stirred by the narrative discourse. Hawthorn relates his observation on fiction to the case that Dorrit Cohn (1999) makes for the distinctiveness of literary fiction. Two of Cohn's points are particularly relevant here: first, only in fictional narratives can narrators possess accurate insight into the consciousness of characters apart from themselves; second, in nonfictional narratives such as testimonies the distinction between author and narrator does not make the same kind of sense as it does when applied to fictional texts (Cohn, 1999; Hawthorn, 2023).

Appropriating these observations on nonfiction and fiction, I specify that although the "ontological landscapes" (Pavel, 1986, p. 139) created by a novel's narrative discourse conjure up compelling realities, those imagined or invented realities are related, however indirectly, to historical reality. In the four novels I interpret, the Holocaust is a significant aspect of this reality. Yet although I approach the novels as narrative presentations of the Holocaust, I do not disregard the elements of fictionality, that is, of the "intentionally signaled invention in communication" (Zetterberg Gjerlevsen, 2016) that characterize them. I hope to demonstrate that, when related to and conditioned by the Holocaust as a historical fact, the communicated invention that forms an integral part of the novels' discourse is a rich resource. Hawthorn is right to argue that the discourse of narrative fiction can engender real emotions and prompt ethical questions, including questions I discuss in this book. But the novel achieves this in ways that differ from the narrative communication of a testimony. One example of this generic difference is that, as my analyses show, a novel's narrative ethics emerges from and is often complicated by the characters and narrators' conflicting values as well as the variable relations between these values and those of the narrative discourse.

This is not to deny that, as the concept of fictionality suggests, the borderline between the two genres can be blurred. Studies of the interrelations between narrative and the mind indicate that in the dynamic processes of narrative world construction, "we use both nonfictional and fictional narrative techniques and strategies of interpretation" (Brockmeier, 2013, p. 124). The weight I attach to the genre of testimony is one reason, in this discussion of Holocaust narratives, I still choose to broadly distinguish between nonfiction and fiction. While my justification for the distinction is partly heuristic, it is in part also ethical. The combination of genres and media that I discuss is challenging: since my chosen texts present the Holocaust in different ways, I need to develop an approach that, while consistent, is sufficiently flexible to respond to the variants of narrative presentation that the texts exhibit. One reason I start by discussing Holocaust testimonies is that I want my discussion to be informed and colored by my "moral relationship" (Clendinnen, 2002, p. 170) with the Holocaust survivors who bear witness. Yet it is a key element of my argument that we also need other forms of narrative communication about the genocide of the Nazis against the Jews. Wiesel, who has claimed that "there is no such thing as Holocaust literature . . . the very term is a contradiction," has nevertheless written the trilogy *Night*, *Dawn*,

The Accident—widely read and influential Holocaust narratives that many critics consider to be a blend of memoir and novel.[34]

Lawrence Langer was the first literary scholar to defend Holocaust writing as art, discussing what he called the "aesthetics of atrocity" in literary works by writers who had lived through the Holocaust, either as survivors of persecution or as bystanders (1975, p. 22).[35] Imre Kertész's *Fatelessness* (1975/2004) succeeds in transmuting the horrors of the concentration camp (Kertész was a Holocaust survivor). *Fatelessness* possesses several elements of fictionality, including Kertész's invention of a narrator who is similar to and yet different from himself, who uses irony when telling about his camp experience, and whose functions as narrator blend into those of the protagonist. Kertész's ingenious combination of these narrative devices contributes decisively to the narrative ethics of *Fatelessness* (Miller, 2011).[36] Authors who have not themselves experienced the Holocaust can also use fictionality in ways that can further our understanding of the genocide. As the temporal distance from the Holocaust increases, there is a sense in which, as Gadamer (2013) suggests, the interpretive potential (or capacity) of both authors and readers can be strengthened.

I hope that, combined with my interpretations of the novels by Littell, Ishiguro, and Erpenbeck, my analysis of Sebald's novel in Chapter 6 will show how narrative fiction can contribute to the continuing task and necessity of remembering the Holocaust. *Austerlitz* provides a rich illustration of Erll's point that "[l]iterature fills a niche in memory culture, because like arguably no other symbol system, it is characterized by its ability—and indeed tendency—to refer to the forgotten and repressed as well as the unnoticed, unconscious, and unintentional aspects of our dealings with the past" (2011, p. 153). A reason why literature can do this is that narrative and imagination are integrally tied to each other (Andrews, 2014). This characteristic feature of narrative fiction is apparent in all the novels I analyze. Moreover, the interplay of narrative and imagination is a constituent element of the fiction film as well. Discussing Ivory's *The Remains of the Day*, I take a particular interest in the ethical aspects of the film's narrative—and in the ways in which these aspects are related to the Holocaust. Since the medium of the film is different from that of verbal fiction, I allow the characteristic features of the medium to influence my approach (Grønstad, 2016; Haggith & Newman, 2005).

This point also applies to my interpretations of film documentaries in Chapters 2 and 3. For example, I discuss how the film medium enables

Lanzmann to present the complex issue of silence more convincingly and thought-provokingly than, using verbal language, I can do in my presentation of the testimonies in *Time's Witnesses*. As regards my approach to Riefenstahl's *Triumph of the Will*, I want to make explicit the interpretive challenge brought into notice by the film's combination of two genres: film documentary and film propaganda. It is difficult to approach *Triumph of the Will* in a way that gives both these dimensions of Riefenstahl's complex film the critical attention they deserve. In my discussion of *Triumph of the Will* as well as Resnais's *Night and Fog* and Lanzmann's *Shoah*, I develop an approach that, concentrating on selected scenes, identifies and discusses how the combination of narrative elements and film aesthetics creates a complex mnemonic process that stirs a range of ethical questions. Although, in all my analyses, I focus on the narrative ethics of telling and showing, I find that the ethics of telling and showing is constantly related to, and in one sense kept in check by, the Holocaust as the anchor point of the ethics of the told (Phelan, 2017).

As I reread and rewatch my chosen texts, my focus on narrative presentation of the Holocaust inevitably makes me suspend, or consider relatively superficially, other aesthetic and ethical elements that they possess. Yet criticism, including ethical criticism, necessarily involves selection. Moreover, I posit that once one or more aspects of the Holocaust have been identified in a narrative text, the text's narrative ethics becomes important, and so does its presentation of memory. My heuristic justification for highlighting the elements of text that I do is that, in my interpretation, they reveal facets of the Holocaust as integral parts of the narrative discourse. My observations on narrative, memory, narrative psychology, and narrative hermeneutics are all related to and constitute the basis for the approach outlined here. My approach is inspired by my main critical concern: to study the narrative ethics of presentations of the historical event of the Holocaust. Given that the Holocaust occurred, I discuss ways in which we—that is, the cultural community of Europe and beyond—can remember this historical event by narrating about it. Yet although it is essential that "we" remember the Holocaust, and although I am convinced that different forms of narrative can help us to do so, I tend to use "I" rather than "we" in the analyses.

Both as a reader and as a viewer, I approach the Holocaust and narrative presentations of the Holocaust from my perspective as a Norwegian man born after the Holocaust. Thus, my perspective is limited—and inevitably there are aspects of the Holocaust narratives I discuss that are beyond my horizon. And yet, as Gadamer convincingly argues, the limitation of my horizon, which includes the temporal distance between the Holocaust and the third decade of the 21st century, can also be an interpretive gain or advantage.[37] One such gain could be that by being aware of the limitations of my perspective, and thus also of my approach, I may improve my ability, as well as my readiness, to ask questions—and to allow the narratives I discuss to ask me questions. As I have suggested, in discussions of Holocaust narratives, these questions tend to be ethical questions.[38]

Since, as the following analyses show, I often find it difficult to answer ethical questions stirred by Holocaust narratives, they blend into ethical reflection informed by my own values as reader or viewer. Asking myself what these values are, one possible response is to say that they are opposed to the values of Nazi Germany. Thus, I subscribe to the first sentence of Article 1 of the Universal Declaration of Human Rights: "All human beings are born free and equal in dignity and rights." Yet once I have made this statement of values, I need to add that I also have more dubious values of which I am less conscious and which influence my actions, attitudes, and priorities more strongly than I would like to think. They also influence my interpretations of the narrative ethics of Holocaust narratives. This admission takes me back to Fossum's photograph: If I were one of the people watching the *Donau* leaving Oslo on November 26, 1942, with 532 Norwegian Jews on board, would my values have caused or enabled me to fight for the Jews' freedom, thus risking my own life? I am not sure they would.

Outline of Chapters

Chapter 1 discusses the narrative ethics of four testimonies in my edited volume *Time's Witnesses: Women's Voices from the Holocaust* (Lothe, 2017a). One common feature of the first-person narratives by Maria Gabrielsen, Ella Blumenthal, Edith Notowicz, and Olga Horak is the tellers' insistence, doubtless in response to those who deny the fact, that the Holocaust did indeed happen (Cesare, 2023). They can assert this with confidence because they were there, inside the concentration camp, where almost everybody else was murdered. Linked to this common feature is a new role of the narrator, since, as Assmann (2018) observes, the witness's function is related to and constitutes a new mode of storytelling developed to cope with not just individual but also collective trauma after the Second World War and the Holocaust. As narration becomes an act of witnessing in a double sense—the first-person narrator's "I" is entangled with a "we" since the narrator also speaks on behalf of those who perished—storytelling's ethical dimension is accentuated.

Concentrating on the narrative ethics of documentary film, Chapter 2 discusses two films not inspired by a written narrative (as in the case of Ivory's *The Remains of the Day*) but by memories of historical events and processes. I first consider *Triumph des Willens* (1935; *Triumph of the Will*), a documentary film that chronicles the 1934 Nazi Party Congress in Nuremberg. Riefenstahl, who directed, produced, and co-wrote the film, claimed that her task was to filmically present, in an aesthetically appealing way, the historical event of the Congress. Yet *Triumph of the Will* is thoroughly and knowingly complicit in Nazi ideology. Of the texts analyzed in this book, *Triumph of the Will* is the only one created before the Holocaust (although not before significant acts of violence and persecution directed by the Nazis against Jews had been committed). Yet for me as a viewer born after the Second World War, Riefenstahl's film is inevitably associated with the Holocaust. Building on the discussion of *Triumph of the Will*, the chapter turns to the French director Resnais's *Nuit et brouillard* (1956; *Night and Fog*). One of the first attempts to document and remember the Nazi concentration camps by activating and exploring the resources of film narrative, Resnais's film proved hugely influential. A notable aspect of the film is the voice-over commentary written by Jean Cayrol, a French poet who, because he was a member of the French Resistance, was deported to the concentration camp Mauthausen. There is, I argue, a problematic tension in *Night and Fog* between Cayrol's commentary, which hardly mentions that most of the victims of the Holocaust were Jews, and Resnais's use of film footage from the concentration and extermination camps to which Jews were deported.

Chapter 3 considers the French director Lanzmann's *Shoah* as a response to *Night and Fog*; although Lanzmann does not refer to Resnais, the two documentaries are intertextually related. Lanzmann takes issue with several of Resnais's choices—choices that, for both directors, are not just formal but also ethical. While Resnais, via the voice-over commentary written by Cayrol, warns against forgetting the horrors of the concentration camps of the Second World War a decade after the events occurred, Lanzmann, resisting the use of voice-over as well as documentary footage in a film made

30 years later, uses film form to demonstrate the need to remember the Holocaust by talking to people who survived the event. Discussing the narrative ethics of Lanzmann as director and interviewer, as well as that of his interviewees, I concentrate on the interviews with Simon Srebnik, Franz Suchomel, Abraham Bomba, Filip Müller, and Raul Hilberg.

That narrative fiction plays a key role in ethical criticism is illustrated by, for example, Nussbaum's (1992) point that novels such as those discussed in this book may conduct ethical inquiry in ways that are just as important, and possibly more nuanced, than the ethical inquiries of analytic philosophers. As Ricoeur, himself a philosopher, puts it, "The thought experiments we conduct in the great laboratory of the imaginary are also explorations in the realm of good and evil" (1994, p. 164). One such thought experiment is the novel whose narrative ethics I analyze in Chapter 4, the French American author Littell's *Les Bienveillantes* (*The Kindly Ones*). First published in French in 2006, this 1,000-page novel presents the reader with a very considerable challenge since its one and only narrator is a Nazi perpetrator who does not regret, and even cunningly defends, his actions during the Second World War, including his involvement in the Holocaust.

Chapter 5 turns to the British author Ishiguro's *The Remains of the Day* (1989) and Ivory's film adaptation (1993). In common with Littell, Ishiguro uses a first-person narrator who is also the novel's protagonist. In spite of the fact that Stevens, the butler in Ishiguro's novel, is different from Littell's Nazi perpetrator, both authors use constituent elements of first-person narration to present their main characters' memories as a multilayered process that demonstrates the vicissitudes of memory. Stevens's primary mission in life has been to serve Lord Darlington, who, when the novel (and the film) begins, is recently deceased. Embarking on a painful process of remembering what on one level he wants to forget, Stevens reveals—or more precisely, exploiting the resources of verbal fiction and film, Ishiguro and Ivory make Stevens reveal—that he was complicit in antisemitism (and even, I argue, the Holocaust). That this suggestion is stronger in the adaptation than in the novel is partly, though not only, a consequence of the great difference between the two media. Effectively combining elements of film form such as rhythm, repetition, camera angle, and color, Ivory's adaptation gives a rich response to the moral values and ethical dilemmas presented by Ishiguro in the novel.

The book's last two chapters discuss two novels written by authors from Germany, Sebald's *Austerlitz* (2001) and Erpenbeck's *Aller Tage Abend*

(2012; *The End of Days*). It is not coincidental that the epigraph of Erpenbeck's novel is from *Austerlitz*: both novels explore the possibilities as well as the limits of narrative, and both are studies in memory—especially the memory of those who are lost and absent. This said, there are also notable differences between the two. Chapter 6 concentrates on Sebald's presentation of the relationship between the main character, Austerlitz, and the narrator, who first listens to Austerlitz's story and then relays it to the reader. In *Austerlitz*, memory and narrative not only are intertwined but mutually reinforce each other: while Austerlitz's memory (or rather, the thinness of his memory) motivates and even necessitates his narrative, his act of narration brings memories of his parents (or rather, memories of his parents' absence) back to him. Austerlitz's act of narration takes the form of a narrative transmission that approximates to a negotiation between him as a Jewish narrator and a listener or narratee who turns out to be German. Thus, the ethics of the told blends into the ethics of the telling and vice versa. As a character and a narrative instrument in the German author Sebald's service, this German listener becomes a narrator who not only passes Austerlitz's verbal narrative on to the reader but presents the reader with Austerlitz's (or Sebald's) pictures, thus making the reader also a viewer.

Erpenbeck's *Aller Tage Abend* adds another female voice, perspective, and experience to those of Holocaust survivors Gabrielsen, Blumenthal, Notowicz, Horak, as well as to that of the pro-Nazi propagandist Riefenstahl. The novel's starting point is that an infant Jewish child dies in a small town in Eastern Europe. Turning to *Aller Tage Abend* in Chapter 7, I discuss how Erpenbeck, via her third-person narrator, whose perspective approaches those of her focalized characters, asks: What would the child, who was a girl, have experienced had she not died? What would have changed if she had not died? That these questions have an ethical dimension becomes obvious once the reader relates them to the Holocaust. Yet ethics can be an integral aspect of such questions after any child's death. Exploiting the resources of fiction, Erpenbeck explores "the kinds of things that might occur" (Aristotle, 1995, p. 59). Responding as a creative writer to her own questions (presented in an "intermezzo" between parts 1 and 2), Erpenbeck reveals that the girl who died turns out to be alive after all, living with her family in Vienna just after the First World War. She dies again, but reemerges in Moscow in the 1930s and, following another death, as a citizen of East Berlin in the 1960s. After yet another death the reader meets her again, in a nursing home in Berlin after the reunification of Germany in 1989. Here she dies one last time, and the novel ends. Exploiting the possibilities of this repetitive pattern, Erpenbeck shows how the protagonist experiences a series of wars and totalitarian regimes in 20th-century Europe. One formative experience is antisemitism, which she tries to deal with in different ways in her successive lives. For the narrator, whose temporal vantage point and ethical stance approximate to that of Erpenbeck as implied author, the Holocaust becomes a postmemory; for the main character—who remains anonymous for most of the narrative but whose name, the reader learns at the end, is Mrs. Hoffmann—it is a painful, traumatic memory.

Relating the points made in this introduction to those of the following chapters, my "concluding reflections" revolve around the interplay of memory, narrative, and ethics in the texts discussed in the book. One reason it is difficult, and in a way not even desirable, to reach a firm conclusion is that while I hope to show that memory and narrative are interdependent, this interplay, and not least the way in which its ethical aspects are interpreted by the reader or viewer, varies very considerably. This kind of interpretive variation depends in part on and follows from the temporal distance between the text—within which there are further variations between the time of experience (narrated time) and the time of the narration (narrative time)—and the time of reading or viewing. As every ethical situation or challenge is singular, I am hesitant to make generalized, abstract statements based on my interpretations of ethical negotiations, tensions, and conflicts in the texts that I continue to reread and rewatch.

As should, I hope, be clear, it is an important part of the book's rationale that it discusses the narrative ethics of both fictional and nonfictional narratives, including testimonies. Ethical questions are posed differently in these two basic variants of narrative, even though the point of transition between fiction and nonfiction can be blurred. Moreover, the ethical questions—which can be explicit or implicit, and which are associated with a narrative's self-interpretive elements—are also read, seen, and *interpreted* in dissimilar, even conflicting ways by different readers and viewers. My discussion throughout is based on and proceeds from the premise that this point applies equally to verbal (oral and written) and filmic texts, as well as to narrative aspects of visual images. That ethical questions are posed and presented differently in dissimilar narrative genres and media does not mean that narrative ethics is more important in one genre or medium than another. What varies is the ethics of form (Toker, 2010), and the remarkable range of narratives' ethical form and structure is a strong indication of the thematic significance and relevance of ethics in narrative texts. Equally, it forcefully indicates the significance and relevance of memory—for the authors and film directors of these texts, for their narrators, characters, and actors, and for their readers and viewers.

As I end by highlighting narrative fiction as an ethical resource, I hope that my book will, in its entirety, contribute to a justification of the production of fictional accounts of the Holocaust. One nonnegotiable requirement of this kind of justification is that the fictional narrative does not distort or falsely present the historical reality of the Holocaust—as does the propaganda film about Theresienstadt inserted into Austerlitz's narrative in *Austerlitz*. There have been arguments that "only the truth will do" and that so long as there is Holocaust denial (which is probably forever) accounts of the Holocaust should stick strictly to historical facts. Historical studies of the Holocaust continue to be essential, and so do written testimonies as well as testimonies on video or film (as in *Shoah*). Yet my book shows, I hope, that important aspects of this set of historical events can be imparted by fictional stories that, exploiting a range of narrative resources and dramatizing individuals' experiences, can engage the reader or viewer in ways that further his or her interpretive activity. As the last Holocaust survivors are passing away, the importance of such fictional narratives, including the four novels discussed here and Ivory's fiction film *The Remains of the Day*, is growing, and they can hopefully help us to not forget a horrific genocide that it may prove difficult to remember.

Notes

1. The exhibition marked 50 years since the notorious Wannsee conference. The purpose of the conference, held in that Berlin suburb on January 20, 1942, was to ensure the cooperation of administrative leaders of government departments in the implementation of the Holocaust. See Jäckel (2019) and "Wannsee Conference and the 'Final Solution,'" *Holocaust Encyclopedia*, https://encyclopedia.ushmm.org/content/en/article/wannsee-conference-and-the-final-solution
2. In common with Mieke Bal, I understand concepts "not so much as firmly established univocal terms but as dynamic in themselves. While groping to define, provisionally and partly, what a particular concept may *mean*, we gain insight into what it can *do*. It is in the groping that the valuable work lies" (2002, p. 11, original emphasis). Aspects of this "groping" form an integral part of the following interpretations.
3. *Holocaust Encyclopedia* (2024). United States Holocaust Memorial Museum, Washington, DC. https://encyclopedia.ushmm.org/content/en/article/introduction-to-the-holocaust
4. There is a large number of studies of the Holocaust. Eight useful edited volumes are Ambrosewicz-Jakobs (2009), Baumel-Schwartz and Laqueur (2001), Benz (2002), Berenbaum and Peck (2002), Friedman (2012), Hirsch and Kacandes (2004), Levi and Rothberg (2003), and Roth et al. (2001). Raul Hilberg's work (1992, 1999, 2003) is particularly relevant for

me: since Hilberg is interviewed by Lanzmann in *Shoah*, there is a sense in which he combines the functions of historian and witness. Other studies that I have found helpful include Arendt (1951/2017), Beevor (1999), Bruland (2012), Friedländer (1997, 2003, 2007), Gilbert (1987), Kershaw (1998, 2000, 2008), LaCapra (1996, 1998), Roth (2005), and Young (1988, 1993, 2010). Important research on aspects of the Holocaust is being carried out at various research centers in many countries.

5. The concept of the implicated subject is a helpful addition to the typology first proposed by Raul Hilberg (1992) in *Perpetrators Victims Bystanders: The Jewish Catastrophe 1933–1945*. While the roles of perpetrator and victim are relatively easily identifiable, that of bystander is more complex and fluid. In *Bystander Society: Conformity and Complicity in Nazi Germany and the Holocaust*, Mary Fulbrook writes, "Bystanding is socially constructed and can change over time.... In what I call a 'bystander society,' fewer people are likely to stand up and act on 'the courage of their convictions' in face of violence against those ousted from the community and vilified as 'others.' . . . In Nazi Germany . . . these conditions were historically produced, rather than pre-existent" (2023, pp. 2–3). Bystanding involves variants and degrees of complicity, and it can be hard for human beings (and characters in narrative fiction) to admit that by failing to protest or act they were complicit in wrongdoing and violence (see Chapters 5 and 6). Fulbrook is right to draw attention to the collective dimension of bystanding, and by implication also to the blurred transition between individual and collective memory. I also second her attempt to find "some means of making distinctions that allow us to explore the complexity of varieties and degrees of involvement and responsibility" (p. 9). For me as a European born after the Holocaust, Rothberg's concept of the implicated subject is one such means.

6. KZ Stutthof was the first concentration camp that the Nazis erected outside Germany. They started building the camp, which was situated about 50 kilometers to the east of Gdańsk in present-day Poland, in September 1939.

7. In *Narrative in Fiction and Film*, I note that the concept of distance reveals a fundamental characteristic of narrative fiction: while it is "unusually flexible and can present events and conflicts with great intensity, it constitutes itself through a series of distancing means" (Lothe, 2000, p. 35). I now posit that this characteristic applies to different genres and forms of narrative, including all those discussed in this book. While in *Narrative in Fiction and Film* "[t]he term 'distance' . . . refers particularly to the relationship between the narrator and the events/characters in the narrative text" (p. 35), I am now just as interested in the (varying and dynamic) relationship among the characters, between the implied author and both the narrator(s) and the characters, and between the reader and all these narrative agents. I distinguish between temporal distance (which involves a distance between the act of narration and the events or experiences that are narrated), spatial distance (which refers to the distance between the narrative situation and the place where the events unfold), and attitudinal distance (which has a distinctly interpretive dimension as it is connected with the values presented through the narrative discourse). In the following narrative analyses, I relate variants of distance to modulations of perspective.

8. In written narratives as well as film narratives, perspective—which I relate to Genette's (1980, p. 186) question "*Who sees?*"—indicates the vision through which the narrative elements are presented to the reader or viewer. The characters, the narrator(s), and the implied author or film director all contribute to this presentation, which is engendered and shaped through the narrative discourse. Bal notes that "focalization [which broadly corresponds to my use of perspective] has a strongly manipulative effect" (2017, p. 141). My analyses support this point, and they also confirm Bal's accompanying observation: "The way in which an object is presented gives information about the object itself as well as about the focalizer" (p. 140). The reader or viewer's perspective and distance also play a key role in the interpretation of the narrative (Gadamer, 2013; Meretoja, 2018a).

9. Four helpful introductions are Abbott (2020), Bal (2017), Fludernik (2009), and Rimmon-Kenan (2002). Two informative collected volumes are Herman et al. (2007) and Phelan and Rabinowitz (2005). A helpful open access publication is Hühn et al. (2021). For an incisive discussion of narrative and narratology in relation to developments in literary theory, see Culler (2011).

10. There are three main reasons why Phelan's work has influenced this study: first, I find his "chart of constants and variables in narrative communication" (Phelan, 2017, p. 26) helpful in narrative analysis; second, I am attracted to his notion of narrative as a powerful mode not

only of communication but also of exploration, including the exploration of difficult issues and painful memories (Phelan, 2005, 2007); and third, he has made significant contributions to narrative ethics (Phelan, 2014, 2017).

11. For a range of discussions of memory and trauma, particularly in relation to history and literature, see the articles in the following volumes: Bond and Craps (2020), Buelens et al. (2014), Davis and Meretoja (2020), Erll and Nünning (2010), Naguib and Stordalen (2015), Olick et al. (2011), Roth et al. (2001), Seeberg et al. (2013), and Sætre et al. (2017).

12. Erll relates "implicit cultural memory" to the psychologist Daniel Schacter's reflections on "the hidden world of implicit memory . . . when people are influenced by a past experience without any awareness that they are remembering" (Schacter, 1996, p. 161; cf. Erll, 2019, p. 229).

13. Hirsch, M. (2012). See also Hirsch (1997, 2012), Rothberg (2019), and Suleiman (2006).

14. This aspect of Halbwachs's exploration of memory reveals his indebtedness to Henri Bergson's (1896/1988) analysis of human beings' experience of time. Characterizing remembering as an active engagement that is fluid and changing, Bergson drew Halbwachs's attention to the difference between "objective" and subjective apprehensions of the past: "whereas new forms of record keeping measured time and recorded history in increasingly uniform and standardized ways, individual memory was still highly variable, sometimes recording short periods in intense detail and long periods in only the vaguest outline" (Olick et al., 2011, p. 17).

15. It is a chilling thought that since Halbwachs was a victim of the Holocaust, he could not appreciate the connections between his understanding of memory and the (individual as well as collective) challenge of remembering the Nazis' mass murder of six million Jews. After protesting the arrest of his Jewish father-in-law, Halbwachs was detained by the Gestapo in Paris in the summer of 1944 and then deported to the concentration camp Buchenwald, where he died in March 1945.

16. Here, as in the other chapters of this book, the term "ethos" refers to the values of a historical person or a fictional character. The concept of ethos is thus closely related to that of ethics. By a person's or character's "ethos" I mean a relatively stable character quality or value; by a person's or character's "ethics" I mean the complex combination of values, priorities, attitudes, and memories presented and challenged through the narrative discourse. However, the demarcation line between ethos and ethics is blurred. While "[e]thos attributions . . . [are] crucial in interpretation and evaluation processes" (Altes, 2014, p. ix), they are not stable since these processes are dynamic, evolving, and changing as we read and reread the verbal narrative or watch and rewatch the film narrative. See also the remarks on ethics in literature and film in Chapters 4 and 5.

17. Alasdair MacIntyre, whose *After Virtue* (1981/1997) is an important early contribution to narrative ethics, has written an influential history of ethics (MacIntyre, 1998). See also Hawthorn and Lothe (2013) and Lothe (2017d).

18. That narrative fiction plays a key role in these studies is illustrated by, for example, Nussbaum's (1992) point that novels such as those by the British novelist Iris Murdoch may conduct an ethical inquiry in ways that are more nuanced than the ethical inquiries of analytic philosophers, including Murdoch's own philosophical writings (Lothe, 2023b).

19. Toker notes that Hjelmslev's concept of "[t]he *substance of content* . . . can be roughly identified with the subject matter, the fields of reference (mainly, the External Field of Reference)"; "The *form of content* is to be sought in the relationships between the themes, patterns of imagery, the deployment of the motifs as parts of the Internal Field of Reference, and the corresponding shaping of the plot" (Toker, 2010, pp. 2–3, original emphasis). While Hjelmslev's concept of the *substance of expression* is the verbal medium of literary communication, "the *form of expression* is the style and such narrative techniques as the point of view, flashbacks, anticipations, heteroglossia, the monitoring of the flow of information, and the handling of blanks and gaps and of scene and summary" (p. 3, original emphasis). Although this book's focus is on the *form* of content and of expression, I relate the presentation of narrative to the substance of expression (whether verbal or filmic) and to the Holocaust as an essential constituent element of the substance of content.

20. The "ethical moment" in Miller's interpretations of narrative is particularly noticeable in his later work, not least in *The Conflagration of Community: Fiction before and after Auschwitz* (2011) and *Communities of Fiction* (2015).

21. Vetlesen adds, "Part of human agency, then, is an agent's desire to *do evil* in the sense given. I investigate why and in what sorts of social circumstances this desire arises at an individual

level, and how it is channelled—amplified, exploited—into what I call collective evildoing. I argue that such evildoing, in which whole groups are pitted against each other, springs from a combination of character, situation, and structure" (2005, p. 2). He links his approach to that of Jürgen Habermas, who has argued that "what moral and, especially, immoral action means is something we experience and learn *prior to* all philosophy; it confronts us no less compellingly in compassion for the hurt integrity of others than in suffering over one's own afflicted identity or in anxiety at its being endangered" (1994, p. 185, original emphasis).

22. There is an important connection between Løgstrup's concept of care and care as a constituent element of narrative medicine. See Charon (2006, 2017) and Spencer (2023).

23. I comment on aspects of Løgstrup's and Levinas's ethics in the following chapters. Two helpful studies of Levinas are Davis (2007b) and Holte (2015). Grønstad (2016) gives an illuminating discussion of Levinas in relation to film studies. See also Bergo (2019), "Emmanuel Levinas." *Stanford Encyclopedia of Philosophy*, https://plato.stanford.edu/archives/fall2024/entries/levinas/

24. Important as the ethical turn in film studies is, film scholars such as André Bazin (1967), Stanley Cavell (1979), Linda Hutcheon (2013), Siegfried Kracauer (1965), and Robert Stam (2005) have made observations on film and film form that are relevant and helpful, even though these observations may have been made before the "ethical turn" in film studies and even though they are not primarily, or not only, concerned with narrative ethics. Unsurprisingly, the ethical aspect of film studies is more pronounced in the work of scholars who discuss variants of film narrative in which the Holocaust is an issue, including, for example, Steven Spielberg's *Schindler's List* (1993). There is an ongoing and critically productive dialogue between film studies generally and studies of the Holocaust and the moving image (Haggith & Newman, 2005).

25. Brockmeier does so himself, not least in his thought-provoking interpretation of Sebald's *Austerlitz*—an interpretation that serves as a dialogue partner for me in Chapter 6.

26. *Beyond the Archive* is also relevant because of Brockmeier's references to and reflections on Holocaust narrative. Discussing James Young's comparative inquiries on the memory of the Holocaust, Brockmeier highlights one of Young's concluding points: "[A]lthough the very facts of this historically unique crime are documented in great detail and considered to be beyond doubt, there was no such thing as one single event called 'the Holocaust.' Rather, every nation—and sometimes even communities within one nation—construed their memories of it according to traditions, values, and political agendas that were dominant at a certain historical moment in time" (Brockmeier, 2015, p. 16; see Young, 1993). This kind of mnemonic variation accords with Brockmeier's strong narrative thesis. Autobiographical memory "come[s] into being through and in narrative," and memories—individual as well as collective and cultural—change over time. This point also applies to Norwegians', including my own, memory of the Holocaust. One reason Norwegians' view of "this historically unique crime" has changed recently is the publication of Georg W. Fossum's photograph of the *Donau*.

27. While Gadamer identifies and foregrounds the historical situatedness of the ways in which I interpret my experiences, Ricoeur (1984, 1985, 1988) demonstrates that my interpretation of my experiences is essentially a *narrative* interpretation. Ricoeur develops a narrative hermeneutics that draws on the insights of Gadamer's philosophical hermeneutics (Ritivoi, 2006). Considered not only as a theoretical basis for interpretations but also as a way of coming to terms with our historical situatedness and experientiality, narrative hermeneutics has been modified and refined in a range of recent studies (e.g., Andrews, 2014; Brockmeier, 2015, 2022, 2023; Davis, 2018b, 2020, 2023; Freeman, 2010, 2015, 2023; Frie, 2017; Meretoja, 2018a, 2018b, 2021, 2023); I am indebted to all of them.

28. Two current critics who do this are Cassandra Falke and Rita Felski, particularly in Falke's *The Phenomenology of Love and Reading* (2017) and Felski's *The Limits of Critique* (2015). Appropriating the French philosopher Jean-Luc Marion's idea of love as a fundamental dimension of human experience, Falke argues that, albeit in different ways, literature and criticism can be envisaged as acts of love that add, or aim to add, something to the world. Her variant of phenomenological criticism is associated with, though also different from, Felski's critique of the "hermeneutics of suspicion" (2015, p. 9): "Rather than looking behind the text—for its hidden causes, determining conditions, and noxious motives—we might place ourselves in front of the text, reflecting on what it unfurls, calls forth, makes possible" (p. 12). While I am sympathetically inclined toward both these approaches, my own is more accurately indicated by

the variant of hermeneutics that emphasizes "that meanings take shape as we engage in a dia-logue with texts from the horizon our own sociocultural world, and narratives exist in dialogic relations to cultural meaning-systems" (Meretoja, 2018a, p. 28). My addition, or specification, is that I tend to substitute "I/me" for "we/our."

29. Phelan locates the implied author outside the narrative text. Partly because of my focus on nar-rative ethics, I am inclined to agree with this view. I would like to add, though, that regardless of whether the reader or viewer locates the implied author or director inside or outside the text, our knowledge and evaluation of the implied author or director are entirely dependent on our acts of reading or watching that text. Thus, there is a sense in which the implied author or director, though positioned outside the text, is also within it. An unread or unwatched text has an author or director but not (yet) an implied author or director. It does not follow that extratextual knowledge about the author or director is necessarily irrelevant or unhelpful; the close connection that I establish between narrative, experience, and memory can make con-sideration of the historical author or director relevant. I reiterate, though, that my primary concern is with the implied author or director as represented by the narrative discourse that I read or watch. To put this another way, my idea of the text's author or director is based on and made possible by my interpretation of the text. In *Somebody Telling Somebody Else* (2017), Phelan emphasizes the implied author's role more strongly than he does in *Living to Tell about It* (2005) and *Experiencing Fiction* (2007). One reason he does so is that he considers the nar-rator just one of various "resources" (2017, p. 25) on which an author can draw in narrative communication. Yet as the analyses of my four chosen novels show, the narrator is an indis-pensable communicator in narrative fiction. Although the narrator's functions vary from genre to genre, and although several film scholars argue that film has narration but not a narrator, the narrator plays a key role in many narratives. The narrator is "[t]he one who narrates, as inscribed in the text" (Prince, 1991, p. 65). Gerald Prince's use of the word "inscribed" about the narrator is helpful since it brings out that the narrator is part of the diegesis, that is, the world in which the narrated situations and events occur (Lothe, 2000, 2019).

30. Two examples of self-interpretive elements in the following analyses are the verb "serve" in Ishiguro's *The Remains of the Day* (Chapter 5) and the proper name "Austerlitz" in Sebald's novel *Austerlitz* (Chapter 6). While awareness of a text's self-interpretive elements can fur-ther close reading and rereading, or watching and rewatching, of the narrative discourse, the reader's or viewer's identification of a self-interpretive element is already an interpretation (which may be affirmed or may need to be corrected or modified).

31. For example, sometimes the narrative presentation of a particular character's values is so striking that his or her values become one of the most memorable facets of my reading or viewing experience. An example is the values that Lieutenant Voss, a minor character in Littell's (2006/2010) *The Kindly Ones*, expresses in his conversations with Aue, who is the protagonist-narrator in the novel (see Chapter 4). Although I hope that readers of my book will find my interpretation of Voss's values convincing, or at least stimulating, I know that my reading can, and should, be challenged by interpretations that are furthered by approaches and colored by perspectives different from my own.

32. For Ricoeur, this sentence is not just theoretical. Soon after he enlisted in the French army in 1939, he was captured and spent most of the war in prison camps in Germany. There he managed to prepare a translation from German into French of Husserl's *Ideen I* in the margins of the book that he had to conceal from the camp guards. See D. Pellauer and B. Dauenhauer (Summer 2024), "Paul Ricoeur," *Stanford Encyclopedia of Philosophy*, https://plato.stanford.edu/archives/sum2024/entries/ricoeur/

33. It is important to remember that those who were murdered in the Holocaust "have rights that extend beyond merely having their fates registered and made known. These rights include that of having their stories told honestly and accurately, but an important additional right is to a certain privacy, a right not to have that which is most personal unnecessarily displayed for all to witness, not to have those identity-defining boundaries that separate the individual from the public unheedingly crossed" (Hawthorn, 2019, p. 279).

34. Wiesel's statement is from the preface to *Day* (Wiesel, 2004).

35. Later Holocaust scholars and literary scholars have supported and refined Langer's view (Kerner, 2011; Patterson et al. 2002; Vice, 2000).

36. A similar point can be made about Tadeusz Borowski's *This Way for the Gas, Ladies and Gentlemen* (1946/1967; cf. Vice, 2000).

37. While my working definition of distance, and especially temporal distance, is indebted to Gadamer (2013), my conceptualization of empathy is inspired by Meretoja's important point that empathy is not just affect but "a mode of orientation that involved understanding and imagination" (Meretoja, 2021, p. 29). With a view to my interpretations of Holocaust narratives, I specify that while my "mode of orientation . . . involve[s] understanding and imagination," it is predicated on the great temporal distance between me and the Holocaust. Thus, more strongly than, for example, Suzanne Keen (2007), I stress that empathy and distance are not just opposed but also related concepts. As Andrea Deciu Ritivoi observes, "A key aspect of Meretoja's definition of empathy concerns its non-subsumptive function, which uses 'earlier experiences as a starting-point for understanding something new' (2021, p. 27) instead of reducing new experiences to familiar meanings we inherit and perpetuate through our cultural narratives" (Ritivoi, 2023, pp. 206–207). Building on this understanding of empathy and drawing on Ricoeur's (1994) moral philosophy, Ritivoi proposes *solicitude* as a related and complementary concept. She highlights three aspects: "First, solicitude does not assume that understanding of different experiences or different identities is possible, even as it seeks it. Second, solicitude requires a sociopolitical context of equality. And third, solicitude generates both an appreciation for others and a renewed appreciation for oneself" (2023, p. 207; cf. Ritivoi, 2006). Linking Ritivoi's understanding of solicitude as "a moral orientation toward alterity" (2023, p. 207) to Meretoja's conceptualization of empathy as "a mode of orientation," I find that, thus understood, empathy and solicitude are helpful concepts both when I use them explicitly and (more important) when they underlie my interpretations—and perhaps particularly the ethical questions and reflections that these include.

38. Commenting on the nexus of trauma, history, memory, and identity, Dominick LaCapra notes, "The ongoing challenge is to approach the topic without opposing history and memory in a binary fashion but instead by inquiring into more complex and challenging relations between them as well as into what may not be encompassed by the binary" (2016, pp. 375–376). In a way, this is what this book aims to do.

1

Time's Witnesses

Maria Gabrielsen, Ella Blumenthal, Edith Notowicz, and Olga Horak

In his study of photography, *Camera Lucida*, Roland Barthes introduces the concepts of *studium* and *punctum*. While *studium* denotes the "general interest" that the viewer takes in a photograph, an interest that may create "an *average* effect," *punctum* "disturb[s] the *studium* . . . for *punctum* is also: sting, speck, cut, little hole" (1982, pp. 26–27, original emphasis). Barthes finds that *punctum* is often a detail that may complicate, yet also extend, the photograph's meaning. Looking at Georg Fossum's photograph of the *Donau*, the smoke from the ship's chimney becomes a *punctum* for me as I link it to the smoke from the crematoria in Auschwitz, the concentration and extermination camp to which the 532 Norwegian Jews abord the *Donau* were deported. This interpretation moves beyond Fossum's intention: when he photographed the *Donau*, he could not know what would happen to the passengers. My interpretation, which presupposes knowledge about the Holocaust, is also colored by my temporal distance from the date when the photograph was taken, November 26, 1942.

Once I have identified and interpreted the *punctum* of Fossum's photograph—and in fact its identification is predicated on interpretation—it inevitably influences my reading of *studium* as well. Yet it retains its own significance. It has "a power of expansion. This power is often metonymic" (Barthes, 1982, p. 45). For me, the metonymic power of the *punctum* of the smoke above the *Donau* stirs ethical reflection not only on the Holocaust but on the fact that since it also happened in Norway, I am, however remotely and indirectly, implicated in the historical processes and antisemitic attitudes that led to unspeakable crimes committed by a nation close to and admired by my own. The *punctum* of the smoke also makes me reflect on the fact that, of the 772 Jews who were deported from Norway to the Nazi concentration and extermination camps in 1942–1943, only 34 survived (Bruland, 2012). The survivors were men. The approximately 300 women

Memory and Narrative Ethics. Jakob Lothe, Oxford University Press. © Oxford University Press (2025).
DOI: 10.1093/9780197579534.003.0002

and children who were deported from Norway to Auschwitz, more than half of them by the *Donau*, were murdered. For that reason, there are no witnesses for these two groups of Norwegian Jews. Here there is a narrative void—a silence.[1]

This aspect of the smoke rising from the *Donau*, and from the Auschwitz crematoria, establishes the starting point as well as the basis for this chapter. The *punctum* of the smoke draws my attention to the fact that if there are no Holocaust survivors, nobody can bear witness; as nobody can remember what he or she was exposed to, the possibility of testimony is eliminated. None of the women and children who were deported from Norway to Auschwitz in 1942–1943 returned, and the void left by these Jewish women and children who were murdered in the Holocaust can never be filled. But four Jewish women who survived the Holocaust and who settled in Norway after the war tell their stories in *Time's Witnesses: Women's Voices from the Holocaust* (Lothe, 2017a): Maria Gabrielsen, Blanche Major, Edith Notowicz, and Isabella Wolf. So do six Jewish women who, in common with the Norwegian women, were all born in Europe but who later lived (and live) on four different continents: Maria Segal and Judith Meisel in California, Yvonne Engelman and Olga Horak in Sydney, Ella Blumenthal in Cape Town, and Zdenka Fantlová in London. I established contact with these 10 women partly by approaching them directly, partly through introductions and help from colleagues and friends.[2]

The chapter discusses the narrative ethics of four of these testimonies: first-person narratives by Maria Gabrielsen, Ella Blumenthal, Edith Notowicz, and Olga Horak. Considering their stories' ethics as inseparable from the presentation of narrative, I interpret the testimonies as acts of memory. Compared to an artistic testimony such as *If This Is a Man* by the Italian author Primo Levi (1958/2005), the narratives I discuss here may appear simple (Lothe, 2017c). Yet I show that the stories told by Gabrielsen, Blumenthal, Notowicz, and Horak are more complex than they seem to be at first glance. Illustrating variants of first-person narration and of narrative ethics, these testimonies lend support to Jens Brockmeier's (2015) view of narrative as not just representing but also enacting and evoking experience. Significant elements of narrative include narrative distance, repetition, fragment, episode, ellipsis, and threat of narrative collapse. I argue that the combination of these (and additional) elements of narrative makes the stories' ethics more nuanced—and also more challenging for the reader. Noting that, for these women, the distance in time between their act of remembering and the remembered event (the Holocaust) is twice as long as it is for the survivors interviewed by Claude Lanzmann in *Shoah* (see Chapter 3), I discuss the ethical implications of this variation of temporal distance.

In addition to the Norwegian Jewish women I strongly wished to interview, I wanted to meet Jewish women who could tell me about the Holocaust from different perspectives in time and space. Since the Holocaust took place in Europe, it is unsurprising that many survivors wished to remove themselves from that continent. They spread out over the world, and the place from which they tell their story influences their narrative perspective as well as their act of memory. In addition to this spatial variation, there is a variation of temporal perspective resulting from the fact that the women narrating their stories were born between 1921 and 1935. Maria Gabrielsen was sent to Theresienstadt when she was nine years old, and her account is colored by the fact that she experienced the deportation as a child. Similarly, the account given by Ella Blumenthal is influenced by her having been about 20 years old when she was in the camps.

Working on *Time's Witnesses*, I tried to maintain a balance between the need to give the book a unifying structure and the wish to control and influence the narrative situation as little as possible. With this as my starting point, I asked each of the time's witnesses four questions, which I sent to them before our meeting:

1. Can you describe the circumstances that led up to your arrest?
2. Can you tell me how you experienced your imprisonment?
3. Can you say a little about your life after the war?
4. When you look back at your time in the prison camp, what do you feel it is particularly important not to forget, and what can we learn from what you and your fellow prisoners were subjected to?

Although I asked a few additional questions during the interviews, I mainly adopted the role of listener while the women narrated. Transcribing the recorded interviews, I attempted to retain the narrator's tone and her own words and way of telling her story. As how much a time's witness wishes to tell differs from how much she can manage to tell, the testimonies vary in length, and so do the four considered in this chapter. The narrators are the authors of their own life histories; they all read the text, corrected errors, and approved their accounts.

Before turning to the first testimony, I comment on the concepts of "testimony" and "witness" as variants of narrative. For all 10 women relating their stories in *Time's Witnesses*, the need to bear witness to the crimes against humanity committed in concentration and extermination camps by the Nazis during the Second World War is accompanied by the problems associated with doing so: How can a survivor talk or write about events so horrible as to threaten to defy description and render language unusable? In *Remnants of Auschwitz: The Witness and the Archive*, Giorgio Agamben notes:

> In Latin there are two words for "witness." The first word, *testis*, from which our word "testimony" derives, etymologically signifies the person who, in a trial or lawsuit between two rival parties, is in the position of a third party. . . . The second word, *superstes*, designates a person who has lived through something, who has experienced an event from beginning to end and can therefore bear witness to it. (2012, p. 17)

Both these Latin words are applicable to the narratives of Holocaust survivors. Their narratives are examples of *superstes* because they report events from a period of imprisonment experienced by the survivor herself. Moreover, less obviously yet significantly, they can include elements of *testis*, for a survivor's narrative can also deal with the brutal treatment and killings of other prisoners. (Compare the episode that Judith Meisel tells about Chavah and her child.)[3] In the narratives of *Time's Witnesses*, both these facets are observable, and in the narrative discourse they are closely related. Survivors, including the 10 women who combine the functions of protagonist and first-person narrator in *Time's Witnesses*, can become witnesses by telling or writing about their camp experiences. Levinas finds, "Le témoin témoigne de ce qui s'est dit par lui. Car il a dit 'Me voici!' devant autrui" (The witness bears witness by what he tells. Because he has said: "Here I am!" before the other) (1982, p. 105). That this dimension of testimony is decisive is illustrated by all 10 stories in *Time's Witnesses*.

Bearing witness is a communicative act, and the act of bearing witness assumes narrative form. A testimony that is not communicated to somebody is no testimony. However—and this point is argued by many Holocaust scholars—in the case of the Holocaust the communication between the witness and her audience is complicated by the fact that, using language, the witness is attempting to tell or write about an event radically different from normal life (Felman and Laub, 1992; LaCapra, 1998; Langer, 1991; Suleiman, 2006; Davis, 2018a). The vastness and incomprehensibility of the Nazis' crimes seem to be located somewhere beyond the realm of language. Yet this is not just a problem; it is also, as all 10 women realize, a challenge and a possibility. Moreover, although a testimony needs to be communicated to somebody, the 10 women's testimonies need not have specified recipients: they may be made available for as yet unknown individuals to access.

In the testimonies under consideration, the survivors use verbal narrative in order to shape their experience of the Holocaust. More precisely, activating the distinction in German between *Erlebnis* and *Erfahrung*, they employ narrative as a means of remembering, reworking, structuring, and presenting an unheard-of series of events which, against all odds, they survived. By so doing, they are perhaps able to understand their camp experiences a little better, thus possibly transforming their personal suffering into a formative experience for the future, including not only their own future but also that of the listener or reader. The witnesses' understanding of experience, a concept implicit rather than explicitly stated in their narratives, lends support to Hans-Georg Gadamer's (2013; cf. Gadamer, 1975) understanding of *Erfahrung* as oriented toward the future (though it builds on an event of which one is cognizant, *Erlebnis*, in the past).

As an act of narration, bearing witness is both a form of remembering and an act of remembrance. As Lawrence Langer notes in *Holocaust Testimonies: The Ruins of Memory*:

> Testimony is a form of remembering. The faculty of memory functions in the present to recall a personal history vexed by traumas that thwart smooth-flowing chronicles. Simultaneously, however, straining against what we might call disruptive memory is an effort to reconstruct a semblance of continuity in a life that began as, and now resumes what we would consider, a normal existence. (1991, pp. 2–3)

If the narratives told by the 10 women in *Time's Witnesses* illustrate the problem of remembering "a personal history vexed by traumas," they also reveal these women's insistent efforts to reconstruct what Langer calls "a semblance of continuity" in their lives. Seen thus, their stories provide a forceful illustration of narrative's capacity to communicate what is painful to remember and hard to express. Even though the narrators are aware of the difficulty of putting their experiences into words, they use the medium at their disposal, language, to do just that. Considering the challenges they face as narrators, their mastery of language is remarkable.[4] Paradoxically, this kind of linguistic and narrative competence becomes particularly striking at the points of the narrative when it threatens to break down (e.g., when the witness's voice fails).

Narrative form plays a key role in the generation of the testimonies' ethics. "The ethics of form," to appropriate Leona Toker's (2010) phrase, is strikingly apparent in these stories. The values presented though narrative form are very different, ranging from those of the Nazi who kills Chavah's child to those of Chavah. Yet it does not follow that these values are "simple" or "stable." The 10 women in *Time's Witnesses* tell the reader about ethical challenges and dilemmas—difficult choices that had to be made to survive. The true heroes, they told me, were the prisoners who, like Chavah, resisted orders while knowing that they would then be killed.

Maria Gabrielsen

Working on *Time's Witnesses*, I tried to emphasize that while my role was that of editor, the book has 10 authors: each woman becomes an author— and a witness—by telling her story. This approach also applies to the first story presented in the volume, that of Maria Gabrielsen. It is essential that the stories are presented as first-person narratives that, as written text, represent the witness's oral narration as accurately as possible. The source of the narration is the witness, whose authority as author is further underlined by a full-page black-and-white photograph on the page facing the beginning of the narrative text. On the top of this page, that is, the page where the witness's story begins, I give, as editor, a brief introduction to her story; this basic information is complemented by a smaller black-and-white photo of the witness as a young woman. The juxtaposition of two photographs in the same visual field (Figure 1.1) accentuates their narrative dimension: while that on the left page shows us the woman at the time of narration, the photo on the right presents a visual image of the same woman just before or a short time after she experienced the Holocaust. If I look again at the two photographs after having read the testimony, their combined narrative effect is furthered strengthened. Activating the communicative resources of narrative, the testimony is an attempt to negotiate the temporal and spatial distance between the two photographs.

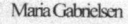

Maria Gabrielsen

Born on 3 January 1934. Deported to Theresienstadt in 1943, where she remained until the end of the war. Lives in Sandefjord, Norway.

I remember being four years old well. We lived at home in Vienna then. We were seven siblings, and we had a good life. Dad was a tailor and worked from home. He used a treadle sewing machine to make suits, and he had customers he supplied. He had a large clothes iron with a lid. Into that he put glowing pieces of coal from the stove. It hissed when he ironed the clothes he had moistened. This fascinated a little girl, and it was from Dad I inherited my interest in sewing.

Dad was Jewish, and his name was Michael Schwarz. Mum's name was Rosa, and she was of German descent. She had converted from Catholicism to Judaism. We lived in a flat in the Simmering district. One day a man suddenly came running out into the hallway where we children were playing. He was holding a baby in his arms, and he shouted: 'It's war! It's war!' He was completely disturbed and tossed the baby into the air. This was the first time I'd heard the word 'war'. I wondered what it was.

From 1938 onwards our situation dramatically worsened. German soldiers marched into Austria on 12 March 1938, and conditions quickly became

27

Figure 1.1   Maria Gabrielsen. In Lothe, J. (2017a), pp. 26–39.

The photograph on the left, taken by photographer Agnete Brun on April 3, 2013, shows Maria Gabrielsen at the time of presenting her testimony, that is, on the day she orally imparted her story to Brun and me as listeners in her home in the small town of Sandefjord, Norway. The smaller photo on the right, which she allowed me to use in the book, depicts Maria as a young woman. In 2024, she still lives at home with her Norwegian husband.

I introduce Maria Gabrielsen's story thus:

Born on 3 January 1934. Deported to Theresienstadt in 1943, where she remained until the end of the war. Lives in Sandefjord, Norway.

Maria begins her story by sharing a memory of her father from 1938, when she was a four-year-old girl in Vienna. This was the year Nazi Germany annexed Austria and, as Maria notes, "our situation dramatically worsened" (p. 27). Although it is difficult to accurately identify the characteristics of a child's language, and although the language and narrative situation of

Maria at that time are inevitably colored by her narration, including her narrative situation in Sandefjord more than 70 years later, elements of a child's experience are observable in her discourse. Consider this example:

> I started school when I was six years old. In the classroom we had to sing for Hitler; there was a picture of him on the wall behind where the teacher was sitting. We also had to pray to Hitler, for he gave us our daily bread. I thought that was strange. At home we had not seen much of the bread from Hitler, and I had realised that Dad did not like him. So I didn't either. (p. 28)

This discourse is simple, yet it is not oversimplified. For me as a listener, it was, and still is, difficult to know how conscious Maria was of using a simple language when telling her reader about this period. But this is not the point here. Rather, what is important is her successful attempt to render important aspects of her memory of the time. With hindsight, the forced adoration of Hitler becomes a formative experience associated with and warning her against the deportation to Theresienstadt in 1943.

Since she was a child when she was deported to the camp, Maria Gabrielsen belongs to "the 1.5 generation," a helpful concept coined by Susan Rubin Suleiman. As Suleiman explains, the 1.5 generation is made up of "child survivors of the Holocaust, too young to have had an adult understanding of what was happening to them but old enough to have been there during the Nazi persecution of Jews" (2004, p. 372). Although all those persecuted by the Nazis experienced bewilderment and helplessness, "the 1.5 generation's shared experience is that of premature bewilderment and helplessness" (p. 373). If this happened to Maria Gabrielsen, there is also a sense in which Suleiman's description of the 1.5 generation applies, as we shall see in Chapter 6, to the fictional character Austerlitz in W. G. Sebald's novel *Austerlitz*.

There is of course a lot that Maria Gabrielsen does not and cannot remember at the time of narration—70 years after her experience of the Nazi persecution of Jews. Yet as the passage shows, she relates what she remembers as accurately as possible. A different passage, also part of the narrative beginning, relates the shock of experiencing what her mother did to her father. Although she was married, Maria's mother entered into a relationship

> with a fervent Nazi called Mathias Schnedlitz. They fell in love and wanted to marry as soon as possible, but to do that, Dad first had to sign the divorce papers. When Dad refused, Mum went to the Gestapo offices and reported

her husband to the Nazis. . . . He was put in a labour camp for a few weeks, and then he was sent to Auschwitz. He was murdered there in the autumn of 1943. (pp. 29–30)

It is a notable aspect of Maria's narration that, after having told me about her mother's betrayal of her husband, she states that most of that information was unavailable to her at the time. This information, acquired much later, influences the way she communicates this part of her testimony to her listener and reader. At the same time, her statement that she "had no idea about this" (p. 30) when it happened makes her narration more credible. As she was a child when her father disappeared, her ignorance is understandable, but it is also comprehensible that she could experience fear of her mother in spite of not knowing what her mother had done. Facets of Maria's story about her mother metonymically represent, as seen from a child's perspective, a vague and yet insistent sensation of the Holocaust— a word unknown to Maria in 1942—as something ominous looming on the horizon. Neither does Maria use the noun "perpetrator"—a word, also unknown to her, that is widely used in Holocaust studies. But she comes close to seeing her mother as a perpetrator whose actions, located outside Auschwitz, are directed against her own family.

Together with her siblings, Maria was deported to Theresienstadt in the spring of 1943.[5] It is, she says, "as if my childhood ends here" (p. 30). Responding to my second question, "Can you tell me how you experienced your imprisonment?", Maria, in common with the other contributors to *Time's Witnesses*, tends to relate episodes that she remembers and is capable of communicating to her audience. While the episode structure is a constituent element of all 10 testimonies in the book, the episodes narrated by Maria are distinguished by an iterative quality less evident in the next three testimonies that I will discuss. This form of repetition tells us something important both about the constant struggle for food and the way the children routinely had to experience the deaths of other inmates:

We had to wait in a long queue to get food. Every now and then children collapsed from exhaustion. When that happened, someone usually came to pull them out of the queue. It was usually pea soup for dinner. It was made from dried yellow split peas. There were a lot of maggots in that soup, but they floated to the top when the soup had come to the boil. We removed the maggots and continued eating. Every other day we were given a piece of bread. . . . The bread was teeming with maggots, and they were alive. (pp. 31–32)

A lot of people were burned in Theresienstadt. They died, and then they were burned. The smoke from the crematorium had a sweetish smell. Every day the guards walked around the camp with two-wheeled flat carts. They tossed the dead onto the cart like sacks of flour and wheeled them to the crematorium. The ashes were placed in boxes. Several of the kids had to stand in a row and heft the boxes of ashes onto a truck. The boxes were all the same size so that they could be neatly stacked on the truck. You couldn't ask what they were going to use the ashes for—you wouldn't get a reply anyway. But for the work we could have a piece of bread, or perhaps even a piece of sausage. Oh, that tasted very good. (p. 32)

Here, as in the passages where she is telling about her experiences at school and about her mother's betrayal of her family, Maria manages to retain—or at least give the reader a glimpse of—her perspective as a child and the way she experienced Theresienstadt as a 10-year-old girl. The element of repetition in these episodes does not mean that her narrative progresses in the normal sense of the word. As the inmates had to struggle to stay alive, each new day became a repetition of the day before. Although Maria hoped to survive, she knew that the end of the war was no guarantee of survival: "What would the Nazis do to us? Perhaps they would kill us before they fled?" (p. 33).

Rereading Maria's testimony, I conclude that her narrative discourse brings out elements of a child's experience of loss. To a certain extent her narration also captures the vicissitudes and limitations of memory. This feature of her story becomes conspicuous when she attempts to tell me something about her mother's betrayal, but as she cannot understand the betrayal, she is unable to do so. I find that since her act of memory—and, as a corollary, her act of narration—revolve around her childhood trauma, and since her mother is at the center of this trauma, this kind of limitation is a narrative strength rather than a weakness, augmenting her story's value as testimony rather than reducing it. Aspects of such limitations and narrative gaps are a characteristic feature of all the stories in *Time's Witnesses*. In the realm of narrative fiction, they are also explored by Sebald in *Austerlitz*.

Many years after she had settled in Norway after the war, Maria was contacted by Helga Arntzen, the leader of Aktive Fredsreiser (Travel for Peace), a company that organizes trips for schoolchildren to the Nazi concentration camps. Maria reluctantly accepted Arntzen's invitation to join Aktive Fredsreiser on a trip to Theresienstadt and Auschwitz:

The first trip was horrible. We first arrived at Theresienstadt. The tour leader asked if I recognised it. "I'm missing the railway tracks," I said. Then they suddenly popped up. I then said: "I'm missing another thing. I'm missing the stream." I had no sooner finished speaking than the stream popped up. That's when I started shuddering. Sure enough, that was the way it used to be. . . . All the time I felt as if someone was grabbing me. It was awful. (p. 38)

Recognition can be a demanding cognitive act, and recognizing a site associated with trauma and loss can be especially painful. While Maria's memory enables her to recognize the camp, that shock-like recognition also does something to her memory, intensifying it through emerging topographical objects that reactivate her traumatic experience. For Maria as for many other Holocaust survivors, it is nearly unbearable to return to the place where she almost lost her life and where she was exposed to systematic violence directed at people who could not defend themselves.

The experience is repeated, and further intensified, when they reach Auschwitz: "That was also terribly difficult. This was where Dad had been deported to" (p. 38). A Catholic priest who volunteered to search for her father's name in the archives of what is now the Memorial and Museum Auschwitz-Birkenau,[6] "found out that Dad had been on four different work details. His health failed, and he was sent to the gas chamber" (p. 38). Maria does not elaborate, and as a listener and reader I think that, at least partly, I can understand why. For Maria, her father is not just a victim but also a hero and an ideal. Conversely, her mother, who betrayed both her husband and her children, represents diametrically opposite values. Both her parents possessed an ethos—a combination of characteristics and values—but the values of her father were radically different from those of her mother. Maria does not use the word "evil" to describe her mother, but, though there may be extenuating circumstances that Maria does not mention, I interpret her mother's acts of betrayal as evil acts. As I establish an ethical linkage between the mother's betrayal of her own family and the values of those responsible for the Holocaust, I consider Maria's mother a Nazi perpetrator. Whether Maria would agree with this interpretation I do not know; it is difficult to make such a statement about your own mother. Her testimony makes me think that her mother's evil act of betraying her family is a consequence, or perhaps rather an effect, of her failure to respond to the command of the Other as represented by the faces of her husband and children. Thus, she avoids the "exceptionable responsibility" that Emmanuel Levinas (1961/1969, pp. 87–88) regards as a defining feature of the command of the Other. Whether consciously or unconsciously, she also fails to respond to, or perhaps does not even perceive or register, the ethical demand that, "intrud[ing] disturbingly into my existence" (Løgstrup, 1997, p. 45), asks me to take care of my neighbor. Although there is a possibility that Maria idealizes her father because he was a victim of the Holocaust, my interpretation of her testimony makes me associate him with the facets of responsibility and care discussed by Levinas and Knud E. Løgstrup. If, hypothetically, I ask myself where I would have been positioned morally if I were Maria's mother or father, I cannot answer. There is a sense in which the fragments of memory that underlie and make possible Maria's narration complicate her attempt to render an extended portrait of her parents. Perhaps she does not even make such an attempt. She has an ardent wish to remember her father, yet her memory of him is unbearably painful. She wishes to forget her mother, yet memories of her and her desertion of her family intrude into Maria's narrative consciousness, causing a different kind of pain. It is remarkable that, given these narrative challenges, she agreed, and managed, to tell her story.

Perhaps, for Maria, her work as a time's witness on trips organized by Aktive Fredsreiser has proved to be a way of negotiating her traumatic memories. As Toker notes, "The relationship between trauma and individual agency—struggles against becoming the product of one's past instead of thoughtfully shaping one's postcamp life—characterizes a number of works by child survivors" (2019, p. 77). For Maria, this kind of struggle includes going to Auschwitz with young people. She makes, she says, a point of telling them "to do everything in their power to keep the Holocaust from being repeated" (Lothe, 2017a, p. 38). On one of these trips to Auschwitz she

> overheard someone who was denying that the Holocaust ever took place. Usually I don't interfere in other people's conversations. But this time I could not help myself—I went over there and told them who I was and what I had experienced. That silenced him. (p. 38)

This kind of speech act—a Holocaust survivor's intervention into somebody's mendacious narrative activity—is a strong indication of the authority of the time's witness. It is also a reminder of the irreplaceable loss, and a growing danger of Holocaust denial, following the passing of the survivors. What silenced the person who, in Auschwitz, was denying the Holocaust was probably his personal encounter with a Holocaust survivor capable of bearing witness to the Nazis' murder of around 1.5 million Jews, including Maria's father, at the very location where they met.

Ella Blumenthal

The fact that Ella Blumenthal (Figure 1.2) is 13 years older than Maria Gabrielsen, and thus was a young woman when she and her family were deported to the Warsaw ghetto, may explain some of the differences between her narration and Maria's.[7] That said, there are also similarities between the two stories; this combination of difference and similarity can tell us

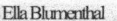

Ella Blumenthal

Born in Warsaw on 15 August 1921. Deported to the Warsaw ghetto in October 1940. Deported to Majdanek in 1943, then to Auschwitz and then to Bergen-Belsen, where she remained until the liberation of the camp on 15 April 1945. Lives in Cape Town.

In spite of surviving the Warsaw ghetto and three death camps, after the liberation I tried to integrate into a normal society, and after I had married, I raised and educated my four children. But I wasn't able to talk about my suffering and fight for survival, because the open wounds were still bleeding.

I was born in Warsaw, the youngest in a family of seven children. My father was a respected and well-to-do textile merchant. My mother and siblings were engaged in the family business. I was a happy teenager until the Germans invaded Poland on 1 September 1939.

After weeks of heavy air raids, the city of Warsaw also fell. There was panic, uncertainty and fear, particularly for Jews. New orders and declarations were coming out daily. All Jewish land was requisitioned; all Jewish bank accounts were closed, blocked. All public gatherings were forbidden; all Jewish schools and synagogues were closed. Food was rationed. Curfew was

43

Figure 1.2 Ella Blumenthal. In Lothe, J. (2017a), pp. 42–54.

something important about distinctive features of narratives of both first-generation and 1.5-generation Holocaust survivors. My introduction to Ella's story reads thus:

> *Born in Warsaw on 15 August 1921. Deported to the Warsaw ghetto in October 1940. Deported to Majdanek in 1943, then to Auschwitz and then to Bergen-Belsen, where she remained until the liberation of the camp on 15 April 1945. Lives in Cape Town.* (p. 43)

As we can see, Ella was deported from the Warsaw ghetto to a concentration camp—and then to other camps. That she survived is almost beyond belief. In this brief discussion of her rich narrative, I comment on its narrative beginning and on one word, "search"—the combination verb and noun that, albeit in different ways, serves as a leitmotif in many verbal and filmic accounts of the Holocaust, including Lanzmann's *Shoah* and Sebald's *Austerlitz*. I also briefly discuss Ella's active participation in the Warsaw ghetto uprising in 1943, linking her narrative presentation of this dramatic incident to her narrative ethics. Drawing on the concluding part of her story, I argue that, for Ella as a Holocaust survivor, there is a connection between a need to distance herself from the Holocaust and a moral obligation to bear witness.

This is how Ella begins her story:

> In spite of surviving the Warsaw ghetto and three death camps, after the liberation I tried to integrate into a normal society, and after I had married, I raised and educated my four children. But I wasn't able to talk about my suffering and fight for survival, because the open wounds were still bleeding. (p. 43)

Ella told me her story in Cape Town in 2012 (with some additional comments in 2013),[8] so there is a temporal distance of 70 years between the time of narration and the time of the narrated events. In more than one way, though, this distance is a gain as well as a drawback. First, it is a prerequisite for the narration to take place at all. Ella was unable to tell anybody about her Holocaust experience until she was past 80, and her story in *Time's Witnesses* is her first published account. Second, the temporal distance enables her to highlight what she finds particularly important to narrate—and thus for the reader to remember.

There is an important sense in which Ella's narrative is a search—a sustained act of narration enabling her, at last, to seek elements of continuity in her life. This kind of search by means of verbal narrative—a narrative search—supports Langer's notion of an act of memory that aims "to reconstruct a semblance of continuity in a life that began as, and now resumes what we would consider, a normal existence" (1991, pp. 2–3). Yet Ella's narrative search also lends credence to Langer's accompanying point that such "disruptive memory" tends to possess elements of narrative that impede chronological progression, thus making the narrative fragmented and causing narrative ellipses and blanks. In different ways and to varying degrees, all the stories in *Time's Witnesses* are distinguished by such ellipses, which are related to and further their episodic quality.

If all of Ella's story assumes the form of a search for a lost family history while at the same time, through this very search, reconstructing "a semblance of continuity" in her life, there is one point, or stage, of her narrative at which the search is highlighted. This passage occurs just after Ella's account of her experience at Bergen-Belsen in the winter of 1944–1945.[9] After having described the horrible conditions under which prisoners lived in the camp, she comments:

> Having survived the uprising in the Warsaw ghetto, Majdanek and Auschwitz, I could not end up on the top of a stack of corpses in Bergen-Belsen now. The will to survival rose up in me with full force once again. I knew that I *had* to survive. And so it was: on 15 April 1945 we were liberated by the British army. (p. 53)

Then follows the passage that includes the key word "search":

> Words cannot express my feeling of freedom, but the most important thing was that we were alive, and that we could start living like human beings again.
>
> In August 1945 I travelled from Bergen-Belsen to Warsaw with an older woman who protected me from the Russian soldiers. I had no money and no passport. My identification was the number tattooed on my arm and a fingerprint on a document I had received in Hannover. I went to Warsaw in search of my family, although I knew that they had all perished in Treblinka.

Yet I still had a spark of hope. One of my brothers managed to leave the Warsaw ghetto with his wife and daughter, and they went to live in a village near Lublin. I had always hoped that my little niece had been saved by the Polish peasants with whom they lived. And from Warsaw I made my way to this village, but at one of the stations I was warned by some Jews that I shouldn't travel any further, as there was a pogrom there and the Poles were killing Jews. I had to return to Warsaw. Later I found out that the three of them—my brother, his wife and their daughter—were among the Jews that were shot in the forest. There was an office where survivors left their names and where they could be reached. I put down my address as Bergen-Belsen. As I found nobody in Warsaw, I returned to Bergen-Belsen. (p. 53)

There are several aspects of this passage that make the reader pause. How could there be pogroms in Poland after the end of the war? How is it possible for a human being to return to Bergen-Belsen, the camp where she almost died? Moreover, as far as the word "search" is concerned, how can one search for somebody one knows is not there? As regards the last question, I suggest that a partial answer, or at least a glimpse of an explanation, is provided by "yet," the first word of Ella Blumenthal's next sentence. That, on a rational level, the search seems hopeless does not mean that there is no "spark of hope" connected with it. This kind of hope is here associated with Ella's existential need to find out as much as possible about family members who against all odds might have survived. It is also related to her search for a "semblance of continuity" in her life, since the survival of a family member, however distant, might enable her to regain at least some of her identity as an independent woman and possibly help her to plan her life in the years ahead.

Challenging the prevalent image of Jews as passive victims of Nazi violence, Ella's testimony is a pertinent reminder of the historical fact of active resistance against deportation to the camps. A notable example of such resistance was the Warsaw ghetto uprising, which the *Holocaust Encyclopedia* describes thus:

On April 19, 1943, the Warsaw ghetto uprising began after German troops and police entered the ghetto to deport its surviving inhabitants. Jewish insurgents inside the ghetto resisted these efforts. This was the largest uprising by Jews during World War II and the first significant urban revolt against German occupation in Europe. By May 16, 1943, the Germans had crushed the uprising and deported surviving ghetto residents to concentration camps and killing centers.[10]

Compare this encyclopedic entry with the following passage from Ella's testimony:

> In 1943 Passover began on an evening in April. I remember my father giving everybody a piece of Matza [the unleavened flatbread which is an important element in this religious festival] which he had saved from the previous year. After reciting the prayers, he prayed to God to save us like He freed the Jews from slavery in Egypt. When the Germans marched in for their routine raids the next morning, they were met with Molotov cocktails, homemade bombs, grenades, and shooting from windows and rooftops. The Warsaw ghetto uprising had started. The Germans were taken by surprise, and they withdrew, leaving behind their dead and injured. Yes, German blood was flowing in the streets of the Warsaw ghetto. (p. 46)

The juxtaposition of these two passages triggers three comments. First, compared to the presentation of this historical event in the *Holocaust Encyclopedia*, Ella's account of the uprising is remarkably fact-oriented and surprisingly accurate. Although she probably obtained later some of the information given in this passage, the accuracy of historical information makes her narrative more reliable, thus also strengthening her narrative authority and contributing to the formation of her narrative ethics. Second, Ella's narrative ethics is also constituted by the way she connects historical information with personal memory. This memory includes that of her father, who, she tells the reader later in her narrative, was murdered in Majdanek.[11] In the last sentence of the passage, "Yes, German blood was flowing in the streets of the Warsaw ghetto," the word "Yes" is semantically charged, suggesting an act of resistance and even a qualified, short-lived success in a desperate situation. Third, in this passage, as in the following description of how, together with other resistance fighters, Ella hid in an underground bunker in the ghetto, her narrative ethics is informed by her father's ethos. The portraits that Ella Blumenthal and Maria Gabrielsen give of their fathers are remarkably similar—both are presented as men who care for their families, oppose war, and detest Nazism.

In Auschwitz and Majdanek—the camp that Ella, her father, and her niece Roma were sent to after having been forced out of the bunker—these qualities were totally useless. In Majdanek,

> which was enclosed by barbed wire, we were surrounded by sentries who pointed their rifles at us. Immediately, older women, children and mothers with babies were separated from us and sent to the gas chambers. And then

it was the turn of the older men. And my father was among them. When he turned back to have a last look at Roma and I, he was hit on the head and bent under the blow. And that was when I saw my father for the last time. I have never, never seen my father again. (p. 49)

After having miraculously survived Majdanek, Ella and Roma were sent to Auschwitz.[12] Their arms were tattooed: "My number was 48 632" (p. 51). When both contracted typhus, their situation became even more desperate, for in Auschwitz sick inmates who could not work were routinely murdered.

One day Roma begged me go to the electric fence with her. "Let us end this struggle. In any case, the only way to survive Auschwitz is through the chimneys. So come, let us join our loved ones." But the will to survive had been awakened in me. I wasn't yet ready to die. I convinced her that we had to carry on so that if we managed to survive, we would be able to tell the world what these murderers had done to us. (p. 51)

More explicitly than any other contributor to *Time's Witnesses*, Ella here identifies her strong wish to bear witness as a motivating factor in the struggle not to perish in Auschwitz. There is an important connection between this wish, which is a constituent element of her narrative ethics, and the key points she makes by way of ending her story:

As I am one of the last generation of eye witnesses, I am now, in the twilight of my days, pouring out the terrors of my life in the Warsaw ghetto and in the three death camps, where disease, malnutrition and random killings were the constants of my life. They worked us to death on starvation rations. We were the slave labour brigade. These scenes will remain forever imprinted in my memory. I will never be able to erase them.

I still often ask myself why *I* was chosen to survive. Twenty-three souls of my immediate family perished. My parents, my brothers, my sisters, their spouses and eight nieces and nephews, including an infant born in the underground bunker in the Warsaw ghetto. I will never find an answer to this question.

So now, by spreading tolerance, learning and understanding, we survivors will be contributing to ensuring that these horrors do not happen again. (p. 54)

There is no reason to question the sincerity of this closing statement, which is documented by her contribution to *Time's Witnesses*. At the time of writing,

103-year-old Ella is still active in her local community in Cape Town. There is a thought-provoking contrast between these acts of bearing witness and her observation at the beginning of her narrative that, for many years after the war, she was unable to talk about her "suffering and fight for survival, because the open wounds were still bleeding" (p. 43).

The increasing temporal distance from the Holocaust does not make Ella forget what she experienced in the camps. The scenes will, she says, "remain forever imprinted in my memory." What the increasing temporal distance does, though, and the spatial distance between Poland and Cape Town may also be a contributing factor here, is to subtly, almost imperceptibly change the experience in a way that gradually makes it narratable. Thus, rather than being the opposite of narrative communication, silence is here a prerequisite for such communication. Paradoxically, silence is thus imbued with an unidentifiable yet significant element of narrative ethics. Silence does not speak, but, in the case of Ella at least, a prolonged silence can enable a Holocaust survivor to speak (Brockmeier, 2015; Levin, 2013: Lothe, 2017b).

Ella's reflections at the end of her story are illustrative of the interrelationship of experience and memory. If her Holocaust experience forms the basis for her memory of the Holocaust, the "scenes" imprinted in her memory enable her not to forget her experience, gradually even allowing her to share it with others. Describing experience as "the result of an integration of what is happening into discourse," Ernst van Alphen suggests "that experience can no longer be seen as strictly individual" (1999, p. 37). Experiences are "not only collectively shared because they are grounded on cultural discourses; this shared background also makes experiences and memories 'sharable'" (p. 37). Ella's acts of bearing witness in Cape Town 70 to 80 years after her Holocaust experience support Alphen's view of memory as "something we produce *as individuals sharing a culture*" (p. 37, original emphasis). Alphen's point accords with Aleida Assmann's (2018) observation that Holocaust testimony deals not only with an individual survivor's traumatic experience but with collective trauma after the Holocaust. This new role of the Holocaust survivor is evident in Ella's concluding reflections.

Edith Notowicz

The Holocaust was a series of historical events that stretched over three years. But no single narrative could hope to capture the enormity of the genocide. As Zdenka Fantlová puts it in her testimony in *Time's Witnesses*,

"There were six million murdered. If they all survived, there would be six million different stories" (Lothe, 2017a, pp. 156–157). While in one sense this comment would seem true, in a different sense it is not. It is true that the narratives would have been different, but not all Holocaust survivors are able to transform their experience into a narrative memory. Whether this kind of inability or failure reduces their identity, I am not sure, though it may problematize their narrative identity by making it more fragmented and less coherent. There is even a troubling sense in which it may problematize the experience: although experience extends beyond narrative, once (or if) remembered it tends to take on narrative shape (Brockmeier, 2015). The enormous challenge of transforming a traumatic experience of this kind into a narrative (however fragmented and disconnected) is a warning against indiscriminate use of the concept of narrative identity. Yet although human identity is not dependent on narrative, narrative can make aspects of human identity clearer to the narrator—and to the listener or reader or viewer.

This brief observation on a complex issue is inspired, and arguably supported, by the witness accounts in *Time's Witnesses*—or, more precisely, by my interpretation of these accounts. A relevant passage here is from the testimony of Edith Notowicz (Figure 1.3), who was born in Hungary and settled in Norway after the war. I introduce Edith's story thus:

> *Born on 16 March 1929. Deported to Auschwitz in May 1944, then on to Hainichen in October 1944 and finally, in April 1945, to Theresienstadt, where she remained until the end of the war. Lives in Trondheim.* (p. 93)

That Edith had not published narratives based on her Holocaust experience prior to our meeting in 2013 is unsurprising given the content, and the implications, of the following quotation. This passage is part of Edith's response to the question "Can you tell me how you experienced your imprisonment?"

> The notorious Doctor Josef Mengele, also known as the "Angel of Death," operated in Auschwitz. I soon made his acquaintance. Mengele used children in his medical experiments. He had a special predilection for twins, but I can't go into details here. It is too horrible for me. He was also interested in finding new methods of sterilisation and thereby preventing the Jewish race from procreating. In the camp he had more than enough test subjects, and I was one of those who were used in Mengele's sterilisation experiments on Jewish girls. There was no question of sedation. The pain is still with me, and in the dead of night it sometimes is as if I am back in the experimentation room in the camp. (p. 96)

Born on 16 March 1929. Deported to Auschwitz in May 1944, then on to Hainichen in October 1944 and finally, in April 1945, to Theresienstadt, where she remained until the end of the war. Lives in Trondheim.

I come from a small rural community in southern Hungary, near the Romanian border. We were a family of five. Dad owned a sawmill; he made sleepers, parquet flooring and other building materials. Mum had studied music in Vienna. She played the piano and took an interest in social work. There was a *Waisenhaus* (home for orphan children) in the nearest town, and Mum was involved in that. She used to give small concerts to raise money for people in need.

Aunts and uncles and several cousins lived close by us. Mum and Dad thought it was important that we kids had respect for both humans and animals, and they taught us from an early age that all humans are equally valuable. At the same time they gave us the freedom to make our own decisions. We were close, and we had a good life. We were not spoiled and got on well with each other. The highlight of the day was when the whole family was gathered around the table to eat. My brother was fourteen years older than me, my sister twelve years older. So I was the youngest, the afterthought.

93

Figure 1.3 Edith Notowicz. In Lothe, J. (2017a), pp. 92–101.

If I did not know that Edith was one of the Jewish girls used in Mengele's sterilization experiments in Auschwitz, this passage would be a glaring example of abuse of storytelling. In a way this part of her narrative is beyond belief, and one indication of the force of this possibility, the possibility of fictional intrusion into a first-person narrative that claims to be a testimony, is that Edith asks herself that very question in the next paragraph:

> Is it true or not? What was the driving force behind the Nazis' intense attempt to exterminate other people? Is it possible that humans can be like this? Often I cannot believe it. But I have been there, so I know it happened. (p. 96)

Although there is a sense in which "I cannot believe it" either, I know that I must do so. For me, the trustworthiness of Edith's story is enhanced by her own disbelief and by the questions she asks. Moreover, the reliability of her narrative is paradoxically strengthened by a narrative ellipsis. Mengele "had a special predilection for twins, but I can't go into details here. It is too horrible for me." This ellipsis approximates paralipsis, a textual lacuna that takes on a particular significance precisely because something is omitted (Toker, 2022). Edith indicates that she knows "details" of Mengele's experiments with twins that she cannot, and does not want to, narrate. As a listener and reader, I respect her decision not to elaborate. I would even argue that the choice of excluding these details from her story increases her authority as a witness who recounts. The omitted parts of her memories of Mengele are reserved for or cannot be excluded from her thoughts and dreams "in the dead of night." That these memories are traumatic does not, however, render Edith's account of Mengele's experiments on Jewish women and children in Auschwitz less credible or less important.[13]

Edith's narrative ellipsis constitutes a blank or gap in her story. A related constituent element of her narrative is that, although she does not use the term "trauma," she refers to "memories" in a way that approximates to trauma:

> Even though it is now more than sixty years since the war ended, many of us still have scars. The nightmares came later, and the anxiety they caused me made my nerves fail. I was only a child when I experienced the worst terrors of war, and I believed that the anxiety would pass when I had become an adult. But the bad memories have haunted me since. (p. 99)

The "bad memories" Edith refers to here are traumatic memories. Haunting her "in the dead of night," they are traces of "the worst terrors of war." Although receding into the past, the traces remain; they are non-erasable. Some scholars, including Alphen (2018) and Bal (1999), make a distinction between trauma and narrative memory. Yet Edith's "bad memories" suggest that, in her experience at least, the two are linked. When she went back to Auschwitz in 2006, participating (as did Maria Gabrielsen many times) in a trip for schoolchildren organized by Aktive Fredsreiser, "the memories grew incredibly powerful, and it was very difficult for me to walk around the camp" (p. 100). The memories are traumatic, but they blend into a more active memory that, including her decision to return to Auschwitz, incorporate her strong wish to share her experience with the young Norwegians on the trip.

It is a common feature of the stories in *Time's Witnesses* that the Holocaust survivors' responses to the last question I asked them, "When you look back at your time in the prison camp, what do you feel it is particularly important not to forget, and what can we learn from what you and your fellow prisoners were subjected to?," include references to people who ignore, or even deny, the Holocaust. Clearly, they are provoked, even shocked by these denials of one of the best-documented crimes in human history. There is a strong sense in which Edith speaks for all Holocaust survivors when, by way of concluding her story, she states:

> It is disconcerting when one hears that somebody denies that the exter-mination of the Jews ever took place. It is particularly awful when these persons manage to trick young people into this web of lies. If a lie is repeated often enough, it can be thought to be true.
>
> I have been imprisoned in Auschwitz myself, and I lost my childhood in Auschwitz. I personally experienced the Nazis' devilry and am one of those who survived this hell, against all odds. All of Europe failed the Jews. What is it going to be like the day the last of us goes? Will there be nothing to check those who deny the Holocaust? (p. 100)

I do not know the answer to these two questions. The questions are not rhetorical, and from my perspective as a European born after the war, I think, or at least hope, I understand her concern. It is true that "Europe failed the Jews"; it is probably also true that Europe may fail again—just as many non-European nations have failed, and continue to fail, to pro-tect their religious and ethnic minorities. If Edith's questions are a key aspect of her narrative ethics, they also reveal her ethical responsibility (Lothe, 2018).

Olga Horak

Ethical responsibility is also an important feature of Olga Horak's (Figure 1.4) story, which I introduce thus:

> *Born on 11 August 1926. Deported to the collection camp Sered in August 1944 and then to Auschwitz. Sent to Kurzbach in October 1944 and then on a death march to Gross-Rosen and Dresden in late December 1944. Sent to Bergen-Belsen in the first days of January 1945 and remained there until the camp was liberated by British and Canadian armed forces on 15 April 1945. Lives in Sydney.* (p. 117)

Olga Horak

Born on 11 August 1926. Deported to the collection camp Sered in August 1944 and then to Auschwitz. Sent to Kurzbach in October 1944 and then on a death march to Gross-Rosen and Dresden in late December 1944. Sent to Bergen-Belsen in the first days of January 1945 and remained there until the camp was liberated by British and Canadian armed forces on 15 April 1945. Lives in Sydney.

We had a well-functioning democracy in Czechoslovakia before the war. After the First World War, Thomas Garrigue Masaryk created a republic which was a wonderful place to live in. Masaryk had been a professor in the USA before the war, and he married an American lady. He was a fine man, and while he was President, Jewish people had good lives. There was no persecution due to religious differences. Everybody lived in harmony.

But it did not last very long, and things changed rapidly in the 1930s. Before the war broke out, in 1938, Czechoslovakia had to cede what the Germans called Sudetenland to Greater Germany. The central part of the country, where I come from, was made into a self-governing puppet republic called the Slovak Republic. The head of state was Jozef Tiso, a Catholic priest. And he had a pact with Hitler to collect and deport all Jewish people who lived

117

Figure 1.4 Olga Horak. In Lothe, J. (2017a), pp. 116–132.

In common with the other time's witnesses, Olga presents the reader with a narrative in which she combines three narrative functions: those of author, narrator, and main character. This kind of narrative combination highlights the two aspects of her ethical responsibility that I want to stress. Although such aspects vary from testimony to testimony, it is a feature of all the stories in *Time's Witnesses*. Like the other nine contributors to the book, Olga is acutely aware of the fact that soon there will be no living survivors of the Holocaust, and thus nobody who can bear witness the way she can because she *was there*. This sense of ethical urgency is connected to the great temporal distance between *Erzählzeit* (narrating time, 2013) and *erzählte Zeit* (narrated time, from the late 1920s onward).[14] Moreover, in common with the other testimonies, Olga's story reveals that the act of bearing witness is both a form of remembering and an act of remembrance. If her narrative illustrates the problem of remembering "a personal history vexed by traumas," it also shows her insistent effort to reconstruct what Langer calls "a semblance of continuity" (1991, p. 2) in her life.

Turning to a brief discussion of three textual examples of these two facets of Olga's ethical responsibility as author, I stress my ethical responsibility as editor; I also emphasize that, for me, this kind of responsibility blends into that which I experienced as a listener to and reader of Olga's story. All the choices I made as editor possessed an ethical element, though this aspect could vary in both scope and kind. For example, how could a privileged Norwegian man born after the Second World War know what questions to ask a Holocaust survivor? The truth is that I could not, and thus I could not be sure that the four questions listed above were the "right" ones. On the other hand, had this problem led me to abandon the entire book project (without questions there would have been no stories), that decision would also have been ethically problematic since the women's testimonies are truly important.

Serving as a motivation to narrate, the "semblance of continuity" that Langer mentions is evident in the first sentences of Olga's account: "We had a well-functioning democracy in Czechoslovakia before the war. . . . There was no persecution due to religious differences. Everybody lived in harmony" (p. 117). This opening establishes a powerful, in one sense almost absolute contrast between the first 12 years of Olga's life and what happened after the German invasion. Life during the war gradually became more difficult until, in August 1944,

[t]here were the carriages waiting for us—cattle carriages—and we were pushed in. This is the way we were transported to Auschwitz. You have probably seen a cattle carriage. What it is made for? To transport horses or cows. . . .

How long it took us to reach Auschwitz, I cannot tell you. For once you are confined in a dark place, you lose your sense of timing. The doors were bolted from the outside. Inside it was horrible. We had no food or water. There was just one bucket which served for necessity. I was a young, modest girl. I could not use it. It was a horrible feeling. When we arrived at Auschwitz, the transport of the human cargo stopped. We did not know where we were. They unbolted the doors, and the guards were shouting and screaming. You know, when they scream *Schnell, schnell! Raus, raus!* ('Quickly! Quickly! Out! Out!') I did not know *why* we had to be *schnell*. What was the hurry for? There was something sick in their minds. (p. 121)

In this passage, Olga's ethical responsibility as author and narrator manifests in two mutually reinforcing ways. First, in not just stating but also attempting to explain why she lost her sense of time inside the cattle carriage, she turns what superficially seems a narrative weakness into a narrative strength, thus increasing her narrative credibility while also accentuating the ethics of her narration. As cognitive narrative theory points out, the way in which the brain receives and processes a myriad of impressions is extremely complicated, and external factors (such as this brutal, inhumane kind of transport) may make it more difficult for the brain to compose plots and arrange temporal sequences that, as Paul Ricoeur puts it, can convert "the existential burden of discordance" (1984, p. 31; cf. Armstrong, 2013) into narrative syntheses that can impose a degree of meaning on life's imbalances—imbalances that, in this case, in the carriage as in the camp, were extreme. How could patterns of action be constructed under such conditions? It is to Olga's credit, and it makes her narration more credible, that she narrates this part of her story as a naked, inexplicable fragment. Her refusal to rearrange the course of events in the light of later knowledge of the mechanism of the Holocaust makes her appear more, not less, responsible. Second, the way Olga conveys her inability to comprehend the Nazis' haste makes the reader glimpse two radically opposed ethical systems. There is a connection between this part of the passage and Levi's (1958/2005) observations in *If This Is a Man* on the guards' attitudes and actions in Auschwitz; after having been deported from Italy, he too arrived in the camp in the autumn of 1944.

Olga's testimony incorporates constituent elements of the fragment and the episode. That her narrative is fragmented and episodic, however, does not make it less convincing as testimony; on the contrary, as in the example considered above, its incompleteness enhances the author's ethical authority. Without a sense of meaningful temporal continuity, events dissolve into unconnected fragments and meaningless episodes; moreover, even if considered *as* fragments and episodes, these elements of events (or nonevents) do not make sense. It does not follow, however, that the fragments and episodes Olga relates are unimportant. Rather, their significance is connected with her inability to ascribe meaning to them; more precisely, she fails to understand the motives and the ethical foundation for the actions of the human agents engaged in the fragmented, or fragment-like, events. This is the case even when the outcome of an event can literally decide between life and death:

> There were many SS (*Schutzstaffel*, a paramilitary organization under the Nazi Party) men waiting on the arrival ramp. They were dressed in immaculate black uniforms and polished boots. One of the SS men sat behind a table. He was in charge of the process of selecting people: sorting out people who were taken to the gas chambers shortly after arriving. He was a young, handsome man. I remember that he wore leather gloves. He was Dr Josef Mengele, the "Angel of Death." . . .
>
> As the line I was in approached the table where Mengele sat, we were ordered to strip completely naked. That was a great shock. It was degrading and humiliating. I was young and would not have undressed in front of anybody. But that was what we had to do. Now we had to form a single line and walk towards Mengele, who looked at us, deciding who was young and fit enough to be sent to the right. Anyone who was not considered good enough by Mengele was sent to the left. Those sent to the left could also be young and healthy, but maybe they had a scar or some insignificant mark. They were not "perfect." So we never knew what to expect.
>
> I approached the table. Mengele looked me up and down like a butcher inspecting meat, and waved me to the right. My mother was a healthy, well-developed woman. She was shown to the right as well. I was 16 ½, and my mother 39. We had passed the first *Selektion* at Auschwitz. (pp. 122–123)

The ethical dimension of Olga's meeting with Dr. Mengele is accentuated by the way in which she reports it: the rendering of facts as she now—in the narrative situation with me in Sydney in 2013—remembers them, the linking of the facts to the shock of having to undress, the comparison of Mengele's look to that of a butcher inspecting meat, the inclusion of the word *Selektion*. Cumulatively, these constituent elements of her narration strengthen her ethics by contrasting it with Mengele's—and by implication with that of Nazism. In addition to *Selektion*, the key word in this passage is "mother": not only do the two women share the experience of meeting Mengele; there is also a strong implication that they share the same values, and that the ethics of Olga's mother have contributed decisively to the formation of her own.

The importance of this point is further strengthened by Olga's narration of an episode just after the liberation of Bergen-Belsen in April 1945. Olga and her mother are waiting to be registered by British soldiers:

> My mother came in front of the table. She received her card. She collapsed. I lost her; she did not make it.
>
> My mother is registered as a survivor. She is not counted as a victim. I was behind her, and of course I was devastated. My mother had survived Auschwitz, Kurzbach, the death march to Dresden, and four months in Bergen-Belsen—only to die just after being registered as a survivor. I had lost her. My mother was 40 years old, and I was 18. Now I was completely alone. (p. 128)

The narration of this episode from Bergen-Belsen is similar to that of the women's meeting with Dr. Mengele. Here too the emphasis is on the actual occurrence, on what happened as remembered by the witness; here, as in the episode from Auschwitz, some words become semantically loaded in a way that enhances their ethical dimension. If *Selektion* is one such word in the earlier passage, in this one the words "completely alone" indicate that without her mother Olga would not have survived the Holocaust. Although different readers interpret narratives in dissimilar ways, I think most would agree that this suggestion at the end of the paragraph has a distinctly ethical element. It is constituted and shaped through narrative form. For me as a listener to Olga Horak's oral rendering of her story, the ethical aspect was strengthened by a long pause after the words "completely alone." The act of narrating how her mother died brought back painful memories that made it difficult for Olga to continue her story. That she eventually did so demonstrates a remarkable strength of will. It also reveals a deep ethical commitment.

The reader might counter that this kind of extratextual information, available to me as listener and editor but not to other readers of Olga's testimony, is irrelevant and potentially even misleading. It may, though, helpfully remind us of one of the strengths of oral narration—a strength that a written narrative does not possess. It also alerts us to the importance of thinking literature across continents; as a European I all too easily forget how important oral narrative traditions still are in other parts of the world, for example in Mali.[15] For me, there was also the editorial and ethical challenge of respecting Olga's pause—a narrative ellipsis impossible to present as written language—and of not asking a question that might make her story less authentic by leading it in a direction she did not choose herself. This possibility of indicating a pause or ellipsis is a narrative resource that oral narration shares with narrative film. In his interview with Abraham Bomba in *Shoah*, Lanzmann presents Bomba's long silence in a way that is aesthetically effective and yet, as I discuss in Chapter 3, ethically problematic.

I conclude this discussion of four Jewish women's stories from the Holocaust by reflecting on their characteristic narrative features and on the ethical challenges of Holocaust testimony. Highlighting the stories' narrative ethics, I am also interested in the testimonies as "cultural memorial forms," to appropriate the title of a thought-provoking editorial by Eneken Laanes and Hanna Meretoja in *Memory Studies* (2021). Finally, I reflect on my role as a listener and reader.

The task of bearing witness to the atrocities committed by the Nazis in their concentration and extermination camps is both important and exceptionally difficult. The survivors are witnesses or, more precisely, they become witnesses by telling about their camp experiences. The women's struggle to become witnesses is evident in all four testimonies discussed in this chapter. Bearing witness is a communicative act; a testimony that is not communicated to somebody is no testimony. This dimension of testimony is decisive. At the same time, there is a troubling sense in which the "real witnesses" of the Holocaust are the victims—those who were murdered by the Nazis. There is a sense in which the Holocaust is "an event without a witness" (Felman & Laub, 1992, p. 80). This view makes the problem of adequately representing and remembering the Holocaust particularly acute. And then the possibility of "inventing facts" (which are never exclusively individual), which Primo Levi mentions in his preface to *If This is a Man* (1958/2005), also becomes a defining feature of testimony. This constituent element of the genre has been theoretically illuminated by Jacques Derrida:

> When a testifying witness, whether or not he is explicitly under oath, without being able or obligated to prove anything, appeals to the faith of the other by engaging himself to tell the truth—no judge will accept that he should shirk his responsibility ironically by declaring or insinuating: what I am telling you here retains the status of literary fiction. And yet, if the testimonial is by law irreducible to the fictional, there is no testimony that does not structurally imply in itself the possibility of fiction, simulacra,

> dissimulation, lie, and perjury—that is to say, the possibility of literature, of the innocent or perverse literature that innocently plays at perverting all of these distinctions. If this possibility that it seems to prohibit were effectively excluded, if testimony thereby became proof, information, certainty, or archive, it would lose its function as testimony. In order to remain testimony, it must therefore allow itself to be haunted. (2000, pp. 29–30)

The testimonies considered in this chapter are "haunted" in this sense. As I mentioned in the discussion of Maria Gabrielsen's story, on a trip with Aktive Fredsreiser to Auschwitz many years after the war she overheard a person denying that the Holocaust ever occurred. Although she went over to him and told him her story, and although it "silenced him," she knows, as do the other women in *Time's Witnesses*, that testimony is no proof. Moreover, if, as Shoshana Felman and Dori Laub (1992) suggest, there is a distressing sense in which proof of the Holocaust vanished with the victims, the absence of the proof that a testifying witness can provide is becoming more complete, and more distressing, as the last Holocaust survivors are passing away.[16] At the same time, at this moment in European history, the authority of the few Holocaust survivors who are still alive and able to speak is further strengthened.

Even though the Holocaust defies comprehension, and even though the six million victims have been silenced, we nevertheless understand more when we read or hear the story of a time's witness. The stories considered in this chapter demonstrate that narrative can be structured in a way approximating the truth, or the kind of truth testimony *can* represent. Such an endeavor is central to the purpose of all the women who tell their stories in *Time's Witnesses*. I sometimes think of a narrative as something that follows silence and is succeeded by silence. Listening to, reading, and rereading these testimonies, I conclude that things are not necessarily that simple. Just as there are innumerable forms of narrative, there are countless variants of silence. Even though the narrative act is active, all forms of silence are not per se passive. Just as the narrative is a strategy for survival, so can silence be. Seen thus, the silences—narrative gaps or ellipses—are an integral part of the stories', as well as their authors', narrative ethics. By survival strategies, I am thinking of various strategies that the time's witnesses, more or less consciously, used to go on living after the war. But the women also had to have survival strategies in the camps—strategies for surviving from one day to the next. Ella Blumenthal's testimony illustrates both these variants. Admittedly, the survivors point out how little they could change things and how much everything depended on good fortune, on sheer luck. But this also meant that it was crucial to choose and act correctly in the situations where this was possible, such as finding the right place in the queue for food. Given the extreme conditions under which the women lived in the camps, these choices and acts often had to be self-centered and egotistic. The women I interviewed made no attempt to deny this. Broadly, the testimonies of *Time's Witnesses* confirm an "ideological confluence" that started in the 1970s: "the tendency in survivor narratives to shift from the ethos of resistance to the ethos of survival. This ethos involves the phenomenon of survivor's guilt" (Toker, 2019, p. 77). The values of Holocaust survivors who tell their stories in *Time's Witnesses* cannot be collapsed into one ethics, nor do the values represented by Chavah's silent protest after her child had been murdered in Stutthof metonymically represent the ethos of Judith Meisel or a different Holocaust survivor. The survivors I talked to and listened to do not consider themselves heroes. The heroes—those who protested and disobeyed orders in the camp—were routinely killed. For Meisel, Chavah is a true hero.

The women who tell of the Holocaust in *Time's Witnesses* try to find words for events and experiences that are so horrific they evade language. Their memories—for example Edith Notowicz's memory of her meetings with Mengele in Auschwitz, or Olga Horak's memory of her mother's death in Bergen-Belsen—are traumatic. As Mieke Bal observes, "Traumatic reenactment is tragically solitary. While the subject to whom the event happened lacks the narrative mastery over it that turns her or him into a proper subject, the other crucial presence in the process, the addressee, is also missing" (1999, p. x). In contrast, "ordinary narrative memory fundamentally serves a social function: it comes about in a cultural context whose frame evokes and enables the memory" (p. x). As a listener to the survivors' stories in *Time's Witnesses*, I was part of such a cultural context. As a second person, I acted as a "witness to a painfully elusive past," thus confirming

> a notion of memory that is not confined to the individual psyche, but is constituted in the culture in which the traumatized subject lives. . . . The acts of memory thus become an exchange between first and second person that sets in motion the emergence of narrative. (p. x)

The emphasis that Bal puts on narrative's (or testimony's) "emergence" is related to and supports my concern with the narrative beginnings of Holocaust narratives. Rereading the narratives, I find that the ethics of their narrative beginnings constitute a strategic point or stage of the narrative— a narrative "threshold" as M. M. Bakhtin understands this concept.[17] For Bakhtin, "the chronotope of *threshold*" (1982, p. 248, original emphasis) marks a crisis or a point of transition where the dimensions of time and space are curiously compressed, thus making the narrator or character pause while at the same time signaling that he or she may need or want to cross the threshold—a crossing or launch that may initiate the autobiographical process (Brockmeier, 2015). As narrative is a strong form of communication and a powerful mode of exploration, the act of narration can take the narrator back to the events she is talking about. This can prove problematic if what she first and foremost needs to do is to put these events behind her and get on with life. If the act of narration can help the Holocaust survivor to negotiate her traumatic memories, it can also reinforce them.

There is no answer for what is right or wrong when it comes to staying silent or speaking out about terrible events and traumatic experiences such as the Holocaust; what may be a good strategy for one survivor is not necessarily so for another. While many Holocaust survivors remained silent for the rest of their lives, it is characteristic of the testimonies considered here that the relation between silence and narrative is more a *both/and* than an *either/or* situation. In *Story and Situation*, Ross Chambers (1984) draws attention to the manner in which, at a deep and frequently unthematized level, the narrator's motivation to narrate is complemented by the listener's (or narratee's) readiness to listen, and that, for both parties, both possibilities of gain and risks of loss are involved. The context of Chambers's observation is narrative fiction,[18] but his point applies equally to the narrative situations in *Time's Witnesses*. By telling fragments of her story, the Holocaust survivor risks reawakening her sense of loss and estrangement, yet her narration may enable her to negotiate that loss. By listening, I (and by implication the reader of the testimony as verbal text and the viewer of a testimony on film) risk losing or being drawn out of a comfortable position of ignorance, yet the act of listening or reading or viewing may further a learning process, thus suggesting the possibility of gaining essential knowledge.

Silence precedes and follows the narratives of the time's witnesses. For most of the contributors to *Time's Witnesses*, a period of more than 50 years passed before they started to talk about their experiences. When they now narrate, the account repeatedly takes them to a point where the act of narration comes to a halt. A pause occurs, which is a form of silence. In an important article titled "The Social Phenomenon of Silence," Irene Levin notes, "Silence is a term for something that is not there, an absence of a phenomenon. . . . A central characteristic of silence is that it becomes a social phenomenon when it no longer exists" (2013, p. 195). Discussing silence and extraordinary events, Levin observes that to stop silence from continuing can be dangerous. The reason is that one does not really know what will happen or come out of it if the silenced experience is not silenced anymore. The moment silence ceases to exist the experience will gain a certain meaning. When we make the unspeakable visible or talked about, it becomes a social reality and one can interact with it. (p. 193)

It is not certain that Ella Blumenthal experienced the time from when she survived the Holocaust up to the point, many years later, when she was able to tell of her experience as being one of imposed silence. Perhaps the question of silence or narration was irrelevant to her survival strategy during this period.

In *The Culture of Confession from Augustine to Foucault*, Charles Taylor (2009) reflects on the ethical implications of Michel Foucault's refusal to consider speech and silence as a dichotomy. Emphasizing the power of speech as well as that of silence, Foucault finds that speech and silence are related to each other in complex social interaction. Thus, for Foucault, "silence can be a position which reflects one's oppression or which demonstrates one's freedom" (Taylor, 2009, p. 197; see Foucault, 1979; Levin, 2013). If the testimonies in *Time's Witnesses* suggest ways in which silence reveals aspects of a human being's freedom, they also support Foucault's accompanying observation that speech and silence are interconnected. An example is the passage, briefly considered above, in which Olga Horak's account of her mother's death just after having been liberated in Bergen-Belsen is followed by silence. A different, equally telling example from *Time's Witnesses* is Judith Meisel's account (discussed in the introduction) of Chavah's use of silence to demonstrate her freedom in Stutthof.

As noted in the introduction, Hanna Meretoja (2017, 2018a) argues convincingly that a narrative does not present the reader or viewer with just one set of values. Rather, a narrative possesses different values. The combination of these values and the values that readers and viewers take along to and activate in their interpretations of narrative complicates the narrative's ethics even further. While I agree that this is the case, and while I also concur with Meretoja's view of narrative as a communicative form that can "reinforce oppressive social structures" as well as "enlarge the space of possibilities in which we can act, think and re-imagine the world together with others" (p. 145), I am repeatedly struck by the ways in which Holocaust testimonies present me with values that are more strongly opposed to one another than in most narratives—in fact opposed to the extent that the possibility of communication and negotiation of these values is eliminated. Moreover, as the values and priorities of Nazism are, for me as the reader of *Time's Witnesses*, associated with evil acts, I consider this association an experiential (i.e., practical, not theoretical) premise for my interpretation. This approach accords with that of Arne Johan Vetlesen (2005), who refers to Jürgen Habermas's (1994, p. 185, original emphasis) statement that "what moral, and especially, immoral action means is something we experience and learn *prior to* all philosophy; it confronts us no less compellingly in compassion for the hurt integrity of others than in suffering over one's own afflicted identity or in anxiety at its being endangered." As a reader and interpreter of the testimonies in *Time's Witnesses*, I am repeatedly confronted with narrative presentations of immoral action. Although I cannot understand how the Holocaust could happen, I understand a little more when I read and reflect on, for example, Edith Notowicz's account (including its ellipsis) of Mengele's medical experiments in Auschwitz.

The women who relate their stories in *Time's Witnesses* are not historians, and their approach is, and must be, different. They were there. They experienced imprisonment. They survived imprisonment. And they have gone on living with the memories from their imprisonment. Now they talk about what they experienced 70 years earlier. It was a world of starvation, disease, death, abuse, suppression, humiliation, and fear. By telling their stories, the women stir up unpleasant thoughts and are reminded of losses against which they have used silence to protect themselves. The act of narration thus demonstrates courage and willpower. There are experiences that the women no longer recall; there are episodes and events they are uncertain about; there are episodes too painful, and still too traumatic, to talk about. But they were there, and they want to talk about what they remember, as they remember it, so that posterity will not forget it (Lothe, 2016). Since there are so few women who can speak from direct experience about the Holocaust, both in Europe in general and in Norway in particular, their accounts have been underrepresented and, as Myrna Goldenberg (2012) has shown, to a certain extent underrated. A narrative not realized through words is difficult to comprehend. Silence is easily overlooked. From this perspective, the women's voices from the Holocaust in *Time's Witnesses* are particularly important.

If the Holocaust survivors start to narrate after a period of silence, they also communicate their stories approaching the demarcation line that will be drawn by their own passing. Looked at from that angle, the space of time for the testimony is short—something the women demonstrate they are conscious of. This form of time-concentration—between the ending of the silence and the ending of the possibility of narrating—gives an edge to the testimonies' narrative ethics by investing them with a sense of urgency which is not just personal but also societal. As long as we have Holocaust survivors among us who are able to communicate their stories—as do Maria Gabrielsen, Ella Blumenthal, Edith Notowicz, and Olga Horak—the Holocaust is close to us.

Notes

1. When Nazi Germany invaded Norway on April 9, 1940, about 2,100 Jews were living in the country. Their situation immediately became precarious. The historian Bjarte Bruland (2012) distinguishes between three phases in the Nazi hunt for the Jews in Norway. The first phase, from April 1940 to January 1942, was dominated by single actions that were not necessarily part of a systematic anti-Jewish policy. In a brief intermediate phase, from January to October 1942, preparations were made for the third phase: the extermination phase of October 1942 to February 1943. During this last phase the Norwegian police carried out a series of arrests of Norwegian Jews, and there were four deportations to concentration and extermination camps. The women and children were in the two largest groups, of which the first was on the *Donau*. The second major deportation of Norwegian men, women, and children took place early in the morning of February 25, 1943. This time, 158 Norwegian Jews were deported on the transport ship *Gotenland*. From Stettin they were sent to Auschwitz via Berlin. They arrived in Auschwitz on March 3. This time also, women and girls, boys under 15 or thereabouts, and men over approximately 45 were gassed immediately after the selection. The situation in Norway thus differs from that in the other Scandinavian countries. As a neutral country, Sweden was not occupied by Nazi Germany, and Swedish Jews were therefore not deported. In Denmark, the Nazis attempted to deport the approximately 8,000 Jews, but thanks to large-scale civilian efforts, the vast majority managed to escape to safety in Sweden in October 1943. In Denmark 481 Jews were arrested and deported to Theresienstadt; of these 52 died.
2. The narratives in *Time's Witnesses* were communicated orally to me. They were recorded on tape and subsequently transcribed and edited. All the time's witnesses read their own text, corrected mistakes, and approved the narrative. The meetings took place on the following dates: Maria Segal on April 15, 2010, and May 11, 2011; Judith Meisel on May 11, 2011; Edith Notowicz on June 11, 2012, and April 17, 2013; Maria Gabrielsen on June 26, 2012, and April 3, 2013; Blanche Major on November 5, 2012; Isabella Wolf on November 29, 2012, and January 25, 2013; Ella Blumenthal on December 12, 2012, and February 19, 2013; Yvonne Engelman on March 13 and 15, 2012; Olga Horak on March 16, 2012; Zdenka Fantlová on September 29, 2012, and May 8, 2013.
3. It is true that, as Agamben observes, a survivor cannot be a third party in the sense of being a neutral observer, but to claim that "his testimony has nothing to do with the acquisition of facts for a trial" (2012, p. 17) seems to me to be going too far—especially if this point is made about all Holocaust survivors. (Agamben's example is Primo Levi.)
4. In addition to their native languages, the women would need some knowledge of German to survive in the camp, and they imparted their stories to me in English.
5. Theresienstadt was located close to the small town of Terezín in the northern part of what is now the Czech Republic. Theresienstadt, which existed from November 1941 to May 1945, was a combination of ghetto, transit camp, and concentration camp. A total of about 140,000 Jews were deported to this ghetto. Of these, almost 90,000 were "sent eastwards." Practically all of these were murdered at Auschwitz, Treblinka, or Majdanek. Maria Gabrielsen and her six siblings were among the 15,000 children who were in Theresienstadt for either a longer or shorter period of time. Many of the children wrote poems and drew pictures; a selection of the drawings is exhibited at the Jewish Museum in Prague. Considering that almost 90% of the

children perished, it is exceptional that Gabrielsen and all her siblings survived. Theresienstadt plays an important role in the narrative ethics of W. G. Sebald's *Austerlitz* (see Chapter 6).

6. *Holocaust Encyclopedia*, http://www.auschwitz.org/en/museum/museum-structure/research-center/

7. Two of the time's witnesses in the book, Maria Segal and Ella Blumenthal, were sent with their families to the Warsaw ghetto, the largest of all the Jewish ghettos established by the Nazis during the war. The ghetto was surrounded by a three-meter-high wall, and after the ghetto was sealed off on November 16, 1940, anyone attempting to escape risked being shot on the spot. Within an area of less than 3% of the total area of Warsaw, the Nazis crammed over 400,000 Jews from the city and the surrounding area. They made up 30% of the population of Warsaw. The Nazis organized the administration of the ghetto via a *Judenrat*. In the Warsaw ghetto this Jewish council was led by Adam Czerniaków, who chose to collaborate with the Nazis. When, in 1942, he realized that collaboration was futile, he took his own life. Raul Hilberg talks about Czerniaków in his interview with Lanzmann in *Shoah* (see Chapter 3; cf. Hilberg, 1999). In the summer of 1942, the Nazis started to deport Jews from the ghetto to camps which, after Germany's invasion of the Soviet Union on June 22, 1941, had been established in the eastern part of Poland. Most of them, 265,000 Jews, were sent to the extermination camp Treblinka. On April 19, 1943, which was the day the Jewish Passover began that year, German forces started the operation to annihilate the ghetto. However, when they entered the ghetto that morning, the Jewish Combat Organization, Żydowska Organizacja Bojowa, under the leadership of Mordecai Anielewicz, launched an attack on the German forces and forced them back onto the other side of the ghetto wall. After three days, the SS returned with reinforcements and blew up one building after another to force the remaining Jews to surrender. The uprising in the Warsaw ghetto was the largest and, symbolically speaking, the most important Jewish revolt in German-occupied Europe. As Blumenthal's testimony records, she participated in the uprising. See *Holocaust Encyclopedia*, https://encyclopedia.ushmm.org/content/en/article/warsaw-ghetto-uprising

8. After reading the first draft, Blumenthal felt that I had misunderstood so much that her interview could not be used as it was. But the most important reason for her not being able to approve the first draft was probably that she was dissatisfied with her own account. By telling her story to me, she had started to recall more of it—by narrating what she had experienced during the war, more memories were coming back to her. When she read my draft text, she did so from a different point of departure than the one she had during the first interview. This, combined with the formative experience of narrating, made a new version necessary. The other time's witnesses, too, expressed the feeling that there was a distance between the oral and written versions of their accounts and made a few adjustments as a result, but none of them felt there was a discrepancy to the extent that Blumenthal did.

9. Bergen-Belsen was a complex of camps with various categories of prisoners: Jews, prisoners of war, political prisoners, Roma, "asocial individuals," criminals, homosexuals, and Jehovah's Witnesses. When the British forces liberated the camp on April 15, 1945, they were met by a dreadful stench. Many thousands of dead prisoners had not been buried. A film made by a team from the BBC that accompanied the British forces shocked Western Europe and North America and is considered one of the most important films in the history of documentaries. Alain Resnais uses film footage from Bergen-Belsen in *Night and Fog* (see Chapter 2).

10. See *Holocaust Encyclopedia*, https://encyclopedia.ushmm.org/content/en/article/warsaw-ghetto-uprising

11. In connection with the revolt in the Warsaw ghetto more than 50,000 Jews were killed. Almost all the approximately 40,000 Jews still alive in the ghetto, including Ella Blumenthal, were deported to Majdanek and to various labor camps. In 1943 Majdanek was the scene of Aktion Erntefest (Operation Harvest Festival), the code name for the massacre in which 18,000 Jews were shot on November 3, 1943. In terms of the number of people killed, this was the largest massacre carried out on a single day during the Holocaust. The largest number of murders during a single 48-hour period took place on September 29–30, 1941, when 33,771 Jews were executed in Babi Yar near Kiev. See *Holocaust Encyclopedia*, https://encyclopedia.ushmm.org/content/en/article/lublin-majdanek-concentration-camp-conditions

   These massacres constitute historical reference points for the fictional character Aue's participation in a massacre of Jews in Jonathan Littell's novel *Les Bienveillantes* (see Chapter 4).

12. Auschwitz was the largest Nazi camp complex, in terms of geographical extent, the number of prisoners, and the number of prisoners killed. About 70% of the prisoners were killed shortly after arriving at the camp. This applied, as mentioned in the introduction, to the Norwegian children, the Norwegian women, and the Norwegian men over about 45 who came to the camp in the autumn of 1942 and winter of 1943. Most of the key personnel of high rank, including camp commandant Rudolf Höss, were first called to testify as witnesses in the Nuremberg trials, after which they were transferred to Poland, where they were put on trial in 1947. The majority were given the death sentence, and Höss was hanged in front of the crematorium at Auschwitz the same year. Auschwitz symbolizes the Nazis' mass extermination of humans they believed did not have a right to life. Auschwitz is also the camp that most people associate with the Holocaust. The most important reason for this is probably that Auschwitz is the Nazi camp where the most people were murdered: a total of 1.1 to 1.3 million people were killed at the camp, most of them ending their lives in the gas chambers. Since the Auschwitz complex was also a camp where prisoners were used as forced labor, some prisoners had a chance (although a very slim one) of survival. They were therefore able to keep memories of the camp alive and later testify as to what had taken place there. This contrasts with Bełżec, Sobibór, and Treblinka, where practically no one survived. As a result, "single purpose" extermination camps have acquired a much smaller place in our cultural memory of the Holocaust, even though, as a percentage, more people were killed there than at Auschwitz. See *Holocaust Encyclopedia*, https://encyclopedia.ushmm.org/content/en/article/auschwitz

13. The German physician and SS captain Josef Mengele was a prominent Nazi doctor who conducted medical experiments that often caused death to the prisoners he selected at Auschwitz. For many Jews and non-Jews, Mengele's postwar life in hiding in South America, where he died in 1979, has come to represent the international failure to bring the perpetrators of Nazi crimes to justice. See *Holocaust Encyclopedia*, https://encyclopedia.ushmm.org/content/en/article/josef-mengele

14. See Scheffel et al. (2014).

15. This example was used by Stephen Greenblatt in a conversation with Ellen Mortensen and Jakob Lothe at the House of Literature in Oslo, June 2016.

16. Ever since the enormity of the Nazi crimes against the Jews became known, there have been repeated attempts to deny that the Holocaust occurred. Even though it is probably the best-documented genocide in human history, Holocaust denialism continues. For a convincing argument against its moral and empirical validity, see Cesare (2023).

17. For an excellent discussion of key issues in Bakhtin's philosophy and criticism, see Erdinast-Vulcan (2013).

18. I will return to Chambers's discussion of the narrative situation in Chapter 6.

2

Leni Riefenstahl's *Triumph of the Will* and Alain Resnais's *Night and Fog*

Although *Triumph des Willens* was released in 1935, four years before the start of the Second World War and seven years before the detailed planning of the Holocaust at the Wannsee conference in Berlin, it has become impossible for people who see the German film director Leni Riefenstahl's film after the war not to associate it with Nazi Germany's systematic murder of six million Jews. Ironically, one of the few who consistently resisted making that connection was Riefenstahl herself. This chapter discusses the narrative ethics of *Triumph of the Will*, Riefenstahl's film about the Nazi Party Congress in Nuremberg in 1934. Relating the film, and its beginning in particular, to Germany's cultural memory of the First World War, I consider it a staged, artful documentary that promotes the values of Nazism. I then proceed to discuss the narrative ethics of a film to which *Triumph of the Will* is intertextually related: the French director Alain Resnais's *Night and Fog* (1956) is one of the first film documentaries that presents, and urges the viewer not to forget, the concentration camps built and run by Nazi Germany.

A critical concern of the section on *Triumph of the Will* is the blend of documentary and propaganda, including the ways in which both these genres are associated with versions and distortions of memory. A main point argued in the part of the chapter that deals with *Night and Fog* is the tension that I identify and discuss between the narrator's commentary and the film's visual images. Both the commentary and the images include aspects of memory, but these mnemonic elements partly contradict rather than reinforce each other. Thus, I argue, a contest ensues not only between the values of Nazism and values that differ from and oppose those of Nazism, but also between different ways of presenting and remembering the Holocaust. This contest reveals a problematic aspect of Resnais's film: the manner in which *Night and Fog* avoids identifying as Jews the majority of the prisoners and the dead in the camps makes me ask whether it is a Holocaust film at all.

Memory and Narrative Ethics. Jakob Lothe, Oxford University Press. © Oxford University Press (2025). DOI: 10.1093/9780197579534.003.0003

Having considered the narrative ethics of Resnais's presentation of images of the dead, most of whom are in fact Jewish victims, I reflect on the film's importance and impact as regards the interplay of individual and collective memory. One conclusion reached in this chapter is that, though extratextual knowledge of the Holocaust makes *Night and Fog* a Holocaust film for me, it is historically and ethically flawed since it does not mention the Nazis' mass murder of millions of Jews.

I first comment on the moving image and the Holocaust, highlighting the concept of film documentary. Noting that film "can be a record of real events that have taken place in the past," Toby Haggith and Joanna Newman claim that the film medium "is a particularly powerful and omniscient kind of record as it appears to require minimal interpretive skills for the viewer to comprehend what is being recalled on the screen" (2005, p. 5). Seen from the perspective of narrative hermeneutics, however, the viewer's comprehension of a film is inseparable from his or her interpretation of that film—and this interpretive activity applies both to documentary film and fiction film. Whether or not I am conscious of my "interpretive skills" (or lack thereof) is not the point here; what is essential is that "to comprehend what is being recalled on the screen" I need to interpret both the moving visual images and the sound (the narrator's voice and the music) that accompanies them. It is true that documentary film participates in what Bill Nichols has termed "the discourses of sobriety"—systems that "regard their relation to the real as direct, immediate, transparent" (1991, pp. 3–4,). Yet utterances presented in a documentary "are always already mediated at the level of the speaking subject whose personal narrative is a product of selection, ordering, interpretation, partisanship, prohibition, character, reflection, and the vicissitudes of memory; and at the level of the media text" (Sarkar & Walker, 2010, p. 7). In *Triumph of the Will*, Hitler's speeches, which feature prominently in the film, are mediated in this way—and Riefenstahl's presentation of them asks the viewer to accept Hitler's interpretation of German history and his role as Germany's savior.

Narrative Beginning

My extratextual knowledge of the Holocaust is insistently present as I interpret Riefenstahl's film. While I regard this kind of presence as inevitable, it is not necessarily unproblematic. For example, my knowledge about the

Holocaust and my temporal distance from the historical event make it more difficult for me to understand how viewers interpreted *Triumph of the Will* before the war. At the same time, *Triumph of the Will* illustrates that temporal distance from the text that I am reading or watching is not necessarily an interpretive weakness (Freeman, 2010; Gadamer, 1960/2013): if I had seen the film in the late 1930s, my interpretation of its narrative ethics would unavoidably have been different from today's.

While I argue that Riefenstahl presents the viewer with constituent elements of her narrative ethics right from the start, I also suggest that the link between narrative ethics and collective memory is particularly striking at the beginning of the film. It does not follow that narrative middles and endings are unimportant. Yet the narrative analyses of all my chosen texts in this book show that a narrative's opening is ethically charged in a special way. When I reread or rewatch a narrative beginning, there is a sense in which it not only preempts but also incorporates the following narrative. The title *Triumph des Willens* is accompanied by this paratext:[1]

> On 5 September 1934, 20 years after the outbreak of the First World War, 16 years after the start of the German suffering, 19 months after the beginning of the German rebirth, Adolf Hitler flew again to Nuremberg to survey his faithful.[2]

Strategically positioned after the title but before the first filmic images, this verbal text—which the viewer reads on the screen and which Riefenstahl presents as the basis and starting point for the film—includes several elements that are self-interpretive because they both provide a basis for and influence my interpretation. From my perspective, two such self-interpretive signs are particularly important. First, it is revealing that when Riefenstahl refers to the First World War, she does not stress the suffering of the German people during the war itself; rather, she highlights the suffering following the peace treaty, signed on June 28, 1919 ("16 years" ago), in the Palace of Versailles, that required Germany to disarm, make territorial concessions, and pay reparations. These requirements led to resentment in Germany, a resentment and sense of national humiliation that Hitler exploited.

The way Riefenstahl relates "the German suffering" to Hitler as manifestation and personification of "the German rebirth" is a self-interpretive sign that blends into a second aspect of the paratext: the viewer is encouraged to remember the First World War and its aftermath in a special way. There are two stages of this request: first, Riefenstahl presents me with a particular version of collective memory; second, she asks me to accept that memory, implying that this is also the memory of all those who participate in her film.[3]

Watching and rewatching the beginning of *Triumph of the Will*, I realize that, had I been a German citizen living in Nuremberg in 1935, I might, to use a term coined by James Phelan, be part of Riefenstahl's "flesh-and-blood audience." If that were the case, I would also become associated with her "authorial audience" (Phelan, 2007, p. 18). However, since I see and interpret the film after the *Second* World War, my memory as a viewer is very different from that of the audience addressed by Riefenstahl. For me, the memory of that war—and of the Holocaust as the nadir of that war—creates not only a temporal but also an attitudinal distance between me as historical viewer and Riefenstahl's implied viewer. Concomitantly, it also creates a distance between Riefenstahl's audience before and after the war. Thus, the paratext (and by implication the film) illustrates one of the key points argued by Maurice Halbwachs: although my memories are individual, they are socially mediated, and they are also formed by my knowledge and by the experience and values that I share with others:

> It is in this sense that there exists a collective memory and social frameworks for memory; it is to the degree that our individual thought places itself in these frameworks and participates in this memory that it is capable of the act of recollection. . . .
>
> One may say that the individual remembers by placing himself in the perspective of the group, but one may also affirm that the memory of the group realizes and manifests itself in individual memories. (Halbwachs, 1992, pp. 38, 40)

Noting that, for Halbwachs, collective and individual memory are "mutually dependent," Astrid Erll highlights the interpretive significance of Halbwachs's distinction between history, which deals with the past, and collective memory, which is oriented toward the interests of the group in the present. As collective memory "proceeds in an extremely selective and reconstructive manner . . . what is remembered can become distorted and shifted to such an extent that the result is closer to fiction than to a past reality" (Erll, 2011, p. 17). Even though Riefenstahl's paratext is not fictional, it includes elements of fiction as it selects and combines historical facts to present Hitler as "the hero of a grand narrative" (Devereaux, 1998, p. 231).

That the narrative beginning of *Triumph of the Will* is rhetorically effective is illustrated by the way it responds to Phelan's rhetorical narrative theory. In *Experiencing Fiction*, Phelan divides a narrative beginning into four parts: *exposition* is "everything, including the front matter, that provides information about the narrative, the characters . . . the setting (time and place), and events of the narrative"; *launch* is "the revelation of the first set of global instabilities or tensions in the narrative"; *initiation* is "the initial rhetorical transactions among implied author and narrator, on the one hand, and flesh-and-blood and authorial audience on the other"; and *entrance* is "the flesh-and-blood reader's multileveled . . . movement from outside the text to a specific location in the authorial audience at the end of the launch . . . [leading to] the authorial audience's hypothesis . . . about the direction and purpose of the whole narrative" (Phelan, 2007, pp. 17–19). As regards the film's exposition and launch, I have noted that the verbal paratext presents the viewer with a carefully designed version of the emergence of a strong, reborn Germany. I am given the information I need—or, more accurately, the information Riefenstahl thinks I need—to make sense of the ensuing narrative. In other words, Riefenstahl asks me to accept and endorse the film's narrative before I start watching it. The director's request is a constituent element of the narrative ethics of the film's beginning; it is an act of persuasion in large part derived from and based on the version of collective memory presented in the paratext. As regards exposition and entrance, the initial rhetorical transactions between Riefenstahl and the film audience start early. Two constituent elements of this part of the beginning, which also serves as a transition to the film's middle, are particularly important.

The first is Riefenstahl's presentation of Hitler's arrival. Positioning the film camera inside the airplane that takes Hitler to Nuremberg, she invites me to associate my perspective with Hitler's (Figure 2.1).

While this kind of perspectival association bothers me, it may have given the audience of 1935 a sense of privilege. Riefenstahl uses a similar technique when, showing how Hitler is enthusiastically greeted by the crowd as his car drives through the streets of Nuremberg, she positions the camera in the car, looking as it were over his shoulder. At the same time, Riefenstahl emphasizes the distance between the audience and Hitler (Nichols, 2010). She presents him as a god-like, Messianic figure who arrives from heaven. As Mary Devereaux notes, the shots of the advancing plane "are intercut with striking aerial footage of Nuremberg—a city representative of the old Germany and of the glorious Teutonic past, its castle a bulwark against foreign

Figure 2.1 Screenshot from *Triumph of the Will*, directed by Leni Riefenstahl (1935)

intruders" (1998, p. 232). The essential point to make here is that, right from the beginning, Riefenstahl establishes a narrative ethics affiliated with, and in large part dependent on, Hitler's ethos. Since I watch the film after the Holocaust, I know more about his ethos than does Riefenstahl's audience in 1935. Yet there is one aspect of Hitler's ethos that, announced already in the film's title, remains prominent throughout: Hitler's, and by implication the German people's, strength of will.

Although it remains unclear in the film what it consists of, Hitler's strength of will, announced in the title and the accompanying paratext,[4] is furthered through a sophisticated choreography that accentuates the interplay of physical movement and music. This interplay becomes a second constituent element of Riefenstahl's narrative ethics. The music, which ranges from themes from Richard Wagner's *Die Meistersänger* via German folk songs to the Nazi Party anthem, includes variants of the march, the musical form whose even meter and strongly accentuated first beats facilitate military marching. Physical movements include Hitler's plane and motorcade, but the most salient movements are those of well-equipped soldiers who, I cannot help thinking, are awaiting the Führer's order to go to war.

Documentary and Propaganda

Before turning to Resnais's *Night and Fog*—a film that, on one level at least, is a postwar response to *Triumph of the Will*—I discuss the concept of documentary and relate it to that of propaganda. I also comment briefly on aspects of aesthetic beauty and evil action. Riefenstahl consistently maintained that her film "is purely historical. . . . It is *film-verité*. It reflects the truth that was then, in 1934, history. It is therefore a documentary. Not a propaganda film" (quoted in Sarris, 1967, p. 461). Riefenstahl herself hardly believed this. Apart from the fact that no narrative can "reflect" history, she knew better than anybody else how much work she had put into editing the film, making it a carefully crafted film narrative whose "principles of organization are governed not by the chronological sequence of the events depicted in the film, but by the demands of the film's narrative vision: the highly selective (and distorted) story about Hitler of which Riefenstahl is the author" (Devereaux, 1998, p. 239). It is certainly true that many documentaries, including *Night and Fog*, are carefully made, and, in common with Riefenstahl, Resnais too presents the viewer with a narrative vision. While his vision includes the horrors of the Nazi concentration camps, Riefenstahl presents Hitler as a savior who will enable Germany to overcome the humiliation after the First World War as well as, and this implication becomes stronger as the film progresses, perhaps engage the nation in an act of revenge. Riefenstahl's selective and manipulative use of Germans' memories of the aftermath of the Great War serves as a basis for and contributes to a narrative ethics that presents the Nazi future as full of promise.

A remarkable fact about *Triumph of the Will* is that "the reality it records is a reality it helped to create" (Devereaux, 1998, p. 239). This important point supports Siegfried Kracauer's "faked reality" charge. In *From Caligari to Hitler*, Kracauer argues that

> from the real life of the people was built up a faked reality that was passed off as the genuine one; but this bastard reality, instead of being an end in itself, merely served as the set dressing for a film that was then to assume the character of an authentic documentary. (2004, p. 301; cf. Rentschler, 1996)

I take Kracauer's term "faked reality" as a synonym of a staged or manipulated reality. The film's problematic status as a documentary is affiliated with its function as propaganda, defined by Bruce Lannes Smith (2024) as "dissemination of information—facts, arguments, rumours, half-truths, or lies—to influence public opinion." Joseph Goebbels, Hitler's fanatical minister for people's enlightenment and propaganda, considered the film

> a magnificent cinematic vision of the Führer, seen here for the first time with a power that has not been revealed before. The film has successfully avoided the danger of being merely a politically slanted film. It has translated the powerful rhythm of this great epoch into something outstandingly artistic; it is an epic, forging the tempo of marching formations, steel-like in its convictions and fired by a passionate artistry.[5]

For Goebbels, the film contributes to and helps to establish the "great epoch" of the Third Reich, and it does so not least through a "powerful rhythm" and a display of "marching formations." As already indicated, these constituent elements of the film contribute considerably to its narrative ethics. It is an ethics that promotes the values of Nazism, particularly as represented by Hitler, yet it is a characteristic of *Triumph of the Will* that these values remain relatively, and in one sense surprisingly, unspecified throughout. One reason Hitler liked the film was that, in common with Goebbels, he appreciated its propaganda effect. Any possible sign of doubt or skepticism about Nazism was, or would have been, removed by Riefenstahl when she distilled her two-hour film from 61 hours of footage. This kind of streamlining of the film's narrative ethics makes it difficult to differentiate between constituent elements of ethics in the narrative discourse. As far as the filmed audience is concerned, they are enthusiastically supportive, whether they are greeting the marching soldiers or listening to Hitler's speeches. As regards the narrative ethics of Hitler as protagonist and that of Riefenstahl as director, producer, and cowriter of the script, they are almost indistinguishable. One possible way of describing this relationship is to say that Riefenstahl uses her film's discourse, including a range of visual and auditory components, to augment and intensify Hitler's rhetoric; she deftly exploits the potential of film narrative to make her protagonist's narrative ethics forceful and convincing.

One reason *Triumph of the Will* succeeds as propaganda while retaining its status as a documentary of the rise of Nazism is the close connection that Riefenstahl establishes between propaganda and persuasion as constituent elements of rhetorical power. Drawing on Antony's speech in Act

III, scene 2 of Shakespeare's *Julius Caesar* as a famous example of the art of persuasion, Jeremy Hawthorn (1987) identifies a number of elements of the technique of persuasion; these elements characterize both Riefenstahl as director and Hitler as protagonist. For example, Hawthorn notes, *"The persuader makes use of non-verbal as well as verbal techniques"* (p. ix, original emphasis); here "verbal techniques" apply most directly to Hitler's rhetorical power, but these techniques are supported and amplified through Riefenstahl's "non-verbal" methods, including camera angle, varying spatial distance between the viewer and Hitler, narrative rhythm, and repetition of key words and phrases. Moreover, *"[t]he persuader seeks always to encourage interpretation"* (p. ix, original emphasis): this is true both of the speeches that Hitler gives in the film and of the way Riefenstahl structures her film around them; "the audience is encouraged to 'join up the facts' in a particular way, and in particular to *categorize* people, or events or beliefs" (p. ix, original emphasis). Indeed, although Hitler does not refer to the Jews directly, he alludes to them when he stresses the distance, and implicitly also the conflict, between members of the Nazi Party and those outside it. This kind of manipulative interpretation is different from the interpretive act that, for Gadamer (1960/2013), builds on the self-interpretive elements that I identify as an integral part of the process of reading or watching. These aspects need not accord with or simply confirm the speaker's expressed intention—whether he or she is a character, narrator, author, or film director. Conversely, for Riefenstahl, the range of interpretive possibilities is limited to the promise and strength of Nazism and to the Führer's genius. For a viewer of *Triumph of the Will* after the Holocaust, however, the elements of Nazism that Riefenstahl suspends or ignores, including the systematic use of violence against those defined as "enemies," force themselves into the memory. Aided by my temporal distance from the film's release in 1935, I am able to build on self-interpretive components unidentifiable by Riefenstahl's audience.

Riefenstahl indicates that Hitler's values are closely related to his ethos, which is presented as integral to his qualities as leader and savior. The last word of the film's title highlights "will," and by implication Hitler's strong, triumphant will is a key aspect of his ethics. Although the film does not specify what "will" means, it becomes increasingly clear that, for Hitler as for Riefenstahl, the "will" of the title is coupled with the Nazi Party's, and by implication Germany's, will to power. This interpretive association is furthered by the film's narrative discourse. Early in the film Riefenstahl stresses

Hitler's humanity: "Even small details, like Hitler stopping his motorcade to accept flowers from a mother and child along the road, are designed to support the film's vision of Hitler as the much-beloved father of the German people" (Devereaux, 1998, p. 232). Gradually, there is a shift of emphasis toward a visual display of power.

Riefenstahl's presentation of Hitler's speeches establishes an important connection to the combination of individual and collective memory in the film's paratext (Figure 2.2).

Although Hitler does not refer explicitly to Germany's defeat in the First World War and to the humiliating terms of the Versailles Treaty, the German audience watching the film in 1935 would probably associate his words about strength, unity, and progress with those events. Thus, one rhetorical aspect of his speech is to count on and appeal to Germany's collective memory. At the same time, Hitler's version of this collective memory is informed by his individual memory, including that of the failed Beer Hall Putsch in 1923 and the following period spent in Landsberg Prison. It is also colored by ideas expounded in *Mein Kampf*, which he wrote at Landsberg.

Figure 2.2 Screenshot from *Triumph of the Will*, directed by Leni Riefenstahl (1935)

The film's visual display of power is associated with and furthered by the way Riefenstahl combines aesthetic and ethical elements. Devereaux finds that

> there is something paradoxical about a work of art that so tightly weaves the beautiful and the morally evil. Indeed, one of the most shocking things about *Triumph of the Will* is that it so clearly demonstrates that beauty and goodness can come apart, not just in the relatively simple sense that moral and aesthetic evaluation may diverge, but in the more frightening sense that it is possible for art to render evil beautiful. (1998, p. 250)

I comment on Devereaux's important point by linking it to the image (Figure 2.3) that shows Hitler—flanked by Rudolf Höss and Heinrich Himmler, two of his strongest supporters—walking toward the camera, with three enormous swastika flags in the background and thousands of soldiers on the left and right of the frame.

Figure 2.3 Screenshot from *Triumph of the Will*, directed by Leni Riefenstahl (1935)

The almost geometrical perfection of the soldiers' positioning suggests that no soldier can be seen as an individual.[6] The image becomes more effective because of the way Riefenstahl has prepared the audience for it. Hitler has descended from heaven to liberate his people—now he is walking toward the audience/the German people in order to implement that task. The image is also beautiful, especially if I take "beautiful" as a synonym of aesthetically pleasing or successful. Aspects of the image that engender this kind of beauty depend in large part on Riefenstahl's use of the film camera: a variant of perspective which includes an angle of vision as well as one of perception, a striking contrast between Hitler in the center and the huge number of soldiers on each side, a remarkable depth of field (with the three flags rising toward the sky, from which Hitler descended at the beginning of the film), and a combined sense of movement and stasis as Hitler, accompanied by a funeral march, is walking toward me while the soldiers are standing at attention (Nichols, 2010).[7] Agreeing with Devereaux that this image is aesthetically beautiful, I am inclined to think that such an impression of beauty can be shared by Riefenstahl's 1935 audience and a viewer who sees the film after the Holocaust. When it comes to the question of evil, there is a greater difference between me and a viewer watching the film in the mid-1930s. I am not arguing that aspects of evil—or, to use my preferred concept, evil action—are absent from the film, and I too find the "the conjunction of beauty and evil . . . unsettling" (Devereaux, 1998, p. 251). And yet, for a viewer with no recourse to extratextual knowledge, there are few signs of evil action in the film. This aspect is bound to be more prominent, and more insistently present, for me than for a pre-Holocaust viewer. Devereaux might counter that one reason *Triumph of the Will* succeeds in rendering evil beautiful is precisely that evil is aesthetically veiled or suspended. Key elements of Nazism were known to many Germans by the time Riefenstahl directed *Triumph of the Will*.[8] In *Mein Kampf*, which sold a million copies in Germany in 1933 alone, Hitler describes Jews as poisoners of society. Ian Kershaw has noted that, in a letter written as early as 1919, Hitler expressed an antisemitism resting on race theory: "'Its final aim,' he concluded, 'must unshakably be the removal of the Jews altogether'" (Kershaw, 1998, p. 125; cf. Kershaw, 2008). How many members of Riefenstahl's German audience had read *Mein Kampf*? This question leads to another one: Had Riefenstahl read her hero's book? For me, this is an ethical question—and it is left unanswered in *Triumph of the Will*.

Riefenstahl's narrative ethics is a major reason she succeeds in promoting Nazi ideology and the values of Nazism. Emphasizing the significance of the film's beginning, I have identified constituent elements of this ethics. These elements—such as Hitler's descent from the sky, the continuous movement of soldiers enthusiastically greeted by large audiences, the use of low camera angle when filming Hitler's speeches, the combination of the film's visual and auditory channels—are aesthetic aspects of *Triumph of the Will*. Yet, contrary to what Riefenstahl maintained, the film's aesthetics not only underlies but also generates its ethics, which is centered on and revolves around the adoration of Hitler as Messianic savior of the German people. There is no doubt that, for Riefenstahl, Hitler is the hero of a grand narrative, the leader of a great nation that remembers, and is preparing to avenge, the defeat suffered in the First World War and the humiliation of the Versailles Treaty. If I were a part of a German audience watching *Triumph of the Will* in 1935, would I have been able to identify and oppose the values of Nazim that it promotes? Although hopefully I would have taken exception to the film's ethics, its alluring aesthetics, which furthers this ethics, would probably have influenced me—though I might not have been conscious of that influence. This question indicates the extent to which Riefenstahl, turning her camera onto real life, molds real life to Nazi ideology through propaganda.[9] *Triumph of the Will* documents not just the Nazi Party Congress in Nuremberg in 1934 but also the Nazi ideology and the Nazis' version of history promoted, most persuasively by Hitler as the film's hero, at that historical event.

Alain Resnais's *Night and Fog*

Watching Resnais's *Night and Fog* after having seen Riefenstahl's *Triumph of the Will* is an experience that is not just thought-provoking but also painful. The experience is thought-provoking because both films are influential documentaries that effectively demonstrate the interplay between aesthetics and ethics—between film form and values presented through that form. Moreover, as both films deal with aspects of human memory and the presentation of memory, they are highly relevant to the concerns of this book. The experience is painful not just because Resnais's film deals with the Nazi concentration camps but also because watching *Night and Fog* I cannot avoid thinking of the implications of the Nazi propaganda in *Triumph of the Will*. To put this another way, my knowledge of the Holocaust, the series of historical events that occurred in 1941–1945, intrudes into and colors my experience not only of watching a French documentary made in 1955 but also a German one released 20 years earlier.

Since *Night and Fog* is an important instance of a film in which the narrative ethics of its *Entstehung* (*genèse*/genesis) as well as its reception are closely related to that of the film itself, I first comment on this aspect of Resnais's documentary. I then proceed to discuss the film's beginning, narrative progression (or rather, lack of such progression), and ending. I argue that *Night and Fog* is a notable example of a film whose narrative ethics is associated with a particular kind of narrative memory that Resnais not only displays but also explores—and to some extent even questions. As I will show, Resnais's use of the Mauthausen survivor Jean Cayrol's written commentary contributes significantly to the film's narrative ethics. Yet, as I also aim to demonstrate, the commentary that accompanies the visual images of camp prisoners and victims of mass murder also *complicates* that ethics since Cayrol does not mention that most of them were in fact Jews. Thus, my interpretation of *Night and Fog* as a Holocaust film depends on my extratextual knowledge of the Holocaust as a historical event.

From this perspective, Resnais's film is an example of a crisis of memory. In *Crises of Memory and the Second World War*, Susan Rubin Suleiman argues that "[a] crisis of memory, as I use that term, is a moment of choice, and sometimes of predicament or conflict, about remembrance of the past, whether by individuals or by groups" (2006, p. 1). I posit that Resnais's *Night and Fog* simultaneously presents and represents such a moment of choice, as well as one of predicament and conflict. Moreover, the film illustrates, and thus supports, Suleiman's accompanying point that "the object of conflict in an affair of memory is the interpretation and public understanding of an event firmly situated in the past, but whose aftereffects are still deeply felt" (p. 1). Resnais's film is an example of a film narrative in which the interpretation of individual and collective memory is related to and furthered by what Suleiman calls "public understanding." Part of the film's originality and significance, as well as its lasting value, is suggested by the ways in which Resnais presents and interprets individual memory as well as a "public understanding" that I consider to be synonymous with collective memory.[10]

One reason the film's *Entstehung* is important is that it evolved from an exhibition—that is, from a public event at which pictures or other objects are shown to the public. Although most exhibitions are not insistently narrative the way a documentary or fiction film is, they often include narrative elements that can inspire a filmmaker. Titled *Resistance, Liberation, Deportation* and curated by Olga Vormser and Henri Michel, the exhibition that proved the germ of *Night and Fog* opened on November 10, 1954, at the Institut Pédagogique National in Paris. The film producer Anatole Daumn was among those invited to the exhibition. Finding that it provided a strong basis for a film, he undertook production for Argos Films. Originally from Warsaw, he also arranged for co-financing by Film Polski (Lindeperg, 2007/2014). Dauman approached Resnais, who eventually signed a contract for the film on May 24, 1955.

Although he found the exhibition curated by Vormser and Michel important, Resnais was skeptical about making the film; in fact, he was so reluctant that he declined offers to direct it until Jean Cayrol, a survivor of the Mauthausen concentration camp, agreed to write the script. Resnais's reluctance tells us something about his ethics, not least if we compare it with Riefenstahl's enthusiasm. More important, it says something about the narrative ethics of the film he would direct if he accepted the invitation to do so. Although Resnais had visited Germany as part of his military service just after the war, he had no camp experience. But Cayrol had, and as a survivor he had communicated his experience in *Poèmes de la nuit et du brouillard* (1946). Reading these poems after having watched *Night and Fog*, I am inclined to interpret Cayrol's script as a kind of continuation of his poems—albeit in a different medium.[11] Perhaps Resnais changed his mind about the film project because he thought that Cayrol's contribution would prove invaluable. This does not mean that the problem of authenticity disappears. Yet it seems that, for Resnais, Cayrol's commentary made the film *more* authentic since it would enable him to present fragments of camp survivors' experiences. However, since Cayrol fails to mention that most of the victims were Jews, this possibility is not realized the way it could have been.

Title and Narrative Beginning (or: Interruption)

The title of a narrative is not just its beginning. A good title, observes Theodor W. Adorno in *Notes to Literature*, is "the microcosm of the work" (2019, p. 284). Using "narrative" as a synonym of "work," I suggest that one reason a title can condense the thematics (including the ethics) of a narrative into a few words is that it lingers in my mind after I have read or seen the narrative; thus, my understanding of a title is a rereading of that title. While this understanding is part of my interpretive activity, a title can also be interpretive—and this applies to the titles of film narratives as well as verbal narratives. Watching a film, the viewer often reads the film's title on the screen before he or she encounters, and immediately begins to interpret, the first visual images. Thus, my interpretation of the title as a verbal text influences my interpretation of the visual images.

Resnais's chosen title, *Nuit et brouillard*, is the French translation of the German *Nacht und Nebel*. In Nazi Germany, this was a term for the handling of prisoners according to a decree promulgated by Himmler on December 7, 1941.[12] The decree meant that enemies of the Reich, and particularly the Jews, would vanish without a trace into *Nacht und Nebel*—night and fog. At a key moment in the film, the visuals cut to a shot of trains arriving at concentration camps in night and fog. Cayrol's text, presented as a voice-over narrated by the French actor Michel Bouquet, tells us that those aboard the trains are doomed to die. There is also a close-up image of the letters "N N" on one of the trains (Figure 2.4).

"night and fog."

Figure 2.4 Screenshot from *Night and Fog*, directed by Alain Resnais (1956)

If I read the title as an allusion, *Night and Fog* invites me to remember two groups of victims. First, Resnais asks me to recall and honor those who perished in the concentration camps of Nazi Germany. Second, he urges me not to forget other individuals and groups of people who are oppressed, tortured, or murdered. This second aspect of the allusion establishes a connection to Cayrol's concluding comments at the end of the film. His observation "We pretend it [the Holocaust] happened only once, at a given time and place" approximates to a warning, suggesting that, for him as well as Resnais, genocide can happen again. This warning is a constituent element of the film's narrative ethics.

However, there is a third group of victims that Cayrol does *not* identify: the six million Jews who perished in the Holocaust. His use of the indefinite pronoun "it" is revealing. Why does he not say "the mass murder of Jews" or "the Holocaust" instead? When, as a viewer of *Night and Fog*, I insert "the Holocaust" in square brackets, that specification is my interpretation of Cayrol's "it." Importantly, I can specify "it" as "the Holocaust" because of extratextual knowledge, that is, knowledge not provided by the film. It is true that the word "Holocaust" (as I define it in the introduction) was not yet in common use in the mid-1950s. But Cayrol could have employed a phrase such as, for example, "the mass murder of Jews." In fact, his voice-over commentary does not mention the word "Jew" at all. Griselda Pollock and Max Silverman write, "The designation 'Jewish' occurs once in the commentary when it speaks of Stern, the Jewish student of Amsterdam (shot 23), although there are visible identifiers of Jewish victims in the image track" (p. 6). Yet it is ethically problematic that the viewer needs extratextual knowledge of the Holocaust or of Jewish identity markers (in particular the Star of David that the Nazis forced the Jews to wear) to determine whether these "identifiers" are "visible."

A possible explanation of Cayrol's conspicuous omission is that, in France as in Norway, the focus of interest in the first postwar years was on resistance to the German occupation rather than on the Nazis' mass murder of Jews (Lindeperg, 2007/2014; Suleiman, 2006).[13] Whether, or to what extent, Resnais supported Cayrol's use of the indefinite pronoun "it" is difficult to know, but his respect for Cayrol as a camp survivor may partly explain why he accepted Cayrol's failure or refusal to identify the majority of those murdered by the Nazis in the concentration and extermination camps as Jews.

I argue that the film's visuals, and particularly Resnais's incorporation of film footage from the camps, draw attention to the Holocaust in a way Cayrol does not (Lindeperg, 2007/2014, p. 104).

Elements of the tension are observable in the screenplay dated June 11, 1955:

1. The camp, deserted in 1955
2. An "algebraic" history of Nazism
3. Himmler's visit to Dachau
4. The convoys
5. Arrival at the camp
6. Quarantine and daily life
7. The locations of the camp
8. Himmler's second visit—continuation of the history of Nazism
9. The proliferation of the system
10. The techniques of extermination
11. The evacuation of the camps—what the Allies found
12. The Auschwitz Museum—the lesson to be learned. (Eisler, 2014, p. xxx)

As *Night and Fog* has no subtitles or subsections, this summary is not part of the film. But it tells me something about its contents, including the "history of Nazism" and the "technique of extermination." Since it also mentions the names of two concentration and extermination camps, Dachau and Auschwitz, it alludes more directly to the Holocaust than Cayrol's commentary. Moreover, the summary tells me something about the film's structure: although it includes elements we would expect to find in a short summary of a narrative's plot or action, including location and time, Resnais departs radically from the expectations of conventional filmmaking. While in many documentaries the combination of past and present is related to and often furthers the film's narrative progression, in *Night and Fog* it "rather occurs as an interruption" (Hebard, 2011, p. 223). This kind of interruption is striking already in the opening shot of an empty field. It is perhaps autumn; the predominant colors are yellow and blue. The camera cranes down, and a fence with barbed wire appears in the visual field (Figures 2.5 and 2.6).

Figure 2.5

Even a peaceful landscape...

Figures 2.5 and 2.6 Screenshots from *Night and Fog,* directed by Alain Resnais (1956)

The camera movement is accompanied by Cayrol's commentary: "Even a peaceful landscape; even a field with crows flying over; even a road with cars, peasants, and couples passing by; even a holiday village with a fair and a steeple can lead the way to a concentration camp" (quoted in Hirsch, 2004, p. 48). As "the camera crosses the fence that separates the camp from the surrounding countryside" (Rothman, 1997, p. 39), the viewer understands, or begins to understand, that the first image of *Night and Fog* is being filmed from behind the barbed wire of Auschwitz. We are thus "presented with a world that can no longer be apprehended in a pure and uninterrupted fashion. . . . Now, in the wake of the camps, the world can only be seen through the prism of camp barbed wire" (Silverman, 2011, p. 201). As the camera is located inside a former concentration and extermination camp looking out at the empty field, Resnais encourages me to relate my perspective as a viewer to that of a camp prisoner. Yet if this kind of encouragement is, as I am inclined to think, an interpretive signal, it is accompanied by a different signal: the suggestion, or beginning demonstration, that these two perspectives are not just extremely different but irreconcilable. If the film begins in the present and relates the present to the past, that past—the world of the camp—is, as Cayrol puts it, "a different planet" (*une autre planète*). On the one hand, the opening suggests that interpretation is essential; on the other hand, the interpretive elements of the opening contradict each other in ways that complicate interpretation. These conflicting interpretive signals do not cancel each other out, however. Rather, while complicating and qualifying each other, they also enrich each other in ways that, as I will show, contribute to the formation of the film's narrative ethics.

Discussing *Night and Fog*, Joshua Hirsch finds that

> the relationship between the present and the past is characterized by the image track in . . . [the] opening shots as one of entrapment. . . . [O]ne is pulled from an apparently harmless present, as if by an irresistible gravitational force, into the black hole of some terrible memory, embodied by the wire that one encounters wherever one turns. (2004, p. 49)

While "entrapment" captures an aspect of the first interpretive signal identified above, Hirsch's well-chosen word is also related, albeit more obliquely, to the second interpretive signal I have identified: as a viewer I am pulled into a "black hole of some terrible memory," although I am acutely aware of my distance from the camps and of my privileged life as a European born after the war. This also becomes a kind of entrapment, reducing my ability to understand. Yet from the perspective of narrative hermeneutics, recognizing this kind of interpretive limitation can, paradoxically, prove an interpretive gain or advantage (Freeman, 2023; Gadamer, 1960/2013; Meretoja, 2018a), not least by advancing a measure of critical humility. The combination of the two forms of entrapment is associated with and furthered by Cayrol's commentary. In contrast to me as a viewer, he has firsthand experience of the camp. His opening words—"Even a peaceful landscape . . . can lead the way to a concentration camp"—are semantically loaded in the way Hirsch indicates: they suggest the "gravitational force" not just of the camp but also of "some terrible memory" of it.

The film's first color segment thus constitutes the first part of a complex narrative beginning that, rather than marking the first stage of a narrative progression, invites the viewer to reflect on the contrast between the beautiful scenery and the fence with barbed wire. As the camera tracks backward to reveal the sign of the past which the fence represents, the combination of that movement and Cayrol's commentary makes me wonder about the film's purpose and direction. What does the contrast between the beautiful scenery and the fence signify? Why is the camera located behind the fence? Why is the field empty? These questions can be asked by all viewers of the segment, including those with no knowledge of the Holocaust. If I know at least something about this historical event, I may ask the same questions, but then they are likely to be accompanied by different questions: How can the scenery associated with a concentration camp be so beautiful? What was it like to look at such scenery from behind a fence with barbed wire? I might even ask a question similar to that asked by Cayrol later in the film: "What hope do we have of capturing this reality?" Although the questions are similar, those asked by a viewer with some knowledge of the Holocaust include an ethical component that is different from and stronger than that of a viewer who does not have this knowledge.

Resnais starts the process of enlightening the viewer about the "history of Nazism" (points 2 and 8 of his summary) by introducing a "documentary flashback" (Hirsch, 2004, p. 49). From the color shot from inside the Auschwitz fence in 1955 the camera cuts to a black-and-white shot from the film discussed in the first part of this chapter, Riefenstahl's *Triumph of the Will*. Hirsch finds that the transition to German soldiers marching at the Nuremberg Nazi Party Congress in 1934

is presented formally as a shock. Almost every conceivable element of the two joined shots undergoes a total reversal at the edit point. Color turns to black and white; clean footage to aged; an eye-level camera position to one on the ground; a moving shot to a stationary one, and simultaneously a stationary mise-en-scène (fence) to a moving one (marching soldiers);

slow, smooth movement (tracking) to fast, jagged movements (soldiers); the incantatory voice-over of the first segment to the staccato.... Thus, the film's movement from the present to the past is not characterized by the ease of mastery, but by the shock of trauma; one is jolted into the past, or, alternately, the past intrudes violently on the present. (2004, p. 50)

Agreeing with Hirsch that this transition is innovative and effective, I also concur with his accompanying point, that it is presented as a shock. As regards the viewer's experience of shock, my interpretation is influenced both by my knowledge of *Triumph of the Will* and by my knowledge of the Holocaust: on a second viewing "the shock of trauma" is accentuated since I link the images of marching soldiers in Riefenstahl's film to later images that Resnais presents of SS guards and prisoners in the camps.

Three aspects of this segment from *Triumph of the Will* are particularly important. First, the segment's abrupt analeptic movement supports Andrew Hebard's view of the film as an "interruption" (2011, p. 223) rather than a narrative with the kind of progression (of plot and characters) that the viewer conventionally expects. It is true that Resnais presents the marching German soldiers as constituent elements of the historical narrative of Nazi Germany—a narrative that, as we have seen, Riefenstahl sought to make as powerful and irresistible as possible. Yet although, considered in isolation, the segment possesses elements of an apparently unstoppable narrative, in *Night and Fog* the function of those narrative components is different from that intended by Riefenstahl. For Resnais, the narrative elements that make out parts of "the history of Nazism" (as he puts it in his summary) engender a film that is predominantly reflective rather than conventionally narrative. *Night and Fog* is a film narrative that questions narrative as we routinely understand it. It is as though, responding to the narrative of Nazi Germany, Resnais moves to the opposite extreme, making an interruption or intervention whose reflective components include uncertainty, incredulity, and doubts about the future. For me, "the history of Nazism" is the most important of these elements since it includes the Holocaust. I reiterate, though, that since Cayrol does not mention the word "Jews," this aspect of my interpretation of *Night and Fog* requires extratextual knowledge.

Second, Resnais's use of a black-and-white shot from *Triumph of the Will* highlights the importance of memory in *Night and Fog*. Discussing the narrative beginning of Riefenstahl's film, I noted the connection she establishes between the humiliating terms of the Versailles Treaty and the promise of a new start in 1933. In *Night and Fog*, this new start—the start of Nazism—is coupled with the concentration camps, and vice versa. Throughout the film, the camps are associated with the narrative trajectory of Nazi Germany. An example is the connection that, later in the film, Resnais establishes between the marching soldiers in *Triumph of the Will* and SS officers on train platforms and in the camps. The former, he suggests, are linked to the latter. Both represent a system of values that underlies and makes possible the processes of deportation (by train) and extermination (in the camps).

Third, while the first and second aspects are important in their own right, they are also significant because of the questions they make me ask. One pressing question is this: How can I sensibly reflect on a historical event that I find incomprehensible? At a different yet linked level, my questions also revolve around the terms I use or have access to when discussing *Night and Fog* as a film narrative about concentration camps. In an essay published several years before Resnais's film, "The Concentration Camps," Hannah Arendt asks a question that addresses both the historical reality of the Holocaust and the concepts we use when attempting to understand this reality:

> There is a great temptation to explain away the intrinsically incredible by means of liberal rationalizations.... We attempt to understand elements in present or recollected experience that simply surpass our powers of understanding. We attempt to classify as criminal a thing which, as we all feel, no such category was ever intended to cover. What meaning has the concept of murder when we are confronted with the mass production of corpses? (Arendt, 1948, p. 745)

There is no adequate answer to Arendt's question. And yet, as I note in the introduction, in order to discuss my chosen texts I see no alternative to using concepts, however inadequate they may be. For example, when I relate the concept of "analeptic movement" to Hebard's term "interruption," a tension arises between Hebard's understanding of interruption and my understanding of analepsis (flashback) as used in narrative theory. For Genette (1980), analepsis is a return, at a given stage of narrative discourse, to an earlier temporal stage of the narrative's story, while prolepsis (foreshadowing) narrates or evokes an event that will occur later.[14] Thus, in literary studies as well as in film studies, analepsis is grounded in a chronological notion of time. But interruption suggests no such temporal rearrangement; rather, "the formal aspects of the archival material serve to interrupt, rather than take over the techniques of the empty camp footage" (Hebard, 2011, p. 224). What we have instead "are overlapping and superimposed 'layers' or 'sheets' of time" (Silverman, 2011, p. 202). Max Silverman finds that this view is supported by Gilles Deleuze's comment on Resnais's film in *Cinema 2*:

> *Night and Fog* could even be thought of as the sum of all the ways of escaping from the flashback, and the false piety of the recollection-image. . . . In Resnais's case, however, this inadequacy of the flashback does not stop his work as a whole being based on the coexistence of sheets of past, the present no longer even intervening as centre of evocation. (Deleuze, 1989, p. 122)[15]

By "the coexistence of sheets of past" Deleuze is presumably referring to the juxtaposition of and alternation between color images of the deserted camp and black-and-white footage of marching German soldiers. (Deleuze is probably thinking of footage from the camps.) I agree that Resnais's rendering of this kind of coexistence contributes to his narrative strategy: although the film presents me as a viewer with worlds that are entirely different, as the "sheets of past" coexist the way they do it becomes increasingly difficult for me to keep them apart.

"Une autre planète"

This difficulty challenges my interpretation of the film's narrative ethics. An essential part of the challenge concerns the relationship between temporal distance on the one hand and reduction of that distance on the other. For Gadamer, it is important "to recognize temporal distance as a positive and productive condition enabling understanding" (1960/2013, p. 308). From this perspective, it is significant that I watch and write about the film in the third decade of the 21st century—the decade when the last Holocaust survivors are passing away. Yet although temporal distance can allow for a new and perhaps more adequate reading of an event (or of a literary or film narrative), there is a possibility that it may be inadequate or even wrong, not least because of my limited knowledge about the Holocaust and my lack of camp experience. Moreover, from the perspective of narrative hermeneutics, the process of interpretation is ongoing, and any interpretation can be improved—supported, refined, or challenged—by later interpretations.

While I agree that temporal distance is not necessarily an interpretive disadvantage, the quality of interruption that Hebard identifies in *Night and Fog* makes me doubt whether my distance from the events furthers my understanding of them. As I continue watching, I discover that the effect of interruption which I noted in the opening segments applies equally to points 3–11 of the summary of Resnais's screenplay. I find it increasingly difficult to distinguish between three temporal dimensions: that of my act of watching and interpreting, that of Resnais's present (with color images of deserted camps), and that of the black-and-white footage that signifies a past that interrupts not only the present of 1955 but also my present as a viewer in the third decade of the 21st century. Thus, while I look at what Cayrol calls "une autre planète," and while I find that metaphor to be entirely adequate, I experience, largely due to his commentary, taking part in his recollection of a world extremely different from my own. Although the world I am forced to look at when watching *Night and Fog* is incomprehensible to me, it still possesses a brutal, frightening reality.

The film's ethics is constituted by two aspects of narrative ethics: the ethics of the telling and the ethics of the told. Watching *Night and Fog*, I tend to link the ethics of the told to the Holocaust, including the ethics of perpetrators, bystanders, and victims, while I associate the ethics of the telling with Resnais's *presentation* of this ethics. As already indicated, in *Night and Fog* these two aspects of narrative ethics, which are helpful when discussing both fiction and nonfiction narratives, are so closely linked that, in the process of watching and interpreting the film, they become practically inseparable. This interplay presents the viewer with an interpretive challenge: am I responding to the ethics of the told or the ethics of the telling? This question, which is not just my question as a viewer but also an interpretive signal made by the film, becomes pressing in the middle of the film narrative, that is, in the rendering of the inhumane, and in one sense unpresentable, conditions of "une autre planète." I am aware that, in making this suggestion, I risk reducing the element of interruption that I have highlighted. Yet although the interruption of the past which Resnais achieves complicates narrative progression, it does not indicate that *Night and Fog* is not a narrative. Rather, it suggests that the film is a particular *kind* of narrative—a film narrative that explores the limitations of narrative and, through this kind of filmic exploration, urges the viewer to reflect on questions that constitute an essential part of the film's narrative ethics.

I highlight two aspects of the ethics of Resnais's rendering of the conditions of "une autre planète." The first concerns his use of documentary black-and-white footage from the camps produced and run by the
Nazis. This footage is primarily used in sections 3–10 of Resnais's summary of the screenplay, that is, in the part of the film which documents
"the techniques of extermination" (stage 10). Although "[i]mages from
the liberation dominate the filmed footage" (Lindeperg, 2007/2014, p.
99; cf. Delage, 2005), those taken by Nazis play a key role by adding
another dimension to Resnais's presentation of memory. Although it was
essential for the Nazis to cover up the systematic, industrial mass murder, it was also important for them to document the crime. This wish,
or need, for documentation is difficult to explain; it could possibly—as
in the case of Franz Suchomel, the Nazi guard at Treblinka interviewed
by Lanzmann (see Chapter 3)—be connected with a perverse sense of
achievement.

While the images taken by Nazis in the camps present the viewer with a
narrative ethics at once frightening and incomprehensible, Resnais employs
the ethics of Nazism as the basis for a contrastive narrative ethics represented not just by him as director and by Cayrol as narrator but also by
the prisoners photographed and filmed by the Nazis. The visual presentation of this contrastive ethics is colored and intensified by Resnais's use of
perspective. In classical narratology, perspective is explained as the agent
that sees, while voice is explained as the agent that speaks (Genette, 1980).
While the voice of Cayrol as narrator is relatively constant throughout, the
perspective varies—and this variation is related to the way Resnais uses the
film camera. In the film segments shot by the Nazis, the perspective is that of
"the Nazi camera" (Silverman, 2011, p. 202). Yet the combination of black-
and-white footage and color images from the filmic present invites me to
relate my perspective as a viewer to that of the prisoner rather than that of
the camera. This effect, which is predominantly ethical, supports Mieke Bal's
(2017) view of perspective—or focalization, which is her preferred term—as
a concept that refers not only to the narrative agent that sees but also to the
person who is being looked at, that is, the focalizer and the focalized. This
perspectival modulation becomes a constituent element of the film's narrative ethics. It makes me ask: What does it feel like to be filmed, and thus
looked at, in this way? What kind of experience does such focalization generate? Although I cannot answer these questions, Resnais asks me to reflect on
them.

My experience of viewing and interpreting *Night and Fog* responds to
and builds on the interpretive signals given by Resnais's combined use of

narrative voice and perspective. An important part of this experience is a recognition of my limited understanding. Yet recognizing my failure to understand, and thus also my inability to share the prisoners' perspective, may itself prove a valuable experience, not least because it incorporates an element of humility. As Gadamer observes, "The truth of an experience [*Erfahrung*] always implies an orientation toward new experience" (1960/2013, p. 364; cf. Gadamer, 1960/1975, p. 338). For me as a viewer of *Night and Fog*, the realization of my inexperience paradoxically augments my understanding of the prisoners' experience. For Gadamer, human beings share the "experience of human finitude. The truly experienced person is one who has taken this to heart, who knows that he is master neither of time nor the future" (1960/2013, p. 365). Although Gadamer is making a general point about experience, I cannot avoid relating it to the "truly experienced" prisoners.

The second aspect of the narrative ethics of "une autre planète" concerns Resnais's use of written text on the screen. This superimposition of verbal on visual signs is associated with the opposed sets of ethics I have just indicated: that of the Nazis on the one hand and that of the prisoners on the other. The first group of verbal signs consists of the letters "N N" and the sentences/phrases "CLEANLINESS IS HEALTH"—"WORK IS FREEDOM"—"TO EVERYONE HIS DUE"—"ONE LOUSE MEANS DEATH." As noted above, "N N" is the acronym for *Nacht und Nebel*, a term used by the Nazis for the treatment of prisoners. Since many of them disappeared, and were meant to disappear, into night and fog, this acronym makes some sense: it refers to a constituent element of the camps' "machinery." The sentences, however, are senseless, even absurd. The most illustrative example is perhaps the sentence above the Auschwitz entrance gate, "ARBEIT MACHT FREI" (WORK IS FREEDOM); in fact, the Nazis murdered the prisoners or forced them to work as slaves until they died.

I highlight these sentences because Resnais's presentation of them makes them integral parts of the film's narrative ethics. One important dimension of this ethics is the abuse of stories, an abuse that formed part of the basis for the Holocaust. As I review the slogans I have just quoted, sentences that force me to read them as I am watching the film and urge me to try to interpret them, the abuse of stories that the phrases signify takes me back to the film's beginning—particularly the footage from Riefenstahl's *Triumph of the Will*. Moreover, I associate them with the two letters "N N." Since Resnais's chosen title is *Night and Fog*, and since the title is the work's microcosm (Adorno,

2019), "N N" condenses that title into two letters. For me, these two letters take on an additional meaning: not only are they an acronym for the film's title, but they also refer to, or make me think of, the initials of the name of a human being—one of the countless prisoners who vanished without a trace in *Nacht und Nebel*, night and fog.

When I read a verbal narrative or watch a film narrative, I read or watch the text's narrative discourse. It is this discourse that forms the basis for my interpretive activity—an activity that begins as soon as I start reading or watching (Brockmeier, 2015; Meretoja, 2018a). The discourse is a complex form of narrative communication, and the ethics of this communication is inseparable from its aesthetic form. The ethics of a narrative is thus attributable to and represented by a series of narrative agents that, as constituent elements of aesthetic form, cumulatively constitute the narrative communication (Phelan, 2007). As regards *Night and Fog*, it would seem necessary to distinguish between the ethics of the persons (human beings or individuals), the narrator, and the director. Yet once I make this distinction, I sense that it is unsatisfactory, potentially even misleading. In narrative theory, the concepts of "person" and "character" are typically connected with and explained by referring to human agency: persons' and characters' ability to act, including the choices they make and their motives for making those choices, is a constituent element of the plot, which typically involves narrative progression. In *Night and Fog* there is, as already indicated, limited progression of this kind. It does not follow that there are no persons or actors in the film, but my interpretation builds on the presentation of person in and through Resnais's original, self-questioning variant of film narrative. In this chapter (as in chapters 1 and 3), I use "person" for the human beings presented in the testimonies and documentaries that I discuss (see introduction). I distinguish between the persons' ethics, the narrator's (Cayrol's) ethics, and the director's (Resnais's) ethics.

The Persons' Ethics

Considering the persons' ethics, I first need to distinguish between those who operated the camp system and the victims of that system. As regards the Nazis and their assistants, their narrative ethics is inseparable from the implementation of the Holocaust in which they are engaged—that is, the evil act of murdering millions of innocent Jews. My use of the word "assistant" necessitates a further distinction between the Nazis' voluntary and involuntary assistants: the ethics of the latter needs to be distinguished from that of the former. Resnais's presentation of the Nazis' ethics focuses on what they did, what they were responsible for. It is as though he shies away from attempting to understand or explain the constituent aspects of this ethics. Yet since he consistently focuses on the Nazi "machine," and particularly on the way it operated in the camps, evil action emerges as a major aspect of the film. A constituent element of this part of the film's narrative ethics is repetition: in the death camps in particular, evil acts are serial.

There is a sense in which the prisoners' ethics is similar, though not identical, because they are all victims of the camp system. But we need to differentiate between groups of victims: the conditions of prisoners in a concentration camp were different from those of an extermination camp such as Auschwitz-Birkenau. Although this kind of difference does not necessarily mean that the ethics of the inmates was dissimilar, the extreme conditions of a death camp challenged the meaning of "ethics" (see Chapter 1) more than those of a concentration camp. Thus, I am skeptical about the way in which Night and Fog tends to collapse concentration and extermination camps into one category; this flaw becomes much graver because it is correlated with the commentary's failure to state that most of those exterminated belonged to a singled-out nationality (Avisar, 1988; Coury, 2002; Michael, 1981).

As a result of the brutal mechanisms of war, deportation, and imprisonment, the prisoners' sense of agency—their ability to initiate and execute their own volitional actions—was virtually eliminated. Resnais's use of footage from the camps shows this convincingly. At the same time, and this is a key component of the film's narrative ethics, the prisoners are not *just* passive and self-oriented; they also, as Cayrol's commentary emphasizes, try to help each other. Such care is related to that shown by Chavah, the mother whose baby was murdered by the Nazi in Stutthof. As Knud E. Løgstrup (1956/1997) notes, this kind of care—care for a vulnerable human being who is utterly dependent on me for his or her survival—is an essential feature of humanity.

In the fragments of verbal text that I have commented on, the sentences and the acronym "N N" are related to a shot that displays a different kind of text: a sheet of paper with handwritten words I cannot read, though I can see that the language is French. The shot is part of a sequence that, as Cayrol explains, shows how prisoners care for each other—even though the extreme conditions of the camp force them to think of themselves and act egoistically to survive.

This shot of written text (Figure 2.7) serves as a counterpoint to the two other text variants. Although I cannot read the text, it makes sense to me: assuming the form of a silent protest against the inhumanity of the camp system, it is a strong indication of human strength and perseverance. Thus it becomes, in my viewing experience, a fragment of persons' ethics diametrically opposed to that extractable from a slogan such as *Arbeit macht frei*. Considered in isolation or used in a different context, this sentence could indicate a very different ethics. To use a helpful term coined by Bal (2002), it is the way it is *framed* in the film that makes it a signifier of Nazi ethics. This point can also be made about the sheet of paper with unintelligible French words written on it: both are framed by and acquire their ethical significance through the conditions of the camp.

The Narrator's Ethics

The ethics of the narrator in *Night and Fog* is complex—particularly because, in my interpretation of the film, Cayrol is not the only narrator. This does not mean that Resnais's use of Cayrol is unimportant; his contribution is

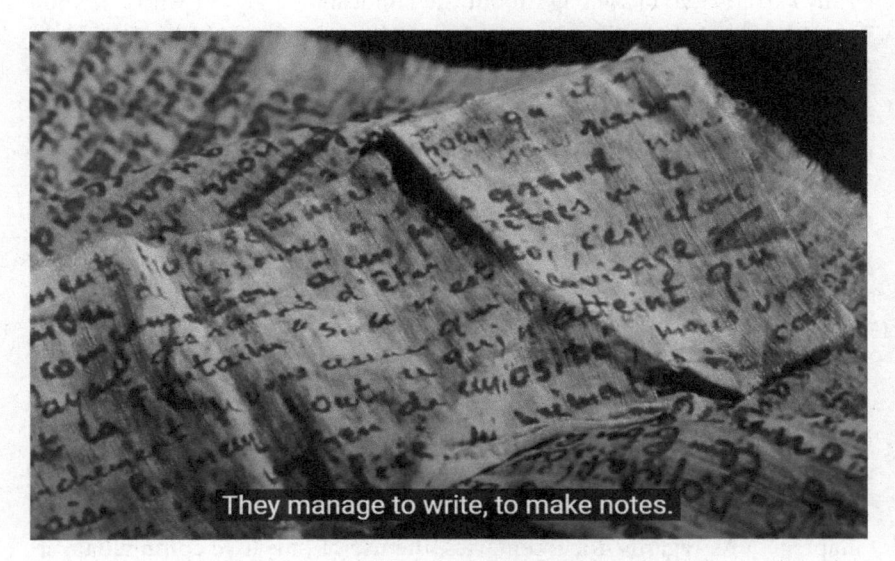

They manage to write, to make notes.

Figure 2.7 Screenshot from *Night and Fog*, directed by Alain Resnais (1956)

invaluable, and Resnais would probably not have made the film had not Cayrol agreed to participate. But it means that there is an additional, invisible narrator—or perhaps, rather, narration—whose ethics approximates to that of Resnais as director.

The comments that accompany the film's opening shots express Cayrol's, and Resnais's, indignation on behalf of the dead. On a second viewing of the narrative beginning, I note an element of warning sparked by Cayrol's commentary. The presence of his narrative voice is strong throughout. He gives the viewer a series of interpretive signals, all of which are related to and follow from his experience of having been a camp inmate himself: he can and does speak with the unique authority of the surviving witness. Thus, his commentary is a kind of testimony, and as such it is difficult to contradict (Davis, 2023; Ricoeur, 2000/2006). An important aspect of Cayrol's narrative ethics is to warn the viewer against the narrative ethics of Nazism. As we recall, such a warning is totally absent from *Triumph of the Will*. At the same time, the warning in Cayrol's commentary is not limited to Nazism; rather, it is leveled at ideologies and systems of power that, abusing stories, use violence to obtain their political and ideological objectives. As a viewer of *Night and Fog*, I subscribe to these components of Cayrol's narrative ethics. But his failure, or unwillingness, to mention who most of those murdered in the camps were makes me critical of this aspect of his ethics. This criticism is prompted by my extratextual knowledge about the Holocaust; a viewer who does not have this knowledge will not gain it by watching the film. Although Resnais uses variants of perspective to simultaneously modify and extend Cayrol's voice-over commentary, it has great authority for the reasons I have suggested. Moreover, Cayrol's voice is not only that of a commentator but also that of an interpreter; he interprets the visual images that I see on the screen but, as noted above, only partly. His omissions characterize, and blemish, his narrative ethics.

Resnais's Narrative Ethics

Most fiction films do not identify and use a narrative voice such as Cayrol's in *Night and Fog*. In fact, many directors consider this narrative device "unfilmic." (Compare the discussion of Ivory's *The Remains of the Day* in Chapter 5.) As regards documentaries, the use of narrative commentary is more common, yet it is unusual to give the narrator a key function like that performed by Cayrol. Both fiction films and documentaries are complex forms of narration, and the constituent elements, visual as well as auditory, of film narration all contribute to the film's narrative ethics. I have noted that while Cayrol's voice is relatively stable throughout, the perspective established by the film, especially the film camera, changes from scene to scene and sometimes even from shot to shot. The perspective not only determines what I see; it also influences how I interpret what I see. While Cayrol's off-screen commentary is part of the film's auditory channel, perspective is part of the visual channel—and both channels form the complex film narration. Discussing fiction as well as nonfiction films, we need to distinguish between the nature of the images and the treatment of them, and as regards the treatment of images, we need to differentiate between cinematography and editing (Lothe, 2000). A key component of cinematography is the camera, and the way Resnais uses the film camera contributes decisively—through variations of spatial distance, angle, and movement—to the formation of narrative perspective. Although perspective is not the only element of the visual channel of *Night and Fog*, and although its key function in the film does not make Cayrol's commentary less important, it furthers and complicates the film's narrative ethics in two linked ways.

First, in a number of shots and sequences the perspective confirms Cayrol's commentary, and vice versa. As we have seen, the film's beginning is an example of this kind of mutual confirmation. Second, there are many instances throughout the film where the perspective does *not* support Cayrol's voice. Sometimes the camera focuses on aspects of the camp system that Cayrol does not comment on; at other times, rather than verbally confirming what the camera makes me see, he interprets what I see in ways that I do not immediately understand. When this happens, I experience friction between my interpretation of an image (or a cluster of images) and Cayrol's. The tension between image (what the camera shows me) and off-screen voice (Cayrol's comments on what I see) illustrates how difficult it is to interpret many of the film's images, particularly those of human beings who are going to be killed or have already been killed. Thus, Resnais's use of the camera, including the perspectival variations which the camera enables him to establish, enhances the film's narrative ethics while at the same time diversifying and complicating that ethics.

The narrative ethics of Resnais as director builds on and proceeds from the various constituent elements of film narration. One such component is the friction between Cayrol's commentary, which avoids the word "Jew," and the images of people whom we may or may not identify as Jews that I see while listening to Cayrol's voice. The film's self-interpretive signs are presented to me as viewer by Resnais, who, drawing on and combining these aspects, gives his film an interpretive direction that influences my own interpretation. It does not follow that my interpretation is not uniquely my own. Moreover, the text may include aspects of self-interpretation that I misinterpret or fail to register. Still, the film's combination of self-interpretive aspects and my own interpretation, which incorporates and builds on them, suggests that the narrative ethics of *Night and Fog* approximates to and represents Resnais's values as director.

In spite of, but also because of, its brevity, *Night and Fog* is a complex film. Its complexity is furthered by the way Resnais combines the ethics of the told and the ethics of the telling. To negotiate the historical reality of the Nazi concentration camps, he selects and combines a series of constituent elements of film narration that invite, even force the viewer not only to confront that reality but also to relate it to the continuing threat and even practice of violence and murder. Memory, including the ethics of memory, plays a key role in this project—and this applies to the ethics of the told as well as to the ethics of the telling. While both these aspects of narrative ethics are significant, I focus, as I do throughout this book, on the ethics of the telling. In *Night and Fog*, this ethics presents the viewer with a form of memory that, as Silverman puts it, "not only merges present and past, here and elsewhere, the particular and the universal, but also unsettles the boundaries between the individual and the collective and between public and private" (2011, p. 207). This curiously indeterminate form of memory is a key component of the film's narrative ethics. I highlight four elements of Resnais's ethics of telling that I find particularly relevant and challenging with a view to the form of memory expounded by and extractable from the film: the use of archival footage produced by the Nazis in the camps, the presentation of the dead, the downplaying of the victims' Jewish identity, and the shot of a French policeman serving as a guard at the internment camp Pithiviers.

As already noted, Resnais uses different kinds of footage, including photographs taken and documentary films made by the Nazis at the time the camps were operative. The main reason this element of Resnais's documentary has been widely discussed is ethical: many viewers and critics of the film have found, and continue to find, that Nazi footage "positions the spectator as a victimizer, potentially eliciting a voyeuristic or sadistic response" (Hirsch, 2004, p. 72). While I accept that this may be one effect of Resnais's use of Nazi footage, and while I also agree that this effect reduces the attitudinal distance between the photographer and the viewer in a way that is ethically problematic, I find that the criticism summarized by Hirsch would have been more convincing had it been more nuanced. Once Resnais had made the decision to use archival footage from the camps, it seems that he wanted to make this documentation as extensive and persuasive as possible, thus presenting segments of footage produced not only by the allied forces but also by the Nazis. Even though the use of Nazi footage may be ethically dubious, it has documentary value. Yet I often find it difficult to ascertain the origin of the footage presented on the screen. To know that origin I need to have extratextual knowledge. On my first viewing of *Night and Fog* I did not know that Resnais employed Nazi footage, and yet I felt that the combination of different kinds of footage, including but not limited to that produced by Nazis, came close to eliciting a voyeuristic response.

This experience leads me to suggest that while Resnais's use of Nazi footage is ethically problematic, as a viewer I am equally concerned with the effects of witnessing events and characters in the camps from any perspective, not just that of a Nazi camera. These effects are related to, and in the case of *Night and Fog* accentuated by, the mechanism of film, and particularly that of the film camera. "The visual is *essentially* pornographic," claims Fredric Jameson; films "ask us to stare at the world as though it were a naked body" (1992, p. 1, original emphasis). In *Night and Fog*, the voyeuristic aspect of film presents the viewer with an interpretive challenge for the ethics of the told as well as Resnais's ethics of the telling. Film's voyeuristic aspect also challenges my perspective because the camera connects it to the agent who sees.

This pernicious effect was the main reason Lanzmann excluded historical images (footage) from *Shoah* (see Chapter 3). Jean-Jacques Delfour has argued that Lanzmann would refuse to use film shot by the Nazis "because it *contains and legitimizes* the Nazi position; to watch it would necessarily mean inhabiting that spectatorial position, exterior to the victims, thus adhering *filmically, perceptually*, to the Nazi position itself, and then fixing its image in memory" (2000, p. 14, original emphasis). In fact, my "spectatorial position [is] exterior to the victims" whether or not the film segment is shot by a Nazi. Moreover, as Libby Saxton writes of Resnais's use of filmic perspective, "[t]he contention that Nazi films and photographs legitimize a unitary voyeuristic-sadistic perspective disregards the fact that our identifications are, as Judith Butler has pointed out, not fixed but plural, fluid and unstable" (2011, p. 144; cf. Butler, 1990). I would add that not only is my identification fluid and unstable; it is also qualified, even opposed by a strong need to distance myself from what the camera forces me to look at.

Saxton finds that "Delfour's reasoning conflates optical perspectives—the spatial positions from which we view—with figurative ones—our affective and ethico-political identifications" (2011, pp. 144–145). Yet in the act of viewing and thus also of interpreting the film, optical and figurative perspectives are closely related to each other. While my optical perspective is colored by my "affective and ethico-political identifications," these identifications are also colored, possibly even changed by my optical perspective—what I see on the screen. This point applies not least to my affective identification, even though, as I have noted, my empathy with the prisoners in the camps is accompanied by a need to distance myself from them. The point may also apply to my ethicopolitical identification: watching the film from the optical perspective that Resnais forces me to adopt, and from my own limited perspective as a viewer with no camp experience, I find that the act of viewing and interpreting *Night and Fog* does something to my own ethics. Although I find it difficult to specify what this "something" is, one of its constituent elements is the question which Cayrol asks at the end of the film: "Who is responsible?" I return to this question by way of concluding this chapter.

While Resnais uses Nazi photographs to show the functioning—the "machine"—of the concentration camps when they were in operation, he adds footage taken by the Allies to show us the camps at their liberation: "Certain images from this latter period are used anachronistically to evoke the prisoners' everyday lives under the Nazi regime" (Saxton, 2011, p. 145). This is one of the ways Resnais frustrates the viewer, contradicting the sense of progression and ending that I tend to attach to liberation. Moreover, Resnais repeatedly returns to the present of 1955, juxtaposing footage from the war with images of the deserted camps. He thus establishes a variant of repetition as the film keeps returning to, and in one sense revolves around, its narrative beginning. These elements of *Night and Fog* all contribute to the formation of Resnais's narrative ethics. So does, as I have attempted to show, persons' ethics as well as that of Cayrol as narrator. Other aspects of Resnais's film also serve as constituent elements of its ethics. I have mentioned the camera and the cinematographer who guides it (and Resnais, who instructs his cinematographers, Ghislain Cloquet and Sacha Vierny, how to do this). One important aspect not mentioned so far is the film music by Hanns Eisler. Since the characters in the film do not or cannot speak, the soundtrack of *Night and Fog* consists of two components: Cayrol's narration and Eisler's music. His score for Resnais's film accompanies Cayrol's commentary while at the same time accompanying the visual images that I see on the screen. A variant of atonal music that does not adhere to the traditional harmonic concept of a key or mode, Eisler's score for *Night and Fog* is difficult to describe verbally. As I interpret the visual image, I also interpret the music. I find that the music does not make it easier to come to terms with the images; rather, my experience is that the music makes me more, not less, disturbed by what I see. The music accentuates my sense of shock and disbelief, yet it also stirs a feeling of resignation and melancholia.[16]

Images of the Dead

Nowhere in *Night and Fog* is my sense of incomprehensibility and shock greater than in the scenes where Resnais forces me to look at images of dead bodies: human beings murdered by the Nazis. The reason I did not include these in my discussion of the ethics of the persons (human beings who serve as actors) in the film is that I tend to think of a person as someone who is alive. But Resnais challenges this view; there is one large group whose contribution to the film's narrative ethics is decisive, even though I cannot adequately describe it: the dead. The acute presence of the dead presents me with an interpretive challenge. Although the dead in *Night and Fog* are no longer human beings, they would have been had they not been murdered. As Resnais repeatedly forces me to look at close-up images of dead bodies, I find them so unique, and so different from each other, that it becomes impossible not to think of them as individuals. As we all know, the dead cannot communicate, but as the Nazis and the living prisoners do not speak either, there is a sense in which this fundamental difference between the living and the dead is reduced. In a perceptive essay titled "Resnais and the Dead," Emma Wilson is concerned "with modes of response to images of pain and suffering, with the difficult questions the film raises about the exposure and defamiliarization of the bodies of once known and loved others" (2011, p. 127). Discussing the ethics of this kind of exposure, Wilson refers to a passage in Griselda Pollock's *Encounters in the Virtual Feminist Museum*:

> I am of the opinion that the archive of the photographic inventory of Nazi atrocities cannot and should not be publicly exhibited. Each image contains known or knowable individuals, not merely anonymous corpses or walking skeletons whose horrifying neglect and reduction to anonymous numbers is part of the profound horror of this event. If we wish to resist participating in fascism's rupture of the most ancient marker of humanity's self-consciousness, namely the consideration for the human dead, we must return to each body its status as a potentially known, beloved, valued, possibly brilliant, certainly mourned human being whose degradation and torture has served its first and immediate purpose as evidence and must now be sheltered in the decent obscurity of archival entombment not allowed to those who in being "disappeared" remain unburied and worse. (Pollock, 2007, p. 194; cf. Silverman, 2006)

As Wilson notes, it is difficult to disagree with these important words. They are relevant not just for *Night and Fog* but also for Lanzmann's *Shoah*, which consistently refuses to make use of "the photographic inventory of Nazi atrocities." And yet at this stage of my interpretation I am inclined to think that Resnais's film would have been less powerful, and possibly also less important, had he decided not to show us the dead the way he does.

One attractive feature of Wilson's discussion is her readiness to qualify, even question points made in her earlier work on *Night and Fog*. Such readiness accords with a guiding principle of narrative hermeneutics: "[T]he discovery of the true meaning of a text or a work of art is never finished; it is in fact an infinite process" (Gadamer, 1960/2013, p. 309). For Gadamer, this ongoing process is an integral aspect of the historicity of all human understanding. The process is infinite not least because, as the temporal distance between the text and the reader or viewer increases, the relationship between the text's self-interpretive elements and my own interpretation of it changes. One of the reasons for this change is my own experience, which "always implies an orientation toward new experience" (p. 364). Drawing on her own experience, including the experience of watching and writing about *Night and Fog* and that of reading and reflecting on Pollock's discussion, Wilson concentrates on "imaginary moves between the family photograph, memento or memory image and the nauseous, surreal, body images Resnais exposes in *Night and Fog*" (2011, p. 129). Noting that images of nudity persist throughout, she argues that, despite constantly pointing to what is not seen and what cannot be shown, Resnais aims "to build his film around a logic of escalation and increment in shock" (p. 133). A striking example is the move from shot 229, which shows a column of naked women on the grass, to 230, which depicts four naked women in the foreground. Wilson finds that the image is

> excessive in its presence and in the brute fact of its having been taken. The horror of the revelation of these women's bare, vulnerable, sentient flesh is magnified for the viewer as we see the women closer in the foreground, with the same illusion of sequence and continuity from image to image. Unlike the naked Eve hiding her sex, these women's arms shield their breasts, they cradle themselves in a bare gesture of self-protection or shielding which is then belied by the unspeakable exposure of their pubic hair and of the pale weight of their bodies in contrast to the clothed, armoured surveillant figures behind them. (p. 133)

Wilson comments, "These images disturb me as I approach them" (p. 133).They disturb me too. I sense that, as a viewer, I unwillingly become the witness of an evil act: the murder of these women not because they have done anything wrong but because they are Jewish. Yet my experience is not just that of a witness: as the images are taken by a Nazi photographer, that is, by one of those responsible for the murder, I become implicated in the act since my perspective is linked, in one sense even locked, to that of the Nazi camera. Bal (1991, 2017) has noted that focalization in a narrative need not be connected just with the agent that sees; it can also be associated with the person or object that is being looked at. In this case, however, "the voice-over only speaks of the Nazi torturers even if the images mostly show the victims. So this voice does not speak of what is shown, on the contrary, it speaks of what one doesn't see" (Mondzain, 2007/2010, p. 149). Cayrol's voice-over thus relates my perspective even more closely to that of the Nazi photographer.

I am not sure about Resnais's narrative ethics in this scene. I find the images shocking, but shock does not necessarily lead to ethical action. Wilson is right to note that the full effect of these images, as well as those of dead bodies in the camps, depends on the viewer's extratextual knowledge, including knowledge about the Holocaust not provided by Cayrol as narrator. As Marianne Hirsch observes,

> the Holocaust photograph is uniquely able to bring out this particular capacity of photographs to hover between life and death, to capture only that which no longer exists, to suggest both the desire and the necessity

and, at the same time, the difficulty, the impossibility, of mourning. (1997, p. 20)

The image of the naked women literally hovers between life and death. For me, it is as though they establish a kind of bridge or connection between images of prisoners in the camps and images, particularly toward the end of the film, of the dead. To put this another way, my interpretation of the filmic image which depicts the execution of the naked Jewish women makes it harder for me not to consider the dead as human beings that, in spite of being lifeless corpses, possess individual traits.

This is difficult ethical territory. One interpretive challenge is that if I relate ethical questions to the dead—or, and more precisely, to Resnais's presentation of the dead—these questions turn out to be my questions, and I am not sure whether I am entitled to ask them. In *Haunted Subjects*, Colin Davis considers possible meanings of visiting the dead, or being visited by them:

> The dead return not as adversaries, not to impose regret or remorse, not to possess us or to be possessed by us, but to communicate from their still-signifying secretiveness. . . .
>
> Can the dead speak to us? Is it possible to envisage some sort of mediation between the worlds of the living and the dead without lapsing into mysticism and wish-fulfilment? (2007a, pp. 64, 111)

Davis combines these two questions with a pertinent warning: "[R]estoring speech to the voiceless risks becoming a theft or imposition of meaning rather than a response to radical otherness" (2007a, p. 112). Moreover, I do not know what such speech would consist of except guesses and questions that would be my own only and not those of the voiceless. Davis is right to note that "in the process of attending to the words of the dead, however erroneous or mystified this might be, our own subject position is disturbed" (p. 114). This observation can be extended to include the process of attending to the *images* of the dead; it is as though the images of the dead speak for them. As Resnais forces me to attend to these images, I am disturbed as a viewer. This kind of disturbance includes elements of interpretation, but I am not sure how to interlink and develop them since I fail to identify the self-interpretive elements in Resnais's film narrative to which they could relate and on which they could build. Resnais presents "the corpse as strangely fragile, physically present, inviting a haptic gaze despite the abject untouchability of the corpse" (Wilson, 2011, p. 135). May there, Wilson asks, be ethical gains in this kind of commerce with the dead? Perhaps there may, but I am not sure. For me, one possible ethical gain is linked to the *shock* I experience as Resnais forces me, and as I force myself, to watch the images of the dead. Even though they are corpses, and even though I am unable to dissociate my perspective from that of the perpetrator, the shock I experience signals, I hope, a wish as well as a need to distance myself from the ethical system of Nazism, including Nazism's glorification of violence and hatred of the Jews. This need for attitudinal distance is, I hope, furthered by an ethical impulse.

In one important sense, "the other is always with us. Because the other is susceptible to death, she or he may of course die; but this does not mean that the other ceases to impinge on the world of the living" (Davis, 2007a, p. 116). Davis links this key aspect of Emmanuel Levinas's account of death to Levinas's accompanying point that "[b]ecause I am invested with responsibility for the other, the death of the other is necessarily my affair" (p. 116). Writing of the caress, Levinas observes that "to love is to fear for another, to come to the assistance of his frailty. . . . The *way* of the tender consists in an extreme fragility, a vulnerability" (1961/1969, p. 256, original emphasis). I relate Levinas's understanding of the caress and of my responsibility for the other to Løgstrup's (1956/1997) notion of human care: care for the other, and particularly for the other who needs my help and assistance. This other is not identifiable with Levinas's more abstract and almost ungraspable idea of the Other. Yet the other whom I meet, and who may need my help, can be a physical manifestation of Levinas's Other.

Part of my unease when watching the images of the dead in the last part of *Night and Fog* is stirred by my sense of helplessness as I am confronted with and yet cannot reach the dead bodies. As I rewatch and reflect on Resnais's film, images of the dead keep haunting me like specters. Jacques Derrida has noted that

> the very thing one is deprived of, as much in spectrality as in the face which looks at images or watches films or television, is indeed tactile sensitivity. The desire to touch, the tactile effect or affect, is violently summoned by its very frustration. (2002, p. 115)

The absence of tactility is striking in Resnais's display of the dead. It frustrates my will for contact with "the departed other and his or her fleeting photographic trace" (Wilson, 2011, p. 130). Whether this will for contact signals an ethical impulse, I am not sure. I would like to suggest, though, that there is a connection between Resnais's insistent presentation of the dead in the last part of *Night and Fog* and Cayrol's comments on the ways in which the camp prisoners care for each other—and even, though they need to be egoistic to survive, often help each other. That many prisoners do this under the extreme conditions of the camp illustrates a care for the other radically opposed to the Nazis' lack of care. Resnais's presentation of this contrast contributes to his narrative ethics.

Is Resnais's narrative ethics, and thus *Night and Fog*, primarily prompted by and concerned with the Holocaust? And if it is, why does Cayrol's voice-over commentary not support this concern? Or does the film, using the Holocaust as a main example and assuming that the event is known to viewers, make a more general ethical statement, suggesting that, as Silverman puts it, "the thin veneer of everyday life is liable, at all times, to dissolve into the overwhelming trauma of genocide" (2006, p. 7)? Although these questions do not necessarily exclude each other, my response to them does something to my understanding of the film's narrative ethics. In their introduction to *Concentrationary Cinema*, Silverman and Pollock argue that although the Holocaust features prominently in *Night and Fog*, it is not primarily, and definitely not only, a "Holocaust film." The term "concentrationary" derives from a book published in 1946 by David Rousset, *L'Univers concentrationnaire* (The Concentrationary Universe). For Rousset, a French political prisoner who survived the German concentration camp Buchenwald, "a *concentrationary universe* invokes a political system of terror whose aim was to demolish the social humanity of all its actual and potential victims within and beyond the actual sites" (Pollock & Silverman, 2011, p. 18). Pollock and Silverman stress that, from his experience inside Buchenwald,

> Rousset argues that the camp is [a] symptom of the *concentrationary* as an infection of the entire social fabric. . . . [It] is not, therefore, a moment of extreme atrocity that occurred only in one place and at one time to be revealed by the liberators and thus cleaned up and cleared away. The concentration camp system marks the inception and initiating actualization of a new political possibility in modern political life of a form of terror that, as a result of this realized experiment under the Third Reich, will always be with us now that it has been unleashed on the world. . . . Not reducible to a term that signifies an event, such as the Holocaust, the *concentrationary* is the inception of a modern "anti-political," antidemocratic political possibility that must be opposed by understanding its realized configurations, not only in Nazi Germany but also in Stalin's Soviet Union. (pp. 18–19)

Linking the title of their volume to that of Rousset's book, Pollock and Silverman consider concentrationary cinema as a variant of film that aims to visually present aspects of the concentrationary universe. Their appropriation of Rousset's concept is largely convincing, and the way they relate Rousset's idea of the concentrationary universe to Arendt's work on totalitarianism and concentration camps is also thought-provoking. Yet Cayrol's, and by implication Resnais's, failure to verbally identify the Holocaust as the Nazis' mass murder of Jews is problematic; indeed, seen from my perspective it is inexplicable and deeply troubling. As I have attempted to show, there is an unresolved tension in *Night and Fog* between its *visual* narrative ethics, which is at least partly centered on the Holocaust, and the auditory dimension of Cayrol's ethics, which puts emphasis on the concentrationary universe. The visual focus on the Holocaust is established right from the start: the opening shots of *Night and Fog* are taken from within Auschwitz-Birkenau, and as a viewer I remain inside the camp throughout. Yet the viewer's need for extratextual knowledge (of the Holocaust as well as of Auschwitz, the camp that has come to metonymically represent the Holocaust) remains a problem.

One reason the Holocaust is insistently present in Resnais's film is his use of archival material, particularly the succession of images of Jews about to be executed and of dead bodies. As Lindeperg notes, Resnais's editing of the images plays a key role here. An example is the feature of the editing, criticized by some historians, that concerns the film's sequence on the "annihilation":

> Starting with Himmler's visit to Auschwitz in 1942, it is put together in the following way: tracking shot along a line of people rounded up; birds-eye view of a transport; the train at Dachau; photograph from the "Auschwitz Album" showing the selection on the ramp at Birkenau; six photographs of men, women, and children, nude or forced to disrobe before their execution; fixed shots of Zyklon B canisters; color shot of the gas chamber. (Lindeperg, 2007/2014, p. 104)[17]

While this effective montage is the result of Resnais's editing, it is also the product of the script's ambiguities and Cayrol's narrative voice: "By omitting any reference to the Final Solution, the narration implies that the gas chamber was one of the methods of execution that awaited all deportees. Yet, with the exception of the shot of the train full of corpses, filmed during the liberation of Dachau, all the archival material in this sequence refers to the destruction of Europe's Jews" (Lindeperg, 2007/2014, p. 104). For a viewer who knows about the Holocaust, this reference is strong, even though Cayrol does not use the word "Jew" and even though he does not use the word "Holocaust." But is it justifiable to make the reference to the Holocaust dependent on extratextual knowledge? I do not think so.

Individual and Collective Memory

One interpretive challenge here is that, since Cayrol features prominently as narrator in the film, it becomes difficult for the viewer to subsume the narrator's ethics under the ethics of Resnais as director. Part of the reason is, as I have suggested, Resnais's respect for Cayrol—and particularly for his camp experience. A related reason is suggested by the interplay of individual and collective memory. When *Night and Fog* was released in France in 1956, the Holocaust was not such a recognized and haunting part of European collective memory as it had become 20 to 30 years later (when Lanzmann made *Shoah*), and as it still is today. If this collective memory influences my own attitude to the Holocaust, it also colors my reading of the Holocaust as a key aspect of Resnais's film. In my ongoing attempt to interpret *Night and Fog*, aspects of collective and individual memory are intertwined. An illustration of this interplay of variants of memory is provided by a much-discussed image of the camp at Pithiviers, the first internment camp in Vichy France, designed to imprison Jews and to transport them to camps further east, particularly Auschwitz.

From the perspective of a watchtower manned by a guard, I see a fence, barracks, and prisoners (Figure 2.8). As my perspective as a viewer is associated with that of the guard, whose kepi makes him identifiable as a French gendarme, there is a sense in which I become complicit in his act of surveillance. Moreover, there is a sense in which the image suggests, or makes visible, the Vichy regime's complicity in the deportation of approximately 76,000 Jews to the Nazi concentration and extermination camps (Marrus & Paxton, 2019).

I associate the first variant of complicity with the Norwegian Holocaust: I link the image of the French gendarme, part of whose body is outside the image's left frame, to Norwegian policemen who assisted the German occupying force during the process of deportation. While numerous Norwegian policemen willingly contributed to the Norwegian Holocaust, many more

Interned at Pithiviers...

Figure 2.8 Screenshot from *Night and Fog*, directed by Alain Resnais (1956)

Norwegians were complicit in the event. This group perhaps included those who, standing on Vippetangen quai on November 26, 1942, witnessed the *Donau* leaving Oslo harbor with 532 Norwegian Jews on board. Even though the Norwegian Holocaust occurred before I was born, I sense that my "memory" of the event is not just collective but also individual. If I were one of the Norwegians standing on Vippetangen quai, what would I have done to save the Norwegian Jews before they were forced to board the ship? Is there a connection between my lasting concern with the Holocaust and my admission, or suspicion, of being an implicated subject?

The second variant of complicity—which Resnais links to the Vichy regime in France during the German occupation, though Cayrol does not mention the word "Vichy"—is illustrative of what Suleiman, in the second part of the passage from *Conflicts of Memory* quoted above, calls "an affair of memory": "[T]he object of conflict in an affair of memory is the interpretation and public understanding of an event firmly situated in the past, but whose aftereffects are still deeply felt." The image of the French gendarme became an "object of conflict" because French citizens were not yet able or ready to admit that they were implicated in the deportation of French Jews. Before commenting on this conflict, which illustrates part of the complex mechanism of collective memory, I note that here, as in the case of the Norwegian Holocaust, the borderline between individual and collective memory is blurred. When Resnais directed *Night and Fog* in 1955, just 10 years had passed since the liberation of the Nazi concentration camps. Thus, French Jews who saw the film on its release in 1956 would perhaps, as they watched archival footage of Jews who were deported, imprisoned, tortured, and murdered, be looking for lost relatives. They may have done this even though, in common with the fictional character Austerlitz in Sebald's novel, they would know that their relatives had been murdered and their faces, as shown in *Night and Fog*, would probably be unrecognizable. Such an act of viewing—a Holocaust survivor's experience of seeing Resnais's film—is an individual act of memory that contrasts with the variant of collective memory that in the mid-1950s tended to distance itself from Resnais's presentation of the image of the French gendarme.

The Frenchmen critical of the image of the French gendarme included government officials and representatives of the armed forces. On February 29, 1956, a censor board met to decide whether the film, including the controversial image, was suitable for general audiences. According to Lindeperg (2007/2014), a proposal formulated as "replacement of the shot of the gendarme by a photograph of equivalent historical importance and unlikely to cause controversy" was supported by 14 votes, while there were five votes against and one abstention. Lindeberg comments, "This result shows that several members from the film industry voted in favor of the gendarme's disappearance, confirming the division among this group regarding this thorny question" (p. 152). Insisting that images of the collaboration were important for the French public to see, Resnais resisted this censorship (Wilson, 2011). In a compromise, Resnais, supported by the distributor Argos Films, masked the photograph by placing a dark strip over the gendarme's kepi. In exchange, he was allowed to show the bodies of victims, including those filmed by the Allied Forces at Bergen-Belsen, at the end of the film.

It would be an oversimplification to argue that the censors' resistance to this particular image was shared by the French public generally. As representatives of the authorities, the censors seem to have been troubled by the suggestion of complicity which the image indicates. Yet there is a connection between their critical attitude to the image and a similarly skeptical, or perhaps hesitant, attitude of the general public. That this instance of censorship, to the extent it was known, provoked no particular interest tells us something about the collective memory of the Second World War in France in the mid-1950s. It also says something about the challenge of coming to terms with the Holocaust, including the French Holocaust. From the 1970s onward, the situation changed and in the early 1980s

> the photograph of the gendarme embarked on an impressive editorial career: reproduced countless times to illustrate articles and publications on the French state's collaboration, it became a firm favorite, thanks less to what it "documented" than to the air of the times that now allowed denunciation of the taboos of the official account of history. The image's "historical importance" was now derived from its cinematic misadventure. (Lindeperg, 2007/2014, p. 155)

That a controversial film image from *Night and* Fog—a photograph shown for just a few seconds, took on a life of its own and became widely distributed because of the changing "air of the times" is a thought-provoking illustration of the process of collective memory. Responding to (and further illustrating) this process, in 1997 Argos Films released on VHS a "complete version" of Resnais's film in which the original photograph of the French gendarme had been restored (Lindeperg, 2007/ 2014, p. 155).

Three linked aspects of the history of this image, and thus also of *Night and Fog*, are particularly relevant to aspects of collective memory. First, the varying responses to and interpretations of the image of the French gendarme (and thus also Resnais's film) indicate that our memory of the Second World War, and of the Holocaust as the nadir of that war, is not a stable archive. Rather, as Brockmeier (2015) demonstrates in *Beyond the Archive*, it is a complex, ongoing process in which constituent elements of memory and narrative are intertwined. "Memory" as I use the concept here accentuates the constituent element of memory that describes "a particular, complex experience" (p. 118). In "Reaching for Meaning: Human Agency and the Narrative Imagination," Brockmeier (2009) argues that neither experiences nor stories just come upon me; rather, it is I who make and remake them. An experience is already a response, and this response, which inevitably blends into interpretation, tends to involve elements of narrative, particularly when the experience has a temporal dimension (like processes in historical or autobiographical time). In *Beyond the Archive*, Brockmeier emphasizes that "[b]oth making experience and telling stories are not external to human subjectivity but always already belong to the very business of living a life" (2015, p. 119); they are "forms of life," as he describes them (Brockmeier, 2022), using an expression by Ludwig Wittgenstein. Thus, while the narratives I tell about myself may be influenced by established cultural conventions and traditions, I do not simply reproduce them. Instead, I actively engage with them—even though this engagement is limited to my own perspective, and even though this perspective is influenced by the conventions and traditions that color the situation in which I live.

Second, if my experience of looking at the photograph of the *Donau* is an act of individual memory that reminds me of the Norwegian Holocaust, the experience of looking at the image of the gendarme may remind French citizens of the French Holocaust. Although these experiences are instances of individual memory, they are also constituent elements of collective memory; conversely, the collective memory of these two events colors our interpretation of them. The media of photography and film contribute significantly to this combination of individual and collective memory, a combination that approximates Erll's definition of cultural memory (2010a, 2010b, 2011).[18] In *Night and Fog*, the mediated aspect of cultural memory has a distinctly experiential dimension that links it to Alison Landsberg's (2004) concept of prosthetic memory. This form of memory

> emerges at the interface between a person and a historical narrative of the past, at an experiential site such as a movie theater or museum. In this moment of contact, an experience occurs through which the person sutures himself or herself into a larger history. . . . In the process that I am describing, the person does not simply apprehend a historical narrative but takes on a more personal, deeply felt memory of a past event through which he or she did not live. The resulting prosthetic memory has the ability to shape that person's subjectivity and politics. (p. 2)

Although it remains somewhat unclear how such a "deeply felt memory" is constituted, Landsberg's concept has an ethical dimension that is interestingly related to *Night and Fog*. If it is part of Resnais's aim to further the viewer's prosthetic memory, that aim could be one reason for including and presenting the image of the gendarme the way he does.

Third, if Resnais uses the image of the gendarme to further my prosthetic memory, his presentation of the image makes me relate the gendarme, whose perspective I am forced to share, to Nazi officers who, later in the film, also look at people who are interned, imprisoned, or being deported to the camps. There is thus a connection between Resnais's presentation of the gendarme and his filmic rendering of the Holocaust. There is also a link between the image of the gendarme and the challenge I face as a viewer when confronted with the images of camp prisoners—particularly, as I have attempted to show, with images of the dead.

I am haunted by these images, which the film camera allows, even forces me to see. Looking at the dead bodies, I sense that my response is inadequate, perhaps even irrelevant. "The camera," writes Stanley Cavell in *The World Viewed*, "is outside its subject as I am outside my language. The abyss of ready insincerity is fixed, but that is what makes truthfulness possible— and virtuous" (1979, p. 127). Referring to Wittgenstein, Cavell insists that I am responsible for the meaning I attach to my words. Am I also responsible for the meaning I attach to the images I see? In a way I am not, since Resnais chooses the images that I see. Yet my viewing—and, unavoidably, my attempt to interpret—the images of the dead pose an ethical challenge. It is as though the images of the dead bodies eliminate the possibility of coming to terms with them. There may be a connection here between my interpretive challenge as a viewer and Resnais's challenge as a director:

> The documentary film-maker naturally feels the impulse to make his presence known to his audience, as if to justify his intrusion upon his subject. But this is a guilty impulse, produced, it may be, by the film-maker's denial of the only thing that really matters: that the subject be allowed to reveal itself. The denial may be in spirit or in fact, an unwillingness to see what is revealed or an inability to wait for its revelation. But the only justification for the knowledge of others is the willingness for complete knowledge. That is the justice of knowledge. Your position in this is no more localizable beforehand than the knowledge itself is. (Cavell, 1979, pp. 127–128)

Resnais's "impulse" to make his presence known may be one reason he considered Cayrol's narration indispensable. Yet Cayrol's narrative voice may signal that this is a "guilty impulse" linked to the director's need to somehow "justify his intrusion upon his subject." Presenting me with images of the dead, Resnais uses the camera in a way that indicates an attempt to grope for "complete knowledge" of the Holocaust, though it remains unclear what this knowledge is or could be.

Building on my distinction between the film's narration, which I relate to Resnais's work as director, and Cayrol's commentary, which is one element of this narration, I conclude that while Cayrol's narrative voice excludes references to the Holocaust, these references are presented, and thus in one sense reinstated, through the film images from the extermination camps. These images play a crucial role in *Night and Fog*, contributing decisively to the tension between the commentary and the film's complex narration, which includes Resnais's use of archival footage from the camps. This means that while my interpretation of *Night and Fog* is influenced by and to some extent dependent on Cayrol's commentary, it is primarily stirred by the shocking experience of watching images of the prisoners, most of whom are Jews, as well as by my extratextual knowledge of the fact.

I stress that this is my interpretation; many viewers with no knowledge of the Holocaust cannot identify the prisoners as Jews. The discrepancy between the film's auditory channel and its visual channel reveals a tension that is not just aesthetic (as it is an aspect of the film's form and narrative communication) but also ethical. This tension becomes an interpretive challenge: for a viewer like me, who is aided by my extratextual knowledge of the Holocaust when watching *Night and Fog*, the images of starving and dead Jews in extermination camps such as Auschwitz and Bergen-Belsen augment that knowledge—not least by demonstrating and documenting the extreme brutality and violence of the mass murder. But a viewer who does not have this knowledge will *not* learn that six million Jews were murdered in the camps. When the film was released in 1956, most viewers' knowledge of the Holocaust was limited. It can be limited, or even nonexistent, today too, not least among young viewers. This problem is related to and perhaps partly caused by the respect that Resnais had for Cayrol's commentary, a respect earned by Cayrol's experience at Mauthausen concentration camp. Yet the film images show that his commentary is interpretive in a way I find unacceptable: by failing or refusing to identify as Jews the victims I see on the screen, Cayrol distorts rather than documents the history of the Holocaust.

To emphasize the tension between Cayrol's interpretation of the visual images and my own interpretation of those images is not to argue that Cayrol is an unreliable narrator, though his commentary is selective and interpretive. But it is to conclude that the visual images of Jews, and of Auschwitz, question his narrative authority by revealing a glaring omission in his commentary. In my experience of watching and trying to understand *Night and Fog*, Resnais's visual presentation of innumerable dead bodies in the Nazi concentration and extermination camps leads me to conclude that, while *Night and Fog* is a remarkable instance of "concentrationary cinema" (Pollock & Silverman, 2011), it is also a film about the Holocaust. Its most pressing and profoundly ethical question is: Who is responsible?

This question is addressed to those responsible for mass murder and the use of violence generally, including, as Cayrol implies in his concluding comments, France's often violent military activities in Algeria in the 1950s. Moreover, while the question concerns the perpetrators, it is also relevant for the bystanders and for "the implicated subject" (Rothberg, 2019, p. 1), those, including myself, beyond victims and perpetrators who are not innocent when it comes to historical violence.

That said, I also conclude that *Night and Fog*'s status as a Holocaust film would have been less questionable if the question had been specified. Could one reason Cayrol does not state who is responsible be that, had he identified them as Nazis, it would have been more difficult not to identify six million victims as Jews? Here too there is a tension between Cayrol's commentary and the film's visual images; images at the film's end of the dead in Bergen-Belsen and of Nazi guards forced to surrender when the Allied forces liberated the camp in April 1945 relate the question of responsibility unambiguously to the Holocaust.

These images also link the ending of *Night and Fog* to one particular shot presented at the beginning of Resnais's film. This image (Figure 2.9) shows Himmler and Hitler watching one of the many parades in *Triumph of the Will*. In 1935, neither Riefenstahl nor her German audience could know that these two Nazi leaders were probably two of the people who would be most directly responsible for mass murder. I have noted that Hitler chose

Figure 2.9 Screenshot from *Night and Fog*, directed by Alain Resnais (1956)

the film's title; the destruction of the European Jews was an element of his will. For me, this image, which forms part of the narrative discourse of both *Triumph of the Will* and *Night and Fog*, becomes a powerful visual illustration of the range and significance of individual and collective responsibility as an integral part of narrative ethics.

Notes

1. My working definition of "paratext" is influenced by Genette's view of the paratext as a threshold: "More than a boundary or a sealed border, the paratext is, rather, a threshold. . . . [It is] a zone between text and off-text, a zone not merely of transition but also of transaction: a privileged place of a pragmatics and a strategy, of an influence on the public" (1997, pp. 1–2).
2. "Am 5. September 1934, 20 Jahre nach dem Ausbruch des Weltkrieges, 16 Jahre nach dem Anfang des deutschen Leidens, 19 Monate nach dem Beginn der deutschen Wiedergeburt, flog Adolf Hitler wiederum nach Nürnberg, um Heerschau zu halten über seine Getreuten."
3. At the same time, Riefenstahl aligns her presentation of German memory of the First World War with aspects of the collective memory of that war (e.g., the cult of the fallen soldier) in other European countries. See Mosse (1994).
4. According to Devereaux, the film's title was, unusually, chosen by its protagonist (Hitler) and not by its director (1998, p. 228).
5. *Völkischer Beobacther*, May 1, 1935, cited in Welsh (1983, p. 158).
6. It needs to be added that other images of the film capture soldiers and workers as individuals.
7. The achievement of Riefenstahl's camera crew, led by cinematographer Josef "Sepp" Allgeier, is remarkable in this scene.
8. In Sebald's novel *Austerlitz*, Věra tells Austerlitz, who tells his German listener, that Austerlitz's father saw Riefenstahl's *Triumph of the Will* in a cinema in Munich in 1938, and that, as a Czech Jew, he found the film frightening. See Sebald (2002, pp. 239–240).
9. As Nichols observes, "a documentary that distorts facts, alters reality, or fabricates evidence jeopardizes its own status as a documentary" (2010, p. 8).
10. See also Coupechoux (2003), Erll (2011), Laanes and Meretoja (2021), and Olick et al. (2011).
11. Cayrol's poetry collection *Poèmes de la nuit et du brouillard* (1946) may have influenced Resnais's choice of title for his film.
12. It is not coincidental that Himmler's decree was announced less than two months before the Wannsee conference in Berlin on January 20, 1942.
13. It is also possible that Cayrol may have been influenced by friends who were sympathetically inclined toward communism (as a system opposed to fascism and capitalism). As Leona Toker has noted, "the subject of the Holocaust was taboo for long stretches of Soviet history; the transliterated word itself came into use only after *perestroika*" (2013, p. 118).
14. While Genette defines *analepsis* as "any evocation after the fact of an event that took place earlier than the point in the story where we are at any given moment," he designates *prolepsis* as "any narrative maneuver that consists of narrating or evoking in advance an event that will take place later" (1980, p. 40).
15. "*Nuit et brouillard* peut même être considéré comme la somme de toutes les manières d'échapper au flash-back, et à la fausse piété de l'image-souvenir. . . . Dans le cas de Resnais, cette insuffisance du flash-back n'empêche pourtant pas que toute son oeuvre soit fondée sur la coexistence des nappes de passé, le présent n'intervenant même plus comme centre d'évocation" (Deleuze, 1985, p. 160).
16. This interpretive effect does not depend on whether the viewer and listener know anything about Eisler. And yet, although my knowledge of the historical Eisler is limited, what knowledge I have does something to my interpretation of the music—and thus also to my interpretation of *Night and Fog* since the music is an integral part of Resnais's film. Born in Leipzig in 1898, Hanns Eisler grew up in Vienna and studied composition with Arnold Schönberg in the early 1920s. In 1930 Eisler began working with playwright Bertholt Brecht. Together they produced socialist works, and after 1933 Eisler's music was banned by the Nazi Party. After

a period in Hollywood during the Second World War, Eisler returned to Germany and settled in East Berlin, where he became a professor at the Berlin Hochschule für Musik (Betz, 1982). Thus, when Eisler was invited to write the score for *Night and Fog*, that demanding creative task would inevitably rekindle painful memories of the First World War, in which he had participated, and the Second, against which he had warned when he spoke publicly against Nazism in Germany. As these memories are constituent elements of his experience and of his identity, they color his music, contributing to the narrative ethics of his score for *Night and Fog* by prompting, for me as viewer and listener, a sense of incomprehensibility and shock when faced with the brutal facts of historical reality. This kind of auditorily communicated incomprehensibility contributes to the film's narrative ethics.

17. The photographs of the "Auschwitz Album" show the arrival of Hungarian Jews at Auschwitz-Birkenau. The album is a unique document since it is the only surviving visual evidence of the Nazis' mass murder of Jews. See https://www.yadvashem.org/yv/en/exhibitions/album_auschwitz/index.asp

18. As Erll notes, cultural memory is mediated, and the memory-making effect of the media of cultural memory "lies not in the unity, coherence, and ideological unambiguousness they convey, but instead in the fact that they serve as cues for the discussion of those images, thus centering a memory culture on certain medial representations and sets of questions connected with them" (2010b, p. 396).

3

Claude Lanzmann's *Shoah*

Seeing the French film director Claude Lanzmann's *Shoah* after having watched Alain Resnais's *Night and Fog* is a unique experience that I find not only thought-provoking but also moving and, as this chapter aims to show, challenging. While Lanzmann's film from 1985 is a monumental achievement in its own right, and while he does not refer (though he perhaps alludes) to the film released by Resnais 30 years earlier, I consider *Shoah* as a response to *Night and Fog* in two ways. First, while Resnais makes extensive use of footage from the Nazi concentration and extermination camps, Lanzmann consistently refuses to incorporate archival footage into his film. Second, if, as I conclude, Resnais presents me with a filmic rendering of the Holocaust that, mainly because of Cayrol's commentary, is problematically vague, Lanzmann's focus is firmly, even insistently on the Holocaust throughout.

A nine-hour documentary about an unspeakable crime against humanity, *Shoah* has become a key reference point in a thematic strand of film studies increasingly concerned with ethical issues (Grønstad, 2016). The film is a "mixed generic performance" (LaCapra, 2007, p. 193) in which Lanzmann not only rejects the use of archival film footage but also refuses an explanatory (and thus unavoidably didactic) voice-over commentary. Instead, he makes himself (as interviewer and listener) a major presence in the film. His interviewees are mainly Holocaust survivors, some bystanders (notably Poles who lived close to the concentration camps), and some former SS guards and officials. This selection of interviewees accords with and supports the Holocaust scholar Raul Hilberg's (1992) distinction between victim, perpetrator, and bystander. That Hilberg is interviewed by Lanzmann strengthens the film's status as a documentary.

In her preface to the French edition of the screenplay of *Shoah*, Simone de Beauvoir concludes that the film is "[a] sheer masterpiece" (1995, p. vi).[1] Concurring with this assessment, I also second the point she makes at the beginning of her preface: "*Shoah* is not an easy film to talk about" (p. iii).[2] Mindful of the complexity and continuing relevance of Lanzmann's film,

Memory and Narrative Ethics. Jakob Lothe, Oxford University Press. © Oxford University Press (2025). DOI: 10.1093/9780197579534.003.0004

this chapter follows from a premise indebted to an accompanying obser-vation that Beauvoir makes: that *Shoah*'s complexity, including much of its originality and continuing relevance to the challenge of not forgetting the Holocaust, is generated by the filmmaker's relentless execution of an approach that consistently focuses on places, on human voices, and on human faces. All three foci are related to, stirred by, and explored through variants of human memory presented in the form of a single narrative. The chapter discusses the interplay of memory and narrative ethics in Lanz-mann's presentation of three places and four characters. The places are Chełmno, Treblinka, and Auschwitz-Birkenau; the voices and faces are those of Simon Srebnik, Franz Suchomel, Abraham Bomba, and Filip Müller. Considering the ethics of these characters' memories, observations, and reflections, I link their fragments of Holocaust narrative to Lanzmann's nar-rative ethics as director, and thus to *Shoah* as a film and to my ethics as a viewer. Toward the end of the chapter, I elaborate my interpretation of Lanz-mann's ethics by commenting on his interviews with the Czech Holocaust survivor Filip Müller and the historian Raul Hilberg.[3] As I have seen *Shoah* several times, there is a sense in which my interpretation of the film narrative approximates and aims to contribute to an ethics of rewatching.[4]

Provocatively stating that the film "is not a documentary," Lanzmann (1991, p. 96), claims that he wanted to transform the witness into an actor, albeit of the witness's own life and story, thus enabling him (as a direc-tor) to make a film that is not about remembering but about reliving. In common with many commentators, I find this description confusing, and I find it even harder to understand what Lanzmann means by claiming that his film is "a fiction of the real" (Lanzmann, 1990, p. 301). It is cer-tainly true that, as LaCapra has noted, "*Shoah* is not strictly a documentary film in that scenes in it are carefully constructed" (2007, p. 192). Yet scenes are "carefully constructed" in many documentaries, including, as we have seen, Riefenstahl's *Triumph of the Will*. I am inclined to interpret Lanz-mann's statements as a riposte to historians and theorists who, seen from Lanzmann's perspective, tend to present the Holocaust as a series of events that can be explained and understood. For Lanzmann, the Holocaust is an incomprehensible historical occurrence that defies chronological progres-sion and narrative sense-making. Considering his interviewees as actors who communicate aspects of their autobiographical narratives, Lanzmann's focus is consistently on them; his prioritized time is the present. Seen from the perspective of narrative ethics, Lanzmann's provocative statements on his own film are thought-provoking because they make me reflect on the constituent elements of a Holocaust narrative, including the ethics of such a narrative. Yet since I watch and respond to *Shoah* as filmic discourse, my interpretation of the film is not dependent on Lanzmann's statements on it as director. When I refer to Lanzmann, I mean Lanzmann the film's creator. My image of him (and of Riefenstahl and Resnais in the preceding chapter and James Ivory in Chapter 5) is thus similar to that of the implied author. I need to add, though, that my image of Lanzmann is complicated by his own statements on his film as well as his appearances in it. Like Riefenstahl, Lanzmann starts his film by presenting the viewer with verbal text that I am asked to read before seeing the first filmic image. This verbal text is not just an introduction to the following film narrative; it is also a self-interpretive element that influences my act of viewing the film as well as my attempt to understand it. Moreover, as in the case of *Triumph of the Will*, it is ethically charged. If I juxtapose the installments of verbal text presented at the beginning of *Triumph of the Will* and of *Shoah*, I read Lanzmann's narrative prologue as a critical comment on and warning against the Nazi propaganda evident in Riefenstahl's celebration of the German *Wiedergeburt* after the defeat in the First World War.

The verbal text that constitutes the first part of *Shoah*'s narrative beginning is in two parts. The first is a segment of a sentence from Isaiah 56:5, "I will give them an everlasting name" (Lanzmann, 1995, p. ix).[5] Serving as an epigraph, the sentence is a self-interpretive sign in its own right— and yet it is characteristic of *Shoah* that I cannot be sure how to interpret it. The relevant phrase in Hebrew (the Masoretic text) can be transcribed as *shem 'olam 'eten-lo*, literally "an eternal name I will give him/it."[6] The older text, from the Dead Sea Scrolls (also supported by other translations), reads alternatively *'eten-lhmh*, "give them." As verse 4 of chapter 56 makes it clear that "I" is God, one possible interpretation of the epigraph is that God will give the Jews an everlasting name; He will ensure that their name is not forgotten. Thus, God's promise highlights memory, while at the same time drawing attention to the danger of being forgotten. Relating this interpretation of the epigraph to the film I am watching, I immediately think of the Holocaust as a crime against humanity that should not be forgotten. Although this interpretation is not dependent on my knowledge of Lanzmann as director of *Shoah*, I cannot resist linking the "I" of the epigraph not only to God but also to him. Seen thus, Lanzmann's film announces itself as an ambitious attempt to remember not just Jews in general but the Jews who perished in the Holocaust in particular. On this reading, the epigraph is a statement of the director's intention, indicating what he wants to achieve with his film.

Shoah is divided into two parts, "Era 1" and "Era 2," and my interpretation of the epigraph is supported by Lanzmann's choice to present it at the beginning of "Era 2" as well. Accentuating its thematic significance, this repetition also highlights the epigraph's ethical dimension. His film is a sincere attempt to ensure that the viewer will not forget the Nazis' mass murder of six million European Jews.

The second installment of verbal text both extends and specifies the epigraph:

The story begins in the present at Chelmno, on the Narew River, in Poland. Fifty miles northwest of Lodz, in the heart of a region that once had a large Jewish population, Chelmno was the place in Poland where Jews were first exterminated by gas. Extermination began on December 7, 1941. At Chelmno four hundred thousand Jews were murdered in two separate periods: December 1941 to Spring 1944 and June 1944 to January 1945. But the way in which death was administered remained the same throughout: the gas vans. Of the four hundred thousand men, women and children who went there, only two came out alive: Mordechaï Podchlebnik and Simon Srebnik. Srebnik, survivor of the last period, was a boy of thirteen when he was sent to Chelmno. His father had been killed before his eyes in the ghetto in Lodz; his mother died in a gas van at Chelmno. The SS placed him in one of the "Jewish work details," assigned to maintaining the extermination camps and slated in turn for death.

With his ankles in chains, like all his companions, the boy shuffled through the village of Chelmno each day. That he was kept alive longer than the others he owed to his extreme agility, which made him the winner of jumping contests and speed races that the SS organized for their chained prisoners. And also to his melodious voice: several times a week, when the rabbits kept in hutches by the SS needed fodder, young Srebnik rowed up the Narew, under guard, in a flat-bottomed boat, to the alfalfa fields at the edge of the village. He sang Polish folk tunes, and in return the guard taught him Prussian military songs. Everyone in Chelmno knew him: the Polish farm folk and German civilians as well, since this Polish province was annexed to the Reich after the fall of Warsaw, germanized and renamed Wartheland. Chelmno was changed to Kulmhof, Lodz to Litzmannstadt, Kolo to Warthbrücken, etc.

German colonists had settled everywhere in Wartheland, and there was even a grade school in Chelmno itself.

During the night of January 18, 1945, two days before Soviet troops arrived, the Nazis killed all the remaining Jews in the "work details" with a bullet in the head, Simon Srebnik was among those executed. But the bullet missed his vital brain centers. When he came to, he crawled into a pigsty. A Polish farmer found him there. The boy was treated and healed by a Soviet Army doctor. A few months later Simon left for Tel Aviv along with other survivors of the death camps.

I found him in Israel and persuaded that one-time boy singer to return with me to Chelmno. He was then forty-seven years old. (Lanzmann, 1995, pp. 1–2, italics in original)

Rereading this verbal text on my second viewing of the film, I find that, from my perspective, two aspects are particularly important. First, it immediately suggests that the film will revolve around and explore significant aspects of the historical event of the Holocaust. In addition to its importance as a separate camp, Chełmno thus represents all of Nazi Germany's extermination camps. The facts given about Chełmno have an introductory function, as has the information provided about the two Jews who miraculously survived the camp.[7] The introduction signals that I am starting to watch a documentary about the Holocaust, a different name for *Shoah*. It also suggests, particularly in the introduction of Srebnik, that this documentary has a narrative dimension that is distinctly ethical. The second aspect of the verbal text becomes conspicuous in the final paragraph. Its first word, "I," establishes a connection with the "I" of the epigraph. While the final paragraph's "I" unambiguously refers to Lanzmann, that identification makes me read an aspect of Lanzmann's "I" into that of the epigraph too. But what aspect? As I rewatch and try to interpret the film's beginning, it strikes me that the "I" who finds Srebnik in Israel includes, or implies, two further dimensions: Lanzmann as a character who interviews Srebnik and other characters in the film, and Lanzmann as my image (based on several viewings) of the creator of *Shoah*. Shoshana Felman is right to note that Lanzmann here addresses the viewer "from within the very writing on the screen which constitutes the film's silent opening" (Felman & Laub, 1992, p. 253). For Felman, Lanzmann's finding of Srebnik in Israel "embodies in effect a point of arrival in Lanzmann's journey, as well as the beginning—or the starting point—of the journey of the film" (p. 253). Going further, she claims that the finding is *the finding of the film itself* : *Shoah* rethinks, as well, the meaning and the implications of the advent (of the event) of its own finding. To find the film is to find a new possibility of sight, a possibility not just of vision—but of revision. (p. 255, original emphasis)

Simon Srebnik: Return to the Place of Annihilation

I agree with Felman that Lanzmann's finding of Srebnik in Israel is a key moment in the genesis of *Shoah*: not only is Srebnik a Holocaust survivor who can testify; he also allows himself to be persuaded to do so at Chełmno, the place where he was "executed" 40 years earlier. Two linked points follow from this observation. First, as Srebnik returns to the extermination camp where he was shot, there is a sense in which he relives, rather than remembers, his camp experience. Yet as the film images I will go on to discuss show, it does not follow that he does not also remember. The complex movement

from the place of regeneration and the locus of the gathering of Holocaust survivors back to the prehistory of their oppression and suppression, back to the primal scene of their annihilation, is at once a spatial and a temporal return, a movement back in space and time which, attempting to revisit and to repossess the past is also, simultaneously, a movement forward toward the future. (Felman & Laub, 1992, p. 256)

One essential reason Srebnik plays a key role—aesthetically as well ethically—is that he is the only Holocaust survivor interviewed by Lanzmann who performs this double movement.

Second, although Lanzmann does not use the word, the final paragraph of the introductory verbal text introduces the element of trauma. Perhaps the main reason Lanzmann has to persuade Srebnik to return with him to Chełmno is that Srebnik's memories of that place are painful—so painful that he may have needed to forget in order to go on living. Why, then, does he return? A partial answer may be his sense of responsibility as a Holocaust survivor and witness; the need to bear witness trumps the need to protect himself from the trauma. Although Srebnik shares this sense of responsibility with the other Holocaust survivors interviewed by Lanzmann, it is particularly striking in his case because he returns to the primal scene of the mass murder. On a second viewing, the combination of Lanzmann's insistence that Srebnik go back to Chełmno and Srebnik's actual return becomes a strong, early signal that *Shoah* will approximate to a testimony in which the act of bearing witness is closely associated with and stirred by a strong ethical obligation. Although different in kind, this ethical obligation is shared by Srebnik and Lanzmann.

Figure 3.1 Screenshot from *Shoah*, directed by Claude Lanzmann (1985)

As I move from the final paragraph of verbal text to the first filmic images, this signal is further strengthened. I see a man sitting in a small river boat, singing a song in a language I do not understand (Figure 3.1). When Lanzmann interviews the man, I learn that his name is Simon Srebnik, who, as I have just read on the silver screen, survived the Chełmno extermination camp. Since I have also been informed that Srebnik sang Polish folk tunes while forced to row on the River Narew, I relate that information to the song I can hear he is singing as I am watching the images.

Lanzmann thus begins *Shoah* by making the Holocaust survivor Srebnik go through an action he repeatedly performed for the Nazis as inmate of an extermination camp 40 years earlier. Srebnik does not, or cannot, talk much, but his singing is remarkably suggestive. In addition to its intrinsic value as a narrative fragment and an act of memory, it becomes an important leitmotif. In the film's present, Srebnik is singing as a free man; when he sang the same song for the Nazi guards, he knew that his death was imminent. As a viewer I can see Srebnik in a small boat framed by a beautiful and peaceful landscape, but I cannot see the extermination camp that he miraculously survived. And yet in a way I can, for Srebnik's song in the present establishes a forceful link to the same song he sang for the Nazis; moreover, that particular temporal connection is strengthened by the fact that, in spite of the beautiful land-scape, we are in the same place. This kind of tension is an essential part not just of the film's beginning but of *Shoah* overall. Lanzmann creates a pow-erful narrative beginning in which constituent elements of film aesthetics challenge the viewer to ask ethical questions, including difficult questions about the connections between moral values, human action, and the lack of such action.

One aspect of film form that contributes markedly to the ethics of the beginning of *Shoah*, and thus of the whole film, is the emphasis Lanzmann puts on the present both as starting point and as point of reference; the com-bination of the final paragraph and the first images are, as I have indicated, illustrative of this kind of insistence. Observing that the construction of a plotted series of events is a key feature of both factual and fictional film, Jacques Rancière has found this beginning "provocative" (1996, p. 158) since the opening sentence of the verbal text, "The story begins in the present at Chelmno," seems to shy away from or problematically suspend this key feature of film form. In one sense, though, the opening sentence accurately describes the film's opening scene with Srebnik sitting in the boat. For me, Lanzmann's attempt to persuade Srebnik to return is more provocative. Is he morally justified in making Srebnik repeat what the Nazis forced him to do? As already indicated, Srebnik's act of singing must be painful for him as it brings back, and probably intensifies, a traumatic experience. Yet his singing may also be a way of dealing with that experience. And it is a key constituent element of a compelling narrative beginning. There is something enigmatic about Srebnik, whose experience is described as if he died: he "was among those executed." My confrontation, as a viewer, with his unique individuality reminds me that there were more than six million other individuals whose lives were ended by the Holocaust. This kind of representation is constituted by the combination of his song (both the words, which I cannot understand, and the melody, which I find beautiful), the place, and the way in which features of Srebnik's face are accentuated by his singing.

The aesthetic impact of the representation is strengthened by, and to a considerable extent predicated on, the information about Srebnik that

Lanzmann gives the viewer as written text on the screen. Linking Srebnik's song to the narrative of *Shoah*, the information enhances the narrative dimension of the film's opening scene while at the same time problematizing narrative progression. This effect, which contributes to Lanzmann's exploration of trauma, is fortified by Srebnik's appearances later in the film. Although, or because, he does not say much, the camera repeatedly focuses on his face. Thus, for me as a viewer, it is as though his song, the act of singing that constitutes the film's beginning, continues: the opening song, which is already a repetition, is repeated throughout. There is something uncanny, ghostlike about this form of repetition. Distinguishing between two basic forms of repetition, J. Hillis Miller (1982) argues that while the first form progresses from an origin or beginning toward some kind of ending or goal, the second form does not possess a narrative progression of this kind. Rather, the progression of plot is here repeatedly interrupted; the repetition of words, phrases, and elements of plot turn the narrative into fragments located at different temporal stages of the discourse, making the narrative move in circles that do not seem to lead anywhere. Although Miller bases his distinction on the way Gilles Deleuze (1969) opposes Nietzsche's concept of repetition to Plato's, and although he does not use the word "trauma" when describing the second form of repetition, I find that Srebnik's song is an instance of the "ghostly" (Miller, 1982, p. 6) effect of this form. If the song is or becomes part of Srebnik's narrative identity, it also problematizes that identity by repeating, and thus rekindling his memory of, gruesome events that he might intensely want to forget. If the song expresses a painful experience, it also suggests that important aspects of that experience cannot be narrated. Constituted by the language of words, the song is a fragment of a memory that becomes a narrative fragment. Still, "there no doubt is a nonlinguistic dimension to certain experiences" (Brockmeier, 2015, p. 107). I suggest that Srebnik's repetitive act of singing touches on this "nonlinguistic dimension" of experience. And yet, as Brockmeier adds, experiences, whether linguistic or not, occur "within a symbolic space, a space of history and cultural significance. It is this symbolic space that makes them *experience*; without it they remain psycho-physiological processes, bodily sensations, unconscious perceptions" (p. 108, original emphasis). Srebnik's song definitely occurs in "a space of history," as he confirms himself when, looking at the ruins of the crematorium in Chełmno a few scenes later in the film, he says, "This is the place." It is "a space of history" where Srebnik experienced and witnessed the Nazis' mass murder of Jews.

While it proves a great resource for Lanzmann as filmmaker, the act of singing must have been inordinately difficult for Srebnik—as I think, though I cannot be sure, I can glean from his facial expression. Emmanuel Levinas highlights the importance of the human face, stressing the ethical challenge and responsibility represented by my encounter with the face of the Other. As noted in the introduction, for Levinas (1961/1969), the Other's face is not an object; it is, or represents, an expression that affects me in a face-to-face encounter. Although the encounter is not an empirical event, "it may be enacted in any number of empirical events" (Davis, 2007b, p. 48). When, using filmic repetition, Lanzmann activates this radical challenge for me as a viewer, he invites me to reflect on the fact that the Nazis who forced Srebnik to sing must also have seen his face while listening to his singing—and yet they attempted to murder him. Demonstrating that there are different ways of responding to the challenge Levinas identifies, the viewer's encounter with Srebnik accentuates the importance of a third temporal layer in *Shoah*: if Lanzmann in 1985 makes Srebnik repeat, and thus in one sense relive, his singing in the boat in 1944, my experience in 2024 of seeing and reflecting on the narrative presentation of Srebnik furthers my understanding of his trauma while simultaneously reminding me how much of that traumatic experience I cannot understand.

The Holocaust was a massive set of historical events that stretched over three years. But no single narrative could hope to capture the enormity of this event. As Zdenka Fantlová puts it in her testimony in *Time's Witnesses*, "There were six million murdered. If they all survived, there would be six million different stories" (Lothe, 2017a, pp. 156–157). Fantlová's thoughtful comment is true since each survivor's experience and memory of the Holocaust is unique, and it is also thought-provoking since Holocaust survivors can find it extremely difficult, perhaps impossible to transform their experience into a narrative. Although this kind of inability or failure does not reduce their identity as human beings, it may problematize their narrative identity by making it more fragmented and less coherent. There is even a troubling sense in which it may problematize the experience: although experience extends beyond narrative, once (or if) remembered it tends to take on narrative shape. The enormous challenge of transforming a traumatic experience of this kind into a narrative (however fragmented and disconnected) is a warning against indiscriminate use of the concept of narrative identity. Yet although narrative is not a necessary condition for all experience and human identity, narrative can make aspects of human identity, and of experiences that are constituent elements of this identity, clearer to the narrator—and to the listener or reader or viewer.

Rewatching the beginning of Shoah, it seems to me that, as film director and creator of the filmic discourse, Lanzmann is reflecting on these difficult questions—questions about the interplay of memory, experience, narrative, and identity. Or perhaps rather the way he introduces me to and gives a narrative presentation of Srebnik encourages, even urges me to reflect on the questions. Although I cannot give adequate answers to them, the questions are important for at least three reasons that blend into each other and reinforce each other in the interpretive process: prompting me to reflect on the importance of Holocaust testimony, they make me appreciative of and grateful for Srebnik's role as a witness; as they revolve around the Holocaust, they reduce my risk of marginalizing, perhaps even forgetting that historical event; and thinking about the questions, I engage in a variant of ethical reflection that has a value of its own—not least because it can make me more humble as a viewer.

Yes, this is the place.

Figure 3.2

Figures 3.2 and 3.3 Screenshots from *Shoah,* directed by Claude Lanzmann (1985)

Film scholars and Holocaust scholars have written perceptively of the importance of the place or the site in *Shoah* (Didi-Huberman, 2007; Liebmann, 2007b; Vice, 2011). Nowhere in the film is the significance of location, of a particular place as an element of space, greater than here at the beginning. As Lanzmann combines Srebnik's repetitive act of singing in the boat on the River Narew with his act of looking at the site of the crematorium (Figures 3.2 and 3.3), the temporal and spatial aspects of narrative coalesce in a way that accentuates both dimensions. Srebnik says:

It's hard to recognize, but it was here. They burned people here. A lot of people were burned here. Yes, this is the place. No one ever left here again. The gas vans came in here. . . . There were two huge ovens, and afterward the bodies were thrown into these ovens, and the flames reached to the sky.

To the sky?

Yes. It was terrible. No one can describe it. No one can recreate what happened here. Impossible? And no one can understand it. Even I, here, now . . . I can't believe I'm here. No, I just can't believe it. It was always this peaceful here. Always. When they burned two thousand people—Jews every day, it was just as peaceful. No one shouted. Everyone went about his work. It was silent. Peaceful. Just as it is now. (Lanzmann, 1995, p. 3)

"Space contains compressed time," writes Gaston Bachelard in *The Poetics of Space*, "that is what space is for" (1958/1994, p. 8). From his phenomenological perspective, Bachelard develops the notion of "lived space" (*espace vécu*), constituting "the humanely embodied counterpart of the three-dimensional, empty, and basically unoriented spaces of physics and geometry. Lived space is deictically oriented space as perceived and talked about in everyday life" (Buchholz & Jahn, 2005, p. 553). This definition of space presupposes a subject, a man or woman (or, in narrative fiction, a male or female character) who experiences space through his or her existential living conditions. Moreover, this phenomenological understanding of space links the term not only to place but also to time. For Bachelard, our experience of space is associated with identity and identity formation, and this quality of space is closely related to *when* and *how* we inhabit a given space. So it is too for Henri Lefebvre, but in *The Production of Space* Lefebvre (1974/1991) contends, from a Marxist rather than a phenomenological perspective, that space is a social product or a complex social construction that affects social practices. With a view to the space of a concentration camp, their notions of space complement each other: if Bachelard tells me something essential about a prisoner's experience of (barely) living inside the camp, Lefebvre furthers my understanding of the enclosed camp space as a social construction that simultaneously reflects and represents dissymmetrical power relations in which one group of people attempts to control and suppress (or, in the extreme case of the Holocaust, eliminate) another.[8]

As an element of space, place is less abstract in that it is located: places "have fixed objective co-ordinates on the Earth's surface" (Cresswell, 2004, p. 7). Chełmno also had fixed coordinates; it was a place in Europe where several hundred thousand Jews were murdered.[9] What does Srebnik think as he is looking at the remnants of the crematorium? I do not know, but I am struck by three aspects that, as I respond to and try to interpret his act of witnessing, make his testimony credible. First, when Srebnik says, "This is the place," that confirmation of Chełmno's location is supported not only by the verbal text that precedes the first film images but also by my viewing, and my interpretation, of Srebnik's act of singing in the boat on the River Narew.

For me, there is an interpretive connection between his singing, which is a repetition of an act the Nazis forced him to perform 40 years earlier, and his recognition of the place, which is also a kind of repetition following from his return. Second, I am persuaded by his comment "No one can describe it.... And no one can understand it." While I accept both statements as true, I am struck by the way they are informed by his narrative ethics: recognizing that "no one" can describe or understand the Holocaust, Srebnik includes himself as one of the very few who survived Chełmno. This recognition by a Holocaust survivor of the impossibility of understanding the mass murder of six million Jews is closely associated with the challenge of not forgetting the Holocaust. Moreover, it invests his narrative with a measure of humility that, for me as a viewer, paradoxically makes his testimony even more compelling and more convincing than it would have been had he not recognized the great difficulty of his task and his responsibility as a witness.

Third, in my act of seeing and interpreting *Shoah*, Srebnik's words are inseparable from his facial expression. I have referred to the importance that Levinas attaches to the human face, stressing the ethical challenge and responsibility represented by my encounter with the face of the Other. Even though, for Levinas, the Other's face is not an object but an expression that affects me, I find that, as he is looking at the place where the mass murder occurred, Srebnik's face reveals or points to traces of the Other as conceptualized by Levinas. Srebnik's face discloses an element of self-interpretation, signaling to me as a viewer that he is now in the place where, as Lanzmann puts it, he "was among those executed." This self-interpretive sign simultaneously incites and colors my own interpretation by stressing that my interpretive challenge is also an ethical challenge. Srebnik is situated in and approaching a boundary or border that, along with the possibilities and problems of transition associated with it, actualizes Mikhail M. Bakhtin's (1982) critically helpful concept of the chronotope or the chronotopic motif: a place where dimensions of time and space are curiously compressed in a way that can generate not only work and playing activities but also tension, conflict, and pain. Bakhtin considers the chronotope of the threshold to be particularly important. It can be a corridor, a hall, or an entrance that indicates a zone of neutrality—and also one of transition, hesitation, reflection, and memory. The chronotopic motif is in a specific place, while at the same time marking a border between coordinate, superordinate, and subordinate spaces. Constituting yet also complicating Srebnik's act of memory as well as his sense of identity, the chronotope of the threshold delineates the place he is in—a place that, activating painful memories, marks both the entrance to the death camp and his miraculous survival.

There are several reasons Srebnik is a key witness in *Shoah*. Interlinking the film's temporal and spatial dimensions, his act of singing at the film's beginning is remarkably suggestive since it not only repeats an action the Nazis forced him to do 40 years earlier but demonstrates that even a traumatic memory can be retrieved, thus becoming a constituent element of a film narrative. Moreover, the song becomes a leifmotif in the film, particularly because of the way it is contrapuntally related, in my viewing experience, to two instances of song later in the film: Franz Suchomel's song (which I will discuss shortly) about Treblinka, and Filip Müller's account of how moved he was when a group of Czech Jews, refusing the order to undress before entering the gas chamber in Auschwitz, started to sing "the Czech national anthem, and the *Hatikvah*" (Lanzmann, 1995, p. 151). It is also important that Srebnik is the only survivor who agrees to return with Lanzmann to the place of the mass murder.[10] For me, he becomes a personification of the way in which the dimensions of time and space interact in *Shoah*. As they blend into each other in Srebnik's act of witnessing, both when he is singing in the boat and when he is at the threshold of the crematorium, Srebnik's testimony becomes remarkably forceful, urging me to reflect on a historical series of events that I cannot understand yet cannot allow myself to forget.

In asking Srebnik to repeat his act of singing in the boat on the River Narew the way he does, Lanzmann is faced with an ethical challenge since he must have known that it would be painful for Srebnik to do what he has probably tried to forget. I am not claiming that Lanzmann's request was ethically dubious; rather, it is ethically motivated in a positive way, and Srebnik's contribution to *Shoah* is aesthetically and ethically decisive. Yet it is not unproblematic to ask a Holocaust survivor to narrate events from that person's past that unavoidably bring back or reactivate painful memories of evil actions. In the narrative discourse of *Shoah*, this problem assumes dissimilar forms and involves different choices, for Lanzmann as interviewer as well as for the interviewee and for the viewer. When Lanzmann interviews Franz Suchomel, who was a guard at Treblinka extermination camp and thus an active participant in the machinery of the Holocaust, he meets with ethical challenges that differ from those encountered in his presentation of Srebnik.

Franz Suchomel: "All that matters to us now is Treblinka"

It is not difficult to understand why Lanzmann wanted to interview Suchomel. As *Shoah* is an ambitious attempt to present the viewer with evil action on a colossal scale, it is essential to talk to and listen to the narratives of not just victims but also perpetrators—those active in the implementation of the Holocaust. That it is difficult for a film director (or journalist or historian) to do this because perpetrators typically refuse to tell about their contribution to and responsibility for mass murder does not make this task less important. But it activates ethical challenges, and it also illustrates how closely these challenges are linked to the aesthetics of *Shoah*. They are also connected with and follow from a key question asked by the Hungarian journalist Gitta Sereny: "How can we understand the mindset and motives of the people who planned and implemented the genocide?" (quoted in McGlothlin, 2021, p. 1; see Sereny, 2006). Sereny, who in the 1970s interviewed Franz Stangl, former commandant of the extermination camps Sobibór and Treblinka, and Albert Speer, former minister for armaments and war production in Nazi Germany, responds thus to her own question: "Questioning perpetrators . . . is difficult, demanding and immensely costly, to oneself and to others" (2006, p. 121). As Erin McGlothlin observes in *The Mind of the Holocaust Perpetrator in Fiction and Nonfiction*:

> Sereny's need "to know [and] understand" the crimes against humanity that were committed in the Third Reich, the Holocaust, and the Second World War requires her to project herself into the mind of a person who perpetrated them in an attempt to comprehend his experience from the inside, to explore not only "what he *knew*" but also "what he *felt*" (Sereny, 2006, p. 128), and to consider the narrative of his crimes as recounted from his own perspective. (McGlothlin, 2021, pp. 2–3)

Finding this undertaking "intricate," McGlothlin comments that it "necessitates a kind of buffer or filter that helps [Sereny] to manage the exercise of reading the mind of the perpetrator and to avoid merging his perspective with her own" (p. 3). This important point is related to and helps to explain the modulations of Lanzmann's perspective in his interview with Franz Suchomel, who was "SS Unterscharführer" (Lanzmann, 1995, p. 43) at Treblinka. Suchomel makes several appearances in *Shoah*; I choose to focus on Lanzmann's interview with him at the beginning of "Era 2." I link my comments to a passage on this "epoch" in Sue Vice's monograph on the film:

> This time the sequence opens on an acousmatic voice, that is, one whose origin we cannot identify, singing a song about Treblinka. At the same time we see a quiet, sunny street, and a slow zoom towards the parked VW filming van culminates in a close-up on the van's rooftop aerial as it moves and turns in search of a signal from the concealed paluche camera. The very nature of the aerial's questing movement puts us in mind of the perennial search in *Shoah* for traces of the past. At the moment Lanzmann asks Suchomel to sing the "Treblinka song" for a second time—"It's very important. But loud!"—there is a cut to Suchomel's face, in a big close-up which has the characteristic scratchy black-and-white look of images captured by the hidden camera. (Vice, 2011, p. 47)

Lanzmann's interview with Suchomel is framed by and made possible through sophisticated film equipment. The techniques, which Vice accurately describes, are elements of film aesthetics. These are not ethically neutral. Rather, film aesthetics merges with the film's ethics; as Vice's reference to "the hidden camera" indicates, Suchomel does not know that he is being filmed. Before discussing the ethical problems associated with Lanzmann's use of a hidden camera, I want to identify some notable gains of his use of the technique described by Vice.

The Suchomel episodes are among the most effective in *Shoah*. For me, the significance of Lanzmann's interview with the former SS Unterscharführer revolves around and is accentuated by the song that opens "Era 2":

> Looking squarely ahead, brave and joyous,
> at the world,
> all the squads march to work.
> All that matters to us now is Treblinka.
> It is our destiny.
> That's why we've become one with Treblinka
> in no time at all.
> We know only the word of our commander,
> we know only obedience and duty,
> we want to serve, to go on serving,
> until a little luck ends it all. Hurray! (Lanzmann, 1995, p. 95)

Recognizing the importance of Suchomel's song, Lanzmann immediately asks him to repeat it: *Once more, but louder!* Suchomel agrees to do so, claiming that by singing about Treblinka "I'm giving you History. Franz wrote the words. The melody came from Buchenwald. Camp Buchenwald, where Franz was a guard" (Lanzmann, 1995, p. 95). Seen from my perspective, three aspects of Suchomel's Treblinka song are particularly noticeable. First, singing his song twice and thus performing a repetitive narrative act in one sense comparable to that of Srebnik, Suchomel does not seem to regret what he did. Rather, for me as a viewer, Suchomel's singing suggests a sense of achievement, of having participated in an important mission: that of exterminating the Jews. Everything he says in the interview is related to the song, including the remark "The new gas chambers ... Let's see ... They could finish off three thousand people in two hours" (Lanzmann, 1995, p. 52). There is a chilling irony in that the song's title, which for Suchomel refers to his act of traveling to in order to work at Treblinka, also, though Suchomel does not acknowledge this, refers to the fact that many hundred thousand Jews made the same trip, with the decisive difference of having been deported and deprived of the possibility of returning home. This irony becomes even more arresting when Suchomel tells Lanzmann that the Jews "were taught the song. And by evening they had to be able to sing along with it" (Lanzmann, 1995, p. 95).

Second, in spite of, yet perhaps also because of, the poor aesthetic quality of the song, it condenses into a few words several of the constituent elements of the Holocaust: the dedication of the Nazis who implemented and ran "the operation,"[11] the understanding of Treblinka as a contributing factor to "our destiny," and the emphasis on the need for "serving" and the desire "to serve." This second aspect forms the basis for the third: the ironic inversion in the middle of the song. When he claims that he and the other guards have "become one with Treblinka/in no time at all," Suchomel inadvertently gives an accurate description of the fate of the several hundred thousand Jews who were burned in the crematoria located in this place, thus becoming "one with Treblinka in no time at all." To identify this variant of dramatic irony is an interpretive act, and this aspect of my interpretation of Suchomel's song makes me more inclined to read elements of irony into Lanzmann's questions and comments. Irony may signal attitudinal distance—a distance from Suchomel that Lanzmann may feel he needs to conduct the interview (cf. McGothlin, 2021; cf. Lothe, 2020a). Is there a connection, I wonder, between Lanzmann's distance from Suchomel and his lies to him, and what would such a connection tell me about Lanzmann's narrative ethics?

I will respond to this question shortly, but first I note that as I watch the beginning of "Era 2" of *Shoah*, and as I keep watching it over and over again,

I am simultaneously repelled and fascinated by the strangely phantom-like contours of Suchomel's face (Figures 3.4 and 3.5). It is as though he, the former SS guard, emerges from the past, thus contributing to Lanzmann's ambitious aim of making a film that is not about remembering but about reliving. The combination of Suchomel's performance of the Treblinka song and his accompanying remarks reveals distinct features of Nazism's moral values. These values are diametrically opposed to those I glean from Srebnik's song, the song that I have already heard him singing on the River Narew and which becomes a leitmotif throughout. One of these values is a variant of biological racism that considered Jews extremely dangerous—so dangerous that (in camps such as Treblinka and Chełmno) they had to be exterminated. It is not just strange but almost unbelievable that Suchomel, 30 years after the war and presumably with at least a basic knowledge of the Holocaust, seems to defend, or at least not distance himself from and certainly not defy, the gigantic project of mass extermination in which he played an active part. While there is a very considerable distance between *Erzählzeit* (when he is interviewed by Lanzmann) and *erzählte Zeit* (when he was a guard at Treblinka), his moral values seem remarkably constant.

Figure 3.4

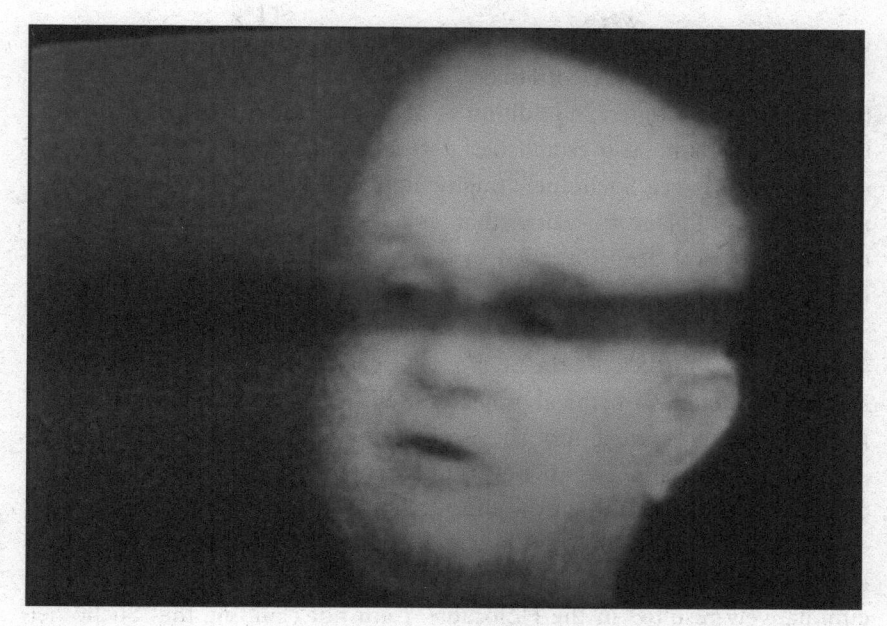

Figures 3.4 and 3.5 Screenshots from *Shoah,* directed by Claude Lanzmann (1985)

These aspects of narrative ethics are primarily linked to Suchomel, who is the narrator in the episode. More indirectly, they are also related to me, since I am the viewer who thinks I can identify them, and since my moral values inevitably influence my understanding of Suchomel's narrative ethics. Even though there is a possibility that my wish, even need to distance myself morally from Suchomel reduces my ability to understand his narrative ethics, I neither can nor want to reduce this attitudinal distance. Thus, I remain, as indicated earlier, simultaneously repelled and fascinated. This kind of need seems to be shared by Lanzmann, whose questions to Suchomel are sometimes colored by a sense of disbelief. His incredulity is associated with the components of narrative ethics identified and briefly discussed above. It is as if, in Lanzmann's presentation of him, Suchomel becomes a personification of constituent elements of the implementation of the Holocaust. I cannot find a single redeeming feature in my understanding of the director's portrait of the earlier Treblinka guard. Whether this is part of Lanzmann's intention I am not sure, though I am inclined to think it is. Aesthetically as well as ethically, the Suchomel scenes, and particularly the one being considered here, enable Lanzmann to erect a frame around the first-person narratives of Holocaust survivors—narratives that assume the form of testimonies. In addition to giving the film a kind of structural balance, this frame also establishes a structural contrast to the survivors' accounts. Moreover, Suchomel's fragment gives the viewer a glimpse of the moral values of Nazism—values that, as far as Suchomel is concerned, do not seem to have been dispelled by a retrospective understanding of the Holocaust.

While Lanzmann's presentation of Suchomel contributes decisively to the aesthetic impact of *Shoah*, the Suchomel scenes thus play a key role in the shaping of *Shoah* as an ethical project as well. Yet precisely since Lanzmann needs Suchomel's contribution, he uses a method that is not just dubious but ethically problematic, possibly even unacceptable. Before considering the ethical challenges resulting from this method, I specify that by "Suchomel's contribution" I mean the ways in which Suchomel, as Lanzmann presents him, gives the viewer a sense of and a partial report on the evil actions that cumulatively resulted in the Holocaust. I am not claiming that Suchomel personifies evil, but I am suggesting that both his words and his facial expression tell us something (though I find it difficult to identify exactly what this is) about the intricate connections between, to appropriate the well-chosen title of Arne Johan Vetlesen's (2005) book, "evil and human agency." As I hope to have shown, the connection is particularly strong in Suchomel's performances of the Treblinka song. In his autobiography, Lanzmann identifies a sudden hardness in the former guard's eyes as he sang, signaling a bodily return to the past (Lanzmann, 2009; cf. Vice, 2011). In common with Vice and many other viewers, I am forcibly struck by what seems a remarkably close fit between the *Erzählzeit* of the old man and the *erzählte Zeit* of the young Treblinka guard. The emphasis on the present "is conveyed not only by the transformation of Suchomel's nostalgia into reincarnation, but also in the choice of location" (Vice, 2011, p. 48). Although I am not sure what Vice means by "reincarnation," she makes an important point in suggesting that Suchomel's act of singing takes him beyond nostalgia and closer to a state and a situation in which he was ready to engage in evil actions. There is, then, no doubt that *Shoah* would have been a less significant and less memorable film if Suchomel's song, which I consider a counterpoint to that of Srebnik, had not been included. Yet this loss does not necessarily justify the use of a hidden camera. This observation takes me to the first ethical challenge in the Suchomel scene: assuming, probably correctly, that had he asked for permission to film, Suchomel would have said no, Lanzmann presents the viewer with a secretly shot film of Suchomel in his apartment. To put this another way, Suchomel is set up. Or, as some viewers might be inclined to say, Lanzmann cheats; though his motive may be laudable, his method is dubious.

Lanzmann might counter by referring to the necessity of including his interview with Suchomel, and he could elaborate by explaining the aesthetic and ethical force of his presentation of the former Treblinka guard. Yet although he would probably find even more arguments for including the Suchomel scene than those I have identified here, the gain of including it does not eliminate the ethical challenge. Moreover, the first ethical challenge is enhanced by a second one: when Suchomel asks Lanzmann to promise that their conversation will not be published and that his name will remain anonymous, Lanzmann makes the promise, thus lying to Suchomel. Again, had he not promised, Suchomel probably would have decided not to talk. Yet that kind of risk does not in itself justify a lie. For Lanzmann as the director of *Shoah*, the challenge approximates to an ethical dilemma: while the gains of interviewing Suchomel and using the former SS guard's (visual and verbal) contribution the way he does is an essential part of his achievement, and not just aesthetically but ethically as well, this achievement comes at a cost since it depends on and necessitates Lanzmann's use of dubious methods.

That said, I am not sure whether Lanzmann himself would have considered the challenge of making Suchomel part of his film an ethical dilemma, particularly if, as is often the case, that dilemma consists of two options that involve or result in divergent courses of action. To put this another way, given the opportunity to talk and listen to a perpetrator of the Holocaust, and given the ethical imperative of that objective, Lanzmann might find it ethically justifiable to use a method that, considered in relative isolation, may include elements that are ethically problematic. One possible reason is that, seen from Lanzmann's perspective, these problematic elements need to be framed by other, perhaps more important ethical considerations. Lanzmann might argue that a decision *not* to interview Suchomel because of the ethical issues I have identified would have been equally problematic, perhaps even ethically indefensible since the gain outweighs the loss. Speaking for myself as one viewer of *Shoah*, I am convinced that the film is aesthetically and ethically strengthened by the Suchomel scenes, which in that sense are ethically justified. Yet it does not follow that Lanzmann's use of Suchomel is ethically unproblematic. Would the deception have been more or less justified had Suchomel said that he deeply regretted his actions and was ashamed of them? I am not sure.

Suchomel's contribution to *Shoah* assumes the form of narrative fragments that build on and revolve around his memories of his time at Treblinka. These memories constitute an experience that, aided and provoked by Lanzmann's questions, Suchomel attempts to give narrative shape. While it is essential to distinguish his fragmented narrative from those of the Holocaust survivors Lanzmann interviews—Suchomel's experience seems less traumatic, and he is keen to defend his former actions as an SS guard—the combination of his song and his comments presents the viewer with aspects of an autobiographical process that "simultaneously unfolds several temporal scenarios that are not conceivable, in fact, not even imaginable, without the forms and practices of narrative" (Brockmeier, 2015, p. 123). Referring to Bruner's (2001) concept of cultural "world-making," Brockmeier underlines "narrative's crucial role in the cultural fabric of meaning that makes up humans' self or identity projects" (2015, p. 123). That narrative plays a crucial role in Suchomel's identity project simultaneously illustrates and supports a key point that Meretoja (2018a) makes in *The Ethics of Storytelling*: the ethics of a narrative, or of a narrative fragment or fragments, is not necessarily an ethics that I embrace as a reader or viewer. With regard to Suchomel, I am appalled by two distinct yet related constituent elements of his narrative ethics: his contribution to the mass murders at Treblinka and his apparent lack of remorse. Conversely, Srebnik's narrative, which is also fragmented, is imbued with an ethics that I respect and admire—even as I realize that Srebnik's experience, including that of his own execution, is so different from mine that my understanding of his narrative ethics is bound to be limited.

This kind of limited understanding influences my interpretation of Srebnik's and Suchomel's narratives, including their narrative ethics. My interpretation is also colored by Lanzmann's narrative ethics as he, the director of *Shoah*, presents these narratives to me as film segments. This point can be extended to include the narrative ethics of the whole film: my understanding of its ethics depends on and is inextricable from my viewing and interpretation of the discourse of *Shoah*. Lanzmann's ethics as director of *Shoah* is much more complex than the ethics of his questions and extratextual comments. Each in his own way, all Lanzmann's interviewees contribute to the formation of this ethics, aspects of which I can identify and reflect on only through my interpretive process as a viewer.

Abraham Bomba: Traumatic Memory as Silence

When Beauvoir writes, "Il n'est pas facile de parler de *Shoah*," she suggests that it is also difficult to interpret *Shoah*. As I understand her comment, she also implies that one reason for this interpretive challenge is suggested by the Holocaust survivor's struggle to transform the memory of his or her camp experience into communicable language. Nowhere in the film is this struggle more evident than in Lanzmann's interview with Abraham Bomba. As critics have noted, this interview is one of the film's most illustrative examples of mise-en-scène: combining various elements of cinematography when he interviews Bomba in Tel Aviv many years after the Holocaust, Lanzmann makes Bomba tell about the work that the Nazis forced him to do as a barber at Treblinka (where he had to cut naked women's hair inside the undressing rooms of the gas chamber) while he is cutting a customer's hair in a barber shop in Tel Aviv. LaCapra finds, "The viewer is, I think, shocked in learning that the barber shop was rented and that the men in it are simply extras who do not understand the language (English) in which the exchange between Lanzmann and Bomba is conducted" (2007, p. 192). This is probably true, but not all viewers will know this—and this extratextual knowledge does not necessarily improve the viewer's understanding of the scene. For me, the mise-en-scène of Lanzmann's interview with Bomba is effective since it frames Bomba's narrative in a way that augments my desire to understand it, even as I sense that I cannot do so. The mise-en-scène furthers the inseparability of dialogue and image; Bomba's painful autobiographical process advances my interpretive process. While the mise-en-scène, including the barber shop as the place of the interview, establishes a connection with the work that Bomba had to do as a barber at Treblinka, Lanzmann stresses the differences between that place and the narrative situation in Tel Aviv. As Vice puts it in her perceptive discussion of this scene:

> When Bomba relates that in Treblinka he wanted to give the women "the imagination that they're getting a nice haircut," so we see him repeat this "imagination" in the present with his "customer." Yet the details of the staging are also significantly different from the past. The "customers" in the present are all men, fitting Bomba's trade as a barber. (2011, p. 55)

Thus, the mise-en-scène enables Lanzmann to strike a balance between proximity on the one hand and temporal, spatial, and attitudinal distance on the other. This combination becomes a constitutive element of his endeavor "to bring the barber to recall the deepest, most repressed bodily memories of that horrific past" (Spitzer, 2004, p. 416).

I focus on the part of the interview in which Bomba attempts to remember and then relate his traumatic memory of one particular act he had to perform as a barber at Treblinka. Significantly, this much-discussed sequence of the interview (and of *Shoah*) is not initiated by Lanzmann but by Bomba himself. When asked by Lanzmann what he felt when he first saw the naked women arriving with their children at the gas chamber, Bomba responds:

> I tell you something. To have a feeling about that . . . it was very hard to feel anything, because working there day and night between dead people, between bodies, your feeling disappeared, you were dead. You had no feeling at all. As a matter of fact, I want to tell you something that happened. At the gas chamber, when I was chosen to work there as a barber, some of the women that came in on a transport from my town of Czestochowa, I knew a lot of them. I knew them; I lived with them in my town. I lived with them in my street, and some of them were my close friends. And when they saw me, they started asking me, Abe this and Abe that—"What's going to happen to us?" What could you tell them? What could you tell?
>
> A friend of mine worked as a barber—he was a good barber in my hometown—when his wife and his sister came into the gas chamber. . . . (Lanzmann, 1995, p. 107)

At this point of his testimony, Bomba's voice fails and his narrative grinds to a halt. A pause of approximately three minutes and 40 seconds, by far the longest in the film, follows. For me, this silence—or blank or gap—is an empty core around which *Shoah*'s narrative discourse revolves and which it hesitantly yet insistently approaches. Although it never reaches, or can reach, this empty core, Bomba's silence takes me uncomfortably close.

Before discussing this film sequence, I make two points about the passage that leads to the silence or, to put it another way, that makes Bomba's narrative break down. First, although it is possible to consider the silence as Bomba's response, or failure to respond, to Lanzmann's question, "What did you feel?" (1995, p. 107), the main basis for the following breakdown of Bomba's narrative is his rejection of the question by stating, "You had no feeling at all." But then he adds, "I want to tell you something that happened." This "something" turns out to be the moment when his friend's "wife and sister came into the gas chamber"; once he has uttered these words he is overwhelmed with feelings and his narrative collapses. At one level, Bomba is thus contradicting himself. As I rewatch the sequence, though, what strikes me is not the contradiction but Bomba's courage: he must know that it will prove difficult "to tell you something that happened," and yet he wants to do this. I am not arguing that Bomba is anticipating the breakdown of his own narrative. Yet the courage he shows by deciding to confront and try to translate into words his most traumatic memories is remarkable. And there is a connection between this courage and the kind of persistence he displays during the long silence that follows.

Second, Częstochowa is a key word in this passage. Bomba's hometown in southern Poland becomes the third of three coordinates: Częstochowa, Treblinka, and Israel. He grew up in the first of these places, he miraculously survived the second, and he now lives in the third—where he is trying to translate his traumatic memories of the second place into words. Combined with the silence that follows, these three elements of space are in line with Bachelard's phenomenological notion of space as "compressed time" (1958/1994, p. 8). As already noted, Bachelard finds that human beings' experience of space is associated with identity and identity formation, and this quality of space is closely related to *when* and *how* we inhabit a given space. In this film segment, and particularly in the silence that it includes, space is indeed "compressed time."

In *The Complete Text of the Acclaimed Holocaust Film*, the segment of silence that follows the breakdown of Bomba's narration is presented thus:

Go on, Abe. You must go on. You have to.
I can't. It's too horrible. Please.
We have to do it. You know it.
I won't be able to do it.
You have to do it. I know it's very hard. I know and I apologize.
Don't make me go on please.
Please. We must go on.
I told you today it's going to be very hard. They were taking that in bags and
    transporting it to Germany.
Okay, go ahead. (Lanzmann, 1995, pp. 107–108)

I have quoted the subtitle of Lanzmann's "complete text—words and subtitles—of my film *Shoah*" (1995, p. vii) to illustrate the great difference between the text of verbal narrative and that of *Shoah* as a film. When Lanzmann writes "complete text" he means the words spoken in the film and the subtitles. But as noted in the introduction, and as I hope to have shown in my discussion of Lanzmann's film as well as those of Riefenstahl and Resnais, spoken words are just one of the many elements that constitute film narration. In this filmic sequence, silence, or the absence of words, is far more important than Lanzmann's presentation of the "complete text" suggests. Thus, the dialogue between Bomba and Lanzmann in the verbal text is misleading. In the film there is no dialogue. After long periods of silence Lanzmann intervenes, repeatedly urging Bomba to resume his narrative (Figure 3.6). Although Bomba says that he cannot do so because it is "too horrible," Lanzmann keeps insisting—until Bomba finally relents and continues.

Figure 3.6 Screenshot from *Shoah*, directed by Claude Lanzmann (1985)

That this sequence of *Shoah* is especially difficult to interpret enhances the need for interpretation. As my approach is indebted to narrative hermeneutics, I look for self-interpretive components that could further my understanding of this scene, but it is hard to identify such elements. While the segment indicates a narrative situation that, according to Ross Chambers's

(1984) definition of this concept, may involve possibilities of gain as well as risks of loss for both Bomba and Lanzmann, I find that as a viewer I am here very much in a hermeneutical "situation . . . [that] represents a standpoint that limits the possibility of vision" (Gadamer, 1960/2013, p. 313); I am at once too close to the narrative situation and too far removed from it. What I can do, though, is use my knowledge of my ignorance, my recognition of my limited horizon, and my temporal and spatial distance from the narrative situation as a basis for my questions: Why does Bomba's narrative collapse? When this happens, why does he not just leave the barber shop? Why does Lanzmann continue to film, focusing the camera on Bomba's face? Why does Bomba finally resume his story? What is the silence's significance—what does it tell us about Holocaust testimony, and about the mechanisms and effects of human memory?

In the context of *Shoah*, these questions are ethical questions. Although I cannot answer them, I can try to use them as a basis for ethical reflection that may possess elements of interpretation. Speaking for myself as one viewer, I find that my difficulty in interpreting Bomba's silence tells me something important about the almost insurmountable challenge of bearing witness to crimes as unspeakable as those Bomba had to experience. Attempting to understand *how* Lanzmann presents Bomba's silence, I note the crucial role of the film camera. Significantly, as Vice observes, "the first shot of Bomba in the sequence is a reflection, although we only realise this when the camera tracks around to focus on him." Vice continues:

The camera is never still for long during this encounter, at times show-ing Bomba from behind, making a 360 tracking shot around him, filming his face in reflection bisected by the seam in the mirror—yet the camera itself is not reflected, making the mirrors seem even less naturalistic and emphasizing the difficulty of capturing Bomba's story. Precisely because of the elaborate set-up, we are mindful that it exists for the sake of a one-time reincarnation of the past. . . . During this sequence in which the camera is invisible, we do not see Lanzmann either; his presence is signalled only by his voice and by Bomba's infrequent glances towards him off-screen, for instance when the barber pleads, "Don't make me go on." Bomba never catches the spectator's look in an eyeline match, and indeed his gaze is directed either down towards the face of the man whose hair he cuts, or away out of shot, as if he can only summon up the past by turning away from the sights of the present. (2011, pp. 55–56)

Vice is right to emphasize the ways in which the camera, as a key element of film form, generates film content (which I use synonymously with a thematics that includes negotiations of ethical questions). It is as though, focalizing Bomba from different angles, the camera is searching for some clue or sign that might explain his silence. Although the camera—or, more accurately, Lanzmann and the cinematographer who steer the camera—does not and cannot give the viewer such an explanation, I agree with Vice that the camera shows how Bomba is turning away from the present, thus perhaps approaching "a one-time reincarnation of the past." In this sequence, the film camera plays such a key role that it becomes almost indistinguishable from the narrative discourse of *Shoah*. Many film scholars have noted that film is a medium limited to surfaces, to the visible. Yet as William Rothman writes in *The "I" of the Camera*, film is also "a medium of mysterious depths, of the inner, the invisible" (1988, p. xv). The sequence when Bomba is silent in *Shoah* supports Rothman's point. Showing me Bomba's face from varying perspectives, the camera (and Lanzmann behind it) invites me to interpret his facial expression. I gather that he may be recalling his lost relatives and friends, but what exactly is he thinking, feeling, and remembering?

As Bomba is experiencing "a reincarnation of the past," his silence suggests that he is enacting his traumatic memory of Treblinka in front of Lanzmann's camera. His traumatic memory becomes part of the silence that lasts for three minutes and 40 seconds. Given that the medium of film has an inbuilt need for movement and progression of action, this is an exceptionally long period of time. Challenging the viewer's patience, it signals that Bomba's silence is as meaningful as it is difficult to verbalize. It is true that, as the "complete text" quoted above suggests, Bomba makes a few comments during the period of silence. But these comments accentuate rather than disrupt the silence, for two reasons. First, they are his response to Lanzmann's requests, almost orders that he resume his story. Second, uttered in a different, much lower voice, they are not part of his story but metacomments on the difficulty of relating that story. One sentence of the final comment is particularly important: "They were taking that [the women's hair] in bags and transporting it to Germany." Bomba murmurs this sentence, which Lanzmann includes in both the French and English editions of "the complete text," in Yiddish. This information is not rendered in the English edition, but the French edition includes a footnote: "Cette phrase murmurée, en yiddish" (This phrase murmured in Yiddish) (Lanzmann, 2001, p. 168).

Since I do not understand Yiddish, the meaning of this sentence eludes me when I watch and rewatch the sequence. As Bomba has already mentioned, just before he refers to the transport from Częstochowa, that "the Germans needed the hair for their purposes" (Lanzmann, 1995, p. 107), the phrase murmured in Yiddish is a repetition. Why does he repeat these words? Does he perhaps find it particularly cruel and upsetting that the Germans, having transported thousands of Jews to Treblinka from different European locations, would then transport the hair of the murdered women to Germany? I do not know, but it is as though, touching base with his Jewish identity in Częstochowa by murmuring this phrase in his native tongue, Bomba finds the strength he needs to continue his story. His following comment is "Okay, go ahead," and when he responds to Lanzmann's next question his voice is louder, reverting to his declamatory voice before it breaks down. Combined with the strength of will that Bomba shows during his silence, his decision and ability to finish the story he has started is a key aspect of his narrative ethics. His silence, including how it begins as well as the way it ends, documents the cost of bearing witness.

As Leo Spitzer observes, the sequence of *Shoah* that presents Bomba's silence "is no longer simply recollection, memory, witnessing. It is acting out a traumatic past in front of the camera, reliving it" (2004, p. 416). Aspects of Bomba's silence support Cathy Caruth's understanding of trauma. Noting "the radical disruption and gaps of traumatic experience," Caruth finds that "there is a response, sometimes delayed, to an overwhelming event or events, which takes the form of repeated, intrusive hallucinations, dreams, thoughts or behaviors stemming from the event" (1995, p. 4). There is also a sense in which Bomba's silence lends support to Caruth's skepticism about storytelling as a way of negotiating trauma since narration may problematically subsume the singular under the general, thus inaugurating the "forgetting of the singularity" (Caruth, 1996/2016, p. 33) of the event. Yet Bomba's silence does not signal a single traumatic event that is a "breach in the mind's experience of time, self, and the world" (p. 3). Rather, Bomba's silence in the barbershop sequence is an act of remembering his forced participation in repetitive events. He recalls the events as well as his experience of them, and the silence is an attempt—in the present, as he is being interviewed by Lanzmann—to negotiate the experience. This attempt includes elements of narrative that, culminating in the phrase he utters in Yiddish, contribute to his resolve to continue his story. Two observations follow from this point. First, the narrative dimension of Bomba's silence becomes more important because of the way it is framed. As his story about his work as a barber in Treblinka takes him to the "something" that he himself wants to tell Lanzmann, and as that story resumes after his long silence, that silence not only problematizes but also gives an edge to his narrative. Lanzmann's use of the film medium contributes significantly to this effect. As Sigfried Kracauer puts it, "in keeping with its recording obligations, film renders the world in motion" (1965, p. 158). Although "the world in motion" is halted and problematized in this sequence, it does not disappear. One reason it does not is that, as a viewer, I expect motion.

Second, from the perspective of narrative hermeneutics, narratives can further genuine understanding

> precisely when they do not concern the comfortable subsumption of new experiences into what we already know, but rather when they involve a process that entails change (of pregiven categories, values, identity). Such change, in turn, is often painful and difficult. (Meretoja, 2018a, p. 115)

Bomba's silence deals with and gives the viewer fragments of a narrative working-through of a "self-altering" experience of injury, murder, and loss (Gilmore, 2001, p. 6). Throughout the sequence, Bomba refers both to the place of Treblinka and to the time when he was "over there" (Lanzmann, 1995, p. 102). I agree with Vice's concluding comment that "it is Lanzmann's achievement to have made these geographical and temporal boundaries vanish. . . . These extraordinary moments of breakdown and return constitute some of the most visible and audible enactments of the past in *Shoah*" (2011, p. 57). The silence in the middle of Bomba's rendering of his traumatic experience makes his testimony unique.

Lanzmann presents the narrative ethics of Srebnik and Bomba in a way that suggests respect, even admiration. There is a sense in which his own narrative ethics as director approximates to the ethics of these two Holocaust survivors: all three share a strong wish to remember and convey through the narrative medium of film the destruction of six million Jews. In the case of Srebnik, I imagine that this wish is an essential reason he allows Lanzmann to persuade him to return with him to Chelmno; with regard to Bomba, I gather that his determination to bear witness is one reason he manages to suffer through the period of silence after the collapse of his testimony. It does not follow that the narrative ethics of these two survivors is identical. While significant aspects of Srebnik's ethics emerge through the repetitive act of singing and his identification of the place where the crematorium was located in Treblinka, I identify constituent elements of Bomba's ethics as I listen to his declamatory voice and as I watch his face during the period of silence. For all the respect he shows the two survivors, Lanzmann's narrative ethics is different from Srebnik's and Bomba's not only because he depends on their testimonies to make his film but also because of his method of film-making. Does he have the right to persuade Srebnik to return to the place where he "was executed" and where he lost all his relatives? Is it ethically justifiable to force Bomba to press on with his narrative after its collapse? Is Lanzmann entitled to make them relive painful memories that they may have needed to suppress to continue to live? And yet "[h]ow else could one access traumatic memory—'deep memory', in Charlotte Delbo's [1990, p. 3] words—without pushing some witnesses insistently, as he did with Bomba, through a barrier of horrific pain?" (Spitzer, 2004, p. 417). Although Spitzer's question is well founded, and although there may be no other way of access-ing Bomba's "deep memory" of the act of cutting the hair of his friend's wife and sister in the Treblinka gas chamber, I find Lanzmann's insistence ethi-cally problematic. There is a sense in which the mise-en-scène is so too: as both the camera and Lanzmann remain invisible, it is as though he is pro-tecting himself from the traumatic situation he has created. Yet I consider the sequence of silence one of the most important and most moving in *Shoah*: Bomba's affect as he is struggling with his "deep memory" stirs an affect in me as a viewer that, however different it is from Bomba's recollection, gives an edge to his narrative as it alerts me to the cost of testimony while at the same time augmenting my understanding of its importance.

If there is an attitudinal distance between Lanzmann and Bomba in this key scene, that distance is much greater in the interview with Suchomel. Lanzmann's narrative ethics here includes elements of irony as well as sar-casm, as when he asks Suchomel, "Warum diese Menschlichkeit?" (Why such humanity?) (Lanzmann, 1995, p. 101). When I link this sarcasm to Lanzmann's secretive filming of Suchomel, and when I also reflect on his blatant lies to him, I wonder about the ethics of his approach. But then, as many critics of *Shoah* have asked, how else but through "surreptitious means" (Spitzer, 2004, p. 417) could Lanzmann have managed to reveal Suchomel's contribution to the Holocaust? This is ethically difficult terri-tory. My tentative conclusion is that Lanzmann's approach may be justifiable since it enables him to make an extraordinary film whose persuasiveness and affective impact as Holocaust testimony would have been considerably reduced had the interviews with perpetrators such as Suchomel not been included.

Filip Müller and Roul Hilberg: The Holocaust Survivor and the Historian

Beauvoir's observation that "*Shoah* is not an easy film to talk about" (1995, p. iii) applies not only to beginning a discussion of Lanzmann's film but also to continuing and ending that discussion. In deciding to focus this chapter on the film's narrative beginning and on Lanzmann's presentation of Srebnik, Suchomel, and Bomba, I have inevitably omitted discussing the narrative ethics of other interviewees as well as Lanzmann's ethics in these interviews. Before concluding this chapter, I briefly indicate how the interviews with the Czech Holocaust survivor Filip Müller and the American historian Raul Hilberg reveal aspects of their narrative ethics that, in addition to their intrinsic value, throw additional light on the ethics of Lanzmann's approach. Müller is a key witness in *Shoah* because he was one of the Sonderkommando members who were responsible for the disposal of the bodies of people who were gassed at Auschwitz-Birkenau. Two features of Lanzmann's narrative ethics become apparent in his presentation of Müller. First, contrasting with and serving as a counterpart to the interview with Bomba, close-ups of Müller's face alternate with shots of open landscapes; this visual alternation is combined with transitions from on- to off-screen sound. Müller's low voice becomes more insistent, and more persuasive, because of the footage that the camera shows us of the outside world. While this footage is not as specific as the place of the crematorium Srebnik is looking at, it is a segment of space that I associate with the landscape of extermination camps in eastern Poland. Significantly, the footage also shows trains moving through this landscape, and I inevitably relate the trains to transports of Jews. For me, one association is particularly strong: the transport of 532 Norwegian Jews from Szczecin to Auschwitz at the end of November 1942. Once I have made this association, I also connect the trains to the *Donau*.

Second, the pattern of Müller's testimony resembles that of Bomba; Müller too "undergoes his own traumatic return" as his testimony takes him "closer and closer to the scene of death itself" (Vice, 2011, p. 82). He recalls the moment when the members of a Czech family at the camp start to sing in the undressing room: "The whole 'undressing room' rang with the Czech national anthem, and the *Hatikvah*. That moved me terribly, that . . . Please stop" (Lanzmann, 1995, p. 151). At this point Müller pauses, crying as he interrupts his narrative and begs Lanzmann to end the interview (Figure 3.7).

Please stop!

Figure 3.7 Screenshot from *Shoah*, directed by Claude Lanzmann (1985)

As Vice observes, "It is as if Müller is weeping in the present as he wept in the past" (2011, p. 83). In contrast to Bomba, however, he is able to continue by telling Lanzmann, and thus me as a viewer, that after he decided to die with his countrymen in the gas chamber they urged him, "[G]et out of here alive, you must bear witness to our suffering, and to the injustice done to us" (Lanzmann, 1995, p. 152). This is perhaps the most explicit reason a Holocaust survivor interviewed by Lanzmann gives for contributing to *Shoah*. There is an ethical connection between three dimensions of bearing witness: first, those about to be gassed urge Müller to survive in order to testify about the Holocaust; second, as a survivor Müller does this by contributing to *Shoah* and by writing a book (Müller, 1979); and, third, Lanzmann conceives of and directs the film in which Müller *can* bear witness. At this point, the link to the film's epigraph is particularly strong. In spite of this ethical connection, though, Lanzmann's narrative presentation of Müller is not ethically unproblematic: Müller's narration takes him to a breaking point, and Lanzmann could have stopped filming when Müller asked him to do so. Yet there is no silence here comparable to the pause, or *Leerstelle*, during which the camera mercilessly records the facial expression of mental torture on Bomba's face as, unable to speak, he is struggling with his most painful memory of Treblinka.

As regards Lanzmann's interview with Hilberg, the narrative discourse of *Shoah* makes me ask: Is this noted historian also a witness? In one sense he is not, since by "time's witness" I mean a Holocaust survivor able to bear witness about his or her camp experience (as do Maria Gabrielsen, Ella Blumenthal, Edith Notowicz, and Olga Horak). Yet when it comes to the task of documenting the Holocaust, studies by historians, including Hilberg's (1961/2003) three-volume study *The Destruction of the European Jews*, are indispensable.

Figure 3.8 Screenshot from *Shoah*, directed by Claude Lanzmann (1985)

Two constituent elements of Hilberg's narrative ethics are particularly relevant to and form part of the basis for Lanzmann's ethics as I extrapolate it from my interpretation of *Shoah*. First, by strengthening the historical basis for the film, Hilberg demonstrates that, in spite of Lanzmann's claim to the contrary, *Shoah* is a documentary (Figure 3.8). The testimonies' reliability is strengthened by Hilberg's explanation of how the transports of Jews were organized; he shows how the survivors' stories are anchored in and form a part of historical reality. Hilberg's emphasis on *showing* is essential. "From the start," he writes in the preface to the revised 1985 edition of his three-volume study, "I have wanted to know how the Jews of Europe were destroyed" (Hilberg, 1961/2003, vol. 1, p. xi). This motivation, which Lanzmann shares, informs the narrative ethics of both *Shoah* and *The Destruction of the European Jews*.

Second, it is relevant for the formation of Lanzmann's narrative ethics as constituted by the film's narrative discourse that Hilberg tells him not only about the Nazis' system of transporting Jews to the camps but also about *The Warsaw Diary of Adam Czerniakow: Prelude to Doom*, a volume he coedited and published in 1999 (Hilberg et al., 1999). Hilberg tells Lanzmann that Czerniaków, who was president of the *Judenrat* (Jewish Council) of the Warsaw ghetto, "kept his diary in daily entries until the afternoon of the day that he ended his life. . . . He didn't save the Jews—in that respect he was like other Jewish leaders—but he left us a record of what had happened to them in a day-by-day fashion" (Lanzmann, 1995, p. 163). For Hilberg as a historian of the Holocaust, Czerniaków's diary is an invaluable source. Yet when he talks about it, his wording and facial expression are different from that of his account of the transport system. Hilberg is clearly moved by the diary; he has enormous respect for Czerniaków's care, under extremely difficult conditions, for the Jewish children entrusted to him; and he shares Czerniaków's indignation with the Germans: "And for the Germans he doesn't have words of disgust. I think he's beyond such words" (Lanzmann, 1995, p. 167).[12] Such an indignation is felt by Lanzmann too, and it carries over to his interview with Dr. Franz Grassler. As deputy to Heinz Auerswald, who was the Nazi commissioner of the Warsaw ghetto, Grassler repeatedly went into the ghetto to visit Czerniaków. The contrapuntal presentation of these two interviews, one with a historian who is commenting on the diary of a Holocaust victim and the other with a Nazi officer in charge of the Warsaw ghetto in which Czerniaków perished, is remarkably effective. While Grassler tones down his role in the Holocaust, noting that "we tend to forget, thank God, the bad times more easily than the good" (Lanzmann, 1995, p. 162), Hilberg expresses his gratitude to Czerniaków for keeping a diary that enables him to record, and thus document and remember, the Nazis' crimes against the Jews in the Warsaw ghetto.

A further gain of Lanzmann's contrapuntal method here is that Grassler's assertion that "[t]he bad times are repressed" (Lanzmann, 1995, p. 162) invites the viewer to compare his evasive comments not only with Czerniaków's diary but also with Suchomel's account of his work as a guard at Treblinka. Where Suchomel willingly tells Lanzmann about his contribution to the Holocaust, Grassler is reticent. Yet as a viewer I infer that, though he was not convicted after the war, Grassler's task of running the Warsaw ghetto places him in Hilberg's category of perpetrator, not in that of bystander. The great contrast between Suchomel and Grassler when it comes to their autobiographical narratives, including their divergent attitudes to memory and forgetting, illustrates the individuality of Holocaust perpetrators as psychological and moral subjects; they are by no means a homogeneous group (see McGlothlin, 2021).

Why is Czerniaków unable to express words of disgust for these crimes? Is it because he is confronted with evil actions of such a magnitude, and executed in such a systematic way, that he cannot find the words to adequately describe them? One critical gain of Vetlesen's *Evil and Human Agency* is his demonstration of the necessity of studying collective evildoing while at the same time being cognizant of the intricate connections between evil actions done collectively and those performed individually (see also Fulbrook, 2023). Vetlesen's awareness of this problem forms part of the basis for his critique of the way Arendt makes generalized comments on evil on the basis of her observations of Adolf Eichmann in *Eichmann in Jerusalem* (Arendt, 1963; Vetlesen, 2005). This chapter has aimed to show that the problem is also encountered by Lanzmann in the making of *Shoah*: while the Holocaust as collective evildoing remains curiously elusive and to a certain extent ungraspable, the examples of individual evildoing, including those of Suchomel and of Grassler, link the industrial mass murder to individual action.

The case of Srebnik illustrates yet also problematizes this point. The Nazis directly involved in and responsible for the operation of the extermination camp Chełmno are absent from Lanzmann's film. Yet although it complicates my interpretation that I cannot see them, this kind of absence is aesthetically and ethically productive: as I listen to Srebnik's song, whose aesthetic qualities are enhanced by the beautiful landscape (a devious beauty, since it was the site of the camp), I know that the Nazi guards listened to the same song. Moreover, presumably they forced Srebnik to sing on the River Narew because they found the song, and Srebnik's performance of it, beautiful. On one level, this is unsurprising; after all, German culture has made seminal contributions to classical music and song. On a different level, the act of listening to Srebnik's song, combined with that of looking at his face, did not prevent the Nazis from shooting him. (That he survived was, seen from their perspective, an unfortunate error—though a minor one considering that more than 99% of the inmates in Chełmno were murdered.)

While Srebrnik accepts the ethical challenge of repeating his act of singing in the place where he was supposed to die, as a viewer I am forced to listen to the same song the Nazis heard him sing. Moreover, I am impelled to accept that while I find Srebnik's singing beautiful, presumably so did they. As there is a sense in which this aesthetic experience takes me uncomfortably close to that of the perpetrators I want to distance myself from, aesthetics blends into ethics. This kind of unwanted attitudinal affinity represents, for me, one of the ethical challenges of watching *Shoah*. Listening to Suchomel's song, I am not struck by the same kind of discomfort. One reason is that I do not find Suchomel's performance of "Wir fahren nach Treblinka" beautiful. Rather, it reminds me of the Nazis' use and abuse of the musical genre of the march—a use anticipated, and in one sense represented, by *Triumph of the Will*. A different, more challenging reason is that the ethical issues I have identified in Lanzmann's lies to the former Treblinka guard inevitably color my viewing of the Suchomel sequences.

As leitmotifs throughout Lanzmann's film, the songs performed by Srebnik and Suchomel are contrapuntal, representative of the victim and the perpetrator, respectively; yet, seen from the perspective of narrative ethics, they are in some ways comparable. If I cannot understand Suchomel's motives, attitudes, and actions, nor can I comprehend those of the Nazi guards who listened to the acts of singing performed by Srebnik. Yet it does not follow from my incomprehension, which signals my inability to interpret this aspect of *Shoah*—that the Nazis had no values. What forcibly strikes me is how different those values are from Srebnik's. This said, I also find it difficult to understand how he could find the strength not only to sing for those he knew would execute him but also to return with Lanzmann to the place of execution, singing the same song again. The importance of song as a leitmotif is further accentuated by the Czech national anthem and the *Hatikvah* that the Czech Jews start to sing in the undressing room of crematorium 2 at Birkenau—a sudden outburst of singing that moves Müller so strongly that, when he recalls the episode, he asks Lanzmann to stop the interview. The song is not just a brave act of defiance; it is also a manifestation of Czech and Jewish identity. This manifestation is narrative, and so is Müller's memory of it: the narrative of his testimony becomes particularly forceful and convincing just at the point where it threatens to break down. So does Bomba's, and so does Srebnik's testimony when, 40 years after the Nazis murdered him, he stands at the threshold of Chełmno.

I conclude this chapter by highlighting two aspects of my interpretation of *Shoah*: distance and silence. As I hope to have shown, each of these words condenses into a concept constituent elements of the film's narrative presentation of Holocaust memory. As this presentation is an ethical project, the two concepts also signal an important dimension of *Shoah*'s narrative ethics. As regards distance from the Holocaust, I have found that while I need to distinguish between spatial and temporal distance, both influence the acts of memory in which Lanzmann's interviewees are engaged. If the combination of temporal and spatial distance may have enabled Srebnik to go on living after the war, it may also have given him the strength he needed to return with Lanzmann to Chełmno. In one sense, his memory of the mass murder that he miraculously survived seems not to have changed; in a different yet related sense, it inevitably has since many years have passed and his camp experience deviates sharply from his postwar experiences. While it is unsurprising that his values are as opposed to those of Nazism on his return to Chełmno as they were when he was a prisoner in the camp 40 years earlier, it is surprising, even shocking that Suchomel's values do not seem to have changed. Why does not the former guard at Treblinka distance himself from the values that underlay and motivated the murder of six million Jews? For me, this is one of the most challenging questions engendered by *Shoah*'s narrative discourse. Could part of the reason be a kind of stubbornness, a reluctance to admit that what he did was wrong—and that he was on the wrong side of history? Or, even more chillingly, does Suchomel still think that what he did was right? His temporal and spatial distance from the Holocaust does not seem to have changed his attitude to and endorsement of the crime to which he contributed. And what about Grassler: how, or to what extent, has his attitude to the Nazis' mass murder of Jews changed? His insistence that "[t]he bad times are repressed" makes it difficult to know.

For Srebnik as for Suchomel and Grassler, as well as for the other victims, perpetrators, and bystanders interviewed by Lanzmann, the combination of temporal and spatial distance is fused with their attitudinal distance from the Holocaust. As I have attempted to show, this aspect of distance is primarily ethical. This observation also applies to Lanzmann, whose "hallucinatory reincarnation of the past in details of the present without appeal to archives . . . [indicates an] absolute, noncomprehending distance from the perpetrator" (LaCapra, 2007, p. 219). While this distance is an integral and significant part of Lanzmann's narrative ethics, I conclude that it also partly explains the strategies that, as the film's director, he employs to make his interviewees speak.[13] Even though, seen from my perspective, the objective is laudable, I find that his methods can be ethically dubious. This criticism applies to his interviews with both perpetrators and victims: he lies to Suchomel to make him talk, and he exerts an almost unbearable psychological pressure on Bomba during the long pause. On the other hand, had these scenes not been part of *Shoah*, the film's power and quality, including its ethical quality, would have been poorer. Neither temporal nor spatial distance is absolute—distance is variable, and it is related to variants of empathy and identification. One remarkable feature of Lanzmann's work as a director is the great contrast—a contrast that I interpret as insurmountable and uncompromising—between his distance from the perpetrator and his empathy with the victim. I want to add, though, that this point applies more directly to Lanzmann as interviewer than to the film as narrative discourse and aesthetic form. The discourse of *Shoah* invites, even urges me to link Lanzmann's comments and attitudes as an actor in his own film to my interpretation of the film as a complex communicative system of visual and auditive signs. It is to Lanzmann's credit that he allows me, as a viewer, to do this; for example, my doubts about the pressure he exerts on Bomba are in no small part generated by my reading of Bomba's facial expression during his period of silence.

But what about my own distance from the subject of *Shoah*? While my temporal and spatial distance from the Holocaust is, as already indicated, considerable, so is my attitudinal distance from the Nazi ideology that made the Holocaust possible. Thus, there is a sense in which my own distance from the subject of the film is similar to that of its director. However, the temporal distance between the Holocaust and me is considerably greater than it was for Lanzmann, who was active in the French Resistance during the war. As *Shoah* is Lanzmann's response to and interpretation of the Holocaust from the temporal vantage point of the mid-1980s, the film illustrates, and thus supports, one of the tenets of narrative hermeneutics: that narrative is "not only an *object* of interpretation: narrative itself is *a mode of interpretation*" (Meretoja, 2018a, p. 44, original emphasis; cf. Meretoja and Freeman, 2023). While Lanzmann's *Shoah* is his mode of interpreting the Holocaust, my mode of interpreting his film narrative is necessarily different from his. One reason is the temporal distance between the Second World War and the third decade of the 21st century. This temporal distance presents me with an interpretive challenge; as I did not experience the war, there is a lot I do not know. Yet I have found that, as Gadamer (1960/2013) suggests, there is a sense in which this distance is an interpretive resource rather than a weakness, not least because it furthers my understanding of how little I understand and, as a corollary, how much I have to learn. In addition to the greater temporal distance from the mass murder, my attitudinal distance from those involved in the Holocaust is also different from Lanzmann's: I am probably more inclined than he would have been to admit that, had I been one of the Polish bystanders he interviews, I might also have been reluctant to admit that I could and should have done more to save the Jews who were murdered in my neighborhood. Inevitably, my interpretation of Lanzmann's interview with the Poles who remember the mass murders at Chełmno makes me think of the people standing on Vippetangen quay in Oslo on November 26, 1942, watching the *Donau* leaving Norway with 532 Jews on board.

Although I know that the people in a photograph cannot speak, I am struck by what I interpret as the silence of the group standing on Vippetangen quay. I associate their silence with that of the Jews aboard the *Donau*, and I also relate it to the many silences in *Shoah*. As Fred Camper has observed, Lanzmann "has infused image-making with a renewed ethical dimension, with a deep respect for his seen and unseen subjects" (2007, p. 109). A key element of *Shoah*'s narrative ethics, silence assumes different forms; moreover, the segments of silence are colored by what comes before and after, as well as by the film's elaborate patterns of repetition. The silences become meaningful because of the way they are framed in and by the film narrative. In his *Theory of Film*, Kracauer notes that "film not only records physical reality but reveals otherwise hidden provinces of it" (1965, p. 158). Through its silence, *Shoah* "reveals otherwise hidden provinces" of the Holocaust.

I have identified and briefly discussed some of the film's silences, including that of Bomba when he is struggling with his traumatic memories. For different reasons, the perpetrators are reluctant to speak, and so are the Polish bystanders. Just as significant are the many film segments in which as viewer I hear nothing, not even noise. In these segments, film's visual and spatial dimensions are accentuated. Yet the silence is not neutral: the segments of silence are self-interpretive elements related to and integrated into Lanzmann's project of remembering and honoring the dead. The silence that accompanies the camera's panning movements across the sites of Chełmno and Treblinka are key aspects of this project. Halting the narrative, the silence contributes to the formation as well as the problematization of that narrative. In my interpretation of *Shoah*, the silences are—or rather, become—empty spaces that, representing the dead, make me recall a colossal crime that I cannot comprehend yet realize that I should not allow myself to forget.

Notes

1. "*Un pur chef-d'œuvre*" (Beauvoir, 2001, p. 14, original emphasis).
2. "*Il n'est pas facile de parler de* Shoah" (Beauvoir, 2001, p. 9, original emphasis).
3. *Shoah* has attracted considerable critical attention. The following books and essays have proved particularly relevant to and helpful for the discussion presented in this chapter: Adams &Vice (2015), Camper (2007), Didi-Huberman (2007), Felman and Laub (1992), LaCapra (2007), Liebman (2007a), McGlothlin (2021), Rothberg (2000), Spitzer (2004), Vice (2011), Walker (2005).
4. This observation also applies to the discussions of film narrative in chapters 2 and 5.
5. "*Et je leur donnerai un nom impérissable. Isaïe, 56, V.*" (Lanzmann, 2001, p. 19, original emphasis).
6. In Hebrew, שֵׁם עוֹלָם אֶתֶּן־לוֹ. As the Hebrew Bible scholar Magnar Kartveit has informed me, an older text from the Dead Sea Scrolls uses *lhmh*, "to them," and the Old Greek, Latin, Syriac, and Aramaic translations all render the word as "to them." It is supposed that *lo*, "to him/it," is an error for the older word *lamo*, "to them," which would explain the later Masoretic version. The literal translation would then be "An eternal name I will give them." Hebrew has a word, "ani" אני, that corresponds to the French pronoun "je" or the English "I"; it is just absent in this sentence—made unnecessary because of the first-person singular verb form. As both verbs of the Hebrew clauses in the verse are first-person singular, there is no noun since the first-person singular makes it clear that the subject is "I." Verses 1 and 4 of chapter 56 unambiguously indicate that the speaking I is the Lord, not the prophet. In the event that Lanzmann also links the "I" to himself as creator of *Shoah*, a Jewish viewer might consider that association a kind of transformation of the metaphorical dimension of memory and name suggested by the relevant part of Isaiah 56:5 to the concrete manifestation of a film.
7. According to the *Holocaust Encyclopedia*, four of the Jewish prisoners at Chełmno survived the war: https://encyclopedia.ushmm.org/content/en/article/chelmno
8. These dissymmetrical power relations changed during the period in which the events that we call the Holocaust occurred; the spatial and temporal aspects of the Holocaust are intertwined. As Tim Cole notes in *Holocaust Landscapes*, there are many "Holocaust landscapes that cover the years 1938 through to 1945" (2016, p. 5).
9. Specifying and anchoring the novel's action in historical places in Central and Eastern Europe, spatial coordinates play a key role in Jenny Erpenbeck's *The End of Days* (see chapter 7).
10. Didi-Huberman argues that Lanzmann wanted Srebnik to do "only one thing, but it was something radical: Srebnik was not to *tell* his story, but would rather *revisit* it" (2007, p. 117, original emphasis). While this was probably part of Lanzmann's intention, it is important to note that the comments Srebnik makes constitute narrative fragments that are related to and to some

extent anticipate those of other Holocaust survivors who speak in the film. An example is Srebnik's identification of the site of Chełmno: "Yes, this is the place."

11. See Lanzmann (1995, p. 93). "Geheime Reichssache": "operation" is a euphemism, as is "the load." Both are repeated in the document that Lanzmann includes in the film.

12. This comment by Hilberg as a historian supports an important point that Ricoeur makes in *Time and Narrative 3* and in *Oneself as Another*. The historian, notes Ricoeur, "brings back to life ways of evaluating which continue to belong to our deepest humanity. In this, history is reminded of its indebtedness to people of the past. And in certain circumstances—in particular when the historian is confronted with the horrible, the extreme figure of the history of victims—the relation of debt is transformed into the duty never to forget" (1990/1994; p. 164; see Ricoeur, 1988). See also Fulbrook (2023), Hilberg (1996), Suleiman (2006).

13. Although, as my discussion shows, I share LaCapra's criticism of some of the film's techniques, I dissent from his assertion that Lanzmann lacks analytical distance from the human subjects he interviews. Janet Walker is right to observe that "Michael Rothberg and Joshua Hirsch are much more cognizant than is LaCapra of *Shoah*'s use of distancing strategies and are therefore much more sympathetic and indebted to Felman's delineation of *Shoah*'s representational limits" (2005, p. 132).

4
Jonathan Littell's *Les Bienveillantes*
(*The Kindly Ones*)

As I hope to have shown in the preceding chapter, a striking aesthetic and ethical feature of *Shoah* is the way in which Lanzmann refrains from making use of archival film footage and instead relies solely and consistently on the presentation of oral witness accounts of the Holocaust. Assuming the form of fragmented, incomplete testimonies, these accounts, spoken by the witnesses and addressed to Lanzmann as interviewer and listener, illustrate a problem of Holocaust narrative: even though (for reasons that may be very different) both victims and bystanders have found it difficult to talk about and publish accounts of their Holocaust experiences, surviving perpetrators have tended not to do so at all. This kind of denial is not difficult to understand since, for a perpetrator of the Holocaust, narration would entail the risk of a trial and a long prison sentence. Yet the relative absence of Holocaust narratives written and published by perpetrators means that we have limited access to narratives that could have told us something important about the perpetrator's motives for participating in the Holocaust and thus about the ideas, attitudes, and values that made the mass murder of six million European Jews possible. Moreover, such narratives might also have incorporated perpetrators' reflections on their involvement in the Holocaust from the temporal vantage point of, say, 2006.[1]

The author of a novel published that year, approximately 60 years after the end of the Second World War, makes use of a first-person narrator who tells the reader about his activity as a former Nazi officer. The French American writer Jonathan Littell's *Les Bienveillantes* (2006/2021), published in English as *The Kindly Ones* in 2009, possesses elements pertaining to all three issues briefly identified above: a former Nazi officer reports on his activities as a perpetrator, discusses the motivations that lay behind his participation in the Holocaust, and reflects on the Holocaust from the perspective of the present day. The fact that this narrative is fictional makes it radically different from firsthand, documentary testimony. I highlight two of these differences. First,

Memory and Narrative Ethics. Jakob Lothe, Oxford University Press. © Oxford University Press (2025).
DOI: 10.1093/9780197579534.003.0005

Littell's novel needs to be distinguished from a Holocaust narrative such as Imre Kertész's *Fatelessness* (1975/2004): although the latter book is often referred to as a novel because of its literary devices and techniques (such as irony and a narrator who does not unproblematically represent Kertész), its ethics and aesthetics are inseparable from the fact that, as historical author and, arguably, also as the implied author, Kertész is an Auschwitz survivor (see Miller, 2011). Second, as a fictional narrative *Les Bienveillantes* is also very different from the relatively few testimonies of Nazi perpetrators that we actually have. In the chapter on *Shoah*, I discussed the example of Franz Suchomel, the former guard at the Treblinka concentration camp who was interviewed by Lanzmann and whose rendering of the song about Treblinka suggests that he experienced no regret but rather a sense of pride or achievement. And yet Lanzmann was forced to (or chose to) lie to Suchomel to make him speak.

The Treblinka guard's defensive attitude, and the fact that there is clearly a lot he does not want to tell Lanzmann, indirectly yet forcibly suggest how fictional accounts can prove to be a great resource in Holocaust narrative. Extending the range of such narratives by enabling and even requiring perpetrators to speak, Littell presents the reader with an extended, detailed account that, though not necessarily frank or reliable, containing omissions and, conversely, psychotic sequences, gives a rich psychological portrait of the protagonist Maximilian Aue—his perspective, actions, dreams, desires, and values. If the issue of ethics looms large in Holocaust narrative, in *Les Bienveillantes* ethical issues are raised on virtually every page, prompting questions such as: What kind of moral authority is represented by and extractable from a fictional narrative whose one and only narrator is an unrepentant Nazi perpetrator? How can the text's moral authority be established in and through a variant of first-person narration that is clearly biased and ethically unreliable? How do I as a reader meet the challenge of identifying, responding to, and reflecting on the ethics of this kind of fictional narrative?

Discussing these issues, this chapter will show how *Les Bienveillantes* illustrates fiction's capacity to identify and explore ethical issues by making them part of and inseparable from the dynamics of telling and reading narratives. Linking Aue's ethics to the ethics of other characters whom he encounters over the course of his narrative, I also relate Aue's ethics to Littell's ethics as implied author. Concentrating on the ethical dimension of reading and interpreting *Les Bienveillantes*, I argue that variants of memory play a key role not only in the formation of Aue's narrative ethics but also in my interpretation of his first-person account. After commenting on three passages from the novel's prologue, titled "Toccata," I discuss Aue's account of eight of his killings. I hasten to add that he is responsible for more than eight killings, yet I posit that the way in which the reader is invited by the implied author to understand these eight is disconcerting and thought-provoking. I then proceed to discuss Aue's involvement in the industrial Holocaust, including his visits to and activities in Auschwitz.[2] While both these parts of the chapter deal with aspects of memory and narrative—there is a strong sense in which Aue's narration is constituted by his memories—the final part addresses the issue of memory more explicitly, focusing on the links between Aue's memories, dreams, and hallucinations and discussing the narrative ethics of these dimensions of his narrative.

Narrative Authority and Reliability

Before turning to "Toccata" I relate the concept of ethics to those of narrative authority and reliability. As regards ethics in literature, two characteristic features apply directly to the critical concerns of this chapter. First, the ethics of a fictional text tends not to assume the form of a fixed, identifiable ethical view, position, or message (Altes, 2014; Meretoja, 2018a). Rather, in narrative fiction ethical issues are typically presented as questions linked to the characters' actions, motives for those actions, and situations of choice involving an ethical component. Second, the ethics of a narrative text such as *The Kindly Ones* is not limited to what the characters do or omit to do, because the telling and the reading of the text also have ethical aspects. Thus, I consider not only the ethics of the told but, primarily, the ethics of telling and the ethics of reading (Phelan, 2017; cf. Lothe, 2013b). Generated by narrative form, these ethical aspects are dynamic and evolving, and their narrative presentation is complemented by the reader's process of interpretation. As Leona Toker has observed, the ethics of narrative form need not entail an expectation that a literary work should have a clear moral message; instead, "aesthetic experience has an intrinsic ethical effect, irrespective of the presence or absence of 'message'" (2010, p. 3; see also Meretoja, 2018a; Toker, 2012). Narrative agents that contribute to this "intrinsic ethical effect" in a work of fiction are the character, the narrator, the implied author, and the reader. In first-person narratives such as this one by Littell, the roles of character and narrator are obviously related, yet although a character's ethos will color his or her narration, the two functions are not identical. One reason I need to distinguish between the roles of narrator and character is that, as my interpretation will show, a first-person narrator's narrative authority may be greater than his or her ethos may lead the reader to assume. One factor contributing to this kind of discrepancy is the question of whether the first-person narrator is or is not reliable.

At the beginning of *The Rhetoric of Fiction*, Wayne C. Booth uses the following example to illustrate narrative authority: "There was a man in the land of Uz, whose name was Job; and that man was perfect and upright, one that feared God, and eschewed evil" (Job 1:1). Booth comments, "With one stroke the unknown author has given us a kind of information never obtained about real people, even about our most intimate friends" (1983, p. 3). Moreover, after Satan's temptation of God and Job's first losses, I read, "In all this Job sinned not, nor charged God foolishly" (Job 1:22). "How," asks Booth rhetorically, "do we know that Job sinned not? Who is to pronounce on such a question? Only God himself could know with certainty whether Job charged God foolishly. Yet the author pronounces judgment, and we accept his judgment without question" (1983, p. 4).

Booth rightly notes that this kind of "artificial authority" (1983, p. 4) has been a constituent element of most narratives until recent times. Extending Booth's point, I would argue that it still is. Even though, in complex contemporary novels such as *Les Bienveillantes*, narrative authority is challenged and questioned in various ways, that kind of complication does not in itself make the issue of narrative authority less important. What it does, though, is to relate it even more closely to ethical questions. As I will show, the authority of Littell in his novel has ethical significance according to the uses to which it is put by the narrator.

The issue of authority is associated with that of reliability. As a reader I conventionally tend to consider the narrator reliable unless or until I encounter textual signals that make me distrust him or her. The defining features of reliability also tend to turn on ethical aspects coupled with the narrator's views, judgments, choices, priorities, and acts of telling; if as a reader I dissent from these, I am inclined to regard the narrator as unreliable (Shen, 2011a). That narrative authority and reliability are linked, however, does not mean that they are identical. One notable difference is that while narrative reliability is primarily associated with and limited to the narrator, narrative authority is an aspect not only of the narrator but also of the implied author. In narrative texts with a knowledgeable, reliable third-person narrator, the narrator's authority can approximate to that of the implied author; even some character narrators can be presented as fully authoritative about some matters (Lanser, 1992).[3]

For the reader of *Les Bienveillantes*, it becomes essential to form an idea of an implied author whose authority can represent an ethical alternative to that of Aue as character and narrator. This is no easy task, however, for Aue's voice and perspective have an authority that, though deeply flawed, is still provocatively insistent, not least since he claims the authority of an eye-witness who is closer to the events than the implied reader or the historical reader. *Les Bienveillantes* begins thus:

> Oh my human brothers, let me tell you how it happened. I am not your brother, you'll retort, and I don't want to know. And it certainly is true that this is a bleak story, but an edifying one too, a real morality play, I assure you. You might find it a bit long—a lot of things happened, after all—but perhaps you're not in too much of a hurry; with a little luck you'll have some time to spare. And also, this concerns you: you'll see that this concerns you.[4]

As we can see, issues of narrative and narrative ethics force themselves on the reader right from the beginning of the narrative discourse. The story is bleak indeed—it is a story about the narrator and main character's participation in the Second World War and the Holocaust. This first-person narrator—whose name is Maximilien Aue and whom, because this is a work of fiction, Littell can take to a series of locations where Aue is involved in decisive events—is the reader's only source of information. As a young German Aue joins the SS, and his work for Himmler and Eichmann earns him a series of promotions; finally, when the Third Reich collapses in May 1945, he kills his protector Thomas. In common with Aue, Thomas Hauser is a highly educated SS officer. Tending to appear wherever he is posted and whenever Aue needs him, Thomas saves Aue's life several times. After killing Thomas, Aue steals his friend's false ID papers and flees to France, where, at the time of narration, he is the director of a factory and has the time to write his memoirs.

This plot summary is based on knowledge of the whole novel, and it is not just selective but also interpretive. Although there is a lot I do not know about Aue when I start reading, as a first-person narrator he assumes, or at least suspects, that as a reader I am likely to regard him as a Nazi perpetrator.

This is probably why he addresses me at once, thus making it more difficult for me to distance myself from him. Seen in this light, the phrase "concerns you," repeated by the narrator and thus singled out as important, takes on a double meaning: not only is Aue going to tell me about the Second World War and the Holocaust, a series of events that ought to "concern" any reader; he is also going to show, or attempt to show, that as a reader I am not as innocent or ethically superior as I may be inclined to think. One meaning of "concerns you" is "this is of interest to you"; the other meaning is "this is about you."[5]

This passage provides an early example of the series of challenges facing the reader of *Les Bienveillantes*: on the one hand, we increasingly feel a strong need to distance ourselves from a narrator and character who turns out to be a murderer; on the other hand, we cannot be sure that, if forced to live under similarly difficult and challenging circumstances, we would have remained ethically unscathed. Consider this passage:

> Once again, let us be clear: I am not trying to say I am not guilty of this or that. I am guilty, you're not, fine. But you should be able to admit to yourselves that you might also have done what I did. . . . If you were born in a country or at a time not only when nobody comes to kill your wife and your children, but also nobody comes to ask you to kill the wives and children of others, then render thanks to God and go in peace. But always keep this thought in mind: you might be luckier than I, but you're not a better person. (p. 20)[6]

Aue is challenging the reader here; rereading the novel, I certainly think I am a better person than he is. What I want to stress is the way in which the implied author uses Aue's accusation to highlight a broader ethical issue. Aue knows that no reader of his narrative can be absolutely sure that he or she would not have committed ethically dubious or even inexcusable acts if subjected, as he was, to the pressures of totalitarianism, war, and the struggle to survive on the Eastern Front. At the same time, Aue also knows that most readers are not killers, as he is; thus there is a double effect of the passage as it also serves as a kind of defensive self-justification on his part. On the first reading of this passage, I do not yet know what Aue has actually done; his accusation therefore hits me more strongly on a first than on a second reading. Yet I do not need to reread the novel to sense that the implied author here asks the reader to carefully consider the issue of ethics as he or she continues reading Aue's narrative. Cautioning me to be wary of the narrator's rhetorical powers, the implied author imbues the narrator with those powers; narrative authority and reliability are both reinforced and put in question in the passage. If Aue's purpose is, as he claims, to "pass the time" (p. 5) by writing his memoirs, the implied author's purposes are clearly much more complex and multifaceted, and they include a distinctly ethical dimension. One reason the implied author's purpose is complex is that, in spite of gradually emerging as something of a monster, Aue cannot simply be written off as a "mad" character who is not to be taken seriously. Nor can we simply regard him as an unreliable narrator, for there is a sense in which his brutal honesty and lack of regret make him more, not less, reliable—and even invaluable—as a reporter.

At the same time, the novel's narrative discourse is a pertinent reminder of the potential danger of equating narrative reliability and narrative authority. That Aue is reliable, at least in parts of the narrative, does not necessarily grant him narrative authority, and certainly not moral authority. Nor is his reliability stable; over the course of his narration he not only misreports, misinterprets, and misevaluates, but also underreports, underinterprets, and underevaluates. Illustrating all six types of unreliability identified by Phelan (2005), Aue's narration can thus be both wrong and insufficient. As regards the ethics of *Les Bienveillantes*, however, it is essential that the narrator's account is not just unreliable: if it were, I would take Aue less seriously as a narrator and as a character, his narrative authority would be impaired, and the ethical challenge of reading and reflecting on the novel would be considerably reduced. One important function of "Toccata" is to grant Aue a combination of narrative authority and reliability that the reader can question as his narration gradually unfolds. Furthering our involvement as readers, the combination is part of a narrative strategy that complicates yet also necessitates the reader's task of constructing an ethics sufficiently different from Aue's to meet the challenge of reading his version—and possibly even to enable the reader to finish the novel.

Perhaps the most successful way in which the implied author establishes Aue's authority in "Toccata" is by making him an apparently reliable recorder of historical facts:

Finally, the highly respected professor Raul Hilberg, a specialist in the matter and one who can hardly be suspected of holding a partisan stance, at least not in favour of the Germans, reaches, after a dense, nineteen-page

demonstration, a final count of 5,100,000, which more or less corresponds
to the opinion of the late Obersturmbannführer Eichmann. So let's settle
for Professor Hilberg's figure, which gives us, to summarize:

Soviet dead .... 20 million
German dead .... 3 million
Subtotal (for the Eastern front) ... 23 million
Endlösung .... 5.1 million (p. 15)[7]

There is no reason not to believe these figures. The war on the Eastern Front
was the most brutal conflict in human history, and historians also see it
as a precondition for the Holocaust. Thus, Aue seems to be reliable here,
and his narrative authority appears strengthened. Littell carried out thorough historical research before writing his novel, and I agree with Susan
Suleiman (2012) that one distinctive feature of the work is the accuracy
of the historical references to the Second World War and the Holocaust.
At the same time, this passage illustrates how Littell can distance himself
from his narrator, thus subjecting him (Aue as first-person narrator and
main character) to variants of irony. For Aue, the incredibly large number
of killed soldiers and civilians somehow does not seem related to his own
involvement in the events of the war. This failure, or refusal, to recognize
his own contribution as an SS officer becomes particularly conspicuous for
the reader who knows something about the two historical persons to whom
Aue refers to support his claim. Eichmann was one of the main architects of
the Holocaust, and later in the novel Aue meets with Eichmann and works
for him. Conversely, the "highly respected professor Raul Hilberg" was a
leading Holocaust scholar whose participation in and significant contribution to Lanzmann's *Shoah* I discussed in Chapter 3. The opening paragraph
of this chapter has already alluded to the three words constituting the title of
Hilberg's second book, his 1992 study, *Perpetrators Victims Bystanders*.[8] This
title is ironically related to Aue—who repeatedly claims to be a bystander
and in some ways even a victim but, as gradually becomes obvious, is
unambiguously a representative of the category of perpetrators.

Aue's Killings

In the novel's fictional universe Aue as protagonist kills other characters
for various reasons and in different ways; cumulatively, the killings reveal

constituent aspects of his ethos. The first killings are a result of Aue's active participation in "the *Grosse Aktion* [that] began on Monday, September 29," in which the Nazis shot several thousand Jews, dumping them into the Babi Yar ravine near Kiev:

> I was petrified, I didn't know what to do. Grafhorst came over and shook me by the arm: "Obersturmführer!" He pointed his gun at the bodies. "Try to finish off the wounded." I took out my pistol and headed for a group: a very young man was sobbing in pain, I aimed my gun at his head and squeezed the trigger, but it didn't go off, I had forgotten to lift the safety catch, I lifted it and shot him in the forehead, he twitched and was suddenly still. To reach some of the wounded, you had to walk over bodies, it was terribly slippery, the limp white flesh rolled under my boots, bones snapped treacherously and made me stumble, I sank up to my ankles in mud and blood. (p. 128)[9]

The most striking aspect of the narration of this horrible scene is perhaps Aue's brutal frankness: not only does he state that he killed a wounded, defenseless man, but he also admits that he was "petrified" and forgot to lift his gun's safety catch. In a way, or up to a point, this kind of frankness strengthens Aue's reliability as a narrator, and in one sense it also supports his narrative authority. The concept of "restricted narration" is helpful here: "[T]he implied author limits the character narrator's function primarily to reliable reporting and uses both the reliability and the restriction to convey interpretations or evaluations that the character narrator remains unaware of" (Phelan, 2017, p. 219).[10] The ethos of Aue's character revealed in this passage comes as a shock to the reader. Assuming the form of a moral reaction, this shocking effect is created not only by the appalling act of killing a wounded man but, equally forcibly, by the following reference to the "slippery" bodies he "had to walk over." If "slippery" reveals a kind of self-centeredness that, under these circumstances, most readers will find disgusting, "had to" suggests that the act of killing was an order he was forced to execute. While in this scene the narrator's reliability in exposing the brutality of his action would appear to strengthen his narrative authority, it reduces his moral authority by revealing his self-centered concern with the problem of walking on the dead bodies.

This effect is further strengthened by Aue's detailed account of a second killing at a later stage of the massacre:

Nearby, another group was being brought up: my gaze met that of a beautiful young woman, almost naked but very elegant, calm, her eyes full of an immense sadness. I moved away. When I came back she was still alive.... I was a rag doll and didn't feel anything, and at the same time I wanted with all my heart to bend over and brush the dirt and sweat off her forehead, caress her cheek and tell her that it was going to be all right, that everything would be fine, but instead I convulsively shot a bullet into her head... since at the thought of this senseless human waste I was filled with an immense, boundless rage, I kept shooting at her and her head exploded like a fruit, then my arm detached itself from me and went off all by itself down the ravine, shooting left and right, I ran after it, waiving at it to wait with my other arm, but it didn't want to, it mocked me and shot at the wounded all by itself, without me; finally, out of breath, I stopped and started to cry. (pp. 129–130)[11]

Rereading this passage, I find it difficult to interpret. If, as Aue indicates, he returns to the Jewish woman because she is beautiful, calm, and sad, why then does he shoot her? If he kills her because of a "boundless rage," where does this rage come from? And finally, how can I interpret his account—which is a variant of narrative memory—of how his arm detached itself from his body, "shooting left and right" and perhaps killing many more Jews? These are ethical questions to which there are no easy answers. By making Aue claim that his arm "detached itself" Littell introduces an unrealistic element of narration that on one level reduces Aue's narrative reliability. Yet at a different level it strengthens his reliability since his claim that his arm detached itself reveals the narrative challenge he encounters as he tries to remember and tell the reader about his involvement in the massacre. Afterward he reflects, "Even the insane butcheries of the Great War, which our fathers or some of our older officers had lived through, seemed almost clean and righteous compared to what we had brought into the world" (pp. 130–131). It is revealing that, in the sentence that follows this indirect yet clear reference to the Holocaust, Aue does not apologize for his crime. Instead, he just adds the sentence "I found this extraordinary" (p. 131).[12] What does he find "extraordinary"? The mass murder of six million Jews, his own contribution as a perpetrator, or his attempt to distance himself from his killings?

One strong indication of Aue's narrative authority here is that of maintaining accuracy of reference. Although Aue is a fictional narrator, much of the information he provides about the historical narrative of the war between Nazi Germany and the Soviet Union is correct. In particular, this scene is a representation of the massacre at Babi Yar on September 29–30, 1941, when 33,771 Jews were killed in a single operation. In making Aue tell us about this historical event the way he does as a fictional narrator, Littell furthers our ethical involvement in the narrative by relating it to one of the most notorious events of the Holocaust. The link is gradually strengthened as Aue's narrative progresses.

This observation also applies partly to what is perhaps Aue's next killing, but here the situation is different since the implied author takes advantage of the possibility granted by fiction to construct a dialogue between Aue and an old *Bergjude* (a Jew from the mountains) for whom he apparently has great respect—and whom he then kills. The Jew, whose name is Nahum ben Ibrahim and who is "a tall old man with a long white beard, still visibly vigorous," addresses Aue "in strangely accented but understandable classical Greek: 'You are an educated man, I see. You must know Greek'" (p. 278).[13] As Aue actually does, the two characters, bizarrely, conduct a conversation in classical Greek on the slopes of the Caucasian mountains. After the conversation, which shows the Jew to be a learned and wise man, Aue orders his assistant to dig a grave and then shoot Ibrahim. As Ibrahim remains calm, smiling, it seems to Aue that he almost wishes to be killed, thus challenging power relations and demonstrating that his ethos is superior to Aue's. Leaning over the grave where Ibrahim lies at the bottom, Aue notices that he is "still smiling a little into his blood-splattered beard; his open eyes, turned toward the wall of earth, were also laughing. I was trembling" (p. 284).[14] Significantly, the victim here emerges as stronger than the perpetrator. Does Ibrahim represent or emerge as a human manifestation of a facet of Emmanuel Levinas's idea of "the Other"? Colin Davis explains that, for Levinas, "the Other remains inviolate and inviolable. The face appears in my world but does not belong to it; I can do it no harm. . . . I may succeed in killing the other, or even innumerable others, but the Other survives. Violence, then, always ends or continues in failure" (Davis, 2007b, p. 51; cf. Levinas, 1961/1969).[15] Aue's reaction may suggest a partial recognition of this curious reversal of power relations. While his ethos is presented as inferior to Ibrahim's, the admission that he "is trembling" humanizes Aue somewhat, thus connecting the ethics of the told closely to the ethics of the telling and making both dimensions even more chilling.

The reader's interpretation of this scene, as painful to read as that of the massacre in the ravine, is aided by a conversation that Aue then has with a linguist, "Leutenant Dr. Voss, who despite his youth is a reputed authority in scientific circles in Germany" (p. 298).[16] After Aue has commented, "We know that racially inferior groups exist, including the Jews,"

> Voss gazed at his coffee with a bitter, sad look. "Doktor Aue. I have always thought of you as an intelligent, sensible man. Even if everything you're telling me is true, explain to me, if you please, what you mean by 'race.' Because for me, that's a concept that is scientifically indefinable and hence without any theoretical value."—"But race exists, that's a fact, our best researchers are studying it and writing about it." . . . Voss suddenly exploded: "They are clowns. They have no competition in serious countries because their discipline doesn't exist and isn't taught there. If it weren't for politics, none of them would have a job or be published!" (p. 300)[17]

As the view on race offered by Voss is much closer to the reader's understanding of this problematic concept than to Aue's, my appropriation of Voss's position strengthens my skepticism about Aue's—and this time not only about his ethos but also about his reliability as first-person narrator. To put this another way, Aue reliably rehearses the view of race held by Nazi Germany's racial anthropologists, but, as Voss points out, these views are unreliable and unscientific.[18] By presenting the conversation between Aue and Voss after Aue's killing of Ibrahim, Voss's authoritative comments expose the murder as an inexcusable act of violence, even though Aue formats it as acceding to the old man's wish. What is curious about Aue's response to Voss as well as to the old Jew is the combination of disagreement with their views and a noticeable respect for them. This respect partly explains why, apparently quite accurately and in some detail, he relays the comments and mini lectures by Ibrahim and Voss to the reader. Is he perhaps more strongly drawn to, persuaded by, and even, subconsciously, worried by their arguments than he is able to admit?

Even though the reader may assume that Aue might have edited out parts of his conversations with Ibrahim and Voss, there is a sense in which the alternative ethical positions represented by them strengthen Aue's reliability but not his authority: by presenting the reader with their views (such as Voss's on "race"), Aue inadvertently makes it possible for us as readers to link our ethics to theirs rather than to his. Aue's recording of the conversations reveals that, in contrast to the implied author, he is unaware of their views' effects. Thus, Aue's narrative rendering of the conversations, and of his act of killing Ibrahim, become constituent elements of the ethics which the reader needs to construct—that is, an ethics that is distinctly different from Aue's yet wholly dependent on his first-person narration.

That said, aspects of unreliability infiltrate Aue's narration. In addition to the variant of scientific unreliability and flawed authority suggested by Voss's criticism of the Nazis' (including Aue's) view on "race," Aue's conversation with the old Jew Ibrahim reveals an instance of underreporting. After having told him that his name is Ibrahim, the Jew asks Aue what his name is:

> "My name is Maximilien. I come from Germany."—"And who was your father?" I smiled: "Why does my father interest you, old man?"—"How am I supposed to know who I'm talking to if I don't know who your father is?" His Greek, I heard now, contained unusual turns of phrase, but I managed to understand it. I told him my father's name and he seemed satisfied. (p. 279)[19]

By smiling and asking a question in return Aue tries to suppress his honest response to Ibrahim's question about his father. For Ibrahim here touches a nerve: on a second reading of the novel, I know that Aue's relationship with this father is fraught, and I also suspect that there is a connection, albeit an indirect one, between the absence of his father and the killing of his mother. This connection may partly explain the rage he feels when, much later in his narrative, he is looking at a photograph of his father without being able to recognize him (pp. 805–806).

Condensed into a smile, Aue's underreporting in this passage links up with his conversation with his mother at his family home in Antibes—a conversation that takes place just before she is killed. When his mother asks him, "What did you come here for?," Aue replies, "I wanted to see you, that's all" (p. 520).[20] Considered in isolation, this comment would seem to be a straightforward example of unreliable narration, for although Aue is unable or unwilling to admit that he murdered his mother, the following narration makes it quite clear—though clearer on a second reading than a first—that he is the killer of both her and her partner Moreau. Thus, what he "wanted," it seems, is not to see his mother but to kill her. Interestingly, however, his mother's question prompts not just a reply but a narrative comment that precedes it: "Once again, I felt as if I were shrinking; before this imperious voice, these cold eyes, I was going to pieces, I was becoming a fearful child, smaller than the twins" (p. 520).[21] In contrast to the spoken reply, this narrative comment is not unreliable, or at least is less unreliable, since it seems to reveal fragments of traumatic memories. Yet how accurate are his memories—can "a fearful child" be a killer? The evasiveness of this self-characterization is related to the "horror" (p. 530) he feels when describing the murders: "Oh my God, I said to myself, she's been strangled, someone has strangled my mother. . . . [T]he murderer must first have killed Moreau, then come upstairs. Anguish was suffocating me, I didn't know what to do. . . . Call the police? I didn't have time, I had to catch my bus" (p. 531).[22]

If Aue's account of his killings in the *Grosse Aktion* and his killing of Ibrahim establish a narrative authority that is stronger than his moral authority as a character—or, to put this another way, if the narration of these killings of Jews enables the reader to distance himself or herself morally from Aue as character, Aue's presentation of the killing of his mother makes it much harder to differentiate between what he did and his narrative rendering of what he did. The agency of Aue as character infiltrates narrative agency, making it difficult for the reader to ascertain where the first ends and the second takes over. The use of the passive form in the first sentence of the quotation is revealing.[23] While "anguish" supports his description of himself as "a fearful child," the act of murder confirms his mother's remark that, in spite of his father's "disappearance," "it's me you hate" (p. 521).[24] There is a notable difference here between the ethics of the told (the murder itself) and the ethics of the telling (Aue's inability to identify himself as the murderer). The contrast to the narration of the earlier killings suggests that his role as son is different from that as SS officer. Once established, however, the difference is reduced—largely due to the narrative function of Aue's mother.

Aue's mother plays a key role in this section, for two related reasons. First, since on a second reading we cannot but link the hate she identifies in her son to his murder of her, the mother's moral authority increases as her characterization proves to be correct, and as she has not only (alone, in their father's absence) brought up Aue and Una but now also takes care of the twins, who may be their children. Second, the mother relates her son's hatred of her to the SS uniform he is wearing: "You came in that uniform to tell me how much you hate me" (p. 521).[25] Thus, Littell makes a minor character relate the perverse action of an individual—Aue, her own son—to hatred as a constituent element of the SS and of Nazi ideology. Revealingly, when in *Shoah* Lanzmann asks a Nazi perpetrator (who does not know that he is being filmed) why he supported the persecution of the Jews, the key word in his explanation is *Hass* (hatred). The connection between personal hatred and mass murder is one of the most chilling aspects of the Holocaust, and the distancing effect of its bureaucratic organization is subtly yet effectively hinted at by the use of the passive voice in Aue's narration of the matricide which, obviously, he has committed. Aue's ethics thus blends into that of the SS.

The account of the double murder of his mother and Moreau arouses suspicion not only in the reader; back in Germany the case is investigated by two policemen, Weser and Clemens, who both seem convinced that Aue is the murderer. The subsequent pursuit of Aue reveals a further aspect of the implied author's ethics by contrastively exposing that of Nazi Germany: Aue's first killings constitute no crime because the victims are Jews. Yet the exposure of this contrast is problematized, though not eliminated, in the novel's last section: Aue here reports how, though not why, he kills three more characters, none of whom is Jewish.

The first of his killings in this strange, concluding part of the novel is associated with its title, "Gigue," a baroque dance originating from the English jig and imported into France in the mid-17th century. When, desperately fleeing the Russians, Aue and Thomas come across a brick church from which organ music is coming, Aue enters: "An old man, near the altar, was playing Bach's *Art of the Fugue*, the third contrapunctus, I think" (p. 932).[26] Aue, who is knowledgeable about classical music and considers Bach the greatest of all composers, sits down on a pew and listens. When the old man has finished his piece, Aue notices that he wears

an Oberstleutnant's uniform from the other war, with a cross at his neck. "They can destroy everything," he said to me calmly, "but not this. It is impossible, this will remain forever: it will go on even when I stop playing." . . . The music was magnificent. . . . But instead of pacifying me, this music only fuelled my anger, I found it unbearable. I wasn't thinking about anything, my head was empty of everything except this music and the black pressure of my rage. . . . I took out my pistol and shot him in the head. He collapsed forward onto the keys, opening half the pipes in a desolate, discordant bleat. (p. 932)[27]

Shocked by Aue's cruel act of violence, Thomas snarls, "You've gone completely mad!" (p. 932).[28] Although Thomas, whose comment foreshadows

Aue's last killing in "Gigue," may be right, I am not sure Aue is mad in the sense of being insane, though in the act of killing a German whose playing of Bach represents German values at the oppositive extreme of those of Nazi Germany he does seem deranged. I consider Aue's reference to "the black pressure of my rage" a self-interpretive element that, cautioning the reader against oversimplified interpretations of his killings, links them to his hatred of his mother and Moreau as well as to his obsessive love for his sister, Una. There is also, I suggest, a connection between his killings and a self-hatred that, underlying his memoirs, stirs his narration.

Aue's combined hatred and self-hatred also underlies, though it does not explain, his next killing. Having finally managed to return to Berlin, he meets Mihaï, one of his former lovers. When Mihaï starts flirting with him, Aue is provoked by his smile: "This smug, calculating smile drove me out of my mind" (p. 949).[29] He pushes Mihaï into the public bathroom, locks the door behind them, and strangles him by standing on the handle of a mop that he places across Mihaï's neck: "Mihaï's face beneath me became red, scarlet, then purplish-blue . . . his bulging eyes stared at me with terror, his nails scratched my boots" (p. 949).[30] After dragging Mihaï's body into one of the stalls, he cleans the bathroom's floor and walks to the bar "to get a drink" (p. 950).[31] In this case, Aue does not even try to explain why he killed his former lover. He did so, it seems, because of Mihaï's smile.

Even though Aue's failure to explain, let alone justify, his killings is particularly conspicuous in the case of Mihaï, this failure is a characteristic feature of his narration of all his killings. His next and next-to-last murders may at first seem to be an exception to this pattern: acting in self-defense, Aue kills a policeman who is chasing him. In this case, however, I am less sure how reliable Aue's narration is. The reason the policeman is attempting to arrest Aue is because Aue bit Hitler when he was being decorated by the Führer in his bunker in Berlin: "As the Führer approached me—I was almost at the end of the line—my attention was caught by his nose. . . . His foul, fetid breath overwhelmed me: it was too much to take. So I leaned forward and bit into his bulbous nose, drawing blood. Even today I would be unable to tell you why I did this: I just couldn't restrain myself" (p. 960).[32]

Aue's biting Hitler's nose is the reason he kills the policeman who is chasing him because of this attack on the Führer; these acts are thus closely connected. In the fictional universe created by Littell, Aue can certainly bite into Hitler's "bulbous nose, drawing blood." In this sense, this act is not different from his killings. However, the fictional character Aue here refers to historians' failure to report the incident: "Trevor-Roper, I know, never breathed a word about this episode, nor has Bullock, nor any of the historians who have studied the Führer's last days. Yet it did take place, I assure you" (p. 961).[33]

The reader does not need to know Hugh Trevor-Roper's *The Last Days of Hitler* (1947/2013) or Alan Bullock's *Hitler: A Study in Tyranny* (1952/1991) to be struck by Aue's extraordinary claim: how can he, the first-person narrator and main character of a novel, argue that he acted, and thus contributed to the formation of history, in the real world? The "episode" is an example of a self-interpretive sign that both stirs and complicates interpretation. As Aue is a character devised and designed by the implied author, Littell can make him refer to and engage with fictional characters such as his sister, Una (or indeed Aue himself), as well as historical persons such as Hitler. However, when Littell pulls Hitler into the universe of *Les Bienveillantes* by making Aue attack him, Hitler becomes fictionalized in a way that makes Aue's reference to Trevor-Roper and Bullock strange. Although Aue's killing of the policeman is a direct consequence of his attack on the Führer, it is not his intention to kill Hitler; his act of biting him does not seem to be a genuine, desperate attempt to put an end to the war. Rather, his act appears spontaneous, and the episode has surreal and even comic elements. This makes me wonder whether his references to Trevor-Roper are sincere. Is Aue teasing me as a reader here, and does Littell invite me to read the episode as a comic interlude in a bleak narrative?

At the narrative's end, which coincides with the end of the Third Reich and the Russian occupation of Berlin, one of the police officers, Clemens, is eventually able to point his automatic gun at Aue. However, appearing out of nowhere, Thomas shoots Clemens. As Thomas is examining Clemens's body, Aue notices an iron bar:

> I picked it up, weighed it, then brought it down with all my strength on the nape of Thomas's neck. I heard his vertebrae crack and he toppled over like a log, across Clemens's body. I dropped the bar and contemplated the bodies. (p. 975)

Then, in the novel's last paragraph, he notes, "I was sad but I didn't really know why" (p. 975).[34]

Aue's last killing is thus that of his closest friend, his SS colleague and mentor who has been inestimably helpful to him and who has just saved him by killing the policeman who was going to punish him for the murder of his mother. Stealing French identification papers from the pockets of his dead friend's clothes, Aue is able to flee to France and thus, many years later, write the memoirs that he introduces in "Toccata." That he does not seem to regret even having killed his closest friend and the man who saved his life requires the reader to reevaluate Aue's ethos as apparently that of a callous psychopath. Yet his ethos is more complex than such a diagnosis would seem to indicate. Rather than attempting to identify and isolate character features in order to make them the basis for a character description, I regard Aue's ethos—and, at a different yet related level, the novel's ethics—as at once contributing to and inseparable from the narrative presentation of his values, priorities, dreams, and desires.

Aue's Involvement in the Industrial Holocaust

If one significant part of Aue's narrative ethics is closely associated with and delineated by his account of the killings I have discussed, constituent elements of his ethics are also observable in his rendering of the later stages of the Holocaust. While the *Grosse Aktion* in which he participates is the best-known instance of mass shootings of Jews by *Einsatzgruppen*, it was, as many readers will know, the industrial mass murder by using poison gas that enabled the Nazis to exterminate millions of European Jews. I write "many readers" since not all 21st-century readers of *Les Bienveillantes* will know much about the Holocaust. For these readers, Littell's novel provides important, even necessary representation of the Nazis' colossal crime against humanity. Relating this point to my own experience of reading and rereading *Les Bienveillantes*, I too learn about aspects of the Holocaust previously unknown to me—aspects that are deeply distressing and that inevitably color my interpretation of Littell's fictional narrative.

I will highlight the ethics of Aue's account of the industrial, systematized Holocaust by commenting on his narrative presentation of three characters: Adolf Eichmann, Heinrich Himmler, and Rudolf Höss. That these three characters of a fictional narrative are fictionalized portraits of three of the main architects and executioners of the Holocaust illustrates Littell's narrative strategy of making his fictional narrator and main character meet with historical persons who, although Littell thus makes them integral parts of his narrative fiction, anchor that fiction in historical reality. Moreover, Littell uses the meetings and points of contact between Aue, Eichmann, Himmler, and Höss to demonstrate that although Aue no longer kills Jews by shooting them, as he does in Babi Yar, he still contributes to the Holocaust.

Not long after the Babi Yar sequence, Aue makes a comment that establishes a thought-provoking connection between his acts of killing Jews early in the narrative and his involvement in the mass killings by poison gas (Desbois, 2008). The perpetrators'

> violence, their alcoholism, the nervous depressions, the suicides, my own sadness, all that demonstrated that the *other* exists, exists as an other, as a human, and that no will, no ideology, no amount of stupidity or alcohol can break this bond, tenuous but indestructible. This is a fact, not an opinion. (p. 147, original emphasis)[35]

These reflections are stirred by Aue's acts as a perpetrator in the *Grosse Aktion*. This experience, and perhaps particularly that of killing the young Jewish woman, has left a mark on him. Moreover, his thoughts are fueled by all his killings, including of his non-Jewish victims. Although Littell does not reduce the narrative's focus on the Holocaust, he thus establishes a connection between the acts of Holocaust perpetrators and acts of violence directed against human beings who exist as "an other." While part of the experience surfaces in these reflections, other parts, or aspects, influence and color Aue's dreams.

Although Aue's use of the *other* is different from Levinas's abstract concept, I interpret, as my observation on Aue's reaction to his killing of Ibrahim suggests, his understanding of "an other" as a human manifestation of a facet of Levinas's Other. I also read Aue's observation as a recognition that, since Jews are human beings like himself, there is a bond between perpetrator and victim. Under different circumstances, he could have been a victim instead of a perpetrator. Aue continues by explaining that, because of the "indestructible . . . bond" between those who kill and those who are killed, alternatives to mass shootings are being considered: "As Eichmann had explained to me, new methods were being studied" (p. 147).[36] In this way, Littell establishes a connection with Aue's conversations with Eichmann later in the novel. After having barely survived Stalingrad, Aue is assigned to Reichsführer Himmler's personal staff; one of his new tasks is to write reports on the operations of the growing number of concentration camps in which "new methods" are used. A euphemism for mass murder by poison gas, these "new methods," Eichmann explains to Aue, play a key role in "the current progress of the resolution of the Jewish question, and its future perspectives" (p. 545).[37] Eichmann's own task, he specifies, is transporting Jews from different European locations to the camps: "My responsibility stops when the train leaves—the rest I can't talk about" (p. 561).[38]

Although Aue is a fictional character, and although Eichmann too is an invented character in Littell's novel, it is impossible for me not to associate Aue's description of Eichmann, as well as his narrative rendering of their conversation, with the historical Eichmann, who, having managed to flee to South America after the war, was found by the Israeli intelligence agency Mossad in 1960, taken to Israel, tried, and executed in 1962. Moreover, I also relate Aue's account of their conversation and collaboration to Arendt's (1963) much-discussed characterization of Eichmann as a representative of "the banality of evil." For Arendt, who reported on the Eichmann trial in Jerusalem for *The New Yorker*, Eichmann was a relatively simple-minded bureaucrat who organized the logistical operation of the Holocaust.[39] In Littell's novel, Aue too considers Eichmann a simple-minded, in some ways even childish character obsessed with his own achievements, whether he is playing Brahms string quartets, as he does at a reception in his home to which Aue is invited, or taking as many Jews as possible to Auschwitz. Yet although Aue tries to distance himself from Eichmann, they are both SS officers, and they share a strong belief in Nazi ideology. Talking to Aue at the reception in his house, Eichmann connects aspects of Nazism with Immanuel Kant's philosophy:

> "You have read Kant, I imagine? Right now," he went on, rubbing his lips, "I'm reading his *Critique of Practical Reason*. . . . And I've thought a lot about the question of the Kantian Categorical Imperative, especially. You agree with me, I'm sure, in saying that every honest man must live according to this imperative." I drank a mouthful of wine and agreed. Eichmann continued: "The Imperative, as I understand it, says: The principle of my individual will must always be such that it can become the principle of moral law. By acting, man legislates." (p. 566)[40]

That Littell makes his fictional version of Eichmann ask whether his own work—transporting as many Jews as possible to Auschwitz—accords with Kantian ethics, furthers the ethical dimension of his presentation of Nazi perpetrators, not least by strengthening the bond between Eichmann and

Aue. By making Eichmann wonder whether their work is in agreement with the Kantian imperative, Littell highlights the values of Nazism, particularly the hatred of Jews and the systematic attempt to exterminate them. While Eichmann refers to a friend's argument that "in wartime, by virtue if you like of the state of exception caused by danger, the Kantian Imperative is suspended" (p. 566),[41] Aue goes further:

> "But it's quite simple, I think. We all agree that in a National Socialist State the ultimate foundation of positive law is the will of the Führer. . . . Thus Dr. Frank, in his treatise on constitutional law, extended the definition of the *Führerprinzip* in the following way: *Act in such a way that the Führer, if he knew of your action, would approve of it.* There is no contradiction between that principle and Kant's Imperative. (p. 566, original emphasis)[42]

To claim that Hitler's principles and ideas can be reconciled with Kant's moral imperative is not only philosophically false but ethically outrageous. Hitler would certainly "approve" of Eichmann's act of transporting hundreds of thousands of Jews to the extermination camps. While Eichmann seems to be reassured by Aue's interpretation of Kant's moral imperative, I am not.[43] Nor is Aue's attempt to support his view by referring to Hans Frank, the Nazi judge who as governor general of occupied Poland was responsible for the deportation and murder of Polish Jews, convincing. This reference establishes an important point of contact with his conversation with Lieutenant Voss earlier in the narrative. As already mentioned, when Aue claims that "our best researchers" have shown that "race exists" (p. 300), Voss explodes by calling them "clowns" (p. 300). He would no doubt have placed Frank in the same category. In this way, Littell prolongs and strengthens Voss's contribution to an ethical alternative to Nazism.

A key element of Aue's interpretation of Kant is the "*Volk*, whose collective will is expressed by the Führer who represents it"; thus, he claims, "we serve the *Volk* and must serve it as the Führer serves it, with total abnegation" (p. 567).[44] Since the Jews do not belong to, but threaten, the *Volk*, they must be eliminated. This, it seems, is Aue's conclusion, which Eichmann apparently accepts. Reflecting on their conversation a few pages later, however, Aue asks, "And the Kantian Imperative? To tell the truth, I didn't have much of an idea, I had told poor Eichmann pretty much whatever came into my head" (p. 570).[45] Strikingly, Aue here rejects his own interpretation, adding that questions such as that asked by Eichmann no longer interest him. What does this change of mind tell the reader about Aue's ethics? I am not sure, but it does not appear to make him more critical of Nazi ideology.

I have mentioned that my interpretation of *The Kindly Ones* is colored by my extratextual knowledge of Nazism. Yet I have also indicated that I learn more about the historical event of the Holocaust by reading Littell's fictional narrative—or, more precisely, Littell's presentation of his fictional character Aue's rendering of his memoirs as a SS officer. The narrative discourse establishes a contrapuntal pattern in which elements of fiction are punctuated by references to historical persons and events. Thus, while my knowledge of the Holocaust informs my reading of the novel, that reading experience not only changes but augments my understanding of the Holocaust as a historical event. One such event, as already indicated, is the Eichmann trial in Jerusalem. Writing his memoirs in the narrative present, Aue refers to the trial, noting that "when [Eichmann] told his judges that he thought the extermination of the Jews was a mistake, we can believe him . . . but once the decision was made, it had to be seen through to the end" (p. 570).[46] Is Aue thinking of himself here? If he is, that thought would be consistent with his skewed interpretation of the Kantian imperative.

Aue's narrative presentation of his relationship with Himmler differs from that with Eichmann not only because of the former's key position in the Nazi power system but also because Himmler, who reads and appreciates Aue's reports about various aspects of the war on the Eastern Front, in effect becomes Aue's employer. Moreover, when Weser and Clemens start investigating Aue, suspecting him of the double murder of his mother and Moreau, Himmler becomes his protector. That said, as in the case of Eichmann, I cannot interpret Aue's account of his collaboration with Himmler without activating my knowledge of the historical Himmler, who as Reichsführer-SS had a leading role in the Holocaust (Breitman, 1991). This aspect of my interpretation becomes particularly pressing when I read Aue's account of the speeches that Himmler gave in Posen on October 4 and 6, 1943:

> [T]hanks to the chance survival of archives, and the victors' justice, these speeches have become famous far beyond the closed circles for which they were intended; you won't find a book on the SS, the Reichsführer, or the destruction of the Jews in which they aren't cited; if their content interests you, you can easily consult them, in several languages; the October 4 speech was entered as evidence in the Nuremberg trials, under document number 1919-PS (it was obviously in this form I was finally able to study

it in detail, after the war, although I learned its general import in Posen itself). (p. 664)[47]

Because these historical references, as well as those to the Eichmann trial, are historically correct, they strengthen Aue's narrative authority as a fictional character who remembers and reports historical occurrences pertaining to the Holocaust. Yet his rendering is by no means neutral, and two features in particular indicate his perspective in ways that show aspects of his ethos. First, his reference to "the victors' justice" is ironic since it suggests that the victors decide what is just and what is wrong. Had the Nazis won the war, Aue implies, Himmler's two speeches would not have survived, nor would the Holocaust have been considered a crime against humanity. Second, it is revealing that, skeptical as he appears to be about the Nuremberg trials, Aue has "obviously" studied "document number 1919-PS." Why? I suggest one reason is that he is shaken by the way in which Himmler, "with a frankness he has never to my knowledge equaled either before or since . . . outlined the program of the destruction of the Jews" (p. 664).[48] For once, Himmler spoke "without euphemisms, without winks, with simple and brutal words like *kill—exterminate*, he said, *meaning kill or order to have killed*" (p. 665).[49] Aue finds that if Himmler allowed himself to speak of the destruction of the Jews in this brutally direct manner, "then the Führer knew about it, and worse, the Führer had wanted it" (p. 665).[50] Aue is not just shaken by the crude directness of Himmler's speech, however; he is also shocked by what he perceives to be Himmler's reason: to address his SS officers so directly "that none of them could, later on, say that he didn't know, couldn't try to make people think, in case of defeat, that he was innocent of the worst" (p. 666).[51]

Why does Aue refer to "them" when he too, as an SS-Sturmbannführer, was addressed by Himmler in Posen on October 6, 1943? If one reason is that need to distance himself from the other SS officers, that need could be specified as a variant of psychological projection: when he observes that Himmler speaks about the Holocaust "in order to *drag them in*, and they understood it very well, hence their distress" (p. 666),[52] he is distressed to learn that he is dragged in too. There is a curious oscillation in Aue's attitude to the Holocaust: on the one hand, he tells the reader about killing individual Jews, and he collaborates with "my comrade Eichmann" (p. 679) as well as Himmler, the man most closely associated with the Final Solution; on the other hand, as his use of the pronoun "them" in the above passage as well as other elements of and gaps in his narrative suggest, he also attempts to distance himself from the Holocaust. This kind of oscillation tells me something important about Aue: defending his killings and his involvement in mass murder, he is shaken by the deaths of individual Jews, including those he kills himself, as well as by the enormity of the genocide. As Aue continues his story, sometimes apologizing to the reader for its length and the wealth of details, his conflicting values—particularly those of his values that contradict or threaten the values of Nazim that he defends, for instance in his conversations with Voss and Eichmann—present him with an ethical challenge to which he finds it difficult to respond.

This challenge becomes more noticeable in "Menuet (en Rondeaux)," particularly in the parts of that long chapter where Aue tells the reader about his collaboration with Höss, the Kommandant of Auschwitz, Nazi Germany's largest concentration and extermination camp, toward which, in my interpretation of the novel, Aue's narrative gravitates. As his narrative is constituted by his memories, this means that those of his memories which, in spite of his claims to the contrary, may become so painful that he tries to forget them, gradually become more noticeable. Aue's responses to his last individual killings, and to Himmler's Posen speech, spark a mnemonic and narrative crisis. As a result of this crisis, in the last part of the novel he increasingly narrates—or perhaps reveals—fragments of memories as well as lengthy dreams and hallucinations that haunt him.

Stirred by irresistible memories, this form of narrative gravitation—which is associated, though not identical, with the progression of the novel's plot— plays a key role in its narrative ethics. Strengthening the focus on the Holocaust, and thus accentuating the ethics of the told, the narrative is still concerned with the ethics of the telling, both Aue's and Littell's own. While these two dimensions are different, it is not always easy for the reader to keep them apart. Aue's collaboration with Eichmann, Himmler, and Höss contributes to this narrative movement, gradually closing in on the Holocaust and placing Auschwitz at the center of the fictional narrative. One example is the way Aue's introductory comments on Höss are related to his references to Himmler's Posen speeches. As he is a SS officer working for Himmler, on his arrival in Auschwitz Aue is taken directly to Höss: "This officer, after the war, acquired a certain notoriety because of the colossal number of people put to death under his command and also because of the frank, lucid memoirs he wrote in prison, during his trial. Yet he was an absolutely typical officer of the IKL [*Inspektion der Konzentrationslager*, "Inspectorate for

Concentration Camps"], hardworking, stubborn, and of limited abilities" (p. 605).[53]

Three aspects of this remarkable passage are particularly significant. First, even though Aue identifies the number of deaths as "colossal," this adjective is an understatement: approximately 1.1 million Jews were murdered by the Nazis in Auschwitz, and the camp's name has become a symbol of the Holocaust. Since Aue not only visits Auschwitz but works there, observing the activities in the camp and writing reports that are sent to Himmler, he contributes to the industrial mass murder. The importance of Aue's assignment is underlined when Höss personally takes him to the different parts of the camp, explaining their functions and complaining, "Ever since the Reichsführer decided to allocate Auschwitz for the destruction of the Jews, we've had nothing but problems" (p. 608).[54] He specifies that he has been "able to begin building permanent installations, with an adequate reception capacity, only in January of this year. But everything still isn't in perfect running order" (p. 608).[55] For Höss, Auschwitz is not "in perfect running order" because he cannot murder the Jews as fast and effectively as Himmler (and by implication Hitler) wishes. The key point to make here is that Aue does not take exception to Höss's assessment; on the contrary, he silently agrees.

This apparent agreement takes me to the second aspect, which I phrase as a question: If Aue concurs with Höss's view and operation of the camp, why does he emphasize Höss's "limited abilities," and what does he mean by this characterization? Does Aue think that Höss ought to have murdered even more Jews? Or does he find that Höss fails to see that, though all Jews are to be exterminated, those fit to work need to live a little longer to support the war effort? My difficulty in answering these questions strengthens my impression of Aue as a puzzling, enigmatic character who attempts to retain a critical distance from the events in which he participates and the characters he meets. This interpretive challenge becomes even more pressing since his attitudinal distance varies: when Aue meets with the medical officers Eduard Wirths and Josef Mengele, he seems to approve of the latter's "much more efficient ... method" (p. 611).[56] Mengele's work included selections whereby incoming Jews were divided into two groups: while those Mengele and his colleagues considered able to work were admitted into the camp, those deemed unfit for labor (approximately 75% of the total) were killed in the gas chambers. Additionally, "method" could point to Mengele's extremely brutal experimentation with prisoners, including experiments performed on identical twins; it could also refer to his task of supervising the administration of

Zyklon B, the pesticide used for the mass killings in the Birkenau gas chambers. Two of the Holocaust survivors whose testimonies I discuss in Chapter 1, Edith Notowicz and Olga Horak, met with Mengele; I trust their view of the Nazi doctor more than Aue's.

Although the elaboration on "method," a word that Littell makes both Höss and Aue use, reveals extratextual knowledge, I find it impossible not to activate that knowledge in my interpretation. Whether or not this is an interpretive gain, I am not sure. What is certain, though, is that a reader with no knowledge or limited knowledge of Auschwitz will learn about the process of extermination of European Jews by reading the novel. Moreover, as it becomes increasingly clear that Aue's involvement in the industrial Holocaust reveals and is premised on the values of Nazism, the narrative discourse urges me to rethink my own ethics in relation to the Holocaust. This kind of interpretive incentive is intensified by the passage's third aspect I want to highlight: when Aue refers to Höss's "frank, lucid memoirs," could he be thinking of his own memoirs? Are they also "frank"? Importantly, these questions can be asked by a reader who has no knowledge of Höss's autobiography, edited by Martin Broszat (1998) and titled *Kommandant in Auschwitz*. As I have read this book, I inevitably compare the autobiography of a historical person with that of Aue as a fictional character. Moreover, there is, as Anneleen Spiessens (2022) has noted, a combination of similarity and difference between Broszat's function as editor and Littell's role as implied author. On the one hand, although the genre of the novel is different from that of autobiography, they both distance themselves from the values that their protagonists, who are also first-person narrators, express and reveal. On the other hand, they do so in different ways: while Broszat is so active and visible as editor that he virtually establishes a counterdiscourse whose ethics opposes that of Höss's discourse,[57] the ethics of Littell as implied author is less explicitly expressed. It does not follow that Littell's ethical distance from his protagonist is less than Broszat's distance from his; direct comparison of the two narratives is complicated by the generic difference between a historical person's autobiography and Aue's memories as a fictional character. And yet Littell could have distanced himself more clearly from Aue, for example by granting his main character less narrative authority and by reducing his reliability as a first-person narrator. By not doing so Littell challenges me as a reader to construct my own alternative to the values that Aue presents and represents. One constituent element of this narrative strategy is the ethical questions that I identify as a reader and that, in my reading experience, Littell invites me to reflect on. My interpretation of the novel thus becomes an ethical interpretation.

Aue's Memories, Dreams, and Hallucinations

My argument that the narrative ethics of *The Kindly Ones* gravitates toward the Holocaust may appear to be weakened by the novel's last two parts, "Air" and "Gigue." While "Gigue," as already mentioned, includes Aue's account of his killings of three non-Jewish men at the end of the war, "Air" is a kind of surrealistic intermezzo in which Aue relates fragments of his experience in the house where Una lived with her husband. Yet the presence of the Holocaust is acutely felt throughout these two parts, infiltrating both his memories and his stubborn attempt to present them in an extended first-person narrative.

To highlight the Holocaust as a key dimension of "Air" and "Gigue" is to suggest that, more insistently than before, the novel's narrative ethics here revolves around and explores the effects and repercussions of antisemitic attitudes and acts of violence that made this series of historical events possible. This includes Aue, even though he defends his actions by referring to extenuating circumstances. The combination of Aue's account of his killing of Jews in "Allemandes I–II" and his involvement in the industrial Holocaust in "Menuet" demonstrates that as an SS officer he is a Nazi perpetrator who contributes to an unspeakable crime.

Although Aue attempts to distance himself from the Holocaust, the fragments of memory that assume the form of dreams or hallucinations reveal his active participation in the mass murder—and these aspects of memory become more noticeable, and more significant, in the final parts of the novel. Although they may appear to reduce his narrative authority as well as his reliability since they refer to actions, or rather visions, outside the autobiographical narrative that Aue seems to want to convey to the reader, the dreams and hallucinations increasingly force themselves into that narrative. Whether Aue intends this narrative inclusion, I am not sure, but as integral parts of the novel's narrative discourse his dreams and hallucinations indicate, as Meretoja puts it, a gradual "breaking down of *narrative mastery*. This, in turn, is central to the novel's way of taking part in the discussion on the ethics of understanding and narrating the Holocaust" (2018a, p. 241, original emphasis).

I agree with Meretoja's observation that Aue's sense of a loss of narrative mastery is connected with and in part follows from the wound he receives at Stalingrad, and I also concur with her accompanying point that the bullet through his head "acquires a symbolic meaning as it epitomizes a structural hole at the center of the novel" (2018a, p. 241). If historians consider the battle of Stalingrad a turning point in the Second World War, Aue's bullet wound leaves a mark on him not only physically but also metaphorically. The word "Stalingrad" becomes a kind of leitmotif in the second half of the novel, as when, much later in the narrative, Aue and Thomas undress in a public pool in Berlin and he asks Thomas where he got the scar across his belly:

> "In Stalingrad, of course. Don't you remember? You were there." A memory, yes, I had one, and I wrote it down with the others, but I had filed it away in the back of my head, in the attic of hallucinations and dreams; now this scar came to turn everything upside down, I suddenly felt as if I couldn't be sure of anything anymore. (p. 693)[58]

Aue's recognition of a fallible memory does not necessarily make him an unreliable narrator. There is even a sense in which the entanglement of the "narrating I" and the "experiencing I" make him more rather than less reliable since elements of his experiencing "I" include the hallucinations and dreams that, I suggest, not only reveal key aspects of his narrative but also form an essential part of the novel's narrative presentation of the Holocaust. To some extent, Aue himself seems to be aware that his first-person narrative is changing as it moves into the final phase of the war. Addressing the reader, he comments:

> I'm quite willing to tell you a few stories: but then let me just dig at random among my memories and my notes; I've told you, I'm getting tired, I have to start bringing this to an end. . . . [I]f I change my method a little, it's mostly for me, whether you like it or not, another mark of my boundless selfishness, certainly a fruit of my bad education. (p. 783)[59]

Before discussing two examples of Aue's hallucinations and dreams, I note that not only is Aue unable to make a clear distinction between them, but he can also find it difficult to specify when and why they begin and end.

The combination of dream and hallucination that characterizes the following example is sparked by a visual image: a photo of Aue's father, taken just after the First World War. Awaiting Aue on his return to Berlin in the summer of 1944, the old picture, sent to him by his colleague Baumann, makes a strong impression on him:

> This image, I must confess, frightened me: no matter how much I gazed at it, I didn't recognize this man whose face, under his helmet, was reduced to a white spot. . . . I still examined the photo, wracked my memory to collect scraps about my father, about his appearance, but it was as if the details were fleeing each other and escaping me. . . . And now this ambiguous, elusive photograph was ruining whatever memories remained in me, was replacing his living presence with a blurry face and a uniform. Overcome with rage, I tore the photograph into pieces and threw them off the balcony. . . . I was sweating, I wanted to jump out of my skin, which felt too tight for my anger and my anguish. (pp. 805–806)[60]

Aue's reaction to the photograph reminds me of his response to Ibrahim's question about his father. If the old Jew touches a nerve by asking Aue, "And who was your father?" (p. 279), the photo of his father similarly provokes him. Why? Does the image of an unrecognizable man in uniform activate painful memories, and possibly even a sense of loss of identity? Does it remind him of his killing of his father's wife, and perhaps also of his incestuous relationship with Una? Although, or because, Aue cannot understand his reaction to the photo, it takes him into "another muddled, confused narrative" (p. 807)[61] in which images and fragments of memory are blended with dreams and hallucinations. When Helene, a young widow he has become acquainted with in Berlin, comes to help him, he thinks, "[T]his gentleness made me mad with rage: What did this girl want with me?" (p. 813).[62]

Why is Aue angered by Helene's "gentleness" and the help she gives him? Could it be because she cares for him in a way that indicates values diametrically opposed to his own? I suggest that this scene—with the desperate, hallucinating Aue and the caring Helene in a hotel room in Berlin toward the end of the war—becomes important because of the way Littell contrasts Aue's values with Helene's. Crucially, this variant of narrative ethics turns on Aue's memories of his involvement in the Holocaust: his hallucinatory state makes him share his memories with Helene in a new, brutally honest way that comes as a shock to her and perhaps also to himself:

"Where did they go, your Jewish neighbours in Moabit? You've never asked yourself? To the East? We sent them to work in the East? Where? If there were six or seven million Jews working in the East, we'd have built entire cities!" . . . I was raging, I must have been ashen-faced, she seemed to be listening attentively, she didn't move. . . . "We're murdering people, you understand, that's what we do, all of us, your husband was a murderer, I'm a murderer, and you, you're a murderer's accomplice, you wear and you eat the fruit of our labour." She was very pale, but her face showed only infinite sadness: "You are an unhappy man." (p. 816)[63]

Although Aue does not refer to himself as a Nazi perpetrator, here he comes close to admitting that he is one. Revealingly, his self-characterization refers both to his individual killings and to his contribution to the industrial Holocaust that I have discussed. His feverish, hallucinatory state makes him more rather than less reliable since his memory of his killings is not modified or changed by self-serving rationalizations such as those presented in his conversation with Eichmann. His attempt to distance himself from the atrocities fails.

If, as Aue claims, Helene is his "accomplice," are her values compromised, and are her values and Aue's perhaps more similar than I have suggested? I think not, yet I add that it remains unclear how much Helene knows about the Nazis' extermination of the Jews; although she is "very pale," her "infinite sadness" can be associated with the Holocaust as well as with Aue. If, as I suggest, there is a connection between her ethical position and that of Una, that connection enhances the passage's significance by relating it to Aue's fantasies and dreams in Una's house in "Air." Aue's memories of and fantasies about his sister may be the main reason he cannot develop a relationship with another woman.

Although the narrative situations are very different, Aue's accusation of Helene as his accomplice reminds me of Himmler's attempt in his Posen speech to make his SS officers aware of their responsibility for the Holocaust. The most notable difference is that, in contrast to Himmler, Aue uses the word "murderer" about himself and his SS colleagues. To consider Helene an "accomplice" in the mass murder of European Jews, however, is unpersuasive for two reasons. First, although Helene is implicated in the Holocaust, she is distanced from it and appears to know little about it. Second, her remark later in their conversation makes her ethical stance clearer and her opposition to the Holocaust stronger. When Aue says, "[I]f we lose the war, our enemies' revenge will be pitiless," she responds, "I wasn't talking about that. Even if we don't lose the war, we are going to pay. We will have to pay" (p. 818).[64] Indicating an ethical responsibility that Aue does not have, this view is interestingly linked to Kant's moral imperative—while at the same time opposing Aue's interpretation of that imperative in his conversation with Eichmann. For Helene, the Holocaust is an evil act that, regardless of the outcome of the war, will have serious consequences for those involved in it.

Importantly, Una, Aue's sister and the great love of his life, makes a statement on the Holocaust that resembles Helene's. Her husband, von Üxküll, asks Aue, "Do you know why you're killing the Jews? Do you know?" (p. 874).[65] Aues does not answer, but Una replies, "By killing the Jews . . . we wanted to kill ourselves, kill the Jew within us, kill that which in us resembles the idea we have of the Jew" (p. 874).[66] While this comment is striking in itself, it becomes even more remarkable since it is not part of Aue's quasi-causal narrative; rather, it is a memory of a dream or hallucination. According to Aue, this conversation, which he relates at the beginning of "Air," takes place in von Üxküll's home, a "beautiful empty house" (p. 870)[67] where Una and her husband lived until they left because the Russians were advancing from the east. But how can Aue have a conversation with them if they are not there? Commenting on his own account of the events in the house, he admits:

> [W]hen I wrote it, it seemed true to me, equal to the reality, but apparently it doesn't actually correspond to the truth. Why is that the case? Hard to say. It's not that my memories are confused, on the contrary, I have many of them and very precise ones, but many of them overlap and even contradict one another, and their status is uncertain. (p. 870)[68]

If this admission suggests, and in one sense even confirms, that Aue may be an unreliable narrator, in a different sense it makes his narration more reliable as it draws attention to the fallibility of memory and the interdependence of remembering and forgetting (Brockmeier, 2015; Ricoeur, 2000/2006). Moreover, Aue's comment on the uncertain status of his memories indicates that his account of his life is necessarily his own interpretation of that life—and that interpretation is necessarily incomplete, biased, and unresolved. Seen from my perspective as a reader, the passage is thus a self-interpretive sign that influences my interpretation of Littell's novel.

But if Aue is dreaming about or imagining his conversation with von Üxküll and Una in the empty house, why does the conversation include, or even turn on, such a strong criticism of his own Nazi ideology? Could it be because, in his dreams and hallucinations, he silently agrees with this criticism? A partial answer to this question could be that if, as I suggest, the breakdown of narrative mastery that Aue experiences as Stalingrad signals a threat to and growing doubt about his Nazi ideology, it presents Aue with an ethical crisis that, though he reverts to his quasi-causal narrative, he is unable to resolve. While the conversations with Helene and Una reveal aspects of this crisis, these aspects are related to Aue's presentation of a number of characters whose values oppose his. Tellingly, these characters are not only Jews but also non-Jewish Germans. In addition to Helene and Una (and also von Üxküll, whose criticism of the Holocaust may have influenced his wife), the latter group includes Dr. Voss, whose strong indictment of Nazism's view on race may have made a stronger impression on Aue than he is able to admit. The Jews killed by Aue also challenge his values, and thus his ethos. The most obvious example of this ethical challenge may be that of Ibrahim, but the sadness of the young Jewish girl he kills at Babi Yar also makes a stronger impression on him than he is able to admit at this early, pre-Stalingrad stage of his narrative. There is an important connection between his account of this senseless killing and his dream at the end of "Air" of

> that girl we had hanged one winter day in the park behind the statue of Shevchenko, a young and healthy girl bursting with life . . . what right did we have to hang her, how could we hang this girl, and I sobbed endlessly, ravaged by her memory, my very own Our-Lady-of-the-Snows, it wasn't remorse, I didn't have remorse, I didn't feel guilty, I didn't think things could or should have been otherwise, yet I understood what it meant to hang a girl, we had hanged her the way a butcher slaughters a steer, without passion, because it had to be done . . . the girl we had hanged . . . was a young girl who had been a little girl who may have been happy and who was then just entering life, a life full of murderers whom she hadn't been able to avoid, a girl like my sister in a way, someone's sister, perhaps, as I too was someone's brother, and such cruelty had no name, no matter how objectively necessary, it ruined everything, if one could do that, hang a girl like that, then one could do anything . . . there was absolutely no sense to it, and that is why I wept, I didn't understand anything anymore and I wanted to be alone to no longer understand anything. (p. 912)[69]

Observing the process of the industrial Holocaust in Auschwitz and supporting that process by writing reports for Himmler, Aue states, "I hardly
looked at the *Häftlinge* [inmates], it wasn't their individual fate that concerned me, but their collective fate, and in any case they all looked alike, they
were a grey, dirty mass" (p. 851).[70] In glaring contrast to the distanced and
casual attitude of this observation and of his reports, both of which support
his quasi-causal narrative, the memory of the hanged young Jewish girl that
forces its way into his dream in von Üxküll and Una's empty house makes
him cry because of the cruelty of the crime of the Holocaust—a crime for
which he and the other "murderers" of the Nazi regime are responsible. It
does not follow that Aue changes his pattern of violent action; he kills at least
three non-Jewish men, including Thomas, after Thomas has rescued him
from the empty house as the Russians are fast approaching. Yet the fragments
of dream and hallucination establish a counterdiscourse that gradually, particularly in the post-Stalingrad part of the novel, undermines the values that
Aue embraces in his quasi-causal account. This variant of textual dynamics
plays a key role in the formation of the novel's narrative ethics.

Building on the discussion of "Toccata" and Aue's killings, and also drawing on my observations on Aue's participation in the Holocaust and on his
memories, dreams, and hallucinations, I conclude this chapter by linking
the issue of narrative ethics to the different yet interdependent elements of
narrative communication activated and employed in *Les Bienveillantes*. I
concentrate on Aue's combined function as the novel's first-person narrator and main character; as I hope to have shown, this combination is crucial
for the formation of the novel's narrative ethics. While Aue's ethos colors the
way he tells his story, his actions serve as an "indirect presentation" (Lothe,
2000, p. 82) of Aue as a fictional character. Yet as the term "indirect" suggests, Aue's ethos is revealed rather than stated: because he fails to see that
all the killings are in fact murders committed in cold blood, and because he
also falls short of expressing any remorse for his crimes, the reader is faced
with the challenge of constructing an alternative ethos that more accurately
describes him. This challenge is strengthened by the two-way effect of the
novel's character narration: while the character's actions color his narration
of them, the first-person narration produced by this character is the reader's
only source of information regarding his ethos.

The strength of this challenge is further enhanced by Aue's narrative
authority and by the fact that, with the exception of pockets of unreliability

such as the account of the matricide, he appears to be a cognitively reliable narrator insofar as he reports events and actions that can be damaging to him and that are not contradicted by other elements of the narrative. Yet one notable aspect, and arguably a gain, of the variant of first-person narrative Littell employs is to probe the limits of the kind of reliability that Aue represents: although he reliably reports what he does, his narration systematically marginalizes and repeatedly fails to mention the tragic consequences of his evil actions. Can we trust the narration of a character who seems unable to express any regret or issue any apology for the murders of the millions of people he lists in "Toccata," and whose deaths were the direct result of the activities of the Nazi regime that he supported? The challenge of reading this novel becomes an ethical challenge.

Even though aspects of narrative authority and reliability are blended in *Les Bienveillantes*, I conclude that while the issue of reliability is primarily centered on Aue's reporting of what he does and thinks, that of narrative authority is more comprehensive in that it includes the assumptions, positioning, and interpretive signals given by the implied author. Because these have to be constructed by the reader on the basis of Aue's narration, as a reader I am faced with the challenge of imbuing the implied author with an ethos that seems sufficiently different from Aue's to enable me to come to terms with the work, perhaps even in the sense of finding it ethically defensible. The reason many historical readers have found, and continue to find, *Les Bienveillantes* a morally dubious novel is connected with this challenge. This is not just a question of what the reader *can* do but also of what he or she *wants to* do: if the reader of the novel is unwilling, or finds it too difficult, to construct an implied author who can adequately or satisfactorily present an ethical alternative to, and thus overrule, Aue's ethos, that reader may not want to read the whole novel. Moreover, though the reader may find that the implied author represents such an alternative, he or she may conclude that Littell as implied author gives Aue too much space and time to present the long-drawn-out account of his various crimes.

Regardless of the reader's response to this challenge, however, the novel is a forceful demonstration of the importance of the concept of implied author for coming to terms with the ethics of Aue's narration—and thus of the novel as a whole. As first-person narrator Aue is very different from the third-person narrator in Job that Booth refers to in order to illustrate how authority is established in narrative fiction. While the narrator in Job derives much of his narrative authority, including his ethical authority, from his association with the implied author, the first-person narrator Aue establishes part of his authority by providing historically correct information about the Holocaust. This kind of authority—that of reporting, in a work of fiction, historical events and real crimes—is enhanced as a consequence of Aue's narration of his two first killings. Yet the moral gap between him and the implied author and, as a corollary, between him and the reader is gradually widening.

If the demanding task of reading *Les Bienveillantes* is associated with and enhanced by the ways in which the character's ethos colors his narration of the event he takes part in and the murders he commits, the novel is also a forceful demonstration of the reader's need for an alternative ethos represented by the implied author. Consonant with the progression of the narrative, this ethos, that of the implied author, assumes the form of a contrast to Aue's. As Dan Shen points out, in Booth's own formulation the concept of the implied author "is essentially a straightforward one referring at once to the person who writes the text in a particular manner (encoding process) and to the textual message of this writer for the reader to infer (decoding process)" (2011b, p. 86). Both these processes have an ethical dimension, and while the images that readers form of the implied author's ethos may be dissimilar, they will all be marked by an increasing attitudinal distance from the narrator's ethos. Aue's direct address to the reader in "Toccata" is at once deftly manipulative and thoroughly deceitful.

Exploiting the resources and possibilities of narrative fiction, the implied author of *Les Bienveillantes* makes his narrator tell about his life as a Nazi perpetrator in a way that few, if any, historical persons would. If, as noted at the beginning of this chapter, this is one reason for writing the novel, there is also an additional one: the narrative strategy of making the perpetrator the one and only narrator. What is wrenching to the reader is the gradual realization, furthered by Aue's account of his killings and his involvement in the mass murder of Jews, that although our guide may be some kind of monster, he is an individual character and not just a general representative of those responsible for the Holocaust.[71] Experiencing this revelation is an essential part of the challenge of reading *Les Bienveillantes*, strengthening our need to ethically distance ourselves from Aue yet complicating that task. Reading *Les Bienveillantes* is experiencing fiction in a way that not only augments our knowledge of the historical event of the Holocaust but also, painfully and in the face of our resistance, makes us realize that the perpetrators, the monsters, were human beings, whatever this implies about what human beings can be.

It is a further challenge of reading Littell's novel that such a linking of aspects of monstrosity would seem to problematically approximate Aue's assertion that we—that is, the reader he addresses in "Toccata"—could have done what he did under the same circumstances. Refusing the distinctions that serve precisely to draw boundaries between victim, perpetrator, and bystander, Aue launches "an attack on differentiations of any kind" (Razinsky, 2012, p. 47), and this attack is sustained throughout. However, as Liran Razinsky also emphasizes, "although exposed as readers to the idea of non-differentiation of acts of atrocity and violence, we are also engaged in a moral examination. We take a direction that Aue does not" (p. 48).

The task of taking a "direction" different from Aue's is a significant part of the challenge of reading Littell's novel. As a reader of *Les Bienveillantes* I am not only induced but even impelled to distance myself from the ethics of the told; I am also inclined to distance myself from aspects of the ethics of the telling. Yet although Aue's comments, thoughts, and actions serve to establish and sustain the difference between his purpose and Littell's as implied author, the reader's task of occupying Aue's perspective for a thousand pages is so ethically difficult and distasteful that it strains many readers', and also this reader's, relationship with the implied author. Consistently neglecting his own moral responsibility by placing the blame on others (especially his superiors and his parents) and on external factors beyond his control (especially the time when he was born and the country where he was born), Aue is so deftly manipulative and so insistent in his narration that although the implied author "gestures to the reader from behind the first-person narrator" (Toker, 2012, p. 159), we may wonder about the novel's overall purposefulness. Linking this purposefulness not only to the purposes of Littell as implied author but also to "the intrinsic intentionality of the literary medium" (Toker, 2012, p. 154), I conclude by suggesting that *Les Bienveillantes* reveals not just an enriching combination but also a problematic tension between these two dimensions: as the novel's only narrative medium Aue may not only support but also damagingly infiltrate and color the implied author's purposes.

Whether or to what extent Aue's account complicates or perhaps even subverts the implied author's purposes is, however, in large part dependent on my interpretive activity—and particularly on my response to and negotiation of the process of distanciation which Aue's narration necessitates. From the perspective of narrative hermeneutics, whatever knowledge I can gain about the implied author's purposes and the novel's intrinsic intentionality depends on and follows from my own interpretation of the narrative discourse. Rereading this discourse and taking a particular interest in its presentation of memory and of ethical issues pertaining to the Holocaust, I am aware of the great temporal distance between the Second World War and the third decade of the 21st century. Cognizant of the fact that this distance, which includes my lack of war experience, reduces my knowledge of the Holocaust, I am encouraged by Gadamer's (1960/2013) observation that, in some ways at least, my distance from the events of the Holocaust may prove an interpretive strength rather than a weakness. Constituting an essential part of my interpretive situation, this variant of temporal distance is related to my horizon: "the range of vision that includes everything that can be seen from a particular vantage point" (p. 313). Enabling me to see how much I do not know, my horizon can help me to identify aspects of the Holocaust that I want to explore by reading and rereading the discourse of Littell's fictional narrative from my perspective as a European citizen born after the war.

Reflecting on the narrative discourse of Littell's novel, I conclude that one of its most distinctive aesthetic and ethical features is the increasing distance between Aue's presentation of his story in a quasi-causal narrative form and his experience of other—challenging and problematic—aspects of this story. Undermining and questioning the quasi-causal rendering of his memories, these elements give the reader glimpses of memories that Aue has attempted to suppress or forget but that force themselves into his narration in the form of dreams, hallucinations, and fits of anger. I do not want to grade these two dimensions of memory; they are interdependent, and the second follows from or intrudes upon the first. While both dimensions depend on Aue's memories, they activate and reveal different aspects of those memories. As Meretoja puts it, "Engaging with the haunting past proves to be more difficult than Aue initially expects, and the process of telling and recounting involves re-enactment of the traumatic experiences in ways that gradually disintegrate the very form of the narration" (2018a, p. 242). At one level of interpretation, I am not surprised when Aue starts to encounter difficulties as he is recounting the story of his "haunting past." At a different yet related level, given Aue's Nazi ideology and his lack of remorse, I find it surprising that he admits at least some of the problems he meets with as he attempts to make his story into some kind of coherent, quasi-causal narrative. Can I interpret these admissions as signs, or remnants, of his humanity? I am not sure; proclaiming, as he does in the hotel conversation with Helene and in the rendering of his dream of the hanged Jewish girl, that he is a murderer is a statement of fact that does not necessarily make him more human. I conclude, though, that his admission of weakness and of despair, though not of remorse, makes him a less predictable and more complex character who continues to provoke me. His accusation directed at me as reader at the very beginning of his account is difficult to respond to; although I think I am a better person than Aue, I am not certain that, under comparable circumstances, I would not have acted, or failed to act, in morally dubious, perhaps even indefensible ways. *Les Bienveillantes* leaves me with ethical questions that I continue to reflect on—even though I do not expect to be able to give satisfactory answers to them.

Notes

1. On new perspectives on narrative presentations of the perpetrator, including the narrative ethics of such presentations, see especially McGlothlin (2016, 2021). A helpful collection of essays on *The Kindly Ones* is Barjonet and Razinsky (2012). See also Meretoja (2018a), Sanyal (2015), Suleiman (2012), and Troupin (2020).
2. By "industrial Holocaust" I mean the Nazis' mass murder of millions of Jews in gas vans or in stationary gas chambers. See *Holocaust Encyclopedia*, https://encyclopedia.ushmm.org/content/en/article/gassing-operations
3. Such assignments of authority can be problematic, though; compare Joseph Conrad's use of Marlow as first-person narrator in *Heart of Darkness* and Chinua Achebe's indictment of the novella (2006, pp. 342–343), ultimately rejecting both Conrad's and Marlow's authority. At the same time, implied authors can use unreliability to weaken the authority of narrators and strengthen their own. In such cases narrative authority tends to revolve around and be represented by the implied author, whose attitudinal distance from his or her narrator thus becomes apparent.
4. *The Kindly Ones*, p. 3. Further citations to Charlotte Mandell's translation (Littell, 2006/2010) from the French are included in the text. As it is essential to relate the translated text to its origin, and vice versa, the notes give the original French versions of all my quotations. This critical practice also applies to chapters 6 (Sebald) and 7 (Erpenbeck). "Frères humains, laissez-moi vous raconter comment ça s'est passé. On n'est pas votre frère, rétorquerez-vous, et on ne veut pas le savoir. Et c'est bien vrai qu'il s'agit d'une sombre histoire, mais édifiante aussi, un véritable conte moral, je vous l'assure. Ça risque d'être un peu long, après tout il s'est passé beaucoup de choses, mais si ça se trouve vous n'êtes pas trop pressés, avec un peu de chance vous avez le temps. Et puis ça vous concerne: vous verrez bien que ça vous concerne" (Littell, 2006/2021, p. 13). As we can see, Mandell translates the French pronoun *on* (one) as "I." The French *on* is used more often and has a wider semantic range than the English "one," and the meaning of *on* here approximates "I." Yet the fact that the two pronouns are not identical shows that the work of the translator is imbued with an interpretive element. Referring to Gadamer, Theo Hermans notes, "To the extent that language facilitates human interaction and fixes forms of cultural expression more or less permanently, it requires interpretation, time and again" (1996, p. 2; cf. Hermans, 2022). French readers may find that the way Aue addresses the reader ("Frères humains") is an allusion to the French poets François Villon and Charles Baudelaire. There is also, as Colin Davis has informed me, a possible allusion to the Romaniote Jewish Swiss author Albert Cohen, who wrote in French and whose novel about antisemitism is titled *Ô vous, frères humain* (1972). The allusions, which are difficult to retain in the English translation, strengthen the self-conscious literariness of the narrative beginning.

5. The double meaning also exists in the original French text, and in both languages it is accentuated by the use of repetition ("vous concerne").

6. "Encore une fois, soyons clairs: je ne cherche pas à dire que je ne suis pas coupable de tel ou tel fait. Je suis coupable, vous ne l'êtes pas, c'est bien. Mais vous devriez quand même pouvoir vous dire que ce que j'ai fait, vous l'auriez fait aussi. . . . Si vous êtes né dans un pays ou à une époque où non seulement personne ne vient tuer votre femme, vos enfants, mais où personne ne vient vous demander de tuer les femmes et les enfants des autres, bénissez Dieu et allez en paix. Mais gardez toujours cette pensée à l'esprit: vous avez peut-être eu plus de chance que moi, mais vous n'êtes pas meilleur" (2006/2021, p. 37).

7. "Enfin, le très respecté professeur Hilberg, spécialiste de la question et peu suspect de vues partisanes, proallemandes du moins, parvient au bout d'une démonstration serrée de dix-neuf pages au chiffre de 5 100 000, ce qui correspond en gros à l'opinion de feu l'Obersturmbannführer Eichmann. Va donc pour le chiffre du professeur Hilberg, ce qui nous fait, pour récapituler:

Morts soviétiques	20 millions
Morts allemands	3 millions
Sous-total (guerre à l'Est) ...	23 millions
Endlösung	5.1 millions (2006/2021, p. 29)

8. See my comments on these concepts in the introduction; see also Fulbrook, 2023; Rothberg, 2019. Hilberg's first book, *The Destruction of the European Jews*, appeared in 1961. In this landmark study of the Holocaust, Hilberg shows that although the destruction of the European Jews may have the appearance of an indivisible event, it was a complex process of sequential steps taken at the initiative of countless decision makers (Hilberg, 1961/2003; cf. Kershaw, 2008).

9. "Moi, j'étais pétrifié, je ne savais pas ce qu'il faillait faire. Grafhorst arriva et me secoua par le bras: 'Obersturmführer!' Il pointa son pistolet vers les corps. 'Essayez d'achever les blessés.' Je sortis mon pistolet et me dirigeai vers un groupe: un très jeune homme beuglait de douleur, je dirigeait mon pistolet vers sa tête et appuyai sur la détente, mais le coup ne partit pas, j'avais oublié de relever la sûreté, je l'ôtai et lui tirai une balle dans le front, il sursauta et tout subitement. Pour atteindre certains blessés, il faillait marcher sur les corps, cela glissait affreusement, les chairs blanches et molles roulaient sous mes bottes, les os se brisaient traîtreusement et me faisaient trébucher, je m'enfonçais jusqu'aux chevilles dans la boue et le sang" (2006/2021, p. 191).

10. Although my interpretation builds on signals and self-interpretive elements in the narrative discourse, it is given from my own perspective and marked by my temporal distance from the Second World War. On a second reading of the passage, my understanding of its restricted narration is different because I know that Aue is less restricted in his presentation of murders he commits later in the narrative.

11. "Près de moi, on amenait un autre groupe: mon regard croisa celui d'une belle jeune fille, presque nue mais très élégante, calme, les yeux emplis d'une immense tristesse. Je m'éloignai. Lorsque je revins elle était encore vivante . . . j'étais une vulgaire poupée et ne ressentais rien, et en même temps je voulais de tout mon cœur me pencher et lui essuyer la terre et la sueur mêlées sur son front, lui caresser la joue et lui dire que ça allait, que tout irait pour le mieux, mais à la place je lui tirais convulsivement une balle dans la tête . . . car moi à la pensée de ce gâchis humain insensé j'étais envahi d'une rage immense, démesurée, je continuais à lui tirer dessus et sa tête avait éclaté comme un fruit, alors mon bras se détacha de moi et partit tout seul dans le ravin, tirant de part et d'autre, je lui courais après, lui faisant signe de m'attendre de mon autre bras, mais il ne voulait pas, il me narguait et tirait sur les blessés tout seul, sans moi, enfin, à bout de souffle, je m'arrêtai et me mis à pleurer" (2006/2021, pp. 192–193).

12. "Même les boucheries démentielles de la Grande Guerre, qu'avaient vécues nos pères ou certains de nos officiers plus âgés, paraissaient presque propres et justes à côté de ce que nous avions amené au monde. Je trouvais cela extraordinaire" (2006/2021, pp. 193–194).

13. "C'était un vieillard de grande stature, avec une longue barbe blanche, encore visiblement vigoreux . . . et me dit dans un grec classique bizarrement accentué mais compréhensible: 'Tu es un homme éduqué, je vois. Tu dois savoir le grec'" (2006/2021, p. 404).

14. "[S]ouriant toujours un peu dans sa barbe éclaboussée de sang; ses yeux ouverts, dirigés vers la paroi de terre, riaient aussi. Je tremblais" (2006/2021, p. 412).

15. Davis (2007b, p. 51) adds, "Conflict or war are not what Levinas calls 'the first event of the encounter' (Levinas, [1961]/1969, p. 199). Violence can only be a second or secondary response to the revelation that I cannot kill the Other. The original relationship is peace, 'the antecedent and non-allergic presence of the Other.'"

16. "Leutnant Dr. Voss, qui malgré son jeune âge fait figure d'autorité réputée dans les milieux scientifiques en Allemagne" (2006/2021, p. 431).

17. "'Nous savons qu'il existe des groupes racialemant inférieurs, dont les Juifs.' . . . Voss regardait son café d'un air amer et triste. 'Doktor Aue. Je vous ai toujours pris pour un homme intelligent et sensé. Même si tout ce que vous me dites est vrai, expliquez-moi, s'il vous plaît, ce que vous entendez par race. Parce que pour moi, c'est un concept scientifiquement indéfinissable et donc sans valeur théorique.'—'Pourtant, la race existe, c'est une vérité, nos meilleurs chercheurs l'étudient et écrivent à son sujet. Vous le savez bien. Nos anthropologues raciaux sont le meilleurs du monde.' Voss explosa subitement: 'Ce sont des fumistes. Ils n'ont aucune concurrence dans les pays sérieux car leur discipline n'y existe pas et n'y est pas enseignée. Aucun d'entre eux n'aurait un emploi et ne serait publié si ce n'était pour des considérations politiques!'" (2006/2021, p. 435).

18. In *The Origins of Totalitarianism*, Hannah Arendt asserts that "Hitlerism exercised its strong international and inter-European appeal during the thirties because racism, though a state doctrine only in Germany, had been a powerful trend in public opinion everywhere" (1951/2017, p. 206). Arendt's observation is aligned with the comments on racism in Emmanuel Levinas's "Reflections on the Philosophy of Hitlerism," a short text he wrote as early as 1934. Levinas argues that Hitlerism attacks the idea of liberation that was taken up by and served to develop European civilization. For the Nazis, the enemy becomes the one who brought the idea of liberation into the world: the Jew. "And then, if race does not exist, one has to invent it" (Levinas, 1934/1990, p. 69; cf. Cesare, 2023).

19. "'Je m'appelle Maximilien. Je viens d'Allemagne.'—'Et qui était ton père?' Je souris: 'En quoi est-ce que mon père t'intéresse, vieillard?'—'Comment veux-tu que je sache à qui je m'addresse si je ne connais pas ton père?' Son grec, je l'entendais maintenant, comportait des tournures tout à fait inhabituelles; mais j'arrivais à le commprendre. Je lui dis le nom de mon père et il eut l'air satisfait" (2006/2021, p. 404).

20. "'Qu'est-ce que tu es venu faire ici? . . . [J]e voulais vous voir, c'est tout'" (2006/2021, p. 743).

21. "De nouveau, je me sentais rapetisser: devant cette voix impérieuse, ces yeux froids, je perdais tous mes moyens, je redevenais un enfent craintif, plus petit que les jumeaux" (2006/2021, p. 743). The twins are perhaps the children of Aue and his twin sister Una, with whom he had an incestuous relationship when they were children. Una, who is married to the composer Berndt Von Üxküll, plays a key role in Aue's sexual fantasies and hallucinations.

22. "Seigneur, me dis-je, on l'a étranglée, on a étranglé ma mère. . . . [L]'assassin avait dû d'abord tuer Moreau, puis monter. L'angoisse m'étouffait, je ne savais pas quoi faire. . . . Appeler la police? Je n'avais pas le temps, je devais prendre mon car" (2006/2021, p. 758).

23. In making this point I build on the interpretive element embedded in Mandell's translation of "on l'a étranglée" (active) as "she's been strangled" (passive). Thus, my interpretation builds on the translator's interpretation.

24. "'Mais c'est moi que tu hais'" (2006/2021, p. 744).

25. "'Tu est venu dans cet uniforme pour me dire combien tu me hais'" (2006/2021, p. 744).

26. "Un veillard, près de l'autel, jouait *L'Art de la fugue*, le troisème contrepoint, je pense" (2006/2021, p. 1328).

27. "et un uniforme d'Oberstleutnant de l'autre guerre, avec une croix au cou. 'Ils peuvent tout détruire, me dit-il tranquillement, mais pas ça. C'est impossible, ça restera toujours: ça continuera même quand je m'arrêterai de jouer.' . . . La musique était magnifique. . . . Or au lieu de m'apaiser cette musique ne faisait qu'attiser ma rage, je trouvais cela insoutenable. Je ne pensais à rien, ma tête était vide de tout sauf de cette musique et de la pression noire de ma rage. . . . Lorsqu'il les referma d'un coup sec, à la fin de la fugue, je sortis mon pistolet et lui tirai une balle dans la tête. Il s'effondra en avant sur les touches, ouvrant la moitié des tuyaux dans un mugissement désolé et discordant" (2006/2021, pp. 1328–1329).

28. "'Tu es devenu complètement fou!' siffla Thomas" (2006/2021, p. 1329).

29. "Ce sourire fat et calculateur me mit hors de moi" (2006/2021, p. 1353).

30. "Le visage de Mihaï, sous moi, devint rouge, écarlate, puis violacé . . . ses yeux exorbités me fixaient avec terreur, ses ongles griffaient mes bottes" (2006/2021, pp. 1353–1354).

31. "J'allai au bar prendre un verre" (2006/2021, p. 1354).

32. "Au fur et à mesure que le Führer se rapprochait de moi—j'était presque en bout de ligne—mon attention se fixait sur son nez. . . . Son haleine âcre, fétide, acheva de me vexer: c'était vraiment trop à supporter. Alors je me penchai et mordis son nez bulbeux à pleines dents, jusqu'au sang. Aujourd'hui encore je serais incapable de vous dire porquoi j'ai fait cela: je n'ai simplement pas pu me retenir" (2006/2021, pp. 1368–1369).

33. "Trevor-Roper, je le sais bien, n'a pas soufflé mot de cet épisode, Bullock non plus, ni aucun autre des historiens qui se sont penchés sur les derniers jours du Führer. Pourtant, je vous l'assure, cela a eu lieu" (2006/2021, p. 1370).

34. "Je le soulevai, le soupesai, puis l'abattis à toute force sur la nuque de Thomas. J'entendis craquer ses vertèbres et il bascula en avant, foudroyé, en travers du corps de Clemens. Je laissai tomber le barreau et contemplai les corps. . . . J'étais triste, mais sans trop savoir pourquoi" (2006/2021, pp. 1389–1390).

35. "leur violence, leur alcoolisme, les dépressions nerveuses, les suicides, ma propre tristesse, tout cela démontrait que l'*autre* existe, existe en tant qu'autre, en tant qu'humain, et qu'aucune volonté, aucune idéologie, aucune quantité de bêtise et d'alcool ne peut rompre ce lien, ténu mais indestructible. Cela est un fait, et non une opinion" (2006/2021, p. 217).

36. "Comme me l'avait expliqué Eichmann, on étudiait de nouvelles méthodes" (2006/2021, p. 217).

37. "l'état d'avancement de la résolution de la question juive et ses perspectives futures" (2006/2021, p. 779).

38. "Ma responsabilité s'arrête au départ du train, le reste, je ne peux pas en parler" (2006/2021, p. 801).

39. In the ongoing discussion of Arendt's "banality of evil" thesis, several historians and Holocaust scholars have found that Arendt (1963) focuses too much on who Eichmann was rather than on what he did. For example, Alan Wolfe (2011) has criticized Arendt for avoiding, or at least toning down, the enormity of Eichmann's evil actions. See also Cesarani (2006).

40. "'Vous avez lu Kant, je suppose? En ce moment, poursuivit-il en se frottant les lèvres, je lis la *Critique de la raison pratique*. . . . Et j'ai beaucoup réfléchi, surtout, à la question de l'Impératif kantien. Vos êtes, j'en suis sûr, d'accord avec moi pour dire que tout homme honnête doit vivre selon cet impératif.' Je bus une gorgée de vin et acquiesçai. Eichmann continuait: 'L'Impératif, tel que je le comprends, dit: Le principe de ma volonté individuelle doit devenir tel qu'il puisse devenir le principe de la Loi morale. En agissant, l'homme légifère'" (2006/2021, p. 808).

41. "'qu'en temps de guerre, en vertu si vous voulez de l'état d'exception causé par le danger, l'Impératif kantien est suspendu'" (2006/2021, p. 808).

42. "'Pourtant, c'est assez simple, je pense. Nous sommes tous d'accord que dans un État national-socialiste le fondement ultime de la loi positive est la volonté du Führer. C'est le principe bien connu *Führerworte haben Gesetzeskraft*. . . . C'est ainsi que le Dr. Frank, dans son traité sur le droit constitutionnel, a étendu la définition du *Führerprinzip* de la manière suivante: *Agissez de manière que le Führer, s'il connaissat votre action, l'approuverait*. In n'y a aucune contradiction entre ce principe et l'Impératif de Kant'" (2006/2021, p. 809).

43. Eichmann and Aue's conversation about Kant hints at Arendt's analysis of Eichmann's statement, in his court testimony in Jerusalem, that he had attempted to abide by Kant's moral imperative. For me as a reader of Littell's novel, Arendt's explanation of Eichmann's misreading of Kant suggests that Aue misunderstands Kant in a similar way: instead of recognizing that, for Kant, the legislator is the moral self, for Aue and Eichmann, the legislator was Hitler. See Arendt (1963).

44. "le *Volk*, dont la volonté collective s'exprime par le Führer qui le représente. . . . [N]ous servons le *Volk* et devons le servir comme le sert le Führer, avec une abnégation totale" (2006/2021, p. 810).

45. "Et l'Impératif kantien? À vrai dire, je n'en savais trop rien, j'avais raconté un peu n'importe quoi à ce pauvre Eichmann" (2006/2021, p. 815).

46. "et lorsqu'il dit à ses juges qu'il pensait que l'extermination des Juifs était une erreur, on peut le croire . . . mais une fois la décision prise, il fallait la mener à bien" (2006/2021, p. 814).

47. "Par le hasard de la survie d'archives et de la justice des vainqueurs, ces discours son devenus célèbres bien en dehors des cercles fermés auxquels ils étaient destinés; vous ne trouverez pas un ouvrage sur la SS, sur le Reichsführer, ou sur la destruction des Juifs où ils ne soient pas cités; si leur contenu vous intéresse, vous pouvez aisément les consulter, et en plusieurs

langues; le discours du 4 octobre figure tout entier au protocole du grand procès de Nurem-berg, sous la cote 1919-PS (c'est évidement sous cette forme que j'ai enfin pu l'étudier en détail, après la guerre, bien que dans les grande lignes j'en eusse pris connaissance à Posen même)" (2006/2021, p. 949).

48. "avec une franchise qu'il n'a jamais à ma connaissance égalée ni avant ni après, avec fran-chise donc et d'une manière qu'on pourrait même dire crue, y dressait le programme de la destruction des Juifs" (2006/2021, p. 950).

49. "sans euphémismes, sans clins d'œil, avec des mot simples et brutaux comme *tuer—exterminer*, dit-il, *je veux dire tuer ou donner l'ordre de tuer*" (2006/2021, p. 951).

50. "alors le Führer était au courant, et pis, le Führer l'avait voulu" (2006/2021, p. 951).

51. "c'était afin qu'aucun d'entre eux ne puisse, plus tard, dire qu'il ne savais pas, ne puisse tenter de faire croire, en cas de défaite, qu'il était innocent du pire" (2006/2021, p. 952). For a historian's interpretation of Himmler's Posen speech, see Friedländer (2003).

52. "c'était pour les *mouiller*, et ils le comprenaient très bien, d'où leur désarroi" (2006/2021, p. 952).

53. "Cet officier, après la guerre, a acquis une certaine notoriété, en raison du nombre colossal de gens mis à mort sous sa responsabilité et aussi des mémoires francs et lucides qu'il rédigea en prison, lors de son procès. Pourtant c'était un officier absolument typique de l'IKL, travailleur, obstiné et limité" (2006/2021, p. 864).

54. "Depuis que le Reichsführer a décidé d'affecter Auschwitz à la destruction des Juifs, nous n'avons que des problèmes" (2006/2021, p. 869).

55. "J'ai seulement pu commencer à construire des installations permanentes, avec une capacité de réception adéquate, en janvier de cette année. Mais tout n'est pas encore au point" (2006/2021, p. 869).

56. "Pourtant, c'est beaucoup plus efficace que la méthode de Wirth" (2006/2021, p. 873).

57. There is a notable similarity between Broszat's editorial practice and that of the editors of the critical edition of Hitler's *Mein Kampf*. See https://www.mein-kampf-edition.de

58. "'Eh bien, à Stalingrad. Tu ne te souviens pas? Tu étais là.' Un souvenir, oui, j'en avais un, et je l'ai écrit avec les autres, mais je l'avais rangé au fond de ma tête, au grenier des hallucinations et des rêves; maintenant, cette cicatrice venait tout bouleverser, j'avais subitement l'impression de ne plus pouvoir être sûr de rien" (2006/2021, pp. 990–991). While the word *grenier* (attic) establishes a link to Aue's search for items that belonged to him and his sister in their family home in Antibes, *cicatrice* (wound) does not refer just to the physical scar that Thomas got in Stalingrad; it is also a trace or visible sign of a physical or psychic trauma.

59. "Des histories, je veux bien en raconter: mais alors, en piochant un peu au hasard de mes souvenirs et de mes notes; je vous l'ai dit, je fatigue, il faut commencer à en finir. . . . Et c'est pourquoi, je le reconnais, si je change un peu de méthode, c'est surtout pour moi, que ça vous plaise ou non, encore une marque de mon égoïsme sans bornes, fruit certainement de ma mauvaise éducation" (2006/2021, pp. 1119–1120). It is characteristic of Aue that, acknowledging his "égoïsme sans bornes," he blames his education.

60. "Cette image, je dois l'avouer, m'effrayait: j'avais beau la détailler, je ne reconnaissais pas cet homme dont le visage, sous sa casquette, se réduisait à une tache blanche. . . . Et main-tenant cette photo ambiguë et insaisissable ruinait ce qui me restait de souvenirs, remplaçait sa présence vivante par un visage flou et un uniforme. Pris de rage, je déchirai la photographie en plusieurs morceaux et les jetai par le balcon. Puis je vidai mon verre et m'en versai aussitôt un autre. Je transpirais, j'avais envie de bondir hors de ma peau, trop étroite pour ma colère et mon angoisse" (2006/2021, pp. 1151–1152).

61. "puis je repartais dans un autre récit embrouillé et confus" (2006/2021, p. 1154).

62. "Mais cette douceur me mettait hors de moi: que me voulait donc cette fille?" (2006/2021, p. 1162).

63. "'Où sont-ils passés, tes voisins juifs de Moabit? Tu ne te l'es jamais demandé? À l'Est? On les a envoyés travailler à l'Est?' . . . Je rageais, je devais être blême, elle paraissait écouter attentive-ment, elle ne bougeait pas. . . . 'On tue des gens, tu comprends, c'est ce qu'on fait, tous, ton mari était un assassin, je suis un assassin, et toi, tu est la complice d'assassins, tu portes et tu manges le fruit de notre labeur.' Elle était livide, mais son visage ne reflétait qu'une infinie tristesse: 'Vous êtes un malheureux'" (2006/2021, pp. 1166–1167).

64. "'Si nous perdons la guerre, la vengeance de nos ennemis sera impitoyable.'—'Je ne parlais pas de ça. Même si nous ne perdons pas la guerre, nous allons payer. Il faudra payer'" (2006/2021, p. 1170).

65. "Est-ce que vous savez pourquoi vous tuez les Juifs? Le savez-vous?" (2006/2021, p. 1247).

66. "En tuant les Juifs, disait-elle, nous avons voulu nous tuer nous-mêmes, tuer le Juif en nous, tuer ce qui en nous ressemblait à l'idée que nous nous faisons du Juif" (2006/2021, p. 1247).

67. "cette belle maison vide" (2006/2021, p. 1241).

68. "lorsque je l'écrivais, elle me paraissait véridique, en adéquation avec la réalité, mais il semblerait qu'en fait elle ne corresponde pas à la vérité. Pourquoi en est-il ainsi? Difficile à dire. Ce n'est pas que mes souvenirs soient confus, au contraire, j'en garde de nombreux et de très précis, mais beaucoup d'entre eux se chevauchent et même se contredisent, et leur statut est incertain" (2006/2021, p. 1242).

69. "cette fille que nous avions pendue un jour d'hiver dans le parc derrière la statue de Chevtchenko, une fille jeune et saine et resplendissante de vie . . . de quel droit l'avions-nous pendue, comment pouvait-on pendre cette fille, et je sanglotais sans fin, ravagé par son souvenir, ma Notre-Dame-des-Neiges, ce n'était pas des remords, je n'aviat pas de remords, je ne me sentais pas coupable, je ne pensais pas que les choses auraient pu ou dû être autrement, seulement je comprenais ce que cela voulait dire de prendre une fille, nous l'avions pendue comme un boucher égorge un bœuf, sans passion, parce qu'il fallait le faire . . . c'était une jeune fille qui avait été une petite fille peut-être hereuse et qui entrait alors dans la vie, une vie pleine d'assassins qu'elle n'avait pas su éviter, une fille comme ma sœur en quelque sorte, la sœur de quelqu'un, peut-être, comme moi aussi j'étais le frère de quelqu'un, et une telle cruauté n'avait pas de nom, quelle que soit sa nécessité objective elle ruinait tout, si l'on pouvait faire ça, prendre une jeune fille comme ça, alors on pouvait tout faire, il n'y avait plus acune assurance . . . cela ne rimait absolument à rien, et voilà pourquoi je pleurais, je ne comprenais plus rien et je voulais être seul pour ne plus rien comprendre" (2006/2021, p. 1301).

70. "Je regardais à peine les *Häftlinge*, ce n'était pas leur sort individuel qui me préoccupait, mais leur sort collectif, et de toute façon ils se ressemblaient tous, c'était une masse grise, sale" (2006/2021, p. 1216).

71. I am therefore unpersuaded by Littell's claim that Aue is "not so much character as he is a voice, a tone, a gaze" (Nora & Littell, 2007, p. 29). It does not follow, however, that his first-person narration does not include subversive accounts or counterdiscourses. These become, as I have argued, more important after the Stalingrad section. As Orit Yushinsky Troupin puts it, "Such subversions of Aue's ostensibly authentic and coherent life story ironize and delegitimize what on a first reading may seem to be a univocal account of a Nazi officer" (2020, p. 317; cf. Rasson, 2012).

5

Kazuo Ishiguro's *The Remains of the Day* and James Ivory's *The Remains of the Day*

Although Jonathan Littell's *The Kindly Ones* and the British author Kazuo Ishiguro's *The Remains of the Day* (1989/2005) are very different novels, both use narrative fiction to explore how the main character attempts to come to terms with his memory of aspects of the Holocaust. Aue and Stevens, the protagonist of Ishiguro's novel, are dissimilar, in some ways even contrastive characters. And yet, combining the functions of main character and first-person narrator, they both look back at and reminisce about their lives—lives that, albeit to varying extents and in different ways, were marked by the Second World War and the Holocaust.

This chapter will show how Ishiguro makes his narrator, a British man who did not participate in the Second World War, present fragments of his autobiographical narrative in a way that gradually reveals his complicity in the Nazis' unspeakable crime. Identifying and discussing aspects of Stevens's first-person narrative that are related to the Holocaust, I ask how Ishiguro activates and combines constituent elements of first-person narration in ways that interlink narrative and memory, and how this narration raises ethical issues that are also relevant to me as a reader. Focusing on Stevens's ethics as a character and as a narrator, I relate his values not only to the ethics of Miss Kenton and Lord Darlington but also to the ethical challenge prompted by my acts of reading and rereading Ishiguro's narrative discourse. In my analysis, this ethical challenge also becomes an interpretive one: How can I understand a protagonist who as a character is overcome by feelings of loss, love, regret, and disillusionment, yet as a narrator is "complexly reliable and unreliable" (Phelan, 2005, p. 31)? I argue that Stevens's memories and interpretations revolve around the Holocaust as an unmentionable historical fact that, particularly on a second reading, becomes an underlying presence throughout. Concomitantly, the collective memory of the Holocaust in contemporary Europe becomes a major thematic concern—and not only for Ishiguro but also for me as a reader. When I watch, and particularly

Memory and Narrative Ethics. Jakob Lothe, Oxford University Press. © Oxford University Press (2025).
DOI: 10.1093/9780197579534.003.0006

rewatch, James Ivory's adaptation, I find that the Holocaust plays a key role in the film too, challenging me as a viewer to engage in ethical reflection. I discuss Ivory's film in the second part of the chapter.[1]

Ishiguro's *The Remains of the Day*

I begin by summarizing the "focalized series of events" (Bal, 2018, p. 37) of Ishiguro's novel and Ivory's adaptation.[2] Stevens is an aging butler whose primary mission in life has been to serve Lord Darlington, recently deceased. When the novel begins in the mid-1950s, Stevens embarks on a journey from Darlington Hall in Oxfordshire to the west of England, where he hopes to meet a former colleague, the housekeeper Miss Kenton. Driving westward, Stevens starts a process of remembering fragments of his life at Darlington Hall from 1922 onward; increasingly, this mnemonic process also makes him remember, and communicate as first-person narrator, episodes that he may want to forget. The process of remembering is presented as a series of analepses that indicate Stevens was complicit in antisemitism since, responding to Lord Darlington's request, he dismissed two young Jewish women whose work at the estate was exemplary. This happened in 1932. When, about a year later, Lord Darlington admits to Stevens that it was "wrong" to dismiss the Jewish girls, Stevens finds it difficult to admit that, as a butler whose duty it is to serve his employer, he too was wrong. Protesting strongly when Stevens informs her about his decision to dismiss the girls in 1932, Miss Kenton tells him that it is totally unacceptable to dismiss two employees because they are Jewish. When, many years later, Stevens at last meets with Miss Kenton, he hopes to persuade her to return with him to Darlington Hall, taking up again her position as housekeeper and serving, together with Stevens, the estate's new owner, the American Mr. Farraday. However, as her daughter is expecting a baby, Miss Kenton does not want to leave Cornwall. Stevens returns to Darlington Hall alone.

As a summary of a narrative text is necessarily selective, and thus interpretive, it leaves out much, and it does not indicate how the text is presented and focalized as narrative discourse. One essential feature of both the novel and the film adaptation not captured by the summary is the interplay between Stevens's narration as he is driving westward through the English countryside and the different temporal layers of analeptic fragments incorporated into that narration. Given that, in Ishiguro's novel as well as in Ivory's film,

Lord Darlington admits that it was wrong to dismiss the two Jewish girls, and given that, in historical reality, the European Holocaust occurred a few years later, did Stevens, in his eagerness to serve his employer, make a mistake similar to his employer's? Moreover, is it possible that even Miss Kenton, who protested against the act of dismissing the Jewish girls, was implicated in the decision? And if she were, what about me as a reader and viewer? If I were in Stevens's or Miss Kenton's shoes, what would I have done? The way these questions blend into an ethical inquiry is a characteristic feature not only of this chapter but of all the narrative analyses presented in this book. The perhaps obvious yet important reason is that although not all the verbal narratives and film narratives I discuss deal exclusively with the Holocaust, they are all framed by the historical reality of the Second World War and the Holocaust as the nadir of that war. This external frame of reference (Hrushovski, 1984; cf. Toker, 2010) is so strong that it not just colors but influences my interpretations, even though neither Ishiguro nor Ivory uses the word "Holocaust." Asking whether Stevens makes a mistake similar to Lord Darlington's, I will show that this question, which is painful for Stevens and therefore difficult for him to ask, emerges gradually. This gradual revelation of painful memories is at the center of the novel's narrative ethics; rereading the novel, I find that the memories revolve around and are stirred by the Holocaust. As Stevens interprets his experiences as he remembers and narrates them, the narrative discourse includes self-interpretive elements that influence my own interpretation. *The Remains of the Day* illustrates and supports a key point argued by Jens Brockmeier: that "narrative experience is experience interpreted." Ishiguro's novel and Ivory's adaptation also support Brockmeier's accompanying point, that "memories and their interpretations are inherently interconnected elements" (2015, p. 114).

The two properties of storytelling that Mieke Bal emphasizes prove highly relevant to my discussion: "It concerns others, and it is always, at least in part, fictional" (2018, p. 37). Although, as the above summary indicates, Stevens's storytelling revolves around himself, it also concerns others, particularly Miss Kenton and Lord Darlington. Moreover, although it would be misleading to consider Stevens an unreliable narrator, it becomes increasingly clear that his narration draws on fragments of memory. As he includes a number of these fragments, he necessarily excludes others, some of which are perhaps too disturbing for him to remember—and which for that very reason may be significant. Thus, the life narrative he constructs inevitably omits, censors, and places in a positive light parts of the life that he is remembering.

The Remains of the Day is also a rich illustration of Ricoeur's notion of "narrative identity" (1990/1994, p. 140) as not only complex but also dynamic, changing over time, and activating, implicitly or explicitly, aspects of memory. If I cannot conceive of narrative divorced from memory, neither can I think of my own identity without remembering something before the stage or point of my life where I am now. There is a link here between my situation as a reader and that of Stevens as a first-person narrator. This connection is an integral part of Ishiguro's narrative ethics.

My discussion concentrates on the textual segments where the question of the dismissal of the Jewish girls, and thus the connection to the Holocaust, is most prominent. I argue, though, that this issue infiltrates all of Stevens's narration, complicating and yet curiously motivating his narrative venture. I also suggest that this dimension of Ishiguro's novel—as well as of Ivory's adaptation—is particularly important with a view to the interplay of memory and narrative, accentuating aspects of narrative ethics.

Narrative Beginning and Miss Kenton's Letter

The novel begins thus:

> It seems increasingly likely that I really will undertake the expedition that has been preoccupying my imagination now for some days. An expedition, I should say, which I will undertake alone, in the comfort of Mr Farraday's Ford; an expedition which, as I foresee it, will take me through much of the finest countryside of England to the West Country.[3]

A beginning, notes Edward W. Said in *Beginnings*, is difficult to pinpoint, and the meaning of a narrative beginning can be hard to ascertain: "For in the act of asking a question about the meaning of a beginning, I seem to have discerned vague outlines of significance where very little had been suspected" (1975, p. 29). A beginning may include a kind of motivation, and a motivation (however vague) may incorporate ethical elements. Rereading the beginning of Ishiguro's novel, I am struck by the semantic range of the word "expedition": Stevens is not just driving toward the West Country; he is also embarking on an expedition, or journey, into his past. That spatial and temporal aspects of narrative are intertwined right from the beginning becomes clearer about a page later, when Stevens admits that his "expedition" is motivated by a letter he has received from a certain Miss Kenton. He hastens to add, "But let me make it immediately clear what I mean by this; what I mean to say is that Miss Kenton's letter set off a certain chain of ideas to do with professional matters here at Darlington Hall" (p. 5). Although the last part of this sentence may be true on one level, on a different yet related level it is not. Stevens may be thinking of practical matters, but he is primarily thinking of Miss Kenton. In fact, this sentence is an early illustration of the truth of the question Miss Kenton asks her superior at a crucial point later in the narrative: "Why, Mr Stevens, why, why, why do you always have to *pretend*?" (p. 162, original emphasis). The consequences of pretense are among the novel's ethical concerns. One aspect of Stevens's need to pretend is his tendency to project his memories onto those of Miss Kenton, as when he finds that her letter is imbued with "a deep nostalgia for her days at Darlington Hall" (p. 50). So they may be, but this is nostalgia he shares because, though he cannot or does not manage to express this verbally, he has been missing her terribly since she left in 1936.

The reason I interpret Stevens's opening remarks the way I do is that, rereading the novel, I build on and activate my knowledge of the whole text. As I have read Stevens's narrative presentation of his relationship with Miss Kenton, I know that it was, and probably still is, complicated—and that these complications were in large part caused by his inability to communicate his feelings. Writing about the "magical quality" of the view from the second floor of Darlington Hall, Miss Kenton adds:

> If this is a painful memory, forgive me. But I will never forget that time we both watched your father walking back and forth in front of the summerhouse, looking down at the ground as though he hoped to find some precious jewel he had dropped there. (p. 52)

"Painful" is a word Stevens cannot or is unable to use, but when he starts the next paragraph by noting, "It is something of a revelation that this memory from over thirty years should have remained with Miss Kenton as it had done with me" (p. 52), I understand that "this memory" is distressing for him too. Asking *why* the memory—or rather, their shared memory—is painful, I find that the narrative discourse gives no clear answer. Yet it gives a partial answer that turns on or revolves around questions of value and priorities in the main characters' lives. Robert Eaglestone observes that "Ishiguro's characters are bound by their actions and the chain of reactions that follow, and this leads to attempted justifications, regrets, a desire for consolation, and forms of working-through or coming to terms, or the failure of these" (2023, p. 188). If Miss Kenton's "painful memory" possesses an element of resignation that signals a sense of lost opportunities, that recognition of a lost opportunity—of a relationship with Miss Kenton—is perhaps even stronger for Stevens than it is for her.

In interpreting Stevens's references to Miss Kenton's letter in this way I build on the text's self-interpretive elements. These are of two kinds. First, there is Stevens's interpretation, including his insistence that his reason for visiting Miss Kenton is "professional" rather than personal: "Miss Kenton's letter set off a certain chain of ideas to do with professional matters here at Darlington Hall." Second, as this example indicates, the narrative discourse suggests a different interpretation that builds on, and yet moves beyond that given by Stevens. Thus, my interpretation of the narrative's beginning not only incorporates but also questions aspects of Stevens's interpretation. Miss Kenton's letter plays a key role here in three linked ways: it motivates him to undertake the trip; it activates his memories and makes him communicate them to the reader; and it stirs him to focus on aspects of his memories, and of his life, that raise ethical issues.

As the narrative is launched by a letter and Stevens's interpretation of that letter, Stevens is predominantly a *reader* at the outset of the narrative. Not only is his reading of the letter already an interpretation: it becomes increasingly clear that he selectively refers to and quotes from passages in the letter that support his interpretation. The narrative text thus begins by referring to a different text that also includes narrative elements (as Miss Kenton is presumably writing about her life after she left Darlington), but most of this text remains unknown to me since Stevens gives me just glimpses of it. The parts of the letter that Stevens does not or cannot pass on to me as a reader constitute a paralipsis, that is, something the narrator has deleted from or does not include in his narration (Genette, 1980; cf. Toker, 2022). This paralipsis is significant since it suggests that his real reason for embarking on the trip is a wish, or hope, that, after all the years that have passed since Miss Kenton left Darlington Hall, a relationship with her might prove possible after all.

Stevens's Journey Westward—and into His Past

The combination of Stevens's first-person narration and excerpts of dialogue incorporated into this narration establishes a narrative pattern that contributes decisively to the novel's narrative ethics. The analepses gradually become longer as Stevens, driving westward toward Miss Kenton, is increasingly absorbed in his memories:

> But I see I am becoming preoccupied with these memories and this is perhaps a little foolish. This trip represents, after all, a rare opportunity for me to savour to the full the many splendours of the English countryside, and I know I shall greatly regret it later if I allow myself to become unduly diverted. (p. 70)

This does not mean, however, that the passages in the narrative present that record "this trip" become unimportant. Tensions and inconsistencies between statements and reflections can be ethically revealing, and so are Stevens's attempts to connect them to each other. This aspect of the novel's ethics becomes, as I will show, particularly important toward the end of the narrative.

Following the "Prologue: July 1956 Darlington Hall" (p. 1), the novel is divided into six parts.[4] The analepsis that includes Stevens's memory of the dismissal of the Jewish girls is presented at the beginning of "Day Three—Evening Moscombe, near Tavistock, Devon" (p. 151). The Jewish girls' dismissal from Darlington Hall is not only a revealing example of how an event blends into and is colored by the narrator's experience of that event; it also shows how Stevens is haunted by fragments of memory that prove inseparable from that experience. Although Stevens finds it difficult to come to terms with this particular event, I argue that his interpretation of it gradually changes as his narration progresses, thus constituting a self-interpretive element on which my own reading draws. This gradual change, of which Miss Kenton and Lord Darlington are important precursors, is illustrative of the narrative ethics of The Remains of the Day.

Temporally situated in 1932–1933, the analepsis in which Stevens communicates his memory of the dismissal of the Jewish girls consists of four parts; these are contrapuntally related in a way that complicates and challenges Stevens's ethos of professionally serving the good and presumably infallible leader. At the center of the analepsis is the request that, after having summoned Stevens to his study, Lord Darlington makes:

> "I've been doing a great deal of thinking, Stevens. A great deal of thinking. And I've reached my conclusion. We cannot have Jews on the staff here at Darlington Hall."

"Sir?"

"It's for the good of this house, Stevens. In the interests of the guests we have staying here. I've looked into this carefully, Stevens, and I'm letting you know my conclusion."

"Very well, sir."

"Tell me, Stevens, we have a few on the staff at the moment, don't we? Jews, I mean."

"I believe two of the present staff members would fall into that category, sir."

"Ah." His lordship paused for a moment, staring out of his window. "Of course, you'll have to let them go."

"I beg your pardon, sir?"

"It's regrettable, Stevens, but we have no choice." (pp. 154–155)

That Stevens asks Lord Darlington not just one but two questions is a strong indication that he is genuinely surprised by the request. Just *how* surprised is difficult to ascertain, partly since, remembering and narrating the "episode" (pp. 146, 158), he is searching for extenuating circumstances. These include, he thinks, the unhealthy influence that Mrs. Carolyn Barnet – a "glamorous lady" (p. 153) with antisemitic attitudes – exerted on Lord Darlington in numerous conversations with him at Darlington Hall in the summer of 1932. When Stevens then proceeds to tell Miss Kenton that it is his "duty" (p. 156) to dismiss the Jewish girls, she responds:

"Mr Stevens, I am outraged that you can sit there and utter what you have just done as though you were discussing orders for the larder. I simply cannot believe it. You are saying Ruth and Sarah are to be dismissed on the grounds that they are Jewish?"

"Miss Kenton, I have just this moment explained the situation to you fully. His lordship has made his decision and there is nothing for you and I to debate over."

"Does it not occur to you, Mr Stevens, that to dismiss Ruth and Sarah on these grounds would be simply—*wrong*? I will not stand for such things. I will not work in a house in which such things can occur." (p. 157, original emphasis)

When Stevens replies by referring to his "professional duty," Miss Kenton reiterates, "I am telling you, Mr Stevens, if you dismiss my girls tomorrow, it will be wrong, a sin as any sin ever was one and I will not continue to work in such a house" (p. 157). Stevens does not or cannot say that Miss

Kenton is not right. His only recourse is to his "duty" as a butler. By using and repeating the word *wrong*, Miss Kenton highlights the ethical dimension of the decisions that Lord Darlington and Stevens make. For her, it is wrong to dismiss an employee because he or she is Jewish—or, more broadly, because of his or her ethnic affiliation. While her ethical position makes her oppose the dismissal of Ruth and Sarah—it is revealing that, in contrast to Stevens, she uses their first names—her act of protest in a specific situation tells me something important not only about her work ethics but about her values and priorities in life.

Ishiguro's use of dialogue, or direct discourse, simultaneously shapes and accentuates the narrative ethics of this passage. If Ishiguro he had decided to make Stevens report or summarize the part of the analepsis that presents the dismissal, Miss Kenton's response to the decision might not have been included—or it might have been toned down and made less forceful. By making dialogue part of the analepsis Ishiguro augments the ethical dimension not only of this encounter but of the novel overall.[5]

Both in the passage considered here and later in the novel, the dialogue that Stevens reports has ethical components that challenge his own ethics. I interpret this aspect of his narration, which is a sustained act of remembrance, as a belated attempt or need to negotiate issues he has been confronted with and choices he has made—choices that, though he may be unable to state this explicitly, he now regrets. Moreover, the fact that he sometimes admits that he is unsure whether he remembers the dialogue correctly makes his narration more reliable.

Reading and rereading the passage in which Miss Kenton considers the dismissal of Ruth and Sarah to be wrong, I align my ethical position with Miss Kenton's. Thus, in this narrative situation there is an attitudinal alliance between me as a reader of the novel and Miss Kenton as a character in the novel. As I experience that Miss Kenton's ethos is linked to my own ethos, I tend to think that, at this stage of Stevens's narration, Miss Kenton's ethos is closer to the implied author's ethics than is Stevens's.[6] Conversely, I gather that there is a considerable, and perhaps increasing, attitudinal distance between Stevens and the implied author. Such a distribution of ethical affinity and distance becomes part of my interpretation of the passage. While the interpretation may be plausible, it needs to be qualified as the narrative progresses. Developing and refining his narrative ethics through Steven's narration, Ishiguro makes me connect the ethical dilemmas and conflicts observable in this passage to those of later dialogues. It does not follow that

Miss Kenton was not right to say it was wrong to dismiss Ruth and Sarah. But her ethical position, as well as those of Stevens as protagonist and Ishiguro as implied author, become more nuanced as Stevens's narration continues.

Stevens's challenge is that, for him, the word "wrong" does not mean the same as it does for Miss Kenton when she considers the decision of dismissing Ruth and Sarah "wrong." Although he seems genuinely surprised by Lord Darlington's request, he thinks it would be wrong not to implement it. Precisely for this reason he is presented with an ethical issue when, about a year later, Lord Darlington returns to "the matter" that Stevens calls a "very minor episode in the thirties" (p. 146):

> "Oh, Stevens," he said to me. "I've been meaning to say to you. About that business last year. About the Jewish maids. You recall the matter?"
> "Indeed, sir."
> "I suppose there's no way of tracing them now, is there? It was wrong what happened and one would like to recompense them somehow."
> "I will certainly look into the matter, sir. But I am not at all certain it will be possible to ascertain their whereabouts at this stage."
> "See what you can do. It was wrong, what occurred." (p. 159)

Admitting that he made a grave mistake, Lord Darlington does something that, according to Stevens's theory of leadership, he should by all accounts be incapable of doing. That a readiness to admit a mistake requires a measure of courage, and that it is a sign rather than a qualification of good leadership does not seem to strike Stevens in this narrative situation. Moreover, in common with Miss Kenton, whose protest against the dismissal Lord Darlington probably does not know of, Darlington repeats the word "wrong."

A word that is repeated in literary discourse, notes Hillis Miller (1982) in *Fiction and Repetition*, does not necessarily become true, but it almost certainly becomes more important. In this instance, the word "wrong" becomes both true and important. An unexpected ethical alliance thus emerges between Stevens's superior, Lord Darlington, and his subordinate, Miss Kenton. Caught in the middle, Stevens becomes complicit in a "matter" more challenging than his own use of the word "episode" (p. 158) suggests. As the passage indicates, Stevens does not explicitly state that he concurs with his master's reassessment. I consider his uncertainty about the Jewish girls' "whereabouts at this stage" as a hint that they may perhaps have left England. If they did or were forced to do so because they were wrongly dismissed, there is even the possible implication that they might have perished in the Holocaust. In making this suggestion I may, however, be influenced by my interpretation of Ivory's adaptation, where, as I will show, this implication is much stronger.

The fourth and last part of the analepsis in which Stevens recalls "this episode of the dismissing of the Jewish employees" (p. 163) is the second meeting between Stevens and Miss Kenton. It is, he now tells her, "at least a great comfort to hear his lordship declare so unequivocally that it was all a terrible misunderstanding." He adds that he wants Miss Kenton to know this "since I recall you were as distressed by the episode as I was" (p. 161). At one level, Stevens is not only being economical with the truth; this is a distorted version of the truth. His remark stirs the following riposte:

> "I'm sorry, Mr Stevens," Miss Kenton said behind me in an entirely new voice, as though she had just been jolted from a dream, "I don't understand you." Then as I turned to her, she went on: "As I recall, you thought it was only right and proper that Ruth and Sarah be sent packing. You were positively cheerful about it."
> "Now really, Miss Kenton, that is quite incorrect and unfair. The whole matter caused me great concern, great concern indeed. It is hardly the sort of thing I like to see happen in this house."
> "Then why, Mr Stevens, did you not tell me so at the time? . . .
> Do you realize, Mr Stevens, how much it would have meant to me if you had thought to share your feelings last year? You knew how upset I was when my girls were dismissed. Do you realize how much it would have helped me? Why, Mr Stevens, why, why, why do you always have to *pretend*? . . .
> I suffered so much over Ruth and Sarah leaving us. And I suffered all the more because I believed I was alone." (p. 162, original emphasis)

Stevens is provoked by Miss Kenton's use of the verb "pretend: "Pretend? Why, really . . ." (p. 162). Her use of the word implies that, though he did what Lord Darlington asked him to do, Stevens was surprised by and took exception to his master's decision. Miss Kenton thus suggests that, at one level at least, his action was insincere. She also implies that the attitudinal distance between her and Stevens is less than he pretends it is. Indicating that his support would have alleviated her suffering, she hints at Stevens's unrealized potential as a friend—and possibly even as a partner.

At this point of the narrative discourse, Ishiguro's narrative presentation of the Holocaust intersects with his account of the relationship between Stevens and Miss Kenton. Memory plays a vital role in Ishiguro's fictional exploration of both these aspects of the novel. Moreover, although Ishiguro's rendering of the relationship between Stevens and Miss Kenton contributes decisively to the novel's narrative ethics—and particularly the ethics associated with and accentuated by the dismissal of the Jewish girls—Stevens's first-person narration gradually reveals that ethical questions are part of—or perhaps, rather, force themselves into—his presentation of all the characters he remembers. Thus, aspects of these characters' ethics inform my gradually evolving idea of Stevens's ethics. I specify that my idea of Stevens's values is not limited to questions pertaining to the Holocaust. Yet I argue that Ishiguro presents ethical challenges associated with and sparked by this event in a way that highlights their historical specificity while at the same time demonstrating their continuing relevance. This aspect of *The Remains of the Day* is furthered by Ishiguro's narrative presentation of the characters whose attitudes, actions, and views are variously related to Stevens's ethics. I reiterate that since the ethics of all the characters in the novel need to be extrapolated from Stevens's first-person narration, their ethics is colored by his narration and his interpretation. Yet Ishiguro's narrative method, and particularly his use of dialogue (free direct discourse), enables him to present the reader with a range of values that supplement, support, and challenge Stevens's values.

As noted, Miss Kenton, whose work at Darlington Hall is exemplary and who has taught and cooperated with Ruth and Sarah, cannot believe that Stevens blindly follows Darlington's orders. Miss Kenton senses that Stevens's penchant for putting his sense of duty above his actual feelings has negative consequences not just for himself and for her (it becomes increasingly clear that they were attracted to each other) but for others too. While Stevens thinks it is his duty to do what Lord Darlington has told him to do, Miss Kenton is convinced it is his duty *not* to dismiss Ruth and Sarah "on the grounds that they are Jewish." Elegantly and thought-provokingly, Ishiguro contrasts the values that Stevens attaches to his idea and practice of serving Lord Darlington with those Miss Kenton attaches to her idea and practice of supporting Ruth and Sarah.

Strong as this contrast is, though, it is qualified when Miss Kenton, who tells Stevens that she will resign from her post at Darlington Hall if Ruth and Sarah are dismissed, does not leave after all. When Stevens, "in an ironic tone of voice" (p. 158), reminds Miss Kenton of this inconsistency, she responds,

"It was cowardice, Mr Stevens. Simple cowardice. Where could I have gone? I have no family. . . . I was so frightened, Mr Stevens" (p. 161). Why is Miss Kenton frightened? She may be frightened for the reasons she mentions, but the most important reason may be that she does not want to, or simply cannot, leave Stevens. In my interpretation of this key scene, there is a connection between the use of "frightened" and the verb I have already highlighted, "pretend." If, as I have suggested, she senses that Stevens allowed his ethics of service and duty to overrule his ethical instinct to protest against Lord Darlington's decision, then he too would have acted inconsistently— and then there might have been room or possibility for a mutual support that could have alleviated not only her predicament but also Stevens's; then they would not have been "alone" (p. 162).

Pretend, Regret, Serve

If "pretend" is a key word in the novel's narrative ethics, so is "regret." Significantly, it is Miss Kenton who, realizing that Stevens's father is dying after having suffered a stroke, uses this word too: "But you must come now, Mr Stevens, or else you may deeply regret it later" (p. 108). Stevens accompanies Miss Kenton to his father's room, finding the situation "most distressing. Nevertheless, I must now return downstairs" (p. 108). Thus, he is not present when his father dies a few minutes later. When Miss Kenton tells him, "Mr Stevens, I'm very sorry. Your father passed away about four minutes ago," all he can say is "I see" (p. 110). While this response contributes to Ishiguro's characterization of Stevens, I want to highlight Miss Kenton's care, respect, and affect: "Then for a moment she bowed her head and a sob escaped her" (p. 110). In a way, she does what he should have done—not because she is obliged to but because she believes it is the right thing to do. That Stevens does not say that he regrets not having been present when his father dies does not mean that he may not do so. Aspects of his tendency to pretend may be operative here too. If pretense is also in play in his memory of the dismissal of Ruth and Sarah, he may regret that decision as well. Furthermore, he may regret having missed the opportunity to develop a relationship with Miss Kenton.

A major reason my attempt to say something about Miss Kenton's values takes me back to Stevens's is that Ishiguro presents their values contrastively, not least by making Miss Kenton use the words "pretend" and "regret" about Stevens. In my interpretation, regret is felt by Miss Kenton as well. If she is in love with Stevens, is her inability to express this love one reason she refers to her failure to leave Darlington Hall after the dismissal of Ruth and Sarah as "cowardice" (p. 161)? If Stevens failed to express his feelings, did Miss Kenton fail to express hers? Was she secretly in love with Stevens even though she married a different man, Mr. Benn, after she left? When they finally meet again in Weymouth, Miss Kenton is widowed. She confesses to Stevens, "[Sometimes] you get to thinking about a different life, a *better* life you might have had. For instance, I get to thinking about a life I might have had with you, Mr Stevens" (p. 251, original emphasis). I am not suggesting that this idea or wish on Miss Kenton's part is directly related to the act of dismissing Ruth and Sarah. Yet it may partly explain why Miss Kenton uses the word "pretend" about Stevens—it is as though she gleans from his dismissal of the Jewish girls that, in this instance at least, Stevens's idea of service makes him do something he considers morally wrong. If Miss Kenton senses this, then perhaps she also understands why Stevens decides to leave his dying father to serve Lord Darlington's guests.

While it may be true that, as Stevens tells Miss Kenton, "I know my father would have wished me to carry on just now" (p. 111), his decision not to be present at his father's deathbed may appear morally indefensible. Revealingly, it seems that Stevens himself is experiencing his absence as heartless: as he is serving the guests downstairs, Mr. Cardinal—a young journalist who is the son of one of Lord Darlington's closest friends—asks him twice, and Lord Darlington once, whether he is "all right" (p. 109). Although he assures both that he is, Lord Darlington is probably correct to observe, "You look as though you're crying" (p. 110). When Stevens responds by referring to the "strains of a hard day," those strains include his father's death in his absence.

There is no doubt that, for Stevens, his father was not just a father but also a mentor and, as far as the profession of butler is concerned, an ideal. I highlight an analeptic episode that, turning on the words "serve" and "dignity," is related to Stevens's decision to dismiss Ruth and Sarah.[7] Stressing that the episode demonstrates the "special quality" that his father "came to possess" (p. 41) as a butler, Stevens starts by explaining, "I am one of two brothers.... [M]y elder brother, Leonard, was killed during the South African War while I was still a boy . . . in a particularly infamous manoeuvre" (p. 41). The information that Stevens, who is reticent about his own background, had a brother who served and died for the British Empire in the South African War of 1899–1902 is interesting in itself, and its relevance for my discussion is strengthened when Stevens adds:

> Not only was it alleged that the manoeuvre had been a most un-British attack on civilian Boer settlements, overwhelming evidence emerged that it had been irresponsibly commanded with several floutings of elementary military precautions, so that the men who had died—my brother among them—had died quite needlessly. (p. 41)

I am not claiming that the act of serving as a butler is directly comparable to that of serving as a soldier. But I am suggesting that, given the great importance Stevens attaches to "serve," the fact that they both served leaders who made serious mistakes constitutes a self-interpretive element in the novel's narrative discourse. The connection between this episode and the "very minor episode" (p. 146) in which Ruth and Sarah are dismissed—the key event around which the novel's plot revolves—is strengthened when Stevens proceeds to relate that, about 10 years later, his father had to serve as a butler while hosting the general who was responsible for the maneuver in which his elder son lost his life. Although he

> was obliged to suffer intimate proximity for four days with the man he detested . . . so well did my father hide his feelings, so professionally did he carry out his duties, that on his departure the General had actually complimented Mr John Silvers on the excellence of his butler and had left an unusually large tip in appreciation—which my father without hesitation asked his employer to donate to charity. (pp. 42–43)

Stevens uses this example of his father's service as a basis for his definition of dignity: "'[D]ignity' has to do crucially with a butler's ability not to abandon the professional being he inhabits" (p. 43). His use of the episode is surprising because the general, a despicable character who "took full opportunity to relate anecdotes of his military accomplishments" (p. 43), was responsible for the father's loss of his son and for his other son's loss of his brother. Yet Stevens's use of the example is also characteristic because his understanding of "serve" and "dignity" does not allow for qualitative differentiation when it comes to leadership. For Stevens, it is a requirement or defining feature of a butler as a "professional being" that he serve all his employers, including the man responsible for the death of his brother. Even though Stevens presents the general and Lord Darlington as contrastive characters, on a second reading I know that, by dismissing Ruth and Sarah, Darlington (and Stevens) are responsible for putting two employees who performed their acts of service professionally in a perilous situation.

A curious caveat associated with Stevens's understanding of dignity is his skepticism about butlers who are not English: "Continentals are unable to be butlers because they are as a breed incapable of the emotional restraint which only the English race is capable of" (p. 44). This statement is not only nationalist; it is racist. Whether this kind of racism plays a part in his dismissal of the Jewish girls I am not sure, but it reveals an aspect of Stevens's ethos that might make him less inclined to protest against Lord Darlington's order. What is also striking, particularly on a second reading, is my realization—and eventually also Stevens's realization—that his restraint may be his main problem in life, linked as it is to the key word "pretend" that Miss Kenton correctly identifies as one of his main character features.

If Stevens's ethics is compromised by his loyalty to Lord Darlington, the latter's ethics is compromised—and, in due course, collectively condemned—by his sympathy for Germany and Nazi Germany. One reason Lord Darlington's and, by implication, Stevens's attitude to Germany (in the 1920s) and Nazi Germany (in the 1930s) contributes to Ishiguro's narrative ethics is his way of relating their attitudes to that of Mr. Cardinal, the young journalist who often visits Darlington Hall. In an analepsis presented toward the end of the novel, Stevens remembers and relates a conversation between Mr. Cardinal and himself in one of the last meetings organized by Lord Darlington before the war. Ishiguro uses Mr. Cardinal to present Stevens, and the reader, with a contrastive ethics: "You don't understand, Stevens.... Over the last few years, his lordship has probably been the single most useful pawn Herr Hitler has had in this country for his propaganda tricks" (p. 235). Mr. Cardinal's use of the word "propaganda" suggests that, for him, the values of Nazism are opposed to his own values. To put this another way, Mr. Cardinal's comments on Nazism, and on Lord Darlington's attitude to Nazism, approximate the collective postwar British attitude to and memory of Nazism and the Second World War, including the Holocaust. That Mr. Cardinal, in his conversation with Stevens in the late 1930s, knew nothing of these events makes the ethics that underlies his statements on and skepticism about Nazism more prominent and impressive.

Moreover, Ishiguro's rendering of the conversation between Stevens and Mr. Cardinal demonstrates the ethical effect of inserting analeptic fragments into the main narrative about Stevens's journey from Oxfordshire to the West Country. As the "expedition" through the space of the English countryside serves as a catalyst for his memories, these fragments of memory gradually reveal a combination of admitting complicity in Lord Darlington's dealings with Nazi Germany and a stubborn resistance to such an admission, one that rejects possible complicity by referring to his obligation to serve his employer. In the analepsis constituted by Stevens's conversation with Mr. Cardinal, the ethical aspect becomes particularly noticeable because, at this late stage of the narrative discourse, the connection between ethical issues that intrude into or emerge through Stevens's accounts of his fragments of memory and his account of the journey that activates these fragments for him become stronger and more explicit. Having reached Devon, Stevens stays overnight in a village where he reluctantly allows himself to be drawn into a conversation with some of its inhabitants. One of them, Harry Smith, asserts, "Dignity isn't just something gentlemen have. Dignity's something every man and woman in this country can strive for and get" (p. 195). And he continues:

> "That's what we fought Hitler for, after all. If Hitler had had things his way, we'd just be slaves now. The whole world would be a few masters and millions upon millions of slaves. And I don't need to remind anyone here, there's no dignity to be had in being a slave. . . . We won the right to be free citizens. And it's one of the privileges of being born English that no matter who you are, no matter if you're rich or poor, you're born free and you're born so that you can express your opinion freely. . . . That's what dignity's really about, if you'll excuse me, sir." (p. 196)

What makes Smith's definition of dignity very different from Stevens's is his emphasis on democratic freedom and freedom of expression; England, he adds, is "a democracy, and we in this village have suffered as much as anyone fighting to keep it that way" (p. 198). Conversely, for Lord Darlington, "[d]emocracy is something for a bygone era" (p. 208). Significantly, Lord Darlington denounces democracy in an analepsis presented *after* Smith has defended it in the main narrative but *before* the analepsis in which Mr. Cardinal tries to make Stevens see that his employer—although and because he as "a true old English gentleman"—is "out of his depth" (p. 234), being manipulated and maneuvered by the Nazis. While Smith's observations on dignity and democracy accord with Mr. Cardinal's ethical stance, they also confirm and strengthen an important aspect of Stevens's ethos. Recalling "Mr Harry Smith's pronouncements on the nature of 'dignity,'" he finds "there is surely little in his statements that merits serious consideration" (p. 203). While the touch of arrogance and denial in this comment increases my attitudinal distance from Stevens, it also reveals his need to defend the close connection he has established between dignity as he understands it and the act of serving "an employer we judge to be wise and honourable" (p. 211). For Stevens, Lord Darlington is such an employer, and he rhetorically asks:

> How can one possibly be held to blame in any sense because, say, the passage of time has shown that Lord Darlington's efforts were misguided, even foolish? . . . It is hardly my fault if his lordship's life and work have turned out today to look, at best, a sad waste—and it is quite illogical that I should feel any regret or shame on my own account. (p. 211)

Two aspects of this passage are particularly important. First, that Stevens feels a need to defend his definitions and acts of dignity and service so strongly at this late stage of the narrative makes me suspect that the collective memory of the war, including the version of that memory presented by Smith, is exerting a stronger influence on his definitions, or rather axioms, than he is willing to admit. This suspicion, which is distinctly interpretive, is strengthened when I read that Lord Darlington's "life and work have turned out today to look, at best, a sad waste." This sentence goes against the grain of everything that Stevens has said about his employer earlier on in his narrative. Even though he reverts to his habitual praise of Lord Darlington as an honorable gentleman, he does not explicitly contradict the damning characterization of his life as "at best, a sad waste." Although he finds it difficult to admit that the collective memory of Lord Darlington as a Nazi sympathizer is more valid, and thus in one sense truer, than his individual memory of his former employer, the sentence illustrates that, even for Stevens, individual memory is not a stable entity; rather, changing and changeable, it has distinctly narrative features (Brockmeier, 2015).

This point takes me to the second aspect of this passage that I find notable. At this late stage of his narrative, Stevens's view of Lord Darlington is challenged by his memory of the dismissal of the Jewish girls. In contrast to the collective memory of Lord Darlington as a Nazi sympathizer, this is an individual memory that, after Lord Darlington's passing, Stevens shares with very few except Miss Kenton. As he will be meeting Miss Kenton very soon, and as she protested energetically against the dismissal of Ruth and Sarah many years earlier, Stevens may be reminded that he was wrong not to do so too. Although he claims it is "quite illogical that I should feel any regret or shame on my account," probably he feels both. And yet, while regret and shame can be key aspects of a reevaluation and recognition of earlier mistakes, or of complicity in such mistakes, a comment by Stevens at the very end of his narrative makes me unsure about his ability to admit that the act of dismissing the Jewish girls was, as Miss Kenton puts it, "simply—*wrong.*" "Lord Darlington," he claims,

> wasn't a bad man. . . . And at least he had the privilege of being able to say at the end of his life that he made his own mistakes. . . . As for myself, I cannot even claim that. You see, I *trusted.* I trusted in his lordship's wisdom. All those years I served him, I trusted I was doing something worthwhile. . . . Really—one has to ask oneself—what dignity is there in that? (pp. 255–256, original emphasis)

Stevens's use of "trust" is revealing. Although the verb does not replace "serve," it qualifies two of the key components in Stevens's understanding of his work, of his life, and of his identity: if Lord Darlington did not deserve to be trusted, what then about the dignity attached to, and in a way constituted by, the act of serving him? What are the consequences for your dignity, and by implication for your self-respect and your identity, if your employer turns out to be unworthy of the trust that underlies your sustained service? For Stevens, these questions, which he comes close to asking even though he does not explicitly formulate them as questions, are ethical because they concern his values and priorities as a butler and as a man.

That Stevens comes to ask these questions closer to the end of his narration than at its beginning is in itself an indication of the extent to which his ethics—and the novel's ethics, which is different from Stevens's—are a narrative ethics in which his memory plays a key part. Stevens's troubling attempts to come to terms with his memory, an insistent memory that forces its way into his mind as he is driving westward, has consequences for his thoughts about the ethical repercussions of his having been devoted to Lord Darlington. He remembers that he believed he was serving a great man who was influencing the course of history. But he also recalls the dismissal of the Jewish girls and other events, and these memories make him reluctantly admit that his master was not just on the wrong side of history but also fundamentally at fault in a moral sense. Tellingly, and in a way tragically, these memories present themselves to Stevens only as analeptic fragments long after the actual events. Reporting a dialogue between Lord Darlington and Mr. Lewis (an American senator who in a conference at Darlington Hall characterized Lord Darlington as "an amateur" (p. 106) in politics), he qualifies his impression of the dialogue by saying, "It is possible this is a case of hindsight colouring my memory" (p. 90). Thus, he actually and ironically draws attention to the way in which his act of remembering as he is driving westward many years later corrects his memory rather than "colouring" it. If Stevens's use of "trust" at the end of his narration qualifies his earlier references to "serve" and "dignity," the significance of a different verb, "regret," also becomes greater in the novel's concluding chapters. In common with "trust," this word occurs just once, and it similarly qualifies and questions his repeated, in a way insistent use of "serve" and "dignity." I suggest that, while it is related to "trust," the function of "regret" within the novel's ethical register is even greater. One reason for the word's import is that Stevens is unable to utter it himself; an additional reason is that it has a bearing on three painful experiences in his life. Revealingly, all of these are associated with his relationship with Miss Kenton, who uses the word when she urges Stevens come to his father's room to see him before he dies: "But you must come now, Mr Stevens, or else you may deeply regret it later." Stevens does not come—and his inability to admit that he made a grave error in not following Miss Kenton's insistent request reveals how deeply he regrets that decision. Ironically, by serving "the gentlemen proceeding into the smoking room" (p. 109), Stevens cannot serve his father at his deathbed. Although, as I have noted, the irony of the passage is subdued as it is qualified by Mr. Cardinal and Lord Darlington's references to Stevens's signs of distress, which he typically denies when serving port to the guests, he silently admits, and regrets, that he was wrong not to follow Miss Kenton's advice instead of the advice that he thinks his father would have given him.

In my interpretation, Stevens also silently admits that Miss Kenton was right to find the decision to dismiss Ruth and Sarah "simply—*wrong*." However, while Lord Darlington openly admits that it was "wrong" (he inadvertently repeats the word used by Miss Kenton) to dismiss the Jewish girls, Stevens—who was unsure about the decision but did not protest—finds it impossible to state verbally that he too was wrong. When, knowing of the weight Stevens attaches to trust in his employer, I reread the passage in which Lord Darlington admits that he (and by implication Stevens) was wrong to dismiss Ruth and Sarah, I understand better not only Lord Darlington's abuse of Stevens's trust in him but also Stevens's inability to admit his mistake. As his definition of "serve" and "dignity" appears to make it impossible for him to accept and thus come to terms with his own regret, that regret is curiously suspended, forming "a fragment of a memory" (p. 222) that has traumatic facets.

If Stevens regrets not having been present when his father dies, and if he also feels bad about having dismissed Ruth and Sarah, his most painful regret is that of not responding to Miss Kenton's repeated invitations to develop a lasting friendship and perhaps even a marital relationship. Although this aspect of his regret is less central to my critical concern than that stirred by his dismissal of Ruth and Sarah, it reveals a lot about Stevens's values, actions, and priorities. When Miss Kenton asks Stevens, "Why, Mr Stevens, why, why, why do you always have to *pretend*?," she touches a nerve; she and Stevens are aligned in a way Stevens cannot see or is unable to admit. One reason he is incapable of identifying this affinity is that it would seriously challenge his identity as a butler. When he attempts to respond, his recourse to the indefinite pronoun "one" signals that her question makes an impression on him: "Naturally, one disapproved of the dismissals" (p. 162). Once again, his feelings are revealed by silent observation rather than by speech. He recalls looking at Miss Kenton in the dusk of the summerhouse where their conversation takes place: "All I could see of her was her profile outlined against a pale and empty background" (pp. 162–163). There is an important connection between this sentence and Stevens's last visual impression of her: "Only as the bus pulled up did I glance at Miss Kenton and perceived that her eyes had filled with tears" (p. 252).

As implied author, Ishiguro uses Stevens as his main narrative instrument, making him communicate in a way that depends on his memories and reveals his ethics. While the ethics of Ishiguro as implied author draws on the ethics of the novel's characters, it is also combined with, and in one sense dependent on, the ethics of Stevens as first-person narrator. It does not follow that the implied author's ethics is comparable to or signaled by Stevens's ethics; on the contrary, aspects of their ethics would appear very different. I am, however, making a twofold point. First, as the various ethical aspects related to and represented by the different characters are presented by Stevens as first-person narrator, the ethics that forms the basis for the implied author's ethics is narrated and thus colored by Stevens's ethics. Second, while components of the plot, including both events and the characters' experiences and memories of those events, suggest that the implied author's ethics approximates to that of another character whose values deviate from

Stevens's, that other character's values can also be questioned. Indeed, Miss Kenton's characterization of herself as "a coward" does not seem to be contradicted by the implied author.

I conclude that, rather than providing easy answers and stable ethical positions, Ishiguro's ethics consists of or approximates a range of ethical questions raised by the narrative discourse. These questions follow from my interpretation of that discourse: *The Remains of the Day* is a forceful demonstration of Gadamer's point that interpretation is "not merely a reproductive but always a productive activity as well" (1960/2013, p. 307). Moreover, the novel illustrates how and to what extent a narrative's self-interpretive aspects may themselves be infiltrated by interpretation; as I have attempted to show, though in one sense self-interpretive because it is an integral part of the narrative discourse, Stevens's narrative presentation of his memories can be distinctly interpretive. If no narrative is "ethically neutral" (Ricoeur, 1990/1994, p. 140), neither is there an ethically neutral reading, not excepting my own.

Discussions of narrative fiction, including the ethics of narrative fiction, often shy away from or do not explicitly consider the ethics of the historical author. There are good reasons for this kind of critical reluctance, including the risk of diverting critical attention from the complex ethics constituted by the narrative discourse of the novel or short story under consideration. And yet, although the implied author is an image formed by me as a reader, and although, partly for that reason, the links between implied and historical author are indirect and complicated, some knowledge of the historical author may be potentially suggestive, thus possibly enriching my own interpretation. If the reader happens to know, as I do, that Ishiguro was born in Japan a few years after the end of the Second World War, that reader may also know that he spent his first years in the shadow of the atomic bomb dropped on Nagasaki, where his parents lived. In an interview with the BBC after having been awarded the Nobel Prize for literature in 2017, Ishiguro said that growing up in England in a Japanese household was crucial to his writing, enabling him to see things from a different perspective (Gompertz, 2017). In my interpretation of *The Remains of the Day*, Ishiguro's perspective influences the narrative presentation of the Holocaust and of the British Empire. As regards the Holocaust, I have tried to show how it becomes—or rather, how Ishiguro makes it become—an indirect yet significant reference for the three most important characters in the novel: Stevens, Lord Darlington, and Miss Kenton. As I have also attempted to indicate, this kind of indirect reference is a memory, individual as well as collective. With regard to the history of the British Empire, I have commented on the way Ishiguro uses Stevens's story about his elder brother, Leonard, and the British general responsible for the loss of Leonard's life (as well as the deaths of Boer civilians) to suggest that since Stevens approves of his father's decision to serve even the general who in fact caused his son's death, their idea of a professional butler's service includes or necessitates serving a perpetrator.

I am certainly not arguing that Ishiguro equates histories of victimization as different as those of the European Jews in the Second World War and the native populations of the vast areas occupied by Britain as an imperial power. But I am suggesting that Ishiguro's writing incorporates an element of multidirectional memory, thus presenting memory "as subject to ongoing negotiation, cross-referencing, and borrowing; as productive and not privative" (Rothberg, 2009, p. 3). Ishiguro's perspective enables him to use what Michael Rothberg aptly calls "the presence of widespread Holocaust consciousness" (p. 3) as a platform for doing two things simultaneously. Not only does he present the reader with a narrative whose ethics revolves around the main character's fragments of memory of the dismissal of two Jewish girls in England in the 1930s; he also shows how ethical questions following from this dismissal are related—indirectly and via the key word "serve"—to ethical issues in the history of European imperialism. Ishiguro's different—one might almost say unique—perspective enables him, and by implication the reader, to see these issues in a new light, thus stirring ethical reflection. As I have suggested, one reason for this effect, aesthetic as well as ethical, is that Stevens's first-person narration takes the form of a sustained act of memory in which, to appropriate the title of Richard Terdiman's book *Present Past* (1993), the past is made present in a way Stevens apparently dislikes yet reluctantly accepts.

One may counter that I do not need to know anything about Ishiguro as a historical author to make these observations. Concurring with this view, I still think that the biographical knowledge I have about Ishiguro does something to my reading of *The Remains of the Day*, reminding me that interpretation is "a productive activity" (Gadamer, 1960/2013, p. 307) and suggesting that, combined with his imagination as a novelist, Ishiguro's non-European background colors his narrative presentation of memories that stir a range of ethical questions. As Ishiguro's ethics as implied and historical author is affiliated with these questions, and as they are asked or implied by the novel's characters and by Stevens as its narrator, Ishiguro's questions approximate my own questions and reflections. As Stevens gradually reveals more of his values and priorities, I sense that I am increasingly inclined to distance myself from him morally. I hope that I would not have become ethically compromised the way he is when the two Jewish girls are dismissed. I hope that, at the crucial point or stage of the narrative when Ruth and Sarah are dismissed, my ethical stance would be associated with that of Miss Kenton and not that of Stevens, and that I would have protested as energetically as she did. Yet I cannot be sure I would. While Stevens's dismissal of the Jewish girls was ethically wrong, it is understandable that he could make this error. It is true that, as Stevens puts it, we harbor a "desire to make our own small contribution to the creation of a better world" (p. 122):

> [T]he surest means of doing so would be to serve the great gentlemen of our times in whose hands civilization had been entrusted. . . .
>
> A "great" butler can only be, surely, one who can point to his years of service and say that he has applied his talents to serving a great gentleman— and through the latter, to serving humanity. (pp. 122, 123)

The problem with Stevens's attitude—which, for him, becomes a philosophy of life—is that not all "great gentlemen" serve "humanity," even though they claim to do so. At the end of his narration, Stevens comes close to admitting this. And yet it is, as the last page of the novel indicates, difficult for him to conclude that his years of service have been futile. There is, he says, "little choice other than to leave our fate, ultimately, in the hands of those great gentlemen at the hub of this world who employ our services" (p. 257). The novel thus ends on a note of resignation rather than reconciliation.

James Ivory's *The Remains of the Day*

Effectively combining filmic techniques and aspects of film form such as rhythm, repetition, camera angle, and color, James Ivory's film adaptation gives a rich and varied response to the values and ethical dilemmas presented by Ishiguro as verbal fiction. One important reason the complexity of the novel's narrative ethics is retained—or rather, presented independently through the medium of film—is suggested by the quality of acting: both Anthony Hopkins (as Stevens) and Emma Thompson (as Miss Kenton) activate, use, and modify a combination of tempo, speech, gesture, facial expression, and other techniques to retain, and in some ways intensify, the novel's ethical concerns. One notable difference is that, because of the way the film medium operates, the analepses force themselves more insistently into the film's (and Stevens's) present than in the novel. As I will show, the issue of the Holocaust is more explicit, though not necessarily more significant, in the adaptation than in the novel.

Rereading Ishiguro's *The Remains of the Day*, I am aware of the interplay between the main narrative, which presents Stevens's journey from Oxfordshire to the West Country, and the analeptic segments or fragments of memory that this journey makes him or forces him to incorporate into his first-person narration. In line with the work of Dan Shen (2021), I consider this interplay a variant of dual narrative dynamics—a dynamics that, as I have attempted to show, accentuates the novel's ethical dimension. This interpretation, I reiterate, is based on and made possible by a second reading. Although the processes of interpreting a film narrative and a literary (verbal) narrative are different,[8] there is also a dissimilarity between my first and second viewings of Ivory's adaptation of Ishiguro's novel. However, this difference is reduced if I have read Ishiguro's novel before seeing Ivory's adaptation: my knowledge of the analeptic fragments narrated by Stevens will inevitably, even on a first viewing, influence my interpretation of the film. My knowledge of the novel's dual dynamics will enable me to identify and perhaps appreciate that of the adaptation. The need for interpretation is as strong for the viewer of a film narrative as it is for the reader of a verbal narrative, and both these versions of the narrative—both of which present "a focalized series of events" (Bal, 2018, p. 37)—possess interpretive elements to which the viewer or reader responds. Seeing a film, I immediately start interpreting it, whether or not the film is an adaptation. One characteristic feature of Ishiguro's novel is the extent to which and the manner in which Ishiguro not only invites me to interpret Stevens's interpretations of his memories but also incites me to consider ethical ramifications of those interpretations. Making an adaptation in what Dudley Andrew calls the "fidelity and transformation" mode, Ivory responds to this characteristic feature of Ishiguro's novel by activating and interlinking a series of elements of film that further a mode of adaptation in which "it is assumed that the task of adaptation is the reproduction in cinema of something essential about an original text" (1999, p. 455). "Reproduc[ing] . . . something essential" about Ishiguro's novel, Ivory's adaptation is a complex film in whose narrative discourse aesthetic and ethical aspects are intertwined. I will comment on two film segments that present the dismissal of the two Jewish girls in a way that sharpens the film's ethical dimension by connecting it more directly to the Holocaust. Before turning to Ivory's presentation of the dismissal of Elsa and Irma, I briefly discuss the film's opening.

Narrative Beginning: Miss Kenton's Letter

In his *Theory of Film*, Siegfrid Kracauer (1965) submits that the role of cinema is to transform the viewer by presenting spectacles that upset his or her mind; starting to watch a film, I am immediately confronted with a different reality, a world from which I am absent—though it strongly, even confusingly, resembles by own. This reality, this world viewed through the medium of film, depends on and is made possible by the succession of photographs (24 frames per second) that produces an optical illusion of movement. "The aesthetic qualities of photography," explains André Bazin:

> are to be sought in its power to lay bare the realities. It is not for me to separate off, in the complex fabric of the real world, here a reflection on a damp sidewalk, there the gesture of a child. Only the impassive lens, stripping its object of all those ways of seeing it, those piled-up preconceptions, that spiritual dust and grime with which my eyes have covered it, is able to present it in all its virginal purity to my attention and consequently to my love. (1967, p. 15)

This quality of photography is also an aesthetic quality of film. As soon as I start watching "realities . . . [laid bare by] the impassive lens," I am struck by and attracted to the bewildering complexity of that reality—a reality that, partly for that reason, I immediately start interpreting. In *Film and the Ethical Imagination*, Asbjørn Grønstad argues that Bazin's observation on the aesthetic qualities of photography and, by implication, of film "contains the seed of an entire theory of ethics, pivoting around the central premise that the filmic capture of a phenomenon in the real world makes us aware of it in such an acute fashion that deep affections arise" (Grønstad, 2016, p. 47). Finding that Bazin's reflections are related to a key question that Kracauer asks, "[W]hat is the good of film experience?" (Kracauer, 1965, p. 285), Grønstad suggests that while one possible answer is "that film can lead to a process of self-interrogation that interrupts our own narcissism," another response is, or could be, "that film makes us aware of the texture and particularity of physical reality otherwise so easily eclipsed by modern systems of abstraction" (Grønstad, 2016, p. 47). To these two possible answers I would like to add a third: film can make us aware of and stir reflection on the ethical implications and consequences of my own actions, my perspective, my attitude, and my values. One of the things that film can do, and that Ivory's *The Remains of the Day* does, is to demonstrate how closely these and related reflections are associated with and influenced by my experience and my memory.

Starting to rewatch Ivory's adaptation, I see filmic images of a country house located in a large park and of cars driving toward that house. As I relate the images not only to my first act of viewing the adaptation but also to my reading and rereading of Ishiguro's novel, I am surprised when the first sound I hear is the voice of Emma Thompson as Miss Kenton, who is reading out loud a letter she has written to Stevens. Accompanying and gradually explaining the images of the park and Darlington Hall, the letter gives me, in condensed form, relevant information about the characters and the plot which, I gather, the film will present. Yet Miss Kenton's auditory rendering of her letter to Stevens is more than an introduction; it is also an interpretation of the beginning of Ishiguro's novel. I identify two interpretive aspects of the adaptation's beginning that, I suggest, highlight the ethical challenges and questions associated with the dismissal of the Jewish girls. The first aspect concerns Ivory's response to a major challenge he meets when, as film director, he wants to adapt a first-person narrative: although film uses and combines a range of communication channels, including an auditory channel, film communication is essentially visual since the camera records a world similar to and yet different from my own. In Ishiguro's novel, Stevens's voice and perspective color his first-person narration right from the beginning. By making Miss Kenton read out loud her letter to Stevens, who, in the novel, refers to her letter but does not quote from it, Ivory uses voice-over. All three constituents of voice-over narration identified by Sarah Kozloff (1988) are operative here: *voice* determines the medium: we hear a female voice speaking; *over* applies to the relationship between the sound source and the images on the screen: as a viewer I cannot see the person speaking at the time of hearing her voice; *narration* is linked to what is said: somebody communicates elements of a story—introduces, supplements, and comments on what is shown visually (cf. Lothe, 2000). Some film scholars are skeptical about voice-over, considering this aspect of film narration contrived and artificial. However, Ivory's use of voice-over serves the dual purpose of providing the viewer with necessary information and stressing Miss Kenton's position as the film's second protagonist more explicitly than does the novel.

This point is related to the second aspect I want to highlight. Miss Kenton's letter begins thus:

Dear Mr Stevens,

You will be surprised to hear from me after all this time. You have been in my thoughts ever since I heard that Lord Darlington had died. We read in the *Manchester Guardian* that his heirs put Darlington Hall up for sale as they no longer wished to maintain it. The article went on to say that since there were no buyers for such a large house the new earl had decided to demolish it and sell the stone to a local builder for 5000 pounds. We also saw some rubbish in the *Daily Mail* which made my blood boil: "Traitor's nest to be pulled down."

[Cut to visual images of auction at which a portrait is being bought by Mr. Lewis]

I was very relieved to read later on how an American millionaire named Lewis had saved Darlington Hall and you were not to be turned out of your old home after all. Is it possibly the same congressman Lewis who attended his Lordship's conference in 1936?

The letter presents the viewer of Ivory's *The Remains of the Day* with two of the adaptation's main constituent elements: memory and narrative ethics. While the ethical aspect is hinted at when Miss Kenton refers to Lord Darlington's conference in 1936, it becomes more explicit in her quotation from the *Daily Mail*. The newspaper's description of Lord Darlington as a "traitor" and of Darlington Hall as a "traitor's nest" suggests that, in the early 1950s, this is the common view of Miss Kenton's and Stevens's previous employer. This view is a variant on Britain's collective memory of the war, including those who, like Lord Darlington, were on the wrong side of history and on the wrong moral side too. By taking exception to the newspaper's description of Lord Darlington, Miss Kenton not only provides information the viewer needs but also aligns her opinion of her earlier employer with Stevens's view. Although, given Miss Kenton's criticism of Lord Darlington's dismissal of the Jewish girls, this attitudinal alignment is surprising, it is not a weakness of the adaptation. Rather, it is an early indication that, although Ivory's *The Remains of the Day* is an adaptation in the fidelity mode, it is a work of art—aesthetically as well as ethically—in its own right. By sympathizing with

Lord Darlington Miss Kenton signals that, while he made mistakes he later regretted, he was, on the whole, a good employer over the years she spent at Darlington Hall. There is an element of reconciliation, perhaps even forgiveness in her assessment; this element is repeated and strengthened when Miss Kenton and Stevens meet and talk about Lord Darlington at the end of the film. Thus, in addition to giving Miss Kenton a prominent position at the beginning, Ivory makes her letter, which is a brief narrative version of her memory of her years at Darlington Hall, include ethical reflections that are connected with, and in one sense support, those of Stevens. These considerations influence and enrich my interpretation of the two protagonists' relationship later in the film.

Ivory enhances the importance of the letter as a variant on film narration when he links Miss Kenton's letter to Stevens's reply. Beginning the adaptation by presenting the viewer with two letters written and read out loud by the film's two main characters invites me to relate the following narrative more directly to these characters' memories, experiences, and values than I would have been able to do had the letters not been included. Variants of temporal, spatial, and attitudinal distance play a role here. Although Stevens might not admit it, the letters presented at the film's beginning suggest that they are both engaged in what Mark Freeman calls a "project of self-understanding, which [has] hindsight at its very core" (2010, p. 4). As I hope to have shown in my discussion of Ishiguro's novel, if self-understanding occurs, as Freeman convincingly argues in *Hindsight*, "*through narrative reflection, which is itself a product of hindsight*, [hindsight also] *plays an integral role in shaping and deepening moral life*" (pp. 4-5, original emphasis). The way Miss Kenton ends her letter to Stevens is an early indication of this kind of narrative reflection. "I don't know," she writes, "what my future is.... The years stretch before me and if only I knew how to fill them. But I would like to be useful again." Relating Miss Kenton's memories to Darlington Hall and her collaboration with Stevens, this narrative consideration—a combination of resignation and a qualified, vague wish for a better future—is an integral part of Miss Kenton's ongoing "shaping and deepening moral life," which, following Freeman, I understand as "spheres of experience . . . that have to do with fundamental questions about how to live" (p. 5). Since I am rewatching the film and thus know about the ethical issues stirred by Stevens's dismissal of the Jewish girls, and as I also possess knowledge of Stevens's tendency, as Miss Kenton puts it later in the film, to "hide [his] feelings," I gather that his narrative reflections in his letter are more similar to

Miss Kenton's than they first seem to be. His letter, read out loud by Anthony Hopkins as Stevens, includes the following sentences:

> Dear Mrs Benn,
>
> I propose to reach Clevedon on Thursday the 3rd of October around 4pm. . . . Mrs. Benn, I always said you possess an amazing memory. Our new employer is indeed Congressman Lewis, though he's now retired from political life in the United States. . . . But I regret to say we are woefully understaffed for a house of this size. Mrs. Benn, will you permit me once again to sing your praises? Let me state that when you left us to get married, no housekeeper ever reached your standard in any department. . . . I fear I may have been a little unwelcoming at first, even a little short. You presented the most excellent references I have ever seen. Which proved to be well deserved indeed. Though, I do confess, I did have my doubts, on account of your youth.

Although the tone of Stevens's letter is characteristically reserved, I interpret his references to Miss Kenton's professional competence as indirect praise of her as a human being.

Considering the letter as a veiled declaration of love might be going too far, yet there is a connection between his letter at the beginning of the film and a statement he makes later, just before the analeptic scene in which Lord Darlington admits that it was wrong to dismiss the Jewish girls. Responding to Richard Carlisle's question whether Stevens would not rather make his own mistakes rather than executing, and later defending, those made by his employer, Stevens admits, "In a very small way I did make my own mistake. But I might still have a chance to set mine right. In fact, I'm on my way to try and do so now." While at one level this statement too refers to Stevens's wish to reemploy Miss Kenton as housekeeper at Darlington Hall, it signals, more strongly and clearly than does the letter, that he made the colossal mistake of not developing a relationship with the person he probably loved.

Miss Kenton and Stevens's Contest over Values

Starting his adaptation of Ishiguro's novel by presenting the viewer with two letters written by the protagonists, Ivory establishes a basis for the contest over values represented by Stevens's and Miss Kenton's conflicting positions on the issue of the dismissal of the Jewish girls. Neither of the two letters was written by Ishiguro; they are by Ruth Prawer Jhabvala, a British American novelist, short story writer, and screenwriter who for many years collaborated with Merchant Ivory Productions. That Ivory's adaptation is in the fidelity and transformation mode does not require that he restrict himself to using text written by Ishiguro. As I have briefly indicated, the letters serve the dual purpose of introducing the viewer to the film's two protagonists and hinting at aspects of their ethos that reveal facets of their values and memories. If these aspects accord with my interpretation of the beginning of Ishiguro's novel, so does the emphasis on memory as a motor for as well as an integral part of the narrative undertaking. Moreover, as Jhabvala starts with Miss Kenton's letter, she (like Ivory) elevates Miss Kenton's role in the film, giving her a more explicit narrative function while at the same time highlighting her contribution as a main character. This kind of accentuation of Miss Kenton's role in the adaptation has a bearing on her position in the issue of the dismissal of the Jewish girls—and thus, more indirectly yet significantly, the issue of the Holocaust.

I have noted that, in Ishiguro's novel, Stevens's account of his journey is punctuated or interrupted by fragments of memory incorporated into his narrative. Even though the events and experiences of these analepses are as real to me as a reader as are those of the main (or frame) narrative, they are introduced, even excused by Stevens in a way that identifies them as "*external analepsis*: the time of the story in the analepsis lies outside and prior to the time of the main narrative. . . . [T]he narration jumps back to a point in the story before the main narrative starts" (Lothe, 2000, p. 54; see Genette, 1980). External analepsis is a feature of Ivory's adaptation too; for example, Hopkins's oral delivery of Stevens's letter is accompanied by analeptic images of Miss Kenton when she first arrives at Darlington Hall in the early 1920s. Yet there is a notable difference between the functions and effects of external analepsis in verbal fiction and film. While, as already indicated, the analepses in the novel are introduced by Stevens as first-person narrator, watching the film I suddenly confront images that, though I understand that they refer to events that occurred before the main narrative starts, force themselves on me so strongly that I tend to interpret them as a variant of the narrative present. The kinetic force of film, and of the film camera in particular, is so strong that the past appears before my eyes as though it were the present; looking at and trying to interpret film images, it is difficult for me not to think that, though they record something that occurred before the time of the main narrative, they blend into that narrative. Film communicates through a succession of photographic images that, though I know they can be manipulated and artificially designed, refer directly to external reality in a way verbal fiction does not (Bazin, 1967).

Yet although in one sense the projection of reality in Ivory's adaptation makes me relate the film's analeptic sequences more closely to those of the main narrative, in a different sense the parts of the adaptation that describe Stevens's and Miss Kenton's earlier life at Darlington Hall also enable the viewer to peep into a different world—a world in which the Second World War, including the Holocaust, had not yet happened and in which Britain was still an imperial power. A different yet related effect of the analeptic segments is to add credence to, verifying through the projection of reality on the screen, Stevens's first-person narration. To put this another way, watching the film, I am less inclined to question Stevens's selection of the fragments of memories presented to me than I am when reading the novel: assuming a form of filmic present, the memories are there—emerging as constituent elements of the film's reality. Yet it does not follow that the film narration does not invite me to interpret, and sometimes question, Stevens's actions, choices, and attitudes as shown or revealed in the analepses.

The way in which Ivory's adaptation presents reality is relevant for and underlies its narrative presentation of the Holocaust as a series of events in historical reality. I am not arguing that the issue of the Holocaust is less important in Ishiguro's novel than in Ivory's film; as I have attempted to show, the enormity of the Holocaust as a crime against humanity underlies and gives an edge to Stevens's first-person narration. One reason the adaptation refers more directly to the Holocaust is that the way in which film presents a version of reality—that, as a succession of photographs, it "is *of* reality" (Cavell, 1979, p. 16, original emphasis)—is part of a series of choices made by Jhabvala as screenwriter and Ivory as director. The first of these choices, or changes compared to Ishiguro's verbal text, occurs at the beginning of a scene in the library of Darlington Hall. Addressing Miss Kenton, Lord Darlington asks, "Have the young German ladies arrived?" When Miss Kenton replies, "Yes, my Lord, they're just outside," a conversation follows:

LORD DARLINGTON: "I'd like to say hello to them, practice my German."
MISS KENTON: "They speak excellent English, my Lord." [Asks them to enter]
MISS KENTON: "This is Elsa and this is Irma."

LORD DARLINGTON: "Haben Sie eine gute Reise gehabt? I'm just asking if they had a good journey."

ELSA: "It was long."

LORD DARLINGTON: "Was hatten Sie vom Wetter? I'm asking them about the weather."

ELSA: "We are very grateful to you, my Lord, for letting us come here. [Looks at Irma] Our parents are very grateful."

LORD DARLINGTON: "Not at all. Miss Kenton will look after you. Welcome to Darlington Hall. Willkommen zu Darlington Hall."

Presenting the viewer with a scene that is not in the novel, Ivory gives me more information than Ishiguro does about the background of the Jewish girls, whose names are changed from Ruth and Sarah in the novel to Elsa and Irma in the film. That, as Lord Darlington's first question makes clear, they come from Germany may indicate that they are Jewish refugees. On a second viewing, there is a touch of dramatic irony in Lord Darlington's eagerness to demonstrate his knowledge of German: while he recognizes Elsa and Irma as German when welcoming them to Darlington Hall, when he dismisses them he has concluded that, according to Nazi ideology, they are not.

Figure 5.1 Screenshot from *The Remains of the Day*, directed by James Ivory (1993)

Miss Kenton plays a key role in this scene. Not just welcoming Elsa and Irma, she is friendly and supportive in a way Lord Darlington is not. Figure 5.1 depicts an example of film's ability to visually present an element of plot and of plot progression in a way that invests the image with an ethical element. The ethical aspect is strengthened on a second viewing: the combined qualities of friendliness, support, and care that Thompson manages to convey through Miss Kenton's posture and facial expression indicate an ethics that, underlined as it is by the combination of gratitude and vulnerability observable on the faces of the two Jewish girls, is at odds with the ethics of Nazism, of antisemitism, and, as it turns out, of Lord Darlington.

The image of Miss Kenton standing between Elsa and Irma is also an example of the way in which Ivory invites me to relate film communication to the act and challenge of memory. As already mentioned, since I cannot attribute the film narration to which this image contributes to a particular narrator or sender, neither can I easily identify the agent that remembers this scene. Yet variants of memory and forgetting are, as the two opening letters signal, a key aspect of the adaptation too. If, as I am inclined to think, this particular image is part of Lord Darlington's memory of the Jewish girls he employed, then it is presumably a memory of two human beings he let go. And if, as I also suggest, the image is part of Miss Kenton's memory of her care for Elsa and Irma and her readiness to support them, then it is also a memory of her disappointment with Lord Darlington and Stevens—whose memory of the scene when the girls are dismissed because they are Jewish is, revealingly, less accurate and more indirect.

Before presenting the viewer with this key scene, Ivory inserts another scene that provides a partial explanation of Lord Darlington's antisemitism—that is, of a hostile attitude to Jews not noticeable in the scene in which he is welcoming Elsa and Irma to Darlington Hall. This scene, which I will briefly discuss, shows Lord Darlington reading a book in his library (Figure 5.2).

Figure 5.2 Screenshot from *The Remains of the Day*, directed by James Ivory (1993)

In the novel, Stevens vehemently defends his employer against accusations of antisemitism—even though he admits that in the early 1930s some of the guests at Darlington Hall, particularly Mrs. Carolyn Barnet, "came to wield an unusual influence over his lordship" (p. 153). In the adaptation, this "influence" is more specific, and it is also more closely associated with Lord Darlington's agency. As he is reading the book, Elsa and Irma are cleaning the wood-burning fireplace in the library. What is he reading?

> We do the Jews no injustice when we say that the revelation of Christ is simply something incomprehensible and hateful to them. Although he apparently sprang from their midst, he embodies nevertheless the negation of their whole nature. The Jews are more sensitive about this than we are. This demonstration of the deep cleft that separates us Europeans from the Jew is by no means given in order to let religious prejudice, with its dangerous bias, settle the matter, but because I think the perception of two fundamentally different natures reveals a real gulf.

Since the words are being read out loud, they resemble voice-over. And yet, as I noted in my discussion of voice-over in the film's beginning, this variant of film communication requires that, as a viewer, I cannot see the person speaking at the time of hearing his or her voice. Watching this scene, I can see Lord Darlington reading at his desk, and I presume that the words I hear are in his voice. Yet he is not reading the words out loud; had he done this, an awkward situation would have arisen since Elsa and Irma are in the same room. Thus, I connect the words I hear partly with Lord Darlington, partly with the "I" of the written text. In my interpretation of the scene, this kind of double attribution—associating the spoken words of a written text both with the book's author and with its reader—is an original and suggestive way of indicating how, reading a book that Mrs. Barnet may have recommended to him, Lord Darlington allows himself to be influenced by antisemitic ideology.

Considered from the perspective of narrative hermeneutics, the effect of this passage does not depend on the viewer's knowledge of the author's identity. What is essential in Ivory's adaptation is the connection between the passage Lord Darlington is reading and the dismissal of Elsa and Irma—who, as they are in the same room, inadvertently function as an audience ignorant of what their employer is reading. In his discussion of the self and narrative identity in *Oneself as Another*, Ricoeur reflects on the moral problem "grafted onto the recognition of [the] essential dissymmetry between the one who acts and the one who undergoes, culminating in the violence of the powerful agent" (1990/1994, p. 145). Although both Elsa and Irma act to their employer's satisfaction—as Stevens puts it in the following dismissal scene, they "work extremely well"—Darlington's act of reading leads to his act of dismissing them.

Whether or not the viewer knows the identity of the passage's author, Ivory's inclusion of the passage and his presentation of it just before the dismissal scene makes the issue of antisemitism more visible and explicit in the adaptation than in the novel. As Ivory also, via Darlington's welcoming words, makes me understand that the Jewish girls are refugees from Germany, the Holocaust (though the word is not mentioned) is evoked in a way it is not in Ishiguro's novel. It does not follow, however, that Ishiguro's more indirect and more subtle reference to the Holocaust is less powerful or less important. As I argued in the first part of this chapter, it is precisely the subtlety of the Holocaust as a thematic aspect of Ishiguro's *The Remains of the Day* that makes its contribution to the novel's narrative ethics remarkable. After having identified the author of the passage Lord Darlington is reading as Houston Stewart Chamberlain, and after having stated that Ruth Prawer Jhabvala wrote the screenplay from which Ivory's adaptation was made, Michael Lackey claims that Jhabvala "subtly correct[s] Ishiguro by incorporating Chamberlain's flagrantly Christian justification for negating the Jew into *The Remains of the Day*" (2012, p. 335). But Jhabvala is not "correcting" Ishiguro; rather, as screenwriter, she interprets the subtle presentation of antisemitism in Ishiguro's novel by introducing elements of content not in his verbal text, particularly the information about the Jewish girls' German background and the passage from Chamberlain's *The Foundations of the Nineteenth Century* (1912). Moreover, in the event that the viewer would find it helpful to know who wrote the passage Lord Darlington is reading, the relevant knowledge would not be Chamberlain's "Christian justification for negating the Jew" but the fact that, as a British-born German philosopher widely read in Britain in the 1920s and 1930s, he produced a mixture of arguments that, he claimed, supported his antisemitic views (Stackelberg & Winkle, 2002). As these views influenced many British readers, they might also have influenced Lord Darlington. I am not sure, however, whether this kind of extratextual information is needed for my understanding of the narrative ethics of Ivory's film.

Just after this scene, Lord Darlington summons Stevens to the library:

Figure 5.3 Screenshot from *The Remains of the Day*, directed by James Ivory (1993)

Figure 5.4 Screenshot from *The Remains of the Day*, directed by James Ivory (1993)

DARLINGTON: "Stevens, we have some refugee girls on the staff at the moment, I believe."

STEVENS: "We do, my Lord. Two housemaids, Elsa and Irma."

DARLINGTON: "You'll have to let them go, I'm afraid."

STEVENS: "Let them go, my lord?"

DARLINGTON: "It's regrettable, Stevens, but we have no choice. You've got to see the whole thing in context. I have the well-being of my guests to consider."

STEVENS: "My lord, may I say, they work extremely well. They're intelligent, polite, and very clean."

DARLINGTON: "I'm sorry, but I've looked into this matter very carefully. There are larger issues at stake. I'm sorry, but there it is. They are Jews."
STEVENS: "Yes, my lord. Thank you."

The dialogue illustrates how the adaptation highlights ethical questions by combining the words spoken by Lord Darlington and Stevens (and, in the following scene, Miss Kenton) with the visual presentation of them. Four constituent elements of this presentation are perspective, distance, gesture, and facial expression. Aided by Tony Pierce-Roberts's cinematography, Ivory makes the camera focus alternately on the faces of Darlington and Stevens (Figures 5.3 and 5.4). While the spatial distance between camera and character is almost identical, the perspective changes as the camera first focalizes Darlington's face and then, after Darlington has told him to dismiss Elsa and Irma, Stevens's. Demonstrating that, as Bal (2017) shows, perspective applies not only to the agent that sees but also to the agent that is being seen (or focalized), the dialogue also illustrates how closely perspective is connected with gesture. If gesture is a basic expressive aspect of cinema (Gustafsson & Grønstad, 2015; cf. Grønstad, 2020), that expressive dimension is here furthered through the combination of perspectival variation and facial expression. While Darlington's gestures before summoning Stevens indicate that he has perhaps been postponing a difficult decision, his facial expression when asking Stevens to dismiss the girls (Figure 5.3) reveals a grave concern and possibly doubt about the ethics of his decision. Correspondingly, Stevens's gestures (Figure 5.4), both when listening to Darlington and when leaving the room after having uttered the words "Thank you" in a low voice, suggest that he knows the dismissal is indefensible. While in the novel Stevens's surprise, which includes an element of protest, is condensed into the question "Sir?" (155), the corresponding dialogue in the adaptation indicates a stronger and more direct objection. Revealingly, what settles the matter is the word "Jew." In view of the scene's narrative ethics, it is essential that Stevens's words of protest are supported and strengthened by his gestures and facial expression.

If this interpretation establishes a closer connection between Stevens's and Miss Kenton's values than that observable in the novel, part of the reason is the different ways in which the communication systems of film and verbal fiction operate. Not only is Stevens's verbal protest more explicit in the adaptation; it is strengthened by the visual communication I described. Ivory's combination of verbal and visual communication establishes a link between this scene and the later one in which Lord Darlington regrets having dismissed Elsa and Irma. However, while Miss Kenton in that scene senses that Stevens was in fact opposed to their dismissal, when Stevens tells her about Lord Darlington's decision just after it was taken, her protest is primarily directed at the dismissal itself and Stevens's readiness to implement it:

Figure 5.5 Screenshot from *The Remains of the Day*, directed by James Ivory (1993)

MISS KENTON: "I'm amazed you can stand there as if you were discussing [an] order for the larder. I can't believe it! You're saying that Elsa and Irma are to be dismissed because they are Jewish!"

STEVENS: "His Lordship has decided. There is nothing for you and I to discuss."

MISS KENTON: "Do you realize that if those girls have no work they could be sent back to Germany?"

STEVENS: "It is out of our hands."

MISS KENTON: "I tell you, Mr Stevens, if you dismiss my girls tomorrow, it will be wrong! A sin, as any sin ever was one!"

STEVENS: "Miss Kenton, there are many things you and I don't understand in this world of today. His Lordship understands fully and has studied the larger issues at stake—concerning, say, the nature of Jewry."

MISS KENTON: "Mr Stevens, I warn you. If those girls go, I shall leave this house."

STEVENS: "Oh, Miss Kenton, please—"

In this dialogue (direct discourse), to which there is a direct cut after the dismissal scene, Miss Kenton makes her position absolutely clear: dismissing employees because they are Jewish is wrong, it is a sin, and it is morally indefensible (Figure 5.5). Two dimensions of Miss Kenton's protest are interlinked: first, she accuses Lord Darlington and Stevens of having made a grave mistake that is ethically untenable; second, she objects because, since she is also the Jewish girls' employer, she becomes implicated in a decision she is strongly opposed to. In her influential essay "Collective Responsibility," Arendt writes of the "vicarious responsibility for things we have not done" (2003, p. 157). This vicarious responsibility consists of the various indirect, structural, and collective forms of agency that, as Rothberg puts it, "enable injury, exploitation, and domination but that frequently remain in the shadows" (2019, p. 1). Miss Kenton protests so strongly because she finds that, against her will, she becomes "an implicated subject" (p. 1). Linking this concept to the term "complicity," Rothberg aligns his use of that term with Debarati Sanyal's understanding of complicity as a "structure of engagement that produces ethical and political reflection across proliferating frames of reference" (Sanyal, 2015, p. 17). Yet Rothberg adds that "implication is both a more capacious and a more fundamental term for describing . . . forms of indirect participation. . . . Complicity presupposes implication, but implication does not always involve complicity" (2019, p. 13). Miss Kenton may not be complicit in the decision of dismissing Elsa and Irma since she protests energetically against it, but she still feels implicated since she is responsible for the girls and since she realizes that, once unemployed, there is a risk that they can be sent back to Germany.

As in the dismissal scene, the characters' verbal language is colored by visual communication. Strikingly relevant to the issue of ethics, both generally and with a view to antisemitism and the Holocaust in particular, is Miss Kenton's attitude of defiance and the combination of anger directed at Lord Darlington and Stevens on the one hand and care for Elsa and Irma on the other; as Figure 5.5 shows, her facial expression at once confirms and accentuates these aspects of her ethos. As regards Stevens, there is a notable resemblance between the subdued, almost resigned way he accepts Lord Darlington's request and the way in which, clearly shocked, he takes his leave after Miss Kenton has threatened to leave Darlington Hall if Elsa and Irma are forced to do so. The dialogue between Stevens and Miss Kenton after the dismissal scene is framed by that between Stevens and Mr. Benn,

Miss Kenton's future husband, presented just before it. The reason Mr. Benn is visiting Darlington Hall is somewhat unclear, but it appears to be related to his interest in Miss Kenton, whom he describes as "an attractive woman." In the dialogue, Stevens says to Mr. Benn, who is skeptical about Darlington's guests and the conferences he arranges, "In my philosophy, Mr Benn, a man cannot call himself well-contented until he has done everything he can to be of service to his employer. Of course, this assumes that one's employer is a superior person, not only in rank or wealth, but in moral stature." As Lord Darlington's dismissal of Elsa and Irma demonstrates that he is *not* "superior . . . in moral stature," this event would appear to seriously challenge Stevens's "philosophy." Yet although Stevens ventures to politely protest against Lord Darlington's decision, he defers to his habitual philosophy of service. That the word that makes him comply with his employer's request is "Jews" makes his ethical failure all the more serious, revealing not just the shortcoming but the potentially terrible consequences of his philosophy of service.[9]

In Ivory's adaptation, as in Ishiguro's novel, there is a contrapuntal relationship between the dismissal scene and the scene in which Lord Darlington regrets his decision (Figure 5.6):

Figure 5.6 Screenshot from *The Remains of the Day*, directed by James Ivory (1993)

DARLINGTON: "Oh, Stevens, I've been planning to ask you, that business last year about the Jewish maids. I suppose there's no way of tracing them, is there?"

STEVENS: "That would be difficult. I tried to get them a position in Surrey. There was room only for one, and the girls didn't want to be separated."

DARLINGTON: "Well, try anyway, Stevens. One would like to do something for them. It was wrong, what occurred. I'm sorry about it. Very sorry."

In both scenes, Lord Darlington requests a service from his butler; in both, Stevens does as he is told; and in both, or following both, Miss Kenton is upset when Stevens tells her about their employer's wishes and decisions. Yet there are two important differences, both of which further the film's narrative ethics. The first concerns the outcome of Darlington's decision and Stevens's execution of that decision. While in the first scene Stevens does what Darlington asks him to do, in the second he is unable to successfully serve his employer: although he tells Darlington that he will try to trace Elsa and Irma, I understand that the attempt will prove unsuccessful because, curiously preempting Darlington's new request that contradicts the earlier one, Stevens has already tried to help the girls. Why has Stevens attempted "to get them a position in Surrey," and why has he not told Darlington (and probably not Miss Kenton either) about this? In my interpretation, Stevens's attempt to help them reveals an ethical impulse following his recognition that the act of dismissal was wrong. Although part of this recognition, or belated insight, may be embedded in his cautious protest when Darlington asks him to dismiss Elsa and Irma, it is primarily motivated by Miss Kenton's strong objection—a protest that is more effective and has a more lasting effect on him than he readily concedes. Stevens does not need to hear Darlington admit, a year after the dismissal, "It was wrong, what occurred": Miss Kenton immediately identified the act as "wrong." In addition to acknowledging that she was right, her question to Stevens—"Do you realize that if those girls have no work they could be sent back to Germany?"—has probably been a motivating factor in his attempt to trace the girls. Miss Kenton's solidarity with and care for two young Jews in a precarious situation has made an impression on Stevens, challenging his values by making him question, though he is unable to openly admit this, his philosophy of unconditional service to his employer.

The second difference concerns Miss Kenton's reaction when Stevens tells her that Lord Darlington now admits that it was wrong to dismiss the girls:

STEVENS: "His lordship also asked about the Jewish girls."
MISS KENTON: "Elsa and Irma?"
STEVENS: "He wondered where they were. He said it was wrong to dismiss them. I remember you were as upset as I was about it."

MISS KENTON: "As you were? As I recall, you thought it was right and proper that they should be sent packing."

STEVENS: "Now, really, Miss Kenton, that is most unfair. Of course, I was upset. Very much so. One doesn't like to see that sort of thing happening in this house."

MISS KENTON: "I wish you'd told me. It would've helped me to know you felt as I did. Why, Mr Stevens, do you always have to hide what you feel?"

Even though Miss Kenton's use of the phrase "hide what you feel" is not identical with "pretend," the word Ishiguro makes her employ in the corresponding sentence in the novel, the meaning of the questions she asks Stevens in the novel and in the adaptation is nearly the same. The difference, in the novel as in the adaptation, is that while in the dialogue after the dismissal scene Miss Kenton sharpens her protest to the point of threatening to resign, here she recognizes an attitudinal affinity with Stevens. Importantly, this kind of recognition is based on the premise that Stevens is sincere— that he was in fact distressed by the girls' dismissal, though he did not say so.

As Ivory's film narration is characteristically unidentifiable when it comes to the question of who remembers and who the narrator is, my response to both these questions becomes an interpretive response. While it makes sense to consider most of the film's plot, including that of the present as well as the analepses, as remembered—and narratively presented—by Stevens, I find that the memories of Miss Kenton, and to a lesser extent also those of Lord Darlington, play a greater role in the adaptation than in the novel. Although the issue of the Holocaust, and of Lord Darlington's and Stevens's complicity in the ramifications of this series of historical events, is most clearly expressed in the film's analepses, it also underlies the narrative present. Not only are Stevens's memories sparked by his journey and the prospect of meeting Miss Kenton again after 20 years. Additionally, the kinetic force of the images that visually present aspects of Stevens's memories in the film's analepses is so strong that they intrude into Stevens's present in a way that I find even more forceful and unstoppable than in the novel. In the film as in the novel, the analepses include events to whose realization Stevens is proud to have contributed as a butler, but also experiences that are painful because he is realizing that his own contribution, founded in no small part on his philosophy of serving Lord Darlington, has been ethically flawed.

Ivory's Contrapuntal Method

As the film progresses, Ivory's contrapuntal method of interlinking the temporal layers of the film's present and past involves a series of comments and admissions made by Stevens. Made in the narrative present, they are more directly related to Stevens's memories, and his attempt to come to terms with these memories, than earlier in the adaptation. Staying overnight in a village because his car runs out of petrol, Stevens meets with Richard Carlisle, a local medical doctor. Driving Stevens back to his car the following morning, Carlisle asks him, "Wasn't there a Lord Darlington in that appeasement business that got us into the war?" Stevens responds, "I'm sorry, sir, I never knew that Lord Darlington." Hopkins makes Stevens reveal that this conversation is embarrassing for him: looking at Carlisle with some trepidation, he seems to be wondering, perhaps even dreading what his next question might be (Figure 5.7).

Figure 5.7 Screenshot from *The Remains of the Day*, directed by James Ivory (1993)

Why is Stevens lying? Does he silently agree with Carlisle's following comment, that Lord Darlington "was lucky, really, not to be tried for treason"? If Darlington was a traitor, was Stevens one too? Stevens gives no direct answers to these questions. Yet he delivers a partial response in the following dialogue:

STEVENS: "Sir, I must confess, I failed to tell you the truth. I did know Lord Darlington, and I can declare that he was a truly good man. A gentleman through and through, to whom I'm proud to have given the best years of my life."

CARLISLE: "But did you share his opinions? Lord Darlington['s]."
STEVENS: "I was his butler. I was there to serve him. Not to agree or disagree."
CARLISLE: "You trusted him."
STEVENS: "Yes, I did. Completely."
CARLISLE: "Wouldn't you rather make your own mistakes?"
STEVENS: "In a very small way I did make my own mistake. But I might still have a chance to set mine right. In fact, I'm on my way to try and do so now."

Admitting to Carlisle that he just lied to him takes some courage and uncovers a facet of Stevens's ethos: he takes exception to lying, and now he corrects himself by stating that he knew the person he has just distanced himself from. Inadvertently, Carlisle touches a nerve: asking Stevens whether he would not rather make his own mistakes than accepting, and thus appropriating, those made by his employer, Stevens's response makes me think that "my own mistake" refers not so much to his relation to Lord Darlington as to his failure, or inability, to develop a relationship with Miss Kenton. As I read this film dialogue, the sentence "In fact, I'm on my way to try and do so now" is a self-interpretive element that suggests Stevens's inability to respond to Miss Kenton's affection and love is not a mistake made "in a very small way"—it is in fact the greatest mistake of his life. This self-interpretive component is strengthened by the way in which Stevens, standing next to Carlisle, who is filling the car with petrol, is looking into space with an expression of determination yet also, in my interpretation, of resignation.

The dialogue between Stevens and Carlisle in the film's present is associated with and furthers my reading of that between Stevens and Mr. Cardinal in the film's last analepsis. The occasion is a secret meeting, arranged by Lord Darlington, between the British prime minister and the German ambassador. That Ivory uses their historical names, Neville Chamberlain and Joachim von Ribbentrop, emphasizes the fiction film's connection with the tense political situation in Europe in the late 1930s. Stevens knows details of the meeting but, asked by Cardinal, pretends not to. Referring to their longstanding friendship at Darlington Hall, Cardinal, a journalist who can see the war coming and who is upset by the way Lord Darlington is being used as a pawn by the Nazis, insists that Stevens sit down and talk to him, and Stevens reluctantly agrees to do so.

I highlight two dimensions of this scene's narrative ethics. Both are furthered and rhetorically intensified by Hugh Grant's performance as Cardinal

Figure 5.8 Screenshot from *The Remains of the Day*, directed by James Ivory (1993)

(Figure 5.8). First, Cardinal, who in the adaptation as in the novel is one of the first to become skeptical about Nazi Germany in general and the regime's hostility to Jews in particular, thinks it is deeply upsetting that Lord Darlington, who is presented as his grandfather in the adaptation, allows himself to be exploited by, and thus serve, the Nazis. What he finds particularly abominable is the way "the criminals in Berlin" are taking advantage of Lord Darlington's qualities as an English gentleman for whom honor is more important than realpolitik. Without saying so directly, Cardinal hints that there is a link between Stevens's philosophy of serving his employer and Darlington's misguided belief that by collaborating with the Nazis he can further peace in Europe. Both are, Cardinal thinks, incredibly naïve.

Second, as Cardinal shifts the emphasis of their conversation from Darlington to Stevens, he shows that he is worried about him and cares for him in a way that resembles Miss Kenton's attitude. Given that, as is obvious to Cardinal, the values of Nazism are at the opposite extreme to those of Darlington and Stevens, he does not understand the latter's apparent lack of concern:

CARDINAL: "Mr. Stevens, don't you care at all? Aren't you at least a bit curious?"
STEVENS: "It's not my place to be curious about such matters."
CARDINAL: "He's being tricked, Stevens, don't you see? Are you as deluded as he is?"

Marveling at Darlington's and Stevens's failure to see that their values necessitate not just skepticism about the values of Nazism but active resistance to them, Cardinal does not seem to be aware of their responsibility for the dismissal of Elsa and Irma. There is no doubt that, had he known about the dismissal, he would have opposed it as vehemently as Miss Kenton did; his lack of knowledge about this event augments the distance between his ethical stance and those of Darlington and Stevens. The dramatic irony in this part of the dialogue is strengthened by Cardinal's question about Stevens's curiosity. Although he may not know this, his question is spot on: Stevens is in fact extremely curious, and he is particularly curious about Miss Kenton's activities and values. One reason for Stevens's unease during the dialogue is that he senses a strong affinity between Cardinal's attitude to the Nazis and Miss Kenton's.

When Stevens eventually meets with Miss Kenton in Weymouth, there is a sense in which the two temporal layers of Ivory's adaptation coalesce. And yet they do not because, as Stevens and Miss Kenton are looking at each other across the restaurant table (Figure 5.9), most of their conversation consists of sharing memories of their time together at Darlington Hall. Why does the conversation end as abruptly as it does? The reason, I suggest, is that Miss Kenton is asking Stevens a question that he finds unbearably painful in the narrative situation, sitting opposite the woman who was probably the great love of his life and having just been told that she cannot return to Darlington Hall because her daughter is expecting.

Figure 5.9 Screenshot from *The Remains of the Day*, directed by James Ivory (1993)

Stevens's response to the question makes the relevant segment of film dialogue consist of two questions rather than one:

MISS KENTON: "What about his grandson, Mr. Cardinal?"
STEVENS: "Mr. Cardinal was killed in the war. May I have the bill, please?"

On a second viewing of the adaptation, this information—given almost in passing, as a necessary reply to a direct question—makes me see the conversation between Cardinal and Stevens before the war in a new light. If Cardinal lost his life, Elsa and Irma may have lost theirs too. The information about Cardinal's death also makes me appreciate the significance of a black-and-white photograph of a young man that sits on a small table in the bedroom of the pub where Stevens sleeps the night before his conversation with doctor Carlisle. Pointing at the photograph, the pub owner, who has taken Stevens to the bedroom, comments, "Democracy is what we fought Hitler for. We lost quite a few in the war, including our son here. Dunkirk."

That Stevens is asking for the bill as soon as he has told Miss Kenton about Cardinal's death is a strong indication of his grief following that loss. It is also indicative of his tendency, still apparent at the end of the film, to shy away from issues that he perceives as threatening. Yet this narrative situation is different from those in which Stevens and Miss Kenton engaged at Darlington Hall many years earlier. One essential difference is a resignation that, perceivable by me as a viewer, is, I gather, experienced by Stevens and Miss Kenton. For Stevens, it is stirred by the news that Miss Kenton will not return to Darlington Hall. For Miss Kenton, there may be resignation associated with her renewed impression of a man who finds it difficult to express his feelings. This resignation in the narrative present is simultaneously accentuated and modified by the way their conversation—temporally located in the present and spatially in the hotel in Weymouth—is hemmed in by an exchange of memories. Just before she asks Stevens about Cardinal, Miss Kenton mentions Lord Darlington:

MISS KENTON: "We read about the suit for libel. It's a shame. Calling his lordship a traitor. Those papers will print anything. They should have lost the case."

STEVENS: "Yes. When his lordship went to court, he sincerely expected he would get justice. Instead, the newspaper increased in circulation, and his lordship's good name was destroyed forever. And afterwards, quite honestly, Mrs. Benn, his heart was broken."

Why does Miss Kenton defend Lord Darlington? Is it out of respect for her former employer, or does she, in common with Stevens, think that his actions before the war were justifiable? Another reason could be that, in this last meeting with Stevens, she does not want to raise the issue of the dismissal of the Jewish girls. If that is the case, then her reconciliatory comment adds another touch of resignation to their conversation. So does Stevens's reply.

When he says that Lord Darlington's "heart was broken," the viewer who has read Ishiguro's novel is reminded of Stevens's comment after Miss Kenton confesses, "I get to thinking about a life I might have had with you, Mr Stevens." Stevens's reaction is narrated as follows: "Indeed—why should I not admit it?—at that moment, my heart was breaking" (p. 252). Projecting his own feelings onto those of Lord Darlington, Stevens covertly admits what he is unable to communicate: that the tragedy of his life was his failure to respond to Miss Kenton's invitations to form a relationship. That this admission indicates a deep regret does not preclude the possibility that, in common with Lord Darlington, he may also regret his complicity in the dismissal of Elsa and Irma. Combining gesture, tone of voice, tempo, and facial expression, Hopkins makes Stevens's comment that Lord Darlington's "heart was broken" just as rich and suggestive as Stevens's confession "[M]y heart was breaking."

I conclude that if these points of connection between Ishiguro's novel and Ivory's film support my view of *The Remains of the Day* as an adaptation in the fidelity and transformation mode, the way the connections are visually presented confirms their contribution to as well as their dependence on a multifaceted film communication. And if, as I argue in this book, both documentary films and fiction films are distinguished by the overlaying of ethics and aesthetic form, Ivory's adaptation uses this overlaying to explore aspects of antisemitism and the Holocaust in a way that prompts ethical questions as well as ethical reflections. Accentuating the role of memory as a motor for the film's narration of events and experiences in the present as well as in the past, Ivory not only demonstrates memory's importance for the formation and sustainability of human memory; he also shows how memory is a constituent element of narrative identity.

The narrative ethics of Ivory's adaptation is strengthened by the way in which narration in the present is halted by aspects, including repressed aspects, of Stevens's past that intrude into his present. The thrust of these intruding fragments of his memories is ethical. "Film is an inherently ethical medium: it depends upon an ethical encounter between the various individuals engaged in its experience. In revealing others' vulnerability, film requires us to feel in relation to them, to care about what happens, at least to some of them" (Aaron, 2016). Watching and rewatching Ivory's *The Remains of the Day*, I interpret what I see by using my cognitive abilities and aspects of my knowledge and experience, and also by activating facets of affect, empathy, distance, and care. Filmic ethics "can be located neither in the image nor in the viewer but in the precarious space that they share. The name of this space is cinema" (Grønstad, 2016, p. 234). Viewing and responding to "the precarious space" of Ivory's adaptation, I build on the self-interpretive elements expressed through the main characters' attitudes, choices, and values while simultaneously acknowledging that my interpretation is uniquely my own. Yet although the horizon of my interpretation is limited, that "horizon is the range of vision that includes everything that can be seen from a particular vantage point" (Gadamer, 1960/2013, p. 313). Moreover, as Gadamer also remarks, "the discovery of the true meaning of a text or a work of art is never finished; it is in fact an infinite process" (p. 309). I find that my acts of rereading Ishiguro's novel and rewatching Ivory's film confirm the validity of Gadamer's insight.

"My narrative," writes Judith Butler in *Giving an Account of Oneself*, "begins *in medias res*, when many things have already taken place to make me and my story possible in language. I am always recuperating, reconstructing, and I am left to fictionalize and fabricate origins I cannot know" (2005, p. 39). I highlight Butler's observation for two reasons. First, Stevens's narrative clearly begins in medias res. When it starts, most of his life is already behind him. His narrative becomes "possible in language" because of "things [that] have already taken place," and it becomes possible at this point in time because of Miss Kenton's letter, to which, after having read it, he responds "in language." Second, while Butler's observation applies to Stevens, the fact that, using the pronoun "I," she refers to her own narrative is a thought-provoking reminder of the ways in which and the extent to which parts of Stevens's narrative are affiliated with aspects of my own narrative. Although, as I have aimed to show, there are facets of Stevens's ethos that I want or feel a need to distance myself from, the narrative makes me see that although his values may be different from mine, constituent elements of his "autobiographical process" (Brockmeier, 2015, p. 11) resemble my own.

I hope to have shown that, in the novel as in the film, the narrative discourse of *The Remains of the Day* displays and reveals a range of ethical components. As facets of the ethics of the telling and showing, these components are complex and dynamic since they are formed, challenged, and modified by the development of the plot as well as by the interaction of characters and of different temporal layers or dimensions. At the same time, the ethics of the telling is colored by the ethics of the told, including not only the Second World War and the Holocaust but also aspects of the history of the British Empire. As I also hope to have demonstrated, Stevens's values—including his attitudes and priorities as indicated and revealed by his actions or failures to act—are diverse, multifaceted, and at times opposed. In the novel, the combination of and tensions between these ethical elements form the basis for and blend into Ishiguro's ethics as implied author. A key contributor to this textual dynamics is the narrator. As first-person narrator, Stevens tells the reader about his journey while at the same time sharing or revealing fragments of his memory of his life at Darlington Hall. As noted in the introduction, Phelan (2017) considers the implied author to be the main narrative agent of narrative fiction. In *The Remains of the Day* both the narrator and the implied author are indispensable communicators (Lothe, 2019; cf. Lothe, 2023a).

The gap between Stevens as a character (the experiencing self) and Stevens as a narrator (the narrating self) has implications for my interpretation of the novel (Phelan & Martin, 1999). At the same time, there is, as Amit Marcus observes, "a difference between Stevens at the beginning of the narration and at its end" (2006, p. 139); I have found that this difference also influences my reading. The components of his ethos that Stevens stresses early in his narrative, including the key word "serve," are gradually undermined by elements that reveal a more complex and less stable ethics signaled by words such as "pretend" and "regret." Ishiguro's novel shows that "narratives whose narrating character is self-deceived may create an oscillation between (at least) two tenable versions of the story" (Marcus, 2006, 135). While my analysis has suggested that the second version gradually emerges as the more credible, it also supports Marcus's accompanying point that a self-deceived narrating character may additionally give rise to two hypotheses about the *motivation* to narrate:

> One possibility is that the motivation of the narrating character is to reinforce self-deception through narration. . . . According to the second hypothesis, the act of narration is also motivated by a (partly unconscious) desire to face the truth and gain an accurate picture of the course of events that has led to self-deception, thus revising the narrator's life. (pp. 135–136)

I conclude that although the second hypothesis seems strengthened toward the end of Stevens's narration (and further strengthened in an act of rereading), the tension or conflict between two different motivations for telling the story is not resolved. Stevens's conflicting motivations may partly explain why the two versions of the story that the narrative discourse reveals cannot be resolved either. Although the reasons are complex, one reason is Stevens's resignation at the end of his autobiographical narrative.

"Narrative" as I use the concept here refers both to Ishiguro's novel and to Ivory's adaptation: using the narrative techniques and activating the communicative resources of verbal language and film language, respectively, they both explore "the vicissitudes of intention" that Jerome Bruner considers as one of narrative's most important psychological features (1986, p. 17; cf. Bruner, 1987, 1990). If Stevens's main intention has been "to serve," the vicissitudes of that intention are forcefully presented to the reader of Ishiguro's novel as well as the viewer of Ivory's film.

In the narrative discourse of both Ishiguro's novel and Ivory's film, the vicissitudes of intention are blended with those of memory. Commenting on pivotal documentaries and essay films that have appeared since the mid-2000s, Grønstad finds that they "exhibit, all in their different ways, an overriding concern with the mutability of memory and its aesthetic articulations" (2016, p. 182). As a fiction film, Ivory's *The Remains of the Day* exhibits a similar concern, combining its aesthetic articulation with an ethical thrust related to and stirred by the mutability of Stevens's memory. Although neither the novel nor the film mentions the word "Holocaust," in my interpretation it underlies both narratives, furthering their narrative ethics by exploring how, through the painful mnemonic search movements of the novel as well as the film, Stevens, in accord with his intention to serve Lord Darlington, reflects on ways he may be complicit in antisemitism and even (as the adaptation suggests more directly than the novel) in the Holocaust. More precisely, he is forced to reflect on his possible complicity by Miss Kenton's protest against the dismissal of the Jewish girls—and also by his employer's regret of his own decision as well as, on a different yet related level, the collective memory of the Second World War and the Holocaust. As a reader of Ishiguro's novel as well as a viewer of Ivory's adaptation, I conclude that, as a fictional character, Stevens *is* complicit in the historical event of the Holocaust that both Ishiguro and Ivory allude to in the fictional narratives they create. There is a sense in which, in both versions, the Holocaust is the work's determinate absence. I also conclude that Stevens probably knows this, though he is unable to express this insight verbally or even, perhaps, to admit this to himself. Although, as a European born after the war, I can claim that I am not complicit in the Holocaust the way

Stevens is, I cannot conclude I am not implicated at all. One unavoidable consequence of this kind of implication in complex historical processes that include violence and war is that I am obliged not to forget the Holocaust. Using verbal narrative and film narrative, Ishiguro and Ivory deliver forceful responses to this ethical challenge.

Notes

1. Although Ishiguro's narrative fiction has attracted considerable critical attention, few critics approach *The Remains of the Day* (Ishiguro's novel as well as Ivory's adaptation) the way I do. Perceptive studies of Ishiguro's fiction include Beedham (2010), Bennett (2023), Eaglestone (2023) Furst (2007), Schaffer (1998), Teo (2014), and Walkowitz (2001). Phelan (2005) gives as analysis of Ishiguro's novel from the perspective of rhetorical narrative theory; Marcus (2006) discusses the novel from a philosophical perspective. A helpful collection of essays is Bennett (2023). Long and Ivory (2005) presents a series of interviews with James Ivory.
2. As the plot of the 1993 adaptation is close to the novel's, the following summary goes a long way toward covering both the novel and the film.
3. Ishiguro (1989/2005, p. 3). Subsequent page references are given in the text.
4. It is significant that the subtitles indicate both time and place. This aspect of the novel is interestingly related to Jenny Erpenbeck's *Aller Tage Abend* (see Chapter 7).
5. I note that in making this comment I reveal my assumption, or expectation, that a dialogue reported by a first-person narrator is more trustworthy than a comment the first-person narrator makes on that dialogue. It does not follow that the implied author cannot make the first-person narrator construct dialogues that the narrator knows are untrue, that is, opposed to the facts of the fictional universe as he or she knows those facts. Had Stevens done this, he would have been an unreliable narrator in a way he is not. Right from the launch of the narrative, Ishiguro presents Stevens as a character whose narration of his journey westward "in the comfort of Mr Farraday's Ford" (p. 3) is infiltrated by memories of past events and experiences. As regards the novel's narrative ethics, it is essential that the direct discourse included in these memories is interpreted by me as authentic. To put this another way, as a reader of Ishiguro's narrative I am inclined to think that, in the fictional world of which Stevens is a part and through which he moves, the fragments of dialogue constitute the core of his memories. His whole narrative venture is a sustained, in one sense even desperate attempt to negotiate the meanings and implications of the dialogues around which his narration revolves, introducing the fragments of direct discourse, reporting them, and reflecting on them. Brian McHale (2011) writes that direct discourse "is conventionally understood to replicate exactly what the quoted character is supposed to have said or thought. . . . Of course, the 'originality' of direct quotation in fiction is entirely illusory. . . . [M]oreover, so is the independence of the quoted inset, which is always framed by the framing context." Both these aspects of free direct discourse contribute to the ethics of the narrative discourse of *The Remains of the Day*.
6. By "Stevens's ethos" I mean a relatively stable character quality or value, for example his idea and practice of serving Lord Darlington. By "Stevens's ethics" I mean the complex combination of values, priorities, attitudes, and memories presented and challenged through the narrative discourse. As noted in the introduction, the demarcation between ethos and ethics is blurred.
7. That this episode is in fact the third of three analeptic fragments that Stevens relates about his father shows how important his father is to him as an ideal butler. It also shows how essential the ideal of a butler is for his father (p. 43). It is possible that Stevens conceives of his narratee as a butler.
8. In one sense they are even opposed because, as the Russian formalist Boris Eikhenbaum noted as early as 1926, "The cinema audience is placed in completely new conditions of perception, which are to an extent opposite to those of the reading process. Whereas the reader moves from the printed word to visualisation of the subject, the viewer goes in the opposite direction:

he moves from the subject, from comparison of the moving frames to their comprehension" (Eikhenbaum, 1926/1973, p. 123). "Comprehension," as Eikhenbaum uses the word, involves, and arguably necessitates, interpretation. Leitch (2020) provides a useful survey of adaptation studies.

9. These "terrible consequences" evoke the Nazi perpetrators' self-defence: we were just obeying orders. See my discussion of the Nazi guards in the last part of Chapter 2 and of Maximilian Aue in Chapter 4.

6

W. G. Sebald's *Austerlitz*

While Littell in *Les Bienveillantes* designs his main character as a first-person narrator who claims not to regret his involvement in the Holocaust, Ishiguro's *The Remains of the Day* is a thought-provoking fictional exploration of protagonist and first-person narrator Stevens's attempts to come to terms with past actions that, as Miss Kenton puts it, are "wrong" (Ishiguro, 1989/2005, p. 157). A characteristic feature of the German British author W. G. Sebald's novel *Austerlitz* is a strong belief in, yet also a notable distrust of, narrative's potential and value with regard to the challenge of negotiating and not forgetting the Holocaust. On the one hand, it seems clear that, for Sebald, narrative is a powerful mode of exploration. Narrative offers a possibility for identifying and investigating challenging problems associated with, and in large part generated by, the author's childhood and the period of European history, including the Holocaust, that shaped it. For Sebald, narrative is not just a form of memory; it is a way—perhaps the only way—of exploring how human beings' identities and values are shaped by their memories. On the other hand, or perhaps at the same time, Sebald is skeptical about narrative—especially the kind of narrative that tends to simplify, mythologize, and misrepresent historical reality. This danger of misrepresentation is imbued in both fictional and historical narrative, not least as far as the presentation of values is concerned.

Focusing on *Austerlitz*, this chapter will show how Sebald uses narrative fiction—which in this case includes visual images—to present the protagonist's and the frame narrator's sustained attempt to come to terms with the losses and absences resulting from the Holocaust. *Austerlitz* is an extraordinary example of how, in a work of narrative fiction, the two main characters—and also, in ways I will attempt to explain, Sebald as author and I as reader—are engaged in a search for truth, including not only acknowledging that the Holocaust happened but reflecting on how it *could* happen, how it is remembered, and the contest of values involved. "Because," notes Charles L. Griswold, "the narrative in which the truth is told (or partially

Memory and Narrative Ethics. Jakob Lothe, Oxford University Press. © Oxford University Press (2025).
DOI: 10.1093/9780197579534.003.0007

told, as the case may be) is by definition backward looking in part, the issue becomes how we should remember the past" (2007, p. xxiv). For both the frame narrator and Austerlitz, this is very much the issue. Yet "[a]t the same time, the narrative is forward looking in that it is inevitably meant to influence future perspective and perhaps action" (p. xxiv). This dimension of *Austerlitz* becomes, I will suggest, particularly important for the frame narrator—and, by implication, for me as reader as well.

The novel's complex negotiations, set out in the narrative situations and in Austerlitz's prolonged search for his parents, are fictional: the characters are created by Sebald, and so is the plot—or the novel's fragments of plot. And yet the references to historical reality are different from and more insistent than those in *Les Bienveillantes* and *The Remains of the Day*. The most apparent difference is that *Austerlitz* includes a series of visual images, primarily black-and-white photographs, that display, or seem to display, fragments of the physical world. The reader of *Austerlitz* thus also becomes a viewer, and my impression and interpretation of the visual images inevitably colors my interpretation of the verbal text. Since the images incorporated into the verbal discourse of *Austerlitz* are an integral part of the novel's presentation of the interplay of narrative and memory, and since they also contribute significantly to the novel's narrative ethics, I discuss six visual images presented in the novel. My discussion aims to show how the interplay of verbal text and visual image serves not only to obliquely present Sebald's abiding preoccupation with the Second World War and the Holocaust but also urges the reader to reflect on the temporal reach of these historical events, not least the absences they generated in individual lives. Since the book's focus is on variants of narrative presentations of the Holocaust, I choose images that, in dialogue with the verbal text into which they are incorporated and by which they are framed, are associated with the Holocaust in ways that supplement and enrich each other. As I consider the frame narrator as the second main character of the novel, I discuss a visual image that is related directly to his narrative presentation of Austerlitz's account. If, as I argue, the narrative ethics of Austerlitz's fragmented narrative is inseparable from and utterly dependent on fragments of his memory, the frame narrator is also, albeit in a different way, engaged in a demanding process of remembering a gruesome crime that he cannot understand and for which he is not responsible, but to which he feels uncomfortably close.[1]

Visual Images in Verbal Narrative

Before turning to *Austerlitz*, I make four observations on the aesthetic and ethical effects of visual images presented in verbal narrative.[2] These brief comments on a complex issue are related to and inspired by the discussion that follows; they also draw on and supplement my comments on photographs in the Introduction and Chapter 1 and on the film medium in Chapters 2, 3, and 5. My obvious yet important first point is that once a visual image is included in a verbal text, we are confronted not just with what we can term two different media but also with a constellation of and opposition between two aesthetic and communicative registers. The reader also becomes a viewer, and the fact that I am looking at a visual image when reading a verbal narrative affects the way I read both the verbal text next to the visual image and the whole narrative. Silke Horstkotte considers photo-text topography as "a spatial dimension which the photos introduce into the linearity of verbal narrative" (2008, p. 50). In a narrative such as *Austerlitz* this spatial dimension is added to or inserted into that of the verbal narrative itself. Literature, and not least narrative fiction, has a topography of its own—a spatial dimension at once linked and opposed to the temporal one.[3] The topography of a photo-text, or what J. W. T. Mitchell calls "imagetext" (1994, p. 83), is a combination of two topographies, one verbal and one visual, and my construction of the former may be supported or complicated by my understanding of the latter. The relation of the topographies can thus vary across a wide spectrum, with total reinforcement at one end and complete conflict at the other.

Second, since we conventionally relate a photograph to our experience of the external, physical world, the encounter with a photo when reading a verbal narrative, especially a fictional one, raises the issue of authenticity. Broadly, two dimensions are activated here. If one purpose of the narrative is to say something about historical reality (historical events, characters, processes), a photograph can support that purpose. But if, not least in a fictional narrative, the author wants to exploit the photograph's ambiguity, he or she can make it part of "an elaborate play with interdiscursive (inter-textual, intermedial, and intericonic) allusions" (Horstkotte, 2008, p. 50), thus problematizing the notion of authenticity. Importantly, the two dimensions need not necessarily exclude each other; rather, they may coexist in a curiously alogical fashion.[4]

Third, because, as noted above, the presentation and layering of space in embedded photographs and other visual images can relate in different ways to the topography of the storyworld evoked in the verbal narrative, cogent issues of narrative are highlighted. I identify two such issues, both of which possess aesthetic as well as ethical aspects. The former aspect is located at the intersection of narrative, reading, and viewing. If confronted with a visual image when reading a verbal narrative, my reading of the verbal text is temporarily suspended as I look at the image and wonder about its relevance and significance. Thus, the visual image has the potential to disrupt the previous narrative progression but also the potential to enrich it. And yet the image, the textual picture I am looking at, can itself include narrative features—features that may be convergent with, accentuated by, or opposed to the surrounding verbal narrative. Such an imbrication of visual and verbal elements becomes particularly noticeable if, as in the case of *Austerlitz*, the textual pictures are uncaptioned, thus in a way making the verbal text an extended caption and, conversely, turning the pictures into an oblique commentary on the verbal text. This dimension of the first aspect blends into the second: who or what are the narrative agent(s) responsible for the visual images? If I use the verbal narrative as my interpretive starting point, is the relationship between the author and the narrator different as far as the textual pictures are concerned?

Fourth, while most visual images possess an aesthetic aspect, the ethical dimension may be more implicit and may to a larger extent depend on the reader's interpretive activity. Unsurprisingly, as far as the Holocaust is concerned, it is a matter of considerable debate how photographs and other visual images of this series of historical events can and should be presented. As Anette H. Storeide observes, "[A]n unwritten rule has been that the images should not be shown at the expense of the victims and not satisfy the audience's need or greed for sensations and shocking images" (2012, p. 262). If, as the chapters on Resnais's *Night and Fog* and Lanzmann's *Shoah* show, this issue looms large in discussions of these two films, it is also challenging in my interpretation of *Austerlitz*. One reason the question is important is that it highlights the narrative dimension of photographs of this kind: looking at a photo from, say, Auschwitz, the viewer's more or less accurate or comprehensive narrative of Auschwitz is activated; moreover, he or she is forcefully reminded of the close, in this case even insistent interplay of visual image, narrative, and individual as well as collective memory.

One interpretive implication of these observations on visual images and their relation to, as well as incorporation into, a verbal text is to challenge my understanding of narrative fiction, including the narrative ethics of fiction. One of photography's defining features, as well as one of the strongest conventions associated with this medium, is its capacity to visually represent a segment of physical reality at a given point in time. Seen thus, photography, though it can be manipulated in various ways, is a marker of nonfictionality. At the same time, the verbal discourse of *Austerlitz* includes several signposts of fictionality (Lothe, 2022). Two such signposts in Sebald's novel are extensive use of dialogue and what David Gorman calls the "distinguishability" of narrator from author (2008, p. 167; cf. Cohn, 1999). With regard to the latter signpost, though, the distinguishability of Austerlitz from the author is greater than that of the frame narrator from the author. This difference is, as I will show, important for the ethics developed through the narrative discourse.

Sebald as Implied and Historical Author

The combination of visual images and verbal discourse lends indirect yet strong support to the distinction made in this book between the implied and the historical author. When Gorman refers to "author" he seems to be thinking of the implied author—the image of the author that I form when reading a fictional narrative and that I revise and refine when rereading it. As regards the historical author, I consider that notion problematic since extratextual knowledge that I may have of the author's life may distract me from careful reading and rereading of the fictional text that narrative analysis and narrative hermeneutics place at the center of critical attention. And yet, if the text explores, as does *Austerlitz*, motifs of human loss, memory, and possible reconciliation by relating the narrative to historical knowledge of the Holocaust, some knowledge of Sebald as the historical author may become more relevant. This kind of relevance, of whose critical value I am not certain, may be enhanced if, as indicated above, visual images are incorporated into the verbal narrative in ways that may emphasize, though perhaps also complicate, the text's relationship with historical reality. The relevance of the notion of a historical author may also be accentuated by Sebald's use of a frame narrator who, partly because he is a middle-aged German man, becomes the novel's second protagonist. Based on these reflections, I include a sketch of Sebald as historical author.

Born in Bavaria in 1944, the son of a German soldier who returned from a French prisoner-of-war camp only in 1947 and did not speak about his war experiences, Sebald was, literally as well as metaphorically, a child of the Second World War. Interviewed by Maya Jaggi in September 2001, Sebald said, "[M]y parents came from working-class, small-peasant, farm-labourer backgrounds, and had made the grade during the fascist years."

> It was that social stratum where [after the war] the so-called conspiracy of silence was at its most present. Until I was 16 or 17, I heard practically nothing about the history that preceded 1945. Only when we were 17 were we confronted with a documentary film of the Belsen camp. There it was, and we somehow had to get our minds around it—which of course we didn't. It was in the afternoon, with a football match afterwards. So it took years to find out what had happened.

One year after completing his studies of German literature at Freiburg University, Sebald obtained a post at the University of Manchester, and a few years later he took a lectureship in German at the University of East Anglia. He taught at this university until his untimely death in a traffic accident in 2001. In addition to a successful academic career during which he wrote several academic books, Sebald embarked on creative writing, consistently using his native German language. In 1988 he published *Nach der Natur* (Sebald, 1998), a kind of meditation in unrhymed verse on the destruction of nature.[5] It was followed by a series of books in which he combines elements of various genres and media, including black-and-white photographs and other images.

Narrative Beginning

Nowhere in Sebald's work is this combination more striking than in his final book, *Austerlitz* (2001/2003).[6] Its front cover shows a black-and-white photograph of a young boy (Figure 6.1). When I start reading the novel, I cannot know that this is a picture of the novel's protagonist as a child. Yet on page 266 the same photo is reproduced, in smaller format (Figure 6.2), accompanied by the sentence "Yes, and the small boy in the other photograph, said Věra

W. G. Sebald
Austerlitz

Figure 6.1   Front cover of W. G. Sebald, *Austerlitz* (2003)

Schneewolke zu sehen glaubte und bis ich Věra wei-
tersprechen hörte von dem Unergründlichen, das
solchen aus der Vergessenheit aufgetauchten Photo-
graphien zu eigen sei. Man habe den Eindruck, sagte
sie, es rühre sich etwas in ihnen, als vernehme man
kleine Verzweiflungsseufzer, gémissements de déses-
poir, so sagte sie, sagte Austerlitz, als hätten die Bilder
selbst ein Gedächtnis und erinnerten sich an uns,
daran, wie wir, die Überlebenden, und diejenigen,
die nicht mehr unter uns weilen, vordem gewesen
sind. Ja, und das hier, auf der anderen Photographie,
sagte Věra nach einer Weile, das bist du, Jacquot, im
Monat Feber 1939, ein halbes Jahr ungefähr vor dei-

— 266 —

Figure 6.2 Page 266 of W. G. Sebald, *Austerlitz* (2003)

after a while, this is you, Jacquot, in February 1939, about six months before you left Prague" (pp. 258–259).[7] The photograph I am looking at is thus of the novel's protagonist, whose name is Jacquot Austerlitz, but I am not in a position to know this when I start reading. There is a curious connection between this ignorance on the part of the reader and that experienced by Austerlitz himself. In the narrative fabric of the novel, Austerlitz's identity search blends into a prolonged search for this childhood and his parents. Details of his origin have been suppressed for a long time; it has taken him a lot of energy to find out that although he grew up in the Welsh village of Bala, he is in fact a Czech Jew who was sent to Britain when he was only five, on a *Kindertransport* in 1939.[8] His father, Maximilian Aychenwald, fled to France, while his mother, Agáta, remained in Czechoslovakia together with Věra, a non-Jewish friend of the family. At this point of his search, Austerlitz has returned to Prague to explore what happened to him 50 years earlier. He manages to make contact with Věra, who recognizes him immediately, and he does not doubt her statement that he is the boy in the photo. He recognizes "the unusual hairline running at a slant over the forehead, but otherwise all memory was extinguished in me by an overwhelming sense of the long years that had passed" (p. 259).[9]

When I start rereading the narrative, I know that Věra thinks the photograph is of Austerlitz, yet I also know that Austerlitz cannot recollect himself in the picture. Moreover, as it appears in a novel, I assume that Sebald found the photograph somewhere and decided to use it as part of *Austerlitz's* narrative design. The photograph on the cover becomes more important because of the way it is repeated in the narrative: it is, or rather becomes, an integral part of the novel's narrative ethics. According to Věra, it is a visual image of Austerlitz as a small boy; for Austerlitz, however, it is an image of a small boy he cannot recognize. Sebald uses the same photograph twice in a manner that approximates to what Hillis Miller calls the second form of repetition—a form of repetition in which "phantasms" are not grounded in some paradigm or archetype (as in the first form), but are "ungrounded doublings which arise from differential interrelations among elements which are all on the same plane" (1982, p. 6). I posit that, for Austerlitz, the photograph of the boy who is and yet is not he becomes a phantasm that encapsulates his experience of time as curiously nonchronological and confusing. The only way he can learn more about his forgotten past, and thus about his own identity, is by trying to trace his origins. This narrative project develops into a search not only for his parents but also for fragments of memories. As Brockmeier puts it, "[T]he search for what he believes are submerged memories becomes the primary purpose of his life— a quest for something of which he only senses a vague outline" (2015, p. 293). The photograph of himself that he cannot recognize is a visual illustration of this outline. Highlighting the interplay of narrative and memory, the title blends into the photograph and vice versa. For me as a reader and viewer, the photograph also becomes an arresting image of a Jewish child who miraculously survived the Holocaust, thus drawing attention to all those who did not.

The title of Sebald's novel, then, consists of two elements: the word "Austerlitz" and a photograph of an unidentified small boy. This remarkable feature of the title indicates how difficult it is to begin, as well as conclude, a discussion of *Austerlitz*. In this novel, beginning and ending are intertwined, as are the processes of memory, narrating, listening, writing, reading, and viewing. Thus, the relationship between the constituent elements of narrative communication is highlighted, destabilized, and insistently explored through the narrative discourse. As the discourse consists of the frame narrator's account of the fragments of traumatic memory that Austerlitz shares with him, interpretation—and particularly the interpretation of memories—plays a key role in this fragile process of narrative communication.

When I first started to read *Austerlitz*, I thought that the "I" who is speaking might be the main character in the novel:

> In the second half of the 1960s I travelled repeatedly from England to Belgium, partly for study purposes, partly for other reasons which were never entirely clear to me, staying sometimes for just one or two days, sometimes for several weeks. On one of these Belgian excursions which, as it seemed to me, always took me further and further abroad, I came on a glorious early summer's day to the city of Antwerp, known to me previously only by name. Even on my arrival, as the train rolled slowly over the viaduct with its curious pointed turrets on both sides and into the dark station concourse, I had begun to feel unwell, and this sense of indisposition persisted for the whole of my visit to Belgium on that occasion. I still remember the uncertainty of my footsteps as I walked all round the inner city. (p. 1)[10]

Yet although there turns out to be a peculiarly strong resemblance between the first-person narrator and Austerlitz as the novel's main character, this beginning is in fact a frame narrative whose main function is to establish a narrative situation in which the two can meet and in which Austerlitz can talk. The latter thus combines the functions of narrator and protagonist. As noted above, the "I" we first meet is a frame narrator who becomes Austerlitz's listener or narratee. Yet he is more than that. Already here, in the novel's opening paragraph, I note the narrative energy which both prompts and characterizes the searching activity in which the frame narrator is engaged. As he travels to Belgium not just once but "repeatedly," the significance of repetition, of repetitive traveling movements which thus clearly are important to him, is stressed right from the beginning. This sense of restlessly repetitive trips accompanies the narrator even after he has reached Antwerp, the city where he meets Austerlitz in the railway station. Before commenting on Sebald's presentation of this meeting, I ask why he uses a frame narrator of this kind. The narrative gains resulting from this choice resemble the effects of Joseph Conrad's use of a frame narrator in *Heart of Darkness*. Conrad's famous novella from 1899 is one of the strongest intertexts in *Austerlitz*. In both narratives, the main narrator is introduced by a frame narrator, who then becomes a keenly interested listener—a narratee intrigued by the story to the extent of passing it on to the reader. Moreover, in *Austerlitz* as in *Heart of Darkness*, the frame narrator's conventional normality (compared to the protagonist, that is, rather than the reader) makes it easier for me to believe the story that he reports. Due to this "tentacular effect,"[11] as a reader I am drawn into the narrative in a manner comparable to the way in which the frame narrator is irresistibly attracted to Austerlitz's account. There is, especially on a second reading of the novel's beginning, a strong sense in which the frame narrator's attraction to Austerlitz's story is colored, even motivated both by his expectations of its dire content and by his readiness to listen patiently and respectfully to the former's long-drawn-out presentation. On a second reading, "unwell" is a key word in the opening paragraph, preempting the unpleasant feeling of nausea and revulsion resulting from Austerlitz's description of the concentration camp Theresienstadt later in the narrative. As I will suggest shortly, in my interpretation of the novel there is an important connection between the frame narrator's mental and physical response to Austerlitz's story and the need for reconciliation highlighted by that same story.

If the frame narrator's thoughts and feelings seem to resonate with those of Austerlitz already in the opening paragraph, the approximation of the roles of narrator and character becomes even more apparent once the two have met:

> One of the people waiting in the *Salle des pas perdus* was Austerlitz, a man who then, in 1967, appeared almost youthful, with fair, curiously wavy hair of a kind I had seen elsewhere only on the German hero Siegfried in Fritz Lang's *Nibelungen* film. That day in Antwerp, as on all our later meetings, Austerlitz wore heavy walking boots and workman's trousers made of faded blue calico, together with a tailor-made but long outdated suit jacket. Apart from these externals he also differed from the other travellers in being the only one who was not staring apathetically into space, but instead was occupied in making notes and sketches obviously relating to the room where we were both sitting—a magnificent hall more suitable, to my mind, for a state ceremony than as a place to wait for the next connection to Paris or Oostende. (pp. 6–7).[12]

This is the first mention of Austerlitz's name, or more accurately, the first repetition of the name I have read on the book's cover. This repetition is strengthened by the reference to his wavy hair, which the reader has already seen before he or she starts reading, and which, rereading the novel, I know is the only visual fragment Austerlitz thinks he can recognize when looking at the photograph that Věra shows him. Austerlitz is introduced as a matter of course, as though he had always been in this particular place. This is another way of saying that Austerlitz belongs nowhere. For a railway station is a public space characterized by movement—a place that for all its material stability (which it seems important for Austerlitz to register and hold on to) is characteristically experienced by travelers as unstable and transitory, suspended between arrival and departure. Yet the narrative situation it provides proves decisive for Austerlitz's and the narratee's attempts at identity formation. It is also essential that the location of their meeting has a particular history attached to it: an enormous number of Jews were deported from the railway stations of Antwerp and other European cities during the war.

Austerlitz is presented as a traveler, and yet one who stands apart from the others. This is exactly how the frame narrator introduces Marlow in *Heart of Darkness*. I do not want to stress the similarities of two characters as different as Sebald's Austerlitz and Conrad's Marlow. But the two narrative situations strongly resemble each other, and Austerlitz and Marlow both tell tales, or rather fragments of tales, which make an impression on the frame narrator as narratee. In *Story and Situation*, Ross Chambers (1984) draws attention to the way in which, at a deep and frequently unthematized level, the narrator's motivation (and even compulsion) to narrate is complemented by the narratee's readiness to listen, and that, for both parties, possibilities of gain as well as risks of loss are involved. The narrative situations in *Austerlitz* offer ample illustrations of this important point. By telling fragments of his story Austerlitz risks confirming his sense of loss and estrangement, yet his narration may enable him to negotiate that loss. By listening, the narratee risks losing or being drawn out of a comfortable position of ignorance, yet the fact that he not only listens to but also retells what Austerlitz has told him suggests a learning process.

The German Frame Narrator

If I ask what kind of knowledge the frame narrator gains, or hopes to gain, the narrative discourse of *Austerlitz* gives no clear answer. Yet there are various hints that what he seeks is knowledge about the Holocaust. This wish or need may partly explain why he is an "empathetic listener" (Assmann, 2018, p. 210). As Aleida Assmann notes, "Sebald's stages in this novel an ideal match between a victim finally eager to speak and a narrator ready to listen and to record" (p. 212). Furthermore, as the frame narrator learns more about the Holocaust by listening to Austerlitz and passing Austerlitz's story on to the reader, he feels a need for some kind of reconciliation with Austerlitz—and possibly also a need for forgiveness for being implicated in the Holocaust (Lothe, 2011; Rothberg, 2019). If this need is existential since it reveals his uncertainty about his own identity, the narrative project he embarks on is distinctly ethical because it deals with the negotiation of values across a wide spectrum—from those of Nazi perpetrators to those of Agáta, Austerlitz's mother. In the narrative discourse of *Austerlitz*, the frame narrator's need for reconciliation with Austerlitz, and by implication with people of Jewish identity, is paradoxically strengthened by the difficulty, perhaps the impossibility of reaching such a reconciliation. There are three interrelated reasons I make this suggestion. First, although the frame narrator avoids identifying himself as German, it becomes clear that he is in fact a German living in exile. The first reference to his German background occurs early in the novel when he tells of his visit to the Belgian fort Breendonk after his first conversation with Austerlitz in 1967.

Significantly, his visit is stirred by this conversation: the frame narrator notes that if Austerlitz had not mentioned Breendonk, he would probably not have gone there. His visit, in turn, makes it more urgent for him to listen to and learn from Austerlitz.

Breendonk was used as a prison camp by the Germans during the war,[13] and the frame narrator states:

> I could well imagine the sight of the good fathers and dutiful sons from Vils-biburg and Fuhlsbüttel, from the Black Forest and the Bavarian Alps, sitting here when they came off duty to play cards or write letters to their loved ones at home. After all, I had lived among them until my twentieth year. My memory of the fourteen stations which the visitor to Breendonk passes between the entrance and the exit has clouded over in the course of time, or perhaps I could say it was clouding over even on the day when I was in the fort, whether because I did not really want to see what it had to show or because all the outlines seemed to merge in a world illuminated only by a few dim electric bulbs, and cut off for ever from the light of nature. (pp. 29–30)[14]

Although the two facets of this passage that I want to highlight are important in themselves, their significance is enhanced by the way Sebald, via a German narrator and character who in some ways resembles himself, ties them to each other. The first aspect concerns the information about the frame narrator's national identity: he can "imagine the sight of" the German staff at Breendonk because he is a German who for some reason has decided to leave his native land. The second aspect is the reference to his memory of his visit to Breendonk. Why was his memory "clouding over" on the day he visited the fort? Could it be because, coming from Germany, he finds the visit difficult, perhaps almost unbearable? Is it becoming a traumatic memory for him? If so, is there a sense in which other Germans too would experience the memory of a visit to a concentration camp, be it Breendonk or Theresienstadt or Auschwitz, as painful? The way Sebald relates the two aspects to each other supports a point often made in culturally oriented approaches to memory: "Memory is not merely an individual, psychological process that takes place in our 'heads' but always already mediated by culturally and socially shaped memorial forms" (Laanes & Meretoja, 2021, p. 3; cf. Erll, 2011).

Some pages later, in reference to Austerlitz's pedagogic skills and his profession as a lecturer on architectural history, the frame narrator observes:

When I began my own studies in Germany I had learnt almost nothing from the scholars then lecturing in the humanities there, most of them academics who had built their careers in the 1930s and 1940s and still nurtured delusions of power, and I found Austerlitz the first teacher I could listen to since my time in primary school. (pp. 43–44)[15]

He adds that Austerlitz's

comment on what he once later described as his obsession with railway stations . . . was the only hint of his personal life he allowed himself to give me before I returned to Germany at the end of 1975, intending to settle permanently in my native country, to which I felt I had become a stranger after nine years of absence. (p. 45)[16]

Indicating that the frame narrator was born in Germany at the end of the war, these scattered pieces of observation not only highlight his relationship with this native land but also present it as strained and unresolved. Although he cannot bear any responsibility for the atrocities committed by the Nazis, the frame narrator, who remains nameless throughout the novel, represents the postwar German citizen—a generation whose negotiations of collective as well as individual memory are unavoidably colored by the long shadow cast by the Holocaust (Assmann, 2018). At the same time, Sebald's interlinking of the aspects suggests that the frame narrator's memory may be more painful than that of many Germans because their knowledge of the Holocaust is limited. We may wonder whether there is something in the interaction between the frame narrator's German identity and Belgium as a nation overrun by Germany early in the war that brings him to Belgium in search of some form of reconciliation.

This tentative suggestion blends into a second reason the frame narrator may feel a need to be reconciled with Austerlitz (and, by implication, with people of Jewish descent). In the account of his visit to Breendonk, the frame narrator dwells on the *Folterkamer* (torture chamber) that serves as an explanatory note to a graphic illustration of this part of the fort (Figure 6.3). What is striking about these reflections is that, in common with the passage quoted above, the frame narrator fails to reassuringly distance himself from the "SS guards" (p. 29).[17] I relate this failure to the traumatic aspect of his memory of Breendonk, and I also connect it with the challenging process of

mir größer wird. Damals jedenfalls, in jener laut-
losen Mittagsstunde im Frühsommer 1967, die ich,
ohne einem anderen Besucher zu begegnen, im Inne-
ren der Festung Breendonk verbrachte, wagte ich
kaum weiterzugehen an dem Punkt, wo am Ende
eines zweiten langen Tunnels ein nicht viel mehr
als mannshoher und, wie ich mich zu erinnern
glaube, abschüssiger Gang hinabführt in eine der Ka-

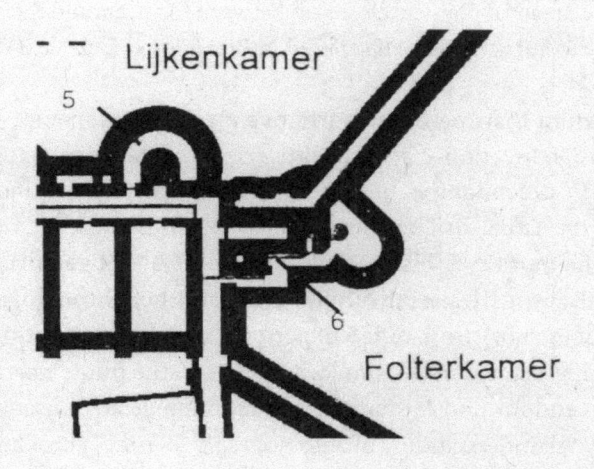

sematten. Diese Kasematte, in der man sogleich
spürt, daß man in ihr überwölbt ist von einer mehrere Meter starken Schicht Beton, ist ein enger, an
der einen Seite spitz zulaufender, an der anderen ab-
gerundeter Raum, dessen Boden um gut einen Fuß
tiefer liegt als der Gang, durch den man ihn betritt,
und darum weniger einem Verlies gleicht als einer

— 40 —

Figure 6.3 Page 40 of W. G. Sebald, *Austerlitz* (2003)

learning about Nazi atrocities stirred by his visit to the fort. The frame narrator's memory here seems to be moving in several directions. On the one hand, the nauseating smell and impression of claustrophobic confinement affects him in a way that brings back painful memories from his childhood: "No one can explain exactly what happens within us when the doors behind which our childhood terrors lurk are flung open" (p. 33).[18] On the other hand:

> It was not that as the nausea rose in me I guessed at the kind of third-degree interrogations which were being conducted here around the time I was born, since it was only a few years later that I read Jean Améry's description of the dreadful physical closeness between torturers and their victims, and of the tortures he himself suffered in Breendonk. (pp. 33–34)[19]

But is it certain that the frame narrator's processes of memory are working in opposite directions? What characterizes the frame narrator's memory of his visit to Breendonk is primarily its complexity: in his narration, his memory of the actual visit becomes inseparable from memories of his childhood and memories of his reading of Améry. Although this mnemonic complexity is distinctly narrative, it is remarkably nonchronological because fragments of memory from different periods of his life blend into each other. There is, I suggest, a curious similarity between the frame narrator's experience at Breendonk and Austerlitz's "nonchronological, nonsequential, and nondirectional understanding of autobiographical time" (Brockmeier, 2015, p. 293) sparked by his visit to Theresienstadt. When he returns to Breendonk at the end of the narrative, after he has listened to Austerlitz's story and relayed it to the reader, his memories of Breendonk are presented and interpreted in a way that, as I will show, poses an ethical challenge not only to him but also to the reader.

One important effect of the narrator's failure to distance himself from the SS guards' acts of torture—or, conversely, his distressing sense of being affiliated with crimes he did not commit—is to simultaneously complicate and accentuate the issue of reconciliation: as the German narrator is pushed into a position approximating that of the perpetrator, his need for reconciliation, and perhaps even some form of forgiveness, becomes more understandable. This need is further strengthened by his reference to Jean Améry (1912–1978), the Austrian-born Jewish writer who, like the fictional character Maximilian (Austerlitz's father), fled to France just before the outbreak of the war. It is historically correct that Améry, having participated in organized resistance against the German occupation of Belgium, was tortured by the Nazis at Breendonk. Later deported to Auschwitz and Buchenwald, Améry was finally liberated at Bergen-Belsen in 1945. Thus, there is a connection between the fate of Améry (a victim and yet a survivor) and the fictional characters of Austerlitz and Maximilian (whose fate is not recorded in the novel, leaving open the possibility that he ended up in Auschwitz); at the time of narrating his story the frame narrator feels he comes close to both.

That the frame narrator also feels irresistibly drawn to Austerlitz is my third reason for suggesting that he has a vague yet strong need for reconciliation. When he notices Austerlitz in the *Salle des pas perdus* in Antwerp, he is curiously drawn to him; he is the one who makes contact, thus initiating their relationship and inviting Austerlitz to talk. Sitting in the same place the next morning, he is hoping that Austerlitz might reappear. As a reader of a work of fiction, I am not surprised when he does—and immediately resumes his story. The narrator is not just a passive listener, however:

> as neither of us knew where the other came from, we had always spoken in French since our first conversation in Antwerp, I with lamentable awkwardness, but Austerlitz with such natural perfection that for a long time I thought he had been brought up in France. (p. 42)[20]

The word "conversation" (which the frame narrator earlier uses on page 37) suggests that although Austerlitz does most of the talking, the frame narrator is actually more active than his own narrative presentation, which focuses on Austerlitz's story, may make us think. Thus, the narrative situations in the novel form the basis for a narrative process approximating to a state of reciprocity imbued with features of reconciliation and possibly also with facets of forgiveness. The qualification signaled by "possibly" is necessary because the issue of forgiveness remains implicit (thus relating it more closely to and making it more dependent on the reader's interpretive activity), and because there is a conspicuous lack of balance between the injured party (Austerlitz, his parents, the Jews of Europe) and the injurer (unspecified perpetrators in Nazi Germany and the occupied territories in whose actions the frame narrator, the author, and the reader may be variously implicated). I will return to this issue in concluding the chapter.

Austerlitz's Search for His Mother

As I read and reread this engrossing, melancholic text, it seems to revolve round and receive a lot of its narrative energy from a sustained search for fragments of the past perceived by Austerlitz as essential to his own autobiographical identity.[21] The railway station metonymically represents that search. The railway station's importance is strengthened by a strong structural connection between the first meeting in the *Salle des pas perdus* in Antwerp and the last one in Paris, to which I will return when discussing the visual image of Gare d'Austerlitz. Its importance is also augmented by the way in which, as an element of space that becomes a spatial as well as a temporal metaphor, it contributes to the novel's narrative ethics by combining aspects of collective and individual memory. Brockmeier observes that as "[m]onuments of mobility but also of migration and flight, [railway] stations are associated with the stories of countless refugees, deportees, and emigrants in the 20th century" (2015, p. 293). Such associations form an essential part of Europe's collective memory of travel by rail, including departures and arrivals marked by experiences of loss as well as hope. A more specific part of this collective memory concerns the deportations by rail to the killing centers in German-occupied Poland. While this collective dimension of railway stations plays a crucial role in *Austerlitz*, it is essential that, as Brockmeier notes, they are also associated with "Austerlitz's own personal past" (p. 293). His is a journey through "Holocaust landscapes" (Cole, 2016). Thus, aspects of collective and individual memory—primarily Austerlitz's memories, but also those of Věra and the frame narrator—are intertwined. Early on in his narrative, the frame narrator mentions that Austerlitz does not tell him much "about his origins and his own life" (pp. 7–8).[22] Yet as already indicated, the question of origin is all-important to Austerlitz. As his search for his parents now, about 50 years after he left Prague, takes him "further and further east and further and further back in time" (pp. 262–263),[23] his conversations with Věra lead him to believe that his mother was taken to the ghetto of Terezín (the German name is Theresienstadt) in late 1942 and then "sent east in September 1944 with one and a half thousand others who had been interned in Terezín" (p. 287).[24] That this transport was to Auschwitz, the Nazi concentration and extermination camp that has become a symbol of the Holocaust, is suggested by the narrative discourse, including the novel's title and the protagonist's name. For me, the fact that the first three and last three letters of Auschwitz and Austerlitz are identical is not just an interpretive signal; it is a self-interpretive element that highlights the significance of the Holocaust: Nazi Germany's industrial mass murder of Jews around which the narrative discourse revolves and toward which it gravitates.

As a reader I do not know why Austerlitz does not search for his mother in Auschwitz; perhaps he feels that a visit to the camp would be too painful. Perhaps, for him, visiting Auschwitz is an unbearable thought because of the over one million Jewish men, women, and children murdered there, including his mother and possibly also his father. "[S]ent east" is as close as he gets to mentioning the toponym. There is a sense in which, in the narrative discourse of *Austerlitz*, Terezín represents all the camps—and Austerlitz's attempt to share his experiences at Terezín with the frame narrator, and thus also with the reader, becomes an effort to reflect on the loss not only of his family but also of the six million Jews murdered in the Holocaust. Thus, individual and collective dimensions of memory are associated with and emerge through attempts to remember in the present. If the narrative of Austerlitz's eastward journey is a delving into his own past, it also becomes a confrontation of past and present events, characters, and objects in which Austerlitz's memory seems as strong, and in one sense as real, as his experience of the present moment.

Nowhere is his experience of the past's insistent presence stronger than in the Terezín section of the novel. Created in large part by the spatial objects he encounters, this effect is strengthened by the way Sebald incorporates the visual image of a map into the verbal discourse. Fascinated by, or perhaps obsessed with, Terezín, Austerlitz, with typical thoroughness, studies an 800-page book "which H. G. Adler, a name previously unknown to me, had written between 1945 and 1947 in the most difficult of circumstances, partly in Prague and partly in London, on the subject of the setting up, development and internal organization of the Theresienstadt ghetto" (p. 327).[25] In the German edition of *Austerlitz*, this sentence is divided into two by the textual picture shown in Figure 6.4.

An example of Sebald's technique of integrating visual images into his verbal discourse, this map invites four comments. First, although not a photograph, this textual picture has a topographical dimension in that it indicates—and makes Austerlitz, the frame narrator, and the reader visualize—an element of space, a place complete with streets, houses, and a surrounding border. However, once I know—or once the narrative I am reading makes me know—that this place was a concentration camp during

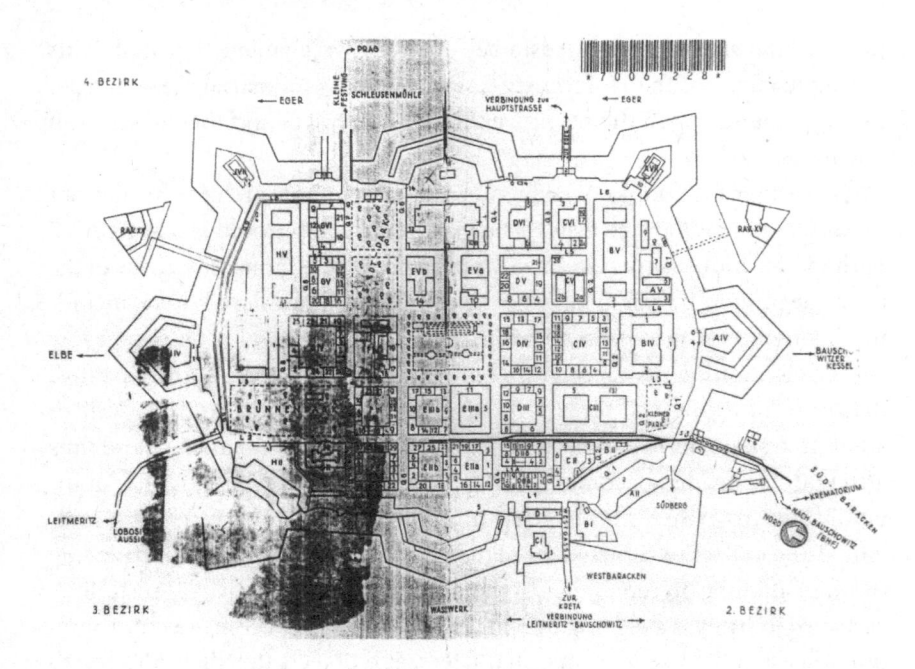

Figure 6.4 Pages 336–337 of W. G. Sebald, *Austerlitz* (2003)

the Second World War, then its topographical shape becomes temporalized and related to European history as well as my own history. Second, as if pre-empting such a reading of the map, Austerlitz attempts to qualify or counter that interpretation by stating that "in its almost futuristic deformation of social life the ghetto system had something incomprehensible and unreal about it" (p. 331).[26] This is as close as the verbal discourse in *Austerlitz* comes to being a caption or caption-like. Third, like most maps, this one too has names written on it. Names, as we well know, have to be read; two names in particular become semantically loaded in the context of the proper names with which they are connected and of the verbal narrative in which they are situated, "BHF" (*Bahnhof*; railway station) and "KREMATORIUM." "BHF" signifies Austerlitz's restless journeys across Europe and those of countless Jews being deported to the extermination camps; "KREMATORIUM" is repeated in the verbal text when Austerlitz relates and the frame narrator reports that the "incinerators of the crematorium, kept going day and night in cycles of forty minutes at a time, were stretched to the utmost limits of their capacity, said Austerlitz" (p. 337).[27]

The map of Theresienstadt makes an impression on me as a reader and viewer. On a second reading, it colors my interpretation of the part of Austerlitz's narrative that deals with his visit to Terezín—and thus with his search for his mother. One dimension of this kind of visual influence on my reading of the novel is to strengthen the narrative fiction's relation to historical reality: the visual image of Terezín—both as a ghetto and camp in its own right and as a transit station for Jews eventually murdered in Auschwitz—demonstrates how, for Sebald, the fictional characters of *Austerlitz* are inspired by and emerge through his knowledge and memory of the Holocaust. The map draws my attention to "the conflagration of community," to appropriate the title of Miller's (2011) study of narrative fiction before and after Auschwitz; as Austerlitz observes, Terezín functions as a curiously cut-off community. But in this "incomprehensible and unreal" community the values of a democratic society are eliminated, resulting in an "almost futuristic deformation of social life" (p. 331). When I look at the map when rereading *Austerlitz*, it becomes a forceful visual illustration of such a "deformation." Moreover, the adjective "futuristic" becomes semantically loaded, suggesting that a deformation of community may recur.

Walking the streets of the small town of Terezín, Austerlitz discovers the so-called Ghetto Museum, where he spends the rest of the day:

> I understood it all now, yet I did not understand it, for every detail that was revealed to me as I went through the museum from room to room and back again, ignorant as I feared I had been through my own fault, far exceeded my comprehension. I saw pieces of luggage brought to Terezín by the internees from Prague and Pilsen, Würzburg and Vienna, Kufstein and Karlsbad and countless other places; the items such as handbags, belt buckles, clothes brushes and combs which they had made in the various workshops. . . . I saw balance sheets, registers of the dead, lists of every imaginable kind, and endless rows of numbers and figures, which must have served to reassure the administrators that nothing ever escaped their notice. (pp. 279–280)[28]

In his discussion of this passage in the chapter of *Beyond the Archive* titled "Beyond Time," Brockmeier writes, "The signs of the past are mute, and the stories behind them remain forever untold" (2015, p. 296). But could it be "that their unrealized meanings, their openness to the narrative imagination are what make them loom so powerfully in the present? For Austerlitz they are mementos without any historical patina, signs of a timeless present" (p. 296). The critical value of Brockmeier's question is enhanced by his reluctance to provide a firm answer to it. As a reader I do not know what the details of the objects displayed in the museum mean; they are indeed mute signs of the past. And yet, as Brockmeier suggests, these mute signs take Austerlitz so close to his mother that he experiences them as part of his present search for her, irresistibly reminding him of Agáta while at the same time confirming her absence.

Generalizing from this and other observations, Brockmeier finds that Sebald's fictional exploration of human memory suggests a view of time that diverts from and thus challenges the conventional distinction in narrative theory between "story time" (the time of the events arranged in chronological order) and "discourse time" (time as presented in the narrative discourse). In *Austerlitz*, discourse time is closely associated with Austerlitz's time in the mind. His journey to Terezín

> has finally demonstrated to Austerlitz that it is impossible to impose any temporal directedness or chronological hierarchy, indeed, any sense of external temporal order on the various layers of his memories, images, ideas, historical and personal reflections, and their ongoing interpretations—the uninterrupted stream of consciousness that went on during the entire visit. (Brockmeier, 2015, p. 296)[29]

Brockmeier is right to emphasize the extent to which Austerlitz's memories, as well as his insistent effort to convey them to the frame narrator in the narrative situations, emerge from a range of constituent elements, including not only the images and signs he is looking at in the museum but his reflections on them as well as his interpretations of them. In my reading experience, these aspects of interpretation are self-interpretive; I build on them in my own interpretation of *Austerlitz*. At the same time, Austerlitz's dual experience of understanding and yet not understanding what he is seeing in Terezín is a warning against overinterpretation because it highlights the insurmountable difference between my own experience and that of Austerlitz as a traumatized Holocaust survivor.

One contributing factor in this warning concerns precisely the distinction between story time and discourse time. Dimensions of story time are activated in the novel: 50 years have passed since Austerlitz escaped to Britain, and in the meantime the Second World War and the Holocaust have occurred. I activate these dimensions as a reader, and in some way, or to some extent, Austerlitz does so too—he is, for example, conscious of the many years that have passed since his childhood in Prague before the war. And yet what is particularly striking in this passage is the way in which, for Austerlitz, objects of the past come painfully close as he is looking at them in the place where the objects' owners were assembled—and then deported and killed. The objects' presence accentuates the absence of those to whom they belonged; they also attract Austerlitz's attention to a future that could have been but was destroyed by the Nazis. My interpretive effort to understand the narrative involves an attempt to construe a kind of chronological progression—though the narrative discourse problematizes, even defies this effort. In this sense, story time is secondary to discourse time; as I argue throughout this book, story time is an integral aspect of my interpretation. Thus, my sense of story time is different from that of another reader and viewer.[30] It becomes part of my "reach for meaning" (Brockmeier, 2015, p. 279) as I read and reread the novel and as I look, and look again, at the visual images it includes. My reach for meaning is an interpretive activity that responds to and is activated by "the vicissitudes of intention" (Bruner, 1986, p. 17) that a narrative presents and explores through its verbal (and in the case of *Austerlitz* also visual) discourse.[31] Interpreting *Austerlitz*, I interpret the frame narrator's interpretation of Austerlitz's autobiographical narrative, which is already an interpretation of fragments of memories of his life. That all these interpretive variants are influenced by psychological features of which the narrative and interpretive agents are more or less conscious makes them more, not less, significant as attempts to negotiate the challenge of not forgetting the Holocaust.

Austerlitz is remarkably modernist in its insistent attempt to problematize oversimplified notions of chronology, linearity, and thematic unity.[32] Moreover, the novel "seek[s] to enact the textual fabric and the temporal dynamics of an autobiographical process" (Brockmeier, 2015, p. 298). One way of rephrasing this point is to suggest that key aspects of autobiography embedded in the novel's narrative discourse sometimes become visible. How and how often this may happen will vary from reader to reader; it will also in part depend on the reader's age, experience, gender, historical knowledge, and biographical knowledge of Sebald's life and works. For me, the autobiographical facet becomes conspicuous in this passage because it calls strikingly to mind a sentence in Sebald's essay collection

Luftkrieg und Literatur.[33] In one of the chapters of this book of nonfiction, the narrating "I," whom the reader is being asked to identify as Sebald, writes:

> I now know that at the time, when I was lying in my bassinet on the balcony of the Seefeld house and looking up at the pale blue sky, there was a pall of smoke in the air all over Europe, over the rearguard actions in east and west, over the ruins of the German cities, over the camps where untold numbers of people were burnt, people from Berlin and Frankfurt, from Wuppertal and Vienna, from Würzburg and Kissingen, from Hilversum and The Hague, Namur and Thionville, Lyon and Bordeaux, Kraków and Łódź, Szeged and Sarajevo, Salonika and Rhodes, Ferrara and Venice—there was scarcely a place in Europe from which no one had been deported to his death in those years. (Sebald, 1999/2004, pp. 71–73)[34]

As we can see, some of these names of European cities occur in both passages. But while in the passage from *Austerlitz* the names Würzburg and Vienna are spoken by Austerlitz to the frame narrator as narratee and then relayed by the latter to the reader, the autobiographical writing of the second passage (whose syntactic structure is similar, not least because of the repetitions of the preposition "from") invites me to relate it much more directly to Sebald as author and first-person narrator. Thus, similar reflections are made by Austerlitz as a Jew, that is, one who has been injured, and by Sebald as a German, that is, somebody who (though he was born in 1944 and thus certainly cannot be made responsible for the crimes) is in some way associated with those who wronged the other. Of course, we should be wary of suspending the generic difference between these two passages. Yet if, as it seems to me, the combination of empathy and distance noticeable in the autobiographical passage suggests a need for reconciliation and perhaps even (a qualified form of) forgiveness, there is a sense in which, in the fictional discourse of *Austerlitz*, this need is transferred to the frame narrator—and by implication also to the reader. This process of narrative transmission is a forceful demonstration of the way memory and narrative ethics interact in the novel's discourse.

Through the long, convoluted sentence that stretches from page 331 to page 342, Austerlitz's first-person narrative—relayed to the reader via the frame narrator—makes a sustained attempt to move beyond the sterile surface of the map of Theresienstadt, groping for signs which could possibly affirm for him the existence of his mother in the camp. Yet although the objects in the Terezín museum are signs of the past, the impression of a timeless present that they make on Austerlitz also colors my interpretation of them. Austerlitz's autobiographical narrative influences my interpretation of that narrative.

At the end of the 10-page-long sentence that frames the map, Austerlitz suddenly mentions that, according to Adler, the Nazis made a film at Theresienstadt, a film Adler never saw "and thought it was now lost without trace" (p. 342).[35] However, Austerlitz eventually manages to obtain "a cassette copy of the film of Theresienstadt for which [he] had been searching" (p. 343).[36] Watching the film, he cannot see his mother, Agáta, anywhere. But then he gets the idea of having a slow-motion copy made. Scrutinizing this artificially extended version, he notices the face of a young woman:
The visual image is accompanied by this passage:

> Around her neck, said Austerlitz, she is wearing a three-stringed and delicately draped necklace which scarcely stands out from her dark, high-necked dress, and there is, I think, a white flower in her hair. She looks, so I tell myself as I watch, just as I imagined the singer Agáta from my faint memories and the few other clues to her appearance that I now have, and I gaze and gaze again at that face, which seems to me both strange and familiar, said Austerlitz, I run the tape back repeatedly, looking at the time indicator in the top left-hand corner of the screen, where the figures covering part of her forehead show the minutes and seconds, from 10:53 to 10:57, while the hundredths of a second flash by so fast that you cannot read and capture them. (pp. 350–351)[37]

The combination of this passage of verbal prose and the visual image of a woman and a man (Figure 6.5) illustrates how the novel's ethics is shaped by aspects of fictionality that reinforce each other in the narrative discourse. There is a strong sense in which Austerlitz's search represents the pain and grief of all those who lost their parents and other close relatives in the Holocaust. This form of generalized ethics is made possible by the way Sebald presents Austerlitz as an invented character whose ethos gradually emerges through the character's narration. As Austerlitz does not exist outside the language and narration of *Austerlitz*, Sebald can give him a unique identity while at the same time making him a representative of all the Jews who became victims of the Holocaust.

alten Herrn, dessen kurz geschorenes graues Haupt die rechte Hälfte des Bildes ausfüllt, während in der linken Hälfte, etwas zurückgesetzt und mehr gegen den oberen Rand, das Gesicht einer jüngeren Frau

erscheint, fast ununterschieden von dem schwarzen Schatten, der es umgibt, weshalb ich es auch zunächst gar nicht bemerkte. Sie trägt, sagte Austerlitz, eine in drei feinen Bogenlinien von ihrem dunklen, hochgeschlossenen Kleid kaum sich abhebende Kette um den Hals und eine weiße Blumenblüte seitlich in ihrem Haar. Gerade so wie ich nach meinen schwachen Erinnerungen und den wenigen

Figure 6.5 Page 358 of W. G. Sebald, *Austerlitz* (2003)

Unusually for *Austerlitz*, the image inserted into this passage is filmic. This means that the visual image we are looking at here is just one frame of the 24 frames per second to which our eyes need to be exposed in order to experience an optical illusion of movement. The temporal dimension of the filmic image is insistent in a way that of a photograph or graphic illustration is not. Yet what I am looking at is a frozen image, an image that insists on moving and yet stands still, suspended in time and space. It is as though Austerlitz is attempting to stabilize or temporarily halt a fleeting, moving image by freezing it in time—first by having the slow-motion copy made, then by making the still copy. As a reader who also becomes a viewer, I participate in this attempt, as do the frame narrator and Sebald as implied author. An attempt to remember, it is also an act of imagination and interpretation, and since the human face I seek to identify is that of Agáta, this interpretive attempt has an ethical dimension (Grønstad, 2016). It is an honest attempt to recover the lost woman in a way that honors her.

Emmanuel Levinas highlights the defenselessness of the human face in a way that illuminates Sebald's description of the visual image. For Levinas (1969), the human face is pure expression that affects me directly; this kind of affect has an ethical dimension as the face I encounter—or more precisely, a manifestation or apparition of the face of the Other—both commands and summons.[38] The human face can appear momentarily, passing by as the face of the unknown woman does in the video Austerlitz is watching. In real life, the image of the face cannot be frozen in time the way Austerlitz freezes it when he has a still copy made. Accentuating the human face's temporal dimension, the impossibility of halting the facial image illustrates the ethical urgency associated with the face—not least if, as in the case of Agáta, it turns out to be utterly defenseless (and this point is valid whether or not the woman in the image is Agáta).

Even though in the fiction the woman in the image may not be Agáta, both she and the unidentified man in the foreground are presumably real human beings who were eventually murdered by the Nazis. Yet although the visual image seems to refer to physical reality, I read it differently because of the invented plot into which it is integrated. It does not follow, though, that the physical reality of the Holocaust, which Theresienstadt metonymically represents, becomes irrelevant to my interpretive attempt: if textual aspects of history are qualified by textual elements of fictionality, in the act of interpretation this fictionality becomes inseparable from the way in which it is framed by and embedded in historical references. Thematically enriching, this kind of ambiguity contributes to the novel's ethics. As already indicated, one of the ways Sebald makes it difficult to disentangle this frozen filmic image from the fiction in which it is embedded is that he makes Austerlitz thinks he can recognize Agáta in a historical film made in Theresienstadt by the Nazis in 1944. As it would seem impossible for a fictional character such as Austerlitz to recognize his mother in a documentary film about people in the real world, there is a sense in which the historical film is fictionalized—even though it connects Austerlitz to historical reality. This insertion of a fictional character into a nonfictional phenomenon is a staple of historical fiction.

As a Nazi propaganda film, the film about Theresienstadt presents a positive picture of the ghetto that is entirely false. I emphasize that in making this last point, I am activating extratextual knowledge that not all readers of *Austerlitz* may have. I am inclined to think that Sebald expects the implied reader to possess this knowledge, but of course not all historical readers will have it. Once I have access to this extratextual information, it becomes part of my interpretation whether I want it or not. Before making the film, the Nazi authorities tidied up the camp and arranged cultural activities to give the viewer the impression of a happy community; after the filming ended, the camp slipped back into its cruel routine. In Sebald's narrative, Austerlitz thinks that "Agáta was sent east in September 1944" (p. 287); in historical reality, both before and after shooting the film at Theresienstadt the Nazis deported a large number of the camp's inmates to Auschwitz. Furthering the novel's ethical dimension, Sebald's incorporation of a frozen image from the documentary into the fiction of *Austerlitz* reveals a strong concern on his part not just with the relations between history and fiction but also with the relations between truth and falsity.

Aspects of fictionality play a key role in the narrative presentation of both relations. On the one hand, the documentary has a historical existence: it was filmed in Theresienstadt, and the camp's inmates feature as nonfictional characters in the film. On the other hand, the film's purpose was not to fictionalize but to lie, while one of the purposes of Sebald's fictional narrative is to capture truths that the documentary either denies or neglects. Titled *Theresienstadt: Ein Dokumentarfilm aus dem jüdischen Siedlungsgebiet* (Theresienstadt: A documentary film from the Jewish settlement area), the film was written and directed by the Jewish actor Kurt Gerron (1944). Forcing Gerron to make the film, the Nazi authorities promised him his life. Filming started on August 16 and was completed on September 11, 1944.

After that Gerron was deported to Auschwitz; he was gassed in Birkenau on October 28, 1944. Thus there is a double sense in which the film was a lie: making Gerron lie about Theresienstadt, the Nazis also lied to him.

As I reread this passage in *Austerlitz* and look again at the visual image linked to it (or, conversely, as I look again at the visual image and relate it to my rereading of the passage), it seems to me that Austerlitz—and in a sense the frame narrator, and Sebald too—are attempting to stabilize or temporarily halt a fleeting, moving image by freezing it in time—first through the slow-motion copy, then by the still copy. As a consequence, my act of reading also grinds to a halt as I am looking at and attempting to interpret the visual image. Although I know that it is part of a film, I tend to interpret it as an image of a woman and a man—that is, as a photograph. Avi Kempinski (2007) finds that by running "the tape back repeatedly" Austerlitz evokes Roland Barthes's notion of the "defeat of Time" (Barthes, 1982, p. 96) in historical photographs; Austerlitz seems to experience a *punctum* whose uncoded intensity and "power of expansion" (p. 45) lead him to believe that the woman in the photo may be his mother.[39] Kempinski writes, "[D]espite this attempt to resuscitate the mother-image through the 'defeat of time,' this faint image ultimately betrays a face, but not the mother's" (2007, p. 466). The two faces in the image seem to be approaching the viewer from an unknown place somewhere in the past, and the lack of textual commentary on the man in the foreground seems conspicuous. He appears to be unknown, yet the reader may wonder whether he may irresistibly remind Austerlitz of his lost father. Although there is something ghost-like about the appearance of the two faces, they do add a human dimension to the map of Theresienstadt, the place where these two human beings were at the time of the shooting of the film. The image contributes to and further extends Austerlitz's attempt to understand at least something of the terrible conditions under which the inmates of the camp lived. As Marianne Hirsch (1997) has shown in *Family Frames*, the appearance of faces, human beings, in a photograph prompts a form of narrativization of it—not least if it is one of family members (cf. Hirsch, 2012).[40] In this textual picture, narrativization is accentuated partly by the way time and space play equally important roles in film, partly by the imprint of temporal markers (numbers) on the frozen image.

In the novel's restlessly searching narrative movements, the fact that Agáta cannot be a narrator strengthens her importance as a character whose ethics is endorsed not only by her son Austerlitz, a Holocaust survivor, but also by the German frame narrator and by Sebald as implied author. A key constituent element of Agáta's ethos is care—care for other human beings generally and for her son in particular. In *The Ethical Demand*, Knud E. Løgstrup argues:

> The demand, precisely because it is unspoken, is radical. . . . The radicality
> of the demand consists, further, in the fact that it asks me to take care of the
> other person's life not only when to do so strengthens me but also when it
> is very unpleasant, because it intrudes disturbingly into my own existence.
> (1997, pp. 44–45)

Under extremely difficult conditions, Agáta replies to the unspoken ethical demand by securing a place for her five-year-old son on a *Kindertransport* to Britain. When she says goodbye to Austerlitz in the railway station in Prague in the summer of 1939, she can hardly expect to see her son again. But she responds to the radicality of the ethical demand by saving his life.

Agáta's contribution to the novel's narrative ethics is further strengthened by the way Sebald relates the filmic image of the woman in the Nazi propaganda film to a different visual image. Searching for information about his mother in the Prague theatrical archives, he comes upon "the photograph of an anonymous actress who seemed to resemble my dim memory of my mother" (p. 353).[41] Věra cannot recognize Agáta in the filmic image, but looking at the photograph, she "recognized Agáta as she had then been" (pp. 353–354). Věra may be right, but it does not follow that Austerlitz is wrong: the memory of his mother sparked by the filmic image and the photograph is qualified by the adjective "faint" (*schwach*) and the verb "imagine" (*vorstellen*), and these qualifications are as significant as the memory itself. Highlighting the insurmountable temporal distance between Austerlitz and his parents, they also accentuate his sense of loss and uncertainty in the present. Different temporal layers are blended in a continuing searching movement that is as important as it appears futile.

Austerlitz's Search for His Father

When, after completing this part of his story, Austerlitz and the frame narrator take leave of each other outside the railway station in Liverpool Street in London, Austerlitz gives his narratee an envelope that contains the photograph of the anonymous actress, who, according to Věra, is his mother. Why does Austerlitz give the German frame narrator a photograph of his mother, who was murdered by German Nazis? I will respond to this question shortly, but first I comment on Austerlitz's information that he is going to Paris "to search for traces of his father's last movements" (p. 354).[42] He and the frame narrator meet again in Paris:

> Curiously enough, said Austerlitz, a few hours after our last meeting, when he had come back from the Bibliothèque Nationale and changed trains at the Gare d'Austerlitz, he had felt a premonition that he was coming closer to his father. As I might know, he said, part of the railway network had been paralysed by a strike last Wednesday, and in the unusual silence which, as a consequence, had descended on the Gare d'Austerlitz, an idea came to him of his father's leaving Paris from this station, close as it was to his flat in the rue Barrault, soon after the Germans entered the city. I imagined, said Austerlitz, that I saw him leaning out of the window of his compartment as the train left, and I saw the white clouds of smoke rising from the locomotive as it began to move ponderously away. (pp. 405–406)[43]

As Austerlitz associates this railway station with his father, like the *Salle des pas perdus* it becomes a catalyst of his memories. And as it is already related to Austerlitz himself through its name, Gare d'Austerlitz constitutes an important aspect of the novel's title.[44] The German words *Zug* and *Bahn/Eisenbahn* ("train" and "road/railway") are semantically loaded for Sebald. On the one hand, they signal travel and possible escape (as in the case of Austerlitz); on the other hand, they are inextricably connected with the transport of Jews to the concentration camps in Germany and occupied Poland.

The combination of the textual picture in Figure 6.6 and its accompanying verbal text makes it even more significant that, as already indicated, the first three and the last three letters of the names Austerlitz and Auschwitz are identical. There is a curious mirror image here: while Austerlitz was saved in 1939, his father, though possibly managing to flee from Paris the following year, did not survive the war. The passage's last sentence is ambiguous in a thematically enriching manner: "clouds of smoke" rise from the locomotive pulling the carriage in which Austerlitz imagines his father is leaning out of the window, and smoke also rose from the chimneys of Auschwitz. In addition to this allusion to one symbolically charged element of the history of the Holocaust, there is, within the fictional fabric of *Austerlitz*, a suggestive link to Austerlitz's reference earlier in his narrative to "a

vor von einem Mitarbeiter des Dokumentationszentrums in der rue Geoffroy-l'Asnier eine Nachricht erhalten habe, derzufolge Maximilian Aychenwald Ende 1942 in dem Lager Gurs interniert gewesen sei, und daß er, Austerlitz, diesen weit drunten im Süden, in den Vorbergen der Pyrenäen gelegenen Ort nun aufsuchen müsse. Sonderbarerweise, so sagte Austerlitz, habe er wenige Stunden nach unserer letzten Begegnung, als er, von der Bibliothèque Nationale herkommend, in der Gare d'Austerlitz umgestiegen

sei, die Vorahnung gehabt, daß er dem Vater sich annähere. Wie ich vielleicht wisse, sei am vergangenen Mittwoch ein Teil des Eisenbahnverkehrs wegen eines Streiks lahmgelegt worden, und in der aufgrund dessen in der Gare d'Austerlitz herrschenden ungewöhnlichen Stille sei ihm der Gedanke gekommen, der Vater habe von hier aus, von diesem seiner Wohnung in der rue Barrault zunächst gelegenen Bahnhof, Paris verlassen bald nach dem Einmarsch der Deutschen. Ich bildete mir ein, sagte Austerlitz, ihn

— 410 —   — 411 —

Figure 6.6 Pages 410–411 of W. G. Sebald, *Austerlitz* (2003)

pest-control officer . . . surrounded by clouds of poisonous white smoke" (p. 255)[45] and to his observation on "a petrochemicals plant half eaten away by rust, with clouds of smoke rising from its cooling towers and chimneys" (p. 263)[46] just after his account (or, more precisely, after Věra's account as reported by Austerlitz to the frame narrator) of his own departure from the Wilsonova station in Prague in 1939. In my interpretation of *Austerlitz*, these references and allusions to smoke remind me of and take me back to the smoke that rises from the chimney of the *Donau* in the photograph by Georg Fossum. A self-interpretive element, the smoke becomes a *punctum* that contributes to my own interpretation.

Unable to find out what happened to his mother, Austerlitz is also incapable of ascertaining how his father ended his life. That they both almost certainly perished in the Holocaust does not make his search less important, however, nor does it reduce his need to tell his story to a listener who may be in need of it. If Austerlitz's narrative is a gesture of solidarity, an act of homage paid to his mother and father, it is also a sustained reflection on the historical reality of war (and the Holocaust within that war), and on the vulnerability and fragility of European civilization. To what extent it is also an act of reconciliation is less certain. Yet aspects of reconciliation emerge in and through the narrative process on which Austerlitz embarks and in which both the frame narrator and the reader participate throughout. This narrative process is a painful yet necessary negotiation of Austerlitz's pre-war memories. It is revealing that while in Terezín Austerlitz is looking at real objects, here he is *imagining* that the sees his father. In both cases, a mnemonic act of negotiation and mediation is taking place. Through this communicative act in this narrative situation, Austerlitz, and Sebald behind him, induce the frame narrator and the reader "to correct for distorted perspective, by adopting something like the standpoint of 'the moral community'" (Griswold, 2007, p. xxii). It will vary from reader to reader how and how much he or she will be able or willing to respond to such an invitation to correct his or her perspective. As the last narrative situation in Paris makes clear, though, the ending of Austerlitz's story makes a strong impression on the frame narrator, thus transforming his attentive listening as narratee into active retelling of the protagonist's story.

Austerlitz and the Frame Narrator

As Austerlitz continues his reflections on the Gare d'Austerlitz, concluding, "I am going to continue looking for my father" (p. 408),[47] the passage just considered blends into the frame narrator's account of how the last narrative situation dissolves:

> It was nearly twelve o'clock when we took leave of each other outside the Glacière Métro station. Years ago, Austerlitz said as we parted, there were great swamps here where people skated in winter, just as they did outside Bishopsgate in London, and then he gave me the key to his house in Alderney Street. I could stay there whenever I liked, he said, and study the black and white photographs which, one day, would be all that was left of his life. (p. 408)[48]

Why does Austerlitz entrust the frame narrator with photographs that mean so much to him, and why does he give him the key to his house in London? Even though the novel gives no clear answer, the reciprocity of injurer and injured is highlighted in both these narrative situations, thus constituting an act of trust and reconciliation, if not of forgiveness. Surely, the frame narrator is no "injurer" in the sense of being a Nazi perpetrator or a representative of Nazi Germany. But he is, I suggest, an implicated subject as Rothberg understands this concept. Neither a victim nor a perpetrator, the frame narrator is "a participant in histories and social formations that generate the positions of victim and perpetrator, and yet in which most people do not occupy such clear-cut roles" (Rothberg, 2019, p. 1). Although there is a great difference between the German frame narrator (who is part of the narrative fiction) and me as a reader (outside the fiction), I have noted that as a Norwegian citizen I am also implicated in histories and social formations that, over the course of history, have generated inequality, suppression, exploitation, conflict, and war. This kind of affinity is perhaps the main reason I am attracted to and fascinated by the frame narrator's project, which I regard as distinctly ethical in its narrative motivation as well as in its orientation toward Austerlitz on the one hand and the reader on the other.

One of the reasons the narrative situations in the novel are important is that by listening to Austerlitz's story the frame narrator becomes more conscious of his role and responsibility as an implicated subject. The narrative presentation of Agáta plays a key role here. Constituent elements of Agáta's ethos serve as the basis for and blend into ethical questions asked by Austerlitz, by the frame narrator, by the implied author—and by the reader. Although the form and direction of these questions will vary, they are influenced, and in part delimited, by the narrative acts performed by Austerlitz and the frame narrator. Revolving around the historical event of the Holocaust, the questions activate, as noted in the introduction, aspects of history, memory, and forgetting. In *History, Memory, Forgetting*, Paul Ricoeur avers that "as the characters of the narrative are emplotted at the same time the story is told, the narrative configuration contributes to modeling the identity of the protagonists of the action as it molds the contours of the action itself" (2000/2006, p. 85). Linking Ricoeur's observation to my discussion of *Austerlitz*, I make two comments. First, the way in which Sebald gives Austerlitz and the frame narrator the dual functions of serving not only as "the characters of the narrative" but also as the narrators of the story (or, more precisely, of fragments of an incomplete story) includes, and in large part depends on, the novel's unique combination of fictional and historical elements. As invented characters and narrators, they become representative in a way that historical persons are not. Second, in *Austerlitz* "the narrative configuration [that] contributes to modeling the identity of the protagonists of the action" is furthered by Sebald's choice of placing his main characters, narrators, and narratees in fragile narrative situations. By using and combining the communicative resources of two main characters and two main narrators, and by anchoring their fictional stories in the historical context of the Second World War and the Holocaust, Sebald explores and narratively presents a variant of fiction that, particularly on a second reading, appears paradoxically strengthened by the ways in which it is ethically formed and sharpened by the historical events it departs from while insistently referring to them. Molding "the contours of the action itself," the narrative of *Austerlitz* configures two contours: the contour of the historical reality of the Second World War and the Holocaust is intertwined with that of the fictional reality of the German narrator-character whose name remains unknown and the Jewish narrator-character whose name on a second reading becomes almost synonymous with Auschwitz and the Holocaust.

As these contours suggest, and as I hope to have shown, *Austerlitz* is a complex narrative presentation of radically different values, ranging from those of Nazi Germany to those of Agáta. Nowhere in the narrative does Sebald make the reader meet with a character who is a Nazi.[49] He does, however, make the entire narrative depend on a frame narrator who is German and who, as a German born at the end of the war, feels distressingly close to awful crimes he did not commit. While Austerlitz is drawn toward the victims of the Holocaust, the frame narrator repeatedly fails to reassuringly distance himself from the perpetrators who made it happen. One textual instance of the frame narrator's sense of uncomfortable approximation to the position of the injurer is, as we have seen, the passage about his visit to Fort Breendonk early in the novel. Rereading *Austerlitz*, I find that already on page 1, his experience of feeling "unwell" is associated with his sense of being an implicated subject. At the very end of the narrative, after the last conversation with Austerlitz and after Austerlitz may have taken his own life, the frame narrator returns to Breendonk 30 years after his first visit, approaching "the dark gate through which, yet again, I could not bring myself to pass even after long hesitation" (p. 412).[50] Instead, he spends some time outside the fortress, reading Dan Jacobson's *Heshel's Kingdom*, a book that Austerlitz has given him and in which Jacobson writes of his search for his grandfather, Rabbi Yisrael Yehoshua Melamed. Traveling to Lithuania, where his grandfather hails from, Jacobson "finds scarcely any trace of his forebears" (p. 414).[51] However, he is forcibly struck by the remnants of the 12 fortresses that the Russians built around the town of Kaunas, "including the notorious Fort IX where [after the German invasion of the Soviet Union in 1941] Wehrmacht command posts were set up and where more than thirty thousand people were killed over the next three years" (p. 415).[52]

It is as though, reading Jacobson's account of his search for his grandfather, the frame narrator's memory of his first visit to Breendonk becomes fused with his narrative transmission of Austerlitz's fragmented narrative about his search for his parents. Reflecting on the last messages that some of those murdered in Fort IX scratched on the wall, the frame narrator notes:

> Others left only a date and a place of origin with their names: Lob, Marcel, de St. Nazaire; Wechsler, Abram, de Limoges; Max Stern, Paris, 18.5.44. Sitting by the moat of the fortress of Breendonk, I read to the end of the fifteenth chapter of *Heshel's Kingdom*, and then set out on my way back to Mechelen, reaching the town as evening began to fall. (p. 415)[53]

Condensing into a few sentences significant ethical concerns and questions discussed in this chapter, this ending is a forceful concluding statement on the importance of the Holocaust in the narrative ethics of *Austerlitz*. The combination of names written by Jews who are about to be murdered and names of European cities from which they were deported resonates, for the frame narrator as for me as reader, with the names and places of Austerlitz's story. The mention of Paris invites me to relate Jacobson's search for his grandfather to Austerlitz's search for his father, who was probably deported to the East—though perhaps to Auschwitz rather than Kaunas. In common with Jacobson, the frame narrator finds it almost incredible that "[t]ransports from the west kept coming to Kaunas until May 1944, when the war had long since been lost" (p. 415).[54] How could the Nazis hate the Jews so strongly that they gave their industrial mass murder priority over everything else, including defending themselves against the advancing Soviet army? How can we explain evil action on this colossal scale? As neither Jacobson nor Austerlitz "finds scarcely any trace of his forebears," how can the frame narrator, a German born in 1944, and I, a reader born after the Holocaust, manage not to forget the victims? How can human values be as different as those of Agáta and those of Nazi perpetrators?

As a reader of the ending of *Austerlitz* I relate the numbers "18.5.44" to the Jews who "kept coming to Kaunas until May 1944"—that is, just a few months before the Red Army retook Kaunas in August that year. But as I know that Sebald was born on May 18, 1944, I associate the date not only with Jewish victims in Kaunas—one of the many places where Jews were murdered in the Holocaust—but also with Sebald as historical author. I am not arguing that this extratextual knowledge necessarily makes my interpretation of the novel more convincing. Yet since I have this knowledge, it makes me link the frame narrator to Sebald as a German born at the end of the war. It does not follow that the frame narrator unproblematically represents Sebald; as a main narrator and the novel's second main character, he is a key component in the novel written by Sebald as implied author. In my interpretation, though, "18.5.44" simultaneously extends and blurs the connections between Sebald as implied and historical author, Austerlitz as main character and narrator, the frame narrator as main character and narrator, and me as reader. As I have attempted to show, these connections essentially revolve around questions stirred by attitudes, decisions, and actions that represent and are motivated by very different values and priorities.

Yet although for some, though not all, readers "18.5.44" may be a self-interpretive element that draws attention to the connection between the frame narrator and Sebald as implied and historical author, its significance is even more complex. Tending to consider the numbers as the birth date of both the frame narrator and Sebald, I read them in two different ways. On the one hand, I interpret the date as the frame narrator's attempt to associate himself with the murdered Jews in Kaunas. On that reading, the date expresses an act of memory distinguished by mourning and a strong sense of loss, while at the same time that act also includes a reflection on the vicissitudes of memory. On the other hand, as I have just read that "[t]ransports from the west kept coming to Kaunas until May 1944," I also relate the date to the Nazis responsible for murdering the Jews. That reading highlights the frame narrator's, and Sebald's, sense of being an implicated subject. It also draws attention to my own responsibility as a reader.

I conclude that, crucial as it is, the frame narrator's experience of being close to as well as distanced from the victims of the Holocaust does not reduce the importance of Austerlitz's story. Austerlitz is the novel's main character, and it is his search for his parents and for his lost identity that makes *Austerlitz* a compelling exemplar of narrative fiction anchored in historical reality. Yet Austerlitz's significance does not make the frame narrator's role less important. Not only does Austerlitz's narrative depend on the frame narrator's dual function as narratee and narrator; as I have aimed to show, his narrative presentation consistently emphasizes and cumulatively strengthens its ethical dimension. If Austerlitz's narrative project is an ethical project, so is the frame narrator's.

I have suggested that as the narrative situations in the novel approximate a kind of negotiation—of memories and losses and of identities and values—between Austerlitz and the frame narrator, that negotiation includes an element of reconciliation. There is also a sense in which, given the frame narrator's understanding of himself as an implicated subject, it may signal his longing for forgiveness. When I venture to use the word "forgiveness" in the context of the Holocaust, it is with a view to the frame narrator—and myself—as an implicated subject who experiences a need for forgiveness not for what I did not do as a bystander but for being "a participant in histories and social formations" (Rothberg, 2019, p. 1) that generate structures of inequality, suppression, violence, and war. I have noted that the frame narrator is both a keenly interested narratee and a conscientious presenter of Austerlitz's story. There is an important connection between the frame narrator's interest in Austerlitz and his need to negotiate aspects of his own past and his German identity. It is as though, in Rothberg's phrase, he "need[s] to reflect on modes of responsibility and justice that exceed the legal frames in which crimes are usually adjudicated" (p. 7). In my reading of *Austerlitz*, the frame narrator's strong interest in Austerlitz incorporates a need for forgiveness and a hope to be forgiven for being German.

Does Austerlitz grant the frame narrator the forgiveness which the latter seems to be hoping for? One reason my discussion has not given a clear answer to this question is that the narrative discourse does not seem to provide one. Yet it does not follow that forgiveness may not be a major thematic concern of the novel. While the frame narrator has problems coming to terms with his German identity, Austerlitz, seeking to reconstruct his identity by searching for his lost parents, tends to regard himself as "a witness to what I could no longer recollect for myself" (p. 311).[55] Yet their relationship is characterized by aspects of trust and friendship. If the frame narrator feels an urge to listen to Austerlitz's story, and if that strong wish signals a need to be forgiven, Austerlitz needs a conversation partner and a listener he can trust. And if, as Griswold observes, "forgiveness requires reciprocity between injurer and injured" (2007, p. xvi), their conversations reveal, I have argued, elements of such reciprocity.[56] In the narrative dynamics of *Austerlitz* these are blended with and simultaneously qualified as well as accentuated by friendship, trust, and a melancholic sensation of the past's pervasive present.

A similarly lasting impression is made on me as reader and viewer. The narrative discourse of *Austerlitz* makes me cognizant of my need for forgiveness by including me in a narrative situation and involving me in a process that, albeit slowly and perhaps modestly, improves the chances of and moves in the direction of an interpersonal moral relation. This relation shows at least some reciprocity between injured (variously represented by Austerlitz and his parents as different kinds of victims) and injurer (represented by and including facets of the frame narrator, Sebald as implied and historical author, and the reader). *Austerlitz* is a novel in which aesthetic form blends into and thus serves to shape the reader's understanding of the ethical issues explored. As Mark McCulloh writes of "Paul Bereyter," a story in Sebald's *The Emigrants*, "We witness this solitary suffering *with* the narrator, as it were, and share his sense of helplessness that life, as we confront its saddest victims, seems intent on forcing upon us" (2003, p. 11, original emphasis). With a view to *Austerlitz*, McCulloh's perceptive point about the narrator's sense of helplessness would apply equally to Austerlitz and the frame narrator. I conclude that, as "a model for the reader of the novel" (Assmann, 2018, p. 213), the frame narrator's sense of helplessness applies to me too.

These points provide the basis for a concluding comment on the historical author. What is unique about Sebald is the way in which his father's silence— a silence that was part of a more general refusal to talk about the immediate past in the Bavarian village where the family lived—gradually, in one sense belatedly motivated him to write a text like *Austerlitz*. If, as Walter Benjamin observes of the narrator in his classic essay "The Storyteller" (1936/1979), the traditional, oral narrator's motivation to narrate is prompted by his or her dramatic experiences away from home—and I note in passing that the experiences of Sebald's father involved both travel and extremely dramatic events—for Austerlitz, and in a way also for Sebald, the need to narrate is caused by the opposite quality of absence. This kind of absence or blank forms an extended *Leerstelle* (a blank or gap), to appropriate a still helpful term coined by Wolfgang Iser (1972, 1978; cf. Hain, 2004).[57] It is this *Leerstelle* that, because it both suspends connectability in the text and draws attention to the underlying narrative of the war (including what caused the war and what it did to those who participated in it as well as to its countless victims), needs to be filled in, or rather, since that is not possible, at the very least addressed and explored. Thus, in *Austerlitz* narrative is a powerful mode not just of communication and explanation but also of exploration of painful memories.

Sebald's combined distrust of and faith in narrative is a recognition of the enormity of the challenge facing anyone attempting to understand the horrors of the Holocaust. It is revealing that Sebald seems to have been unable or perhaps unwilling to think of an alternative approach to this vexed issue. His writings are narratives *quand-même*, narratives in spite of the daunting inexplicability of the problem to be explored, narratives designed—like those of modernist authors such as Conrad, Kafka, and Woolf[58]—to ask difficult questions rather than to provide oversimplified answers. The insurmountable task of producing a "complete" narrative of the history of Austerlitz's family serves as a token and symbol of the fact that a complete narrative of the Holocaust can never be constructed. Fragments point to a lost whole, reminding me of the irreplaceable quality of the lost lives and experiences. In concert with this narrative strategy, forgiveness is also severely challenged in *Austerlitz*. As I hope to have shown, though, the difficulty or even impossibility of forgiving those implicated in the histories and social formations that led to the Holocaust does not, in the narrative discourse of this engrossing text, reduce or suspend their need for forgiveness. For Austerlitz as well as the frame narrator, evil is omnipresent. For both, "a standing challenge is to understand whether and how it is possible to be reconciled to evil. Forgiveness is a prime candidate in part because it does not reduce either to resigned acceptance or to deluded avoidance" (Griswold, 2007, p. xxv). The frame narrator's role is crucial here. His functions are complex, and there is a sense in which he not only represents a facet of the novel's implied author but also serves as a kind of fictional spokesman for Sebald as historical author. Since the injurer's need to be forgiven is enhanced by an unspeakable crime which greatly complicates, perhaps even eliminates any forgiving act on the part of the injured party, the hints at forgiveness which I have identified and discussed are remarkable indeed. Fragile as they are, these aspects emerge from and depend on the strange, and strangely persistent, narrative communication between the novel's German frame narrator and its Jewish protagonist, and by implication also on the narrative communication between these two and me as a reader and viewer.

Notes

1. Three helpful collections of essays on Sebald are Görner (2003), Long and Whitehead (2004), and Patt (2007b). Two important monographs are McCulloh (2003) and Long (2007). In addition to the contributions to Patt's volume, including her introduction, three essays dealing specifically with the issue of visual images and narrative in Sebald are Duttlinger (2004),

Horstkotte (2008), Kilbourn (2004), and Weber (2003). I also draw on and extend points made in Lothe (2008, 2011, 2012, 2020b, 2022).

2. I use the terms "visual image" and "textual picture" synonymously to indicate photographs and photocopied matter (e.g., an illustration or a map) presented in, and thus made a part of, a verbal text. Even though such images are generically and aesthetically very different from the images formed in and by verbal language, the interpretive activity prompted by the reading of Sebald can establish points of contact between the two main variants.

3. In *Topographies* J. Hillis Miller (1995) gives a detailed account of the complexity of the concept.

4. One example of this kind of combination, which presents the reader (and viewer) with a considerable interpretive challenge, is that of the photographs of Vita Sackville-West included in the first edition of one of the major fictional biographies of the 20th century, Virginia Woolf's *Orlando* (1928/1998).

5. The English translation by Michael Hamburger, *After Nature*, appeared in 2001.

6. First published in German by Carl Hanser Verlag in 2001. The visual images I discuss are taken from the original, German edition because the relationship between visual image and surrounding verbal text—a relationship that in my interpretive activity also becomes one between viewing and reading—is sometimes different in the English translation of the novel. Subsequent citations are in parentheses in the text.

7. "Ja, und das hier, auf der anderen Photographie, sagte Věra nach einer Weile, das bist du, Jacquot, im Monat Feber 1939, ein halbes Jahr ungefähr vor deiner Abreise aus Prag" (2001/2003, pp. 266-267).

8. *Kindertransport* (Children's Transport) was the informal name of rescue efforts that from December 1938 until May 1940 brought about 10,000 refugee children, the vast majority of them Jewish, to Great Britain from Germany and Germany-annexed territories, including Czechoslovakia. See *Holocaust Encyclopedia*, https://encyclopedia.ushmm.org/content/en/article/kindertransport-1938-40

9. "Wohl erkannte ich den ungewöhnlichen, schräg über die Stirne verlaufenden Haaransatz, doch sonst war alles in mir ausgelöscht von einem überwältigenden Gefühl der Vergangenheit" (2001/2003, p. 267).

10. "In der zweiten Hälfte der sechziger Jahre bin ich, teilweise zu Studienzwecken, teilweise aus anderen, mir selber nicht recht erfindlichen Gründen, von England aus wiederholt nach Belgien gefahren, manchmal bloss für ein, zwei Tage, manchmal für mehrere Wochen. Auf einer dieser belgischen Exkursionen, die mich immer, wie es mir schien, sehr weit in die Fremde führten, kam ich auch, an einem strahlenden Frühsommertag, in die mir bis dahin nur dem Namen nach bekannte Stadt Antwerpen. Gleich bei der Ankunft, als der Zug über das zu beiden Seiten mit sonderbaren Spitztürmchen bestückte Viadukt langsam in die dunkle Bahnhofshalle hineinrollte, war ich ergriffen worden von einem Gefühl des Unwohlseins, dass sich dann während der gesamten damals von mir in Belgien zugebrachten Zeit nicht mehr legte" (2001/2003, p. 9).

11. Sebald's essay collection *The Rings of Saturn* includes a perceptive essay on Conrad, who, like him, left the European continent and settled in Britain. The term "tentacular effect" was coined by Cedric Watts (1977, p. 33).

12. "Eine der in der *Salle des pas perdus* wartenden Personen war Austerlitz, ein damals, im siebenundsechziger Jahr, beinahe jugendlich wirkender Mann mit blondem, seltsam gewelltem Haar, wie ich es sonst nur gesehen habe an dem deutschen Helden Siegfried in Langs Nibelungenfilm. Nicht anders als bei all unseren späteren Begegnungen trug Austerlitz damals in Antwerpen schwere Wanderstiefel, eine Art Arbeitshose aus verschossenem blauen Kattun, sowie ein massgeschneidertes, aber längst aus der Mode gekommenes Anzugsjackett, und er unterschied sich auch, abgesehen von diesem Äusseren, von den übrigen Reisenden dadurch, dass er als einziger nicht teilnahmslos vor sich hin starrte, sondern beschäftigt war mit dem Anfertigen von Aufzeichnungen und Skizzen, die offenbar in einem Bezug standen zu dem prunkvollen, meines Erachtens eher für einen Staatsakt als zum Warten auf die nächste Zugverbindung nach Paris oder Ostende gedachten Saal" (2001/2003, pp. 14–15).

13. Although technically a prison (SS-Auffanglager) rather than a concentration camp, Breendonk became infamous for maltreatment and torture of prisoners, many of whom were subsequently transferred to and murdered in larger camps in Eastern Europe. In Belgian historical memory, Breendonk soon became and has remained symbolic of the barbarity of the German occupation of the nation. See Pahaut and Maerten (2006).

14. "das waren die Familienväter und die guten Söhne aus Vilsbiburg und aus Fuhlsbüttel, aus dem Schwarzwald und aus dem Münsterland, wie sie hier nach getanem Dienst beim Kartenspiel beieinander sassen oder Briefe schrieben an ihre Lieben daheim, denn unter ihnen hatte ich ja gelebt bis in mein zwanzigstes Jahr. Die Erinnerung an die vierzehn Stationen, die der Besucher in Breendonk zwischen Portal und Ausgang passiert, hat sich in mir verdunkelt im Laufe der Zeit, oder vielmehr verdunkelte sie sich, wenn man so sagen kann, schon an dem Tag, an welchem ich in der Festung war, sei es, weil ich nicht wirklich sehen wollte, was man dort sah, sei es, weil in dieser nur vom schwachen Schein weniger Lampen erhellten und für immer vom Licht der Natur getrennten Welt der Konturen der Dinge zu zerfliessen schienen" (2001/2003, pp. 37–38). "[D]ie vierzehn Stationen" (the fourteen stations) may be an allusion to the 14 stations of the Passion of Christ. Whether or to what extent the allusion would be ironic depends in large part on the reader's interpretation of the three words and the context in which the frame narrator uses them.

15. "Austerlitz ist ja für mich, der ich zu Beginn meines Studiums in Deutschland von den seinerzeit dort amtierenden, grösstenteils in den dreissiger und vierziger Jahren in ihrer akademischen Laufbahn vorangerückten und immer noch an ihrer Machtphantasien befangenen Geisteswissenschaftlern so gut wie gar nichts gelernt hatte, seit meiner Volksschulzeit der erste Lehrer überhaupt gewesen, dem ich zuhören konnte" (2001/2003, pp. 51–52).

16. "diese Bemerkung über seine später einmal von ihm so genannte Bahnhofsmanie gemacht hat, weniger zu mir als zu sich selber, und sie war auch die einzige Andeutung seines Seelenlebens geblieben, die er sich mir gegenüber erlaubte, bis ich Ende 1975 nach Deutschland zurückging mit der Absicht, dort, in der mir nach einer neunjährigen Abwesenheit fremd gewordenen Heimat, auf die Dauer mich niederzulassen" (2001/2003, p. 53).

17. The German term *SS-Leute* (2001/2003, p. 37) is somewhat more inclusive than the English "SS guards."

18. "Genau kann niemand erklären, was in uns geschieht, wenn die Türe aufgerissen wird, hinter der die Schrecken der Kindheit verborgen sind" (2001/2003, p. 41).

19. "Es war nicht so, dass mit der Übelkeit eine Ahnung in mir aufstieg von der Art der sogenannten verschärften Verhöre, die um die Zeit meiner Geburt an diesem Ort durchgeführt wurden, denn erst ein paar Jahre später las ich bei Jean Améry von der furchtbaren Körpernähe zwischen den Peinigern und den Gepeinigten, von der von ihm ausgestandenen Folter" (2001/2003, pp. 41–42).

20. "und da also keiner vom anderen wusste, woher er stammte, hatten wir uns seit unserem ersten Antwerpener Gespräch stets nur der französischen Sprache bedient, ich mit schandbarer Unbeholfenheit, Austerlitz hingegen auf eine so formvollendete Weise, dass ich ihn lang für einen Franzosen hielt" (2001/2003, p. 50).

21. There is a connection between Austerlitz's search for his parents and Ella Blumenthal's search for lost relatives in Poland after the war. See my discussion of Blumenthal's testimony in Chapter 1.

22. "der mir auch in der Folge kaum etwas von seiner Herkunft und seinem Lebensweg anvertraute" (2001/2003, p. 16).

23. "immer weiter ostwärts und immer weiter zurück in der Zeit" (2001/2003, pp. 270–271).

24. "dass Agáta im September 1944 mit eineinhalbtausend anderen in Terezín Internierten nach Osten geschickt worden war" (2001/2003, p. 295).

25. "das H. G. Adler, der mir unbekannt war bis dahin, über die Einrichtung, Entwicklung und innere Organisation des Ghettos von Theresienstadt zwischen 1945 und 1947 unter . . . den schwierigsten Bedingungen teils in Prag, teils in London verfasst und bis zu seiner Veröffentlichung in einem deutschen Verlag im Jahr 1955 mehrfach noch überarbeitet hat" (2001/2003, pp. 335, 338).

26. "weil das Ghettosystem in seiner gewissermassen futuristischen Verformung des gesellschaftlichen Lebens für mich den Charakter des Irrealen behielt" (2001/2003, p. 339).

27. "und die vier, Tag und Nacht in Betrieb gehaltenen und in einem Zyklus von je vierzig Minuten arbeitenden Naphthaverbrennungsöfen des Krematoriums belastet wurden bis an die äusserste Grenze ihrer Kapazität, sagte Austerlitz" (2001/2003, pp. 344–345).

28. "Das alles begriff ich nun und begriff es auch nicht, denn jede Einzelheit, die sich mir, dem, wie ich fürchtete, aus eigner Schuld unwissend Gewesenen, eröffnete auf meinem Weg durch das Museum, aus einem Raum in den nächsten und wieder zurück, überstieg bei weitem mein Fassungsvermögen. Ich sah Gepäckstücke, mit denen die Internierten aus Prag und

aus Pilsen, Würzburg und Wien, Kufstein und Karlsbad und zahllosen anderen Orten nach Terezín gekommen waren, Gegenstände wie Handtaschen, Gürtelschnallen, Kleiderbürsten und Kämme, die sie gefertigt hatten in den verschiedenen Manufakturen . . . Bilanzblätter sah ich, Totenregister, überhaupt Verzeichnisse jeder nur denkbaren Art und endlose Reihen von Zahlen und Ziffern, mit denen die Amtswalter sich darüber beruhigt haben müssen, dass nichts unter ihrer Aufsicht verlorenging" (2001/2003, pp. 287–288).

29. This feature of *Austerlitz* aligns Sebald's novel with "Virginia Woolf's and other modernists' astonishment about the discrepancy between time on the clock and time in the mind" (Brockmeier, 2015, p. 298).

30. This point also applies to the plot summaries I give of the four novels I discuss.

31. For David Herman, storytelling, stories, and storyworlds are "irreducibly grounded in intentional systems," whereas "intentional systems are grounded in storytelling, practices" (2008, pp. 240–241). While I agree with Brockmeier that, drawing on this hermeneutic rationale, "we can view autobiographical narrative as . . . a 'primary resource' for (re)constructing psychological states and, more generally, states of consciousness" (2015, p. 279), I prefer Brockmeier's phrase "reach for meaning" to Herman's "intentional systems." Not only is "reach for meaning" a more accurate description of the different interpretive processes of *Austerlitz*; it is also more closely related to, and thus signals more clearly, the ethical dimension of those processes, including not only those of Austerlitz and the frame narrator but also my own as a reader and viewer.

32. The narrator in Virginia Woolf's modernist "biography" *Orlando* (1928/1998), an original fictional text whose generic experimentation and use of black-and-white photographs are reminiscent of *Austerlitz*, comments on the "extraordinary discrepancy between time on the clock and time in the mind" (p. 91).

33. The German title, *Luftkrieg und Literatur* (1999), is more accurate than that of the English translation (2004). I discuss Sebald's use of visual images in Lothe (2012). See also Horstkotte (2008); Kempinski (2007).

34. "Heute weiss ich, dass damals, als ich auf dem Altan des Seefelderhauses in dem sogenannten Stubenwagen lag und hinaufblinzelte in den weissblauen Himmel, überall in Europa Rauchschwaden in der Luft hingen, über den Rückzugsschlachten im Osten und im Westen, über den Ruinen der deutschen Städte und über den Lagern, in denen man die Ungezählten verbrannte aus Berlin und aus Frankfurt, aus Wupperdal und aus Wien, aus Würzburg und Kissingen, aus Hilversum und Den Haag, Naumur und Thionville, Lyon und Bordeaux, Krakau und Łodz, Szeged und Sarajevo, Saloniki und Rhodos, Ferrara und Venedig—kaum ein Ort in Europa, aus dem in diesen Jahren niemand deportiert worden wäre in den Tod" (Sebald, 1999, p. 78).

35. "die er, Adler selber, sagte Austerlitz, allerdings nie zu Gesicht bekam und die jetzt offenbar vollends verschollen ist" (2001/2003, p. 349).

36. "als es dem Imperial War Museum über das Berliner Bundesarchiv schliesslich gelungen war, eine Kassettenkopie des von mir gesuchten Theresienstädter Films zu beschaffen" (2001/2003, pp. 350–351).

37. "Sie trägt, sagte Austerlitz, eine in drei feinen Bogenlinien von ihrem dunklen, hochgeschlossenen Kleid kaum sich abhebende Kette um den Hals und eine weisse Blumenblüte seitlich in ihrem Haar. Gerade so wie ich nach meinen schwachen Erinnerungen und den wenigen übrigen Anhaltspunkten, die ich heute habe, die Schauspielerin Agáta mir vorstellte, gerade so, denke ich, sieht sie aus, und ich schaue wieder und wieder in dieses mir gleichermassen fremde und vertraute Gesicht, sagte Austerlitz, lasse das Band zurücklaufen, Mal für Mal, und sehe den Zeitanzeiger in der oberen linken Ecke des Bildschirms, die Zahlen, die einen Teil ihrer Stirn verdecken, die Minuten und die Sekunden, von 10:53 bis 10:57, und die Hundertstelsekunden, die sich davondrehen, so geschwind, dass man sie nicht entziffern und festhalten kann" (2001/2003, pp. 358–359).

38. See the comments on Levinas in the introduction and in other chapters of this book.

39. In *Camera Lucida* the concept of *studium* refers to the cultural, linguistic, and relatively conventional interpretation of a photograph, whereas, as I note in Chapter 1, *punctum* denotes the wounding, intensified, subjective, and personally touching detail which establishes a more direct relationship with the object or person within the photo. See Barthes (1982, pp. 26–27).

40. As visual legacies of the Holocaust, photographs of lost family members play an important role in the work of postgeneration artists and writers (Hirsch, 2012).

41. "auf die unbeschriftete Photographie einer Schauspielerin gestossen, die mit meiner verdunkelten Erinnerung an die Mutter übereinzustimmen schien" (2001/2003, p. 360).

42. "denn er stehe nun, so sagte er, im Begriff, nach Paris zu gehen, um nach dem Verbleib des Vaters zu forschen" (2001/2003, p. 361).

43. "Sonderbarerweise, so sagte Austerlitz, habe er wenige Stunden nach unserer letzten Begegnung, als er, von der Bibliothèque Nationale herkommend, in der Gare d'Austerlitz umgestiegen sei, die Vorahnung gehabt, dass er dem Vater sich annähere. Wie ich vielleicht wisse, sei am vergangenen Mittwoch ein Teil des Eisenbahnverkehrs wegen eines Streiks lahmgelegt worden, und in der aufgrund dessen in der Gare d'Austerlitz herrschenden ungewöhnlichen Stille sei ihm der Gedanke gekommen, der Vater habe von hier aus, von diesem seiner Wohnung in der rue Barrault zunächst gelegenen Bahnhof, Paris verlassen bald nach dem Einmarsch der Deutschen. Ich bildete mich ein, sagte Austerlitz, ihn zu sehen, wie er sich bei der Abfahrt aus dem Abteilfenster lehnt, und sah auch die weissen Dampfwolken aufsteigen aus der schwerfällig sich in Bewegung setzenden Lokomotive" (2001/2003, pp. 410–412).

44. See Lothe (2008).

45. "ein Kammerjäger ... verfolgt mich bis heute manchmal in meinen Träumen, wo ich ihn sehe beim Ausräuchern der Zimmer, von giftweissen Schwaden umwölkt" (2001/2003, p. 263).

46. "ein vom Rost zur Hälfte schon zerfressenes petrochemisches Kombinat, aus dessen Kühltürmen und Schloten weisse Rauchwolken aufsteigen" (2001/2003, pp. 271–272).

47. "und werde also weitersuchen nach meinem Vater" (2001/2003, p. 414).

48. "Es ging auf zwölf Uhr, als wir uns verabschiedeten vor der Métrostation Glacière. Früher, sagte Austerlitz zuletzt, sind hier heraussen grosse Sümpfe gewesen, auf denen die Leute Schlittschuh liefen im Winter, genau wie vor dem Bishop's Gate in London, und überreichte mir die Schlüssel seines Hauses in der Alderney Street. Ich könne dort, wann immer ich wolle, sagte er, mein Quartier aufschlagen und die schwarzweissen Bilder studieren, die als einziges übrigbleiben würden von seinem Leben" (2001/2003, p. 414).

49. It should be noted, though, that he comments on the Nazis' frightfully efficient and systematic deportation system.

50. "über die Brücke zu dem finsteren Tor, durch das ich mich diesmal, auch nach längerem Zögern, nicht hineintraute" (2001/2003, p. 418). There is a sense in which the map of Theresienstadt is a visual illustration of this system.

51. "Kaum irgendwo findet Jacobson auf seiner litauischen Reise eine Spur seiner Vorfahren" (2001/2003, p. 420).

52. "1941 kamen sie in deutsche Hand, auch das berüchtigte Fort IX, in dem zeitweise Kommandostellen der Wehrmacht sich einrichteten und wo in den folgenden drei Jahren mehr als dreissigtausend Menschen ums Leben gebracht wurden" (2001/2003, p. 421).

53. "Andere hinterliessen uns bloss ein Datum und eine Ortsangabe mit ihren Namen: Lob, Marcel, de St. Nazaire; Wechsler, Abram, de Limoges; Max Stern, Paris, 18.5.44. Ich las am Wassergraben der Festung von Breendonk das fünfzehnte Kapitel von *Heshel's Kingdom* zu Ende, und machte mich dann auf den Rückweg nach Mechelen, wo ich anlangte, als es Abend wurde" (2001/2003, p. 421).

54. "Bis in den Mai 1944 hinein, als der Krieg längst verloren war, kamen Transporte aus dem Westen nach Kaunas" (2001/2003, p. 421).

55. "und, wenn man so sagen kann, sagte Austerlitz, Zeugnis ablegte von dem, was ich selbst nicht mehr wusste" (2001/2003, p. 320).

56. The expansive understanding of reconciliation, and possibly of forgiveness, that emerges through *Austerlitz*'s narrative discourse could be linked to Myisha Cherry's notion of *radical repair*: "Radical repair addresses the roots of a problem, aims for change, and requires everyone—not just the victim—to help make things right" (Cherry, 2023, p. 5).

57. In narrative fiction and nonfiction, a *Leerstelle* is often manifested in and signaled by a narrative ellipsis. Whether it occurs in a sentence or a paragraph or a larger text segment, the ellipsis can assume the form of a gap that needs to be interpreted to be understood. Lise Patt observes, "If there is a Sebaldian method, in *Austerlitz* we are given its opening line: 'mind the gap' between words, between and in images and text, but most significantly, mind the gaps *in* (not only *between*) signs" (Patt, 2007a, p. 81).

58. For me, there are indirect yet significant links between the lives of these three major modernist writers and the Holocaust. Joseph Conrad, who died in 1924, hailed from Poland, where the

Nazis built their extermination camps. He spent an important part of his childhood in Kraków, a city located near Auschwitz. Although Conrad was no prophet, his narrative presentation in *Heart of Darkness* (1899) of the Belgians' use of Africans as slave labor in the Congo calls the Holocaust to mind. If Franz Kafka had not died of tuberculosis in the same year as Conrad, he would probably have perished in the Holocaust, as did his three sisters, Elli, Valli, and Ottilie. The family of Virginia Woolf's husband, Leonard Woolf, was Jewish. Woolf, who took her own life in 1941, knew that in the event of a German invasion of Britain he would probably be deported to a camp on the continent.

7

Jenny Erpenbeck's *Aller Tage Abend*
(*The End of Days*)

The most obvious point of connection between W. G. Sebald's *Austerlitz* and Jenny Erpenbeck's *Aller Tage Abend* (2012; first published in English as *The End of Days* in 2014) is the epigraph in Erpenbeck's novel:

> We left from here for Marienbad only last summer.
> And now—where will we be going now?
> W. G. Sebald, Austerlitz (Sebald, 2002, p. iii)[1]

The question that concludes the epigraph is asked by Agáta, who, as we recall from the discussion of *Austerlitz* in the preceding chapter, saved her son Austerlitz's life—and who was also a victim of the Holocaust. In the novel, the "now" of the question is related to, and yet also contrasted with, a visit that Austerlitz, his parents, and Věra, a non-Jewish friend of the family, made to Marienbad in 1938. Soon after, it became impossible for them to visit Marienbad because of the increasingly difficult situation for Jews in Czechoslovakia after the German invasion.[2] While in *Austerlitz* the "now" is Austerlitz's memory of a memory that Věra shares with him when they meet in Prague many years after the war, the epigraph of *Aller Tage Abend* does not highlight the complex process of memory as strongly as does the corresponding textual fragment of *Austerlitz*. Yet already on a first reading of the epigraph I was, I think, inclined to link the trip to Marienbad to a good memory, while its closing question made me wonder whether the adjective "good" would apply to the next journey. The qualification "I think" is necessary because, since I read *Austerlitz* before *Aller Tage Abend* was published, there is a sense in which I have never experienced a first reading of the beginning of Erpenbeck's novel.

Encountering an epigraph from a novel I have already read when starting to read *Aller Tage Abend*, I inevitably associate the epigraph's closing question with the destinations of journeys that members of Austerlitz's family

Memory and Narrative Ethics. Jakob Lothe, Oxford University Press. © Oxford University Press (2025).
DOI: 10.1093/9780197579534.003.0008

make, or are forced to make, in Sebald's novel: while Věra stays in Prague, Austerlitz's father, Maximilian, goes to Paris, and Agáta manages to send Austerlitz to England on a *Kindertransport* before she is "sent east in September 1944" (Sebald, 2001/2002, p. 287) and murdered. That the epigraph can generate this response indicates that the novel from which it is taken may give a number of possible answers to the question. Yet it also suggests that the narrative I am starting to read may provide partial answers to the questions that Sebald explores. My extratextual knowledge of the literary text that the epigraph is taken from does not in itself make my reading of *Aller Tage Abend* "better" than that of a reader who does not possess this knowledge. Yet once I have this knowledge I neither can nor wish to eliminate it: my experience of the intertextual relationship between the two novels not only colors but also, as I will show, contributes to my interpretation.[3]

An epigraph is a kind of motto—an attempt made by the author to condense essential thematic aspects of his or her text into a few sentences while at the same time relating them to those of a different text. *Aller Tage Abend* is a work of narrative fiction, and its epigraph is a fragment from another fictional narrative. In *Aller Tage Abend* as in *Austerlitz*, however, narrative fiction is anchored in historical reality; in both, narrative is inseparable from the processes and uncertainties of memory. Moreover, for Erpenbeck as for Sebald, narrative raises ethical issues and challenges. Deeply marked by the violence of the 20th century, the novels' characters are confronted with conflicting values and value systems. So too are the novels' narrators and implied authors, and so am I as a reader.

Having said that, I do not want to make the novels more similar than they are. Both are original works of fiction that identify and explore memories of the Holocaust in innovative ways. One essential difference between the two novels is that while Sebald's focus is predominantly on male characters, Erpenbeck tells the story through the various lives of one female character. Moreover, while Sebald was a German British author who died in 2001, Erpenbeck, born in Berlin in 1967, is a German writer of fiction who belongs to the generation after Sebald.[4] Discussing the narrative ethics of *Aller Tage Abend*, I will highlight textual passages in each of the novel's five parts where aspects of the Holocaust are particularly striking. As I consider several of the questions asked in the narrative as elements of self-interpretation, my interpretation is influenced by those aspects. Paying particular attention to narrative repetition and perspectival variation, the chapter shows how the novel's narrative ethics emerges through Erpenbeck's presentation of the narrator and the characters' fragments of memory. I argue that the narrative ethics of the novel revolves around the word *Birkenwäldchen*, a German noun not included in the English translation of *Aller Tage Abend*. I discuss the significance of this word, which for me becomes a *punctum*, as Barthes understands the concept (see Chapter 1), by connecting it to the challenge of presenting, remembering, and reflecting on the Holocaust in a work of narrative fiction published 70 years after the Nazis' mass murder of six million Jews.

The novel's starting point is that an infant child dies in a small town in Eastern Europe—Brody, in western Ukraine—at the beginning of the 20th century. After describing her family's shock and reaction to the unexpected death, Erpenbeck as implied author, via her third-person narrator whose perspective can be aligned with those of her focalized characters, asks: What would the child, who was a girl, have experienced had she not died? What would have changed if she did not die? That these questions have an ethical dimension becomes obvious once I associate them with the Holocaust. Yet ethics can be an integral part of such questions asked after any child's death. Responding as a creative writer to her own questions and reflections on what could or might happen to the child, Erpenbeck reveals that the girl who died turns out to be alive after all, living with her family in Vienna just after the end of the First World War. She dies again, but reemerges in Moscow in the 1930s and, after another death, as a citizen of East Berlin in the 1960s. After yet another death the reader meets her again in a nursing home in Berlin after the reunification of Germany in 1989. Here she dies one last time, and the novel ends.

In common with earlier plot summaries presented in this book, this one also oversimplifies the novel's narrative discourse, while at the same time including interpretive elements that signal the chapter's critical focus. Exploiting the possibilities of the novel's repetitive pattern, Erpenbeck shows how one fictional character experiences a series of wars and totalitarian regimes in 20th-century Europe. The main character's experience includes antisemitism, which she tries to deal with in different ways in her successive lives. As this experience is shared by her Jewish family, and by implication by many Jewish communities in Eastern Europe and by all Jews, Erpenbeck presents the reader with an artful combination of individual and collective memories. For the narrator—and, outside the fictional universe, for Erpenbeck as implied and historical author—the Holocaust is a postmemory (Hirsch, 2012); for the main character—who remains anonymous for most of the narrative but whose name, the reader learns at the end, is Frau Hoffmann—it is a painful, traumatic memory.

One remarkable feature of *Aller Tage Abend* is that Erpenbeck incorporates different summaries of her main character's life story into the novel's narrative discourse, thus demonstrating the great difference between those summaries and that discourse. The first of these assumes the form of autobiographical sketches that the main character, who at this stage of plot progression is referred to as "Comrade H." (p. 177), writes in Moscow when she is affiliated with the Communist Party. The last summary is presumably composed of fragments of an obituary in a German newspaper after the protagonist's death in East Berlin in the 1970s. I will return to the thematic and interpretive implications of these summaries; the essential point at this stage is the contrast between the novel's narrative discourse and the accounts of the protagonist's life that it includes. This contrast lends support to one of the tenets of narrative hermeneutics: if the act of reading is interpretive, so is the act of writing. While neither activity is neutral, both are shaped by the reader's, and the author's, multilayered perspective. I divide the chapter into four parts, corresponding to and dealing with the four main European locations of the narrative: Brody, Vienna, Moscow, and Berlin.

Brody

The novel's first two sentences reveal key aspects of Erpenbeck's thematic focus as well as her narrative strategy:

> The Lord gave, and the Lord took away, her grandmother said to her at the edge of the grave. But that wasn't right, because the Lord had taken away much more than had been there to start with, and everything her child might have become was now lying there at the bottom of the pit, waiting to be covered up. (p. 5)[5]

There is a tension in this narrative beginning between the fact of a child's death and the mother's defiance of that fact. On a second reading, the phrase "might have become" takes on a proleptic function as books 1–5 show what the child, who turns out to be the narrative's main character, may become in the realm of fiction. Demonstrating the validity of Aristotle's definition of the poet as someone who shows me what "might occur"

(1995, p. 59), Erpenbeck starts by killing off her protagonist and then goes on to resurrect her at the beginning of each of the following books of her novel.

A second feature of the narrative's beginning is Erpenbeck's dual focus on the family—here represented by the mother, her grandmother, and the dead child—and on the death of one individual. One important effect of this kind of dual narrative focus, which is sustained throughout, is Erpenbeck's exploration of collective and individual memory in one and the same narrative movement. Rereading the beginning, I find that one constituent element of this movement is the way the mother's memory of her child is intensified through her act of mourning:

> Now she sits here on this little wooden footstool that her grandmother gave her on her wedding day, she sits with her eyes closed, just as she has seen others sitting in times of mourning.... Today, the child was buried in accordance with Jewish custom, and in accordance with Jewish custom she will now sit for seven days upon this footstool; but her husband will not speak to her. (pp. 8–9)[6]

The mother's memory of her child is intensified through her act of mourning. Extended in time and halting plot progression, Erpenbeck's portrayal of the mourning mother on the wooden footstool joins the death of a child—the narrative's first event—with a period of mourning that, lasting for seven days, may or may not include the mother's reflections but almost certainly includes fragments of memories. The significance of this pause or gap in a narrative that has just begun is illuminated by Jacques Derrida's descriptions of mourning in *The Work of Mourning* and *Mémoires: For Paul de Man*. In the latter book, Derrida writes:

> Mourning is impossible, and for *us* most of all. The "trace of the other," the other who has died and that remains *other*, is at once inside and outside of us, marking a gap that *moves* in "us," as "us"—living who sign our name. (1989, p. 49, original emphasis)

It is a distinctive feature of Derrida's late work that, as Pamela Osborn puts it, "the multiple losses described become gaps which both simultaneously imply meaning *and* deny narrative stability so that the text becomes *haunted* by absence and undecidability" (2012, p.113, original emphasis).

The narrative of *Aller Tage Abend* is haunted in this sense. While the gaps in the narratives of all five books are intensified and radically widened by the gaps between them, all the books—including their endings, each of which presents the reader with the protagonist's death—activate aspects of loss and mourning. Throughout the narrative, the interplay of memory and mourning, or, more precisely, the way in which fragments of memory include and often seem to be constituted by elements of mourning is a major aspect of the novel's narrative ethics.

Thinking that her absent husband may be at church, praying for the soul of their dead child, the mother asks, "And where can their child's soul go now? To purgatory? Paradise? Hell? . . . Maybe on the other side of life there is nothing at all?" (p. 9).[7] I read an ethical dimension into these questions since the first one makes me think of the novel's epigraph, and since I know that the child is actually the main character who over the course of her life, or lives, will be going to various places, and whose decision to go to Moscow in particular is in large part motivated by her communism.

There are two more reasons these questions are relevant to my analysis. First, the narrative of *Aller Tage Abend* includes a series of questions that are associated with a character's perspective: focalized through the character's thoughts and memories, they are colored by his or her experiences, actions, thoughts, attitudes, and values. However, as already indicated, Erpenbeck as implied author presents the questions, and indeed the whole narrative, by using an unidentified third-person narrator as her primary communicative instrument. Even though this narrator has access to many of the characters' thoughts and memories, there is a lot she does not know, or does not tell the reader, about them. The third-person narrator is no identifiable character, but she has values that influence her narrative presentation. Although I refer to the narrator as "she" because of the gender of Erpenbeck as author, and although the third-person narrator's ethics often approximates to and represents the implied author's ethics, I distinguish between these two variants or manifestations of ethics in the narrative. One reason this distinction is necessary is that the narrator's ethics is variable and in one sense unstable: while it can present one or more facets of the implied author's ethics, it can also blend into and become virtually indistinguishable from the ethics of the character whose actions, attitudes, and values she observes and reports. While Erpenbeck can make her narrator show empathy with a character, she can make the narrator distance herself from a different character (or from the same character at a different stage of the plot). The narrative presentation of the mother's questions as she is mourning her child suggests that the third-person narrator is emphatically related not only to the mother but also to her deceased child. When the child turns out not to be dead in alternative plotlines, this kind of attitudinal connection between the third-person narrator and the main character of the narrative she presents is strengthened.

Second, the questions are important because they not only highlight religious thoughts but also suggest how these can include religious doubts and uncertainties about the future. It is significant that, following her mother's (the protagonist's grandmother's) advice, the mother of the deceased child has distanced herself from Judaism by marrying a Christian man (Mueller, 2014). And yet, according to the Halacha,[8] both she and her child (the deceased child who becomes the novel's protagonist) are Jewish because her mother is. Under the Nuremberg race laws, the protagonist is a *Mischling*, a "mixed-race person," because two of her grandparents are Jewish.[9] These implications, which partly presuppose extratextual knowledge, become stronger on a second reading of the novel's beginning. Rereading the opening, I am more appreciative of the connection between the mother's questions and the protagonist's realization after having noticed that her mother tries to shelter her children from antisemitic attitudes in Vienna in book 2, that "she, too, was of Jewish descent" (p. 89).[10] This connection illustrates how constituent elements of collective and individual values and traditions are intertwined in the novel's narrative discourse. As the narrative progresses, it becomes increasingly clear that so are collective and individual aspects of memory.

By not using the word "Holocaust" Erpenbeck signals that her characters'—and perhaps also her narrator's—knowledge of the Nazis' mass murder of Jews is limited. Thus, the characters remember fragments of events that Erpenbeck invites me to relate to a word that her third-person narrator does not employ. Perhaps, in common with the characters to whose perspectives her narration is related, the narrator does not know the word "Holocaust" either. Yet as a reader I do, and this knowledge inevitably informs my interpretation.

In addition to their intrinsic value, the aspects of Jewish faith and tradition apparent in the opening of book 1 provide a partial background for the narrative presentation of a pogrom that the mother's Jewish parents experienced many years earlier. One day people suddenly throw stones at their house. The father shouts at Andrei, whom he recognizes:

But Andrei didn't hear him—or pretended not to, which was more likely, since he knew perfectly well who lived in the house he was throwing stones at. Then one of Andrei's stones came hurtling thorough a window pane, passing just a hair's breadth from [her mother's] head, and crashed into the glass-fronted bookcase behind her, striking Volume 9 of the leather-bound edition of Goethe's *Collected Works* that her husband's parents had given him as a gift when he finished school. *No breath of air disturbs the place,/Deathly silence far and wide./O'er the ghastly deeps no single/Wavelet ripples on the tide.* (p. 12)[11]

The mother barely survives, but her husband is killed with an axe: "Then she is a Jewish widow holding Death by the hand" (p. 14).[12] They are both victims of physical violence. As the attack is entirely unprovoked, Erpenbeck invites me to look for a different kind of motive or cause. This is an interpretive activity: I read the killing of the Jewish man as an act or manifestation of antisemitism. And yet to what extent or in what way can antisemitism explain this incident? It is not easy, neither for the Jewish woman who survives nor for me as a reader, to relate the antisemitism that underlies the attack to a concrete motive. The hatred of Jews, this time expressed even by Andrei, "whom she has known since he was a baby" (p. 14),[13] appears to be as strong as it is inexplicable. What seems certain, though, is that the unprovoked attack is a demonstration of contesting values. As Colin Davis (2018b) has noted, ethics is the domain of such a contest. In this case, the contest spirals into a conflict in which the weaker part suffers because of the stronger part's violence.

Taking my interpretation one step further, I suggest that, at this early stage of the narrative, Erpenbeck presents me with an event that resembles the Holocaust in three ways: it is directed at Jews, it is violent, and it is hard to explain. There is a thought-provoking relation between this event and later ones in which other family members are murdered, albeit under different conditions and not with a family member present as a witness. If the event is an example of physical violence resulting from and made possible by the "essential dissymmetry between the one who acts and the one who undergoes" (Ricoeur, 1990/1994, p. 145), my interpretation of the event is also dissymmetric: I find it more difficult to identify the beliefs of the attacker than those of the attacked. The reason is not just that, given my knowledge of the Holocaust and the religious tolerance of the society in which I live, I oppose the violent act of Andrei and his friends. The narrative discourse suggests two more reasons. The first is indicated by the name "Andrei," which is the only first name identified in book 1—and one of the few in the whole novel. On page 12 alone, "Andrei" occurs nine times. Why? Perhaps because both the mother, who becomes the protagonist's grandmother, as well as her husband, who is murdered, think of Andrei as a neighbor and friend—as someone whose participation in the attack they find shocking and inexplicable. They appeal to those of Andrei's values that, according with their own, should make it impossible for him to murder a neighbor who has done him no harm. In my reading experience of the passage, these values resemble my own; I share the empathy with the Jewish couple implicitly expressed by the narrator.

The second specific reason the passage gives me for appreciating the Jewish couple's values is the combination of a surname and a book title, "Goethe's *Collected Works.*" The stone thrown by Andrei that almost kills the grandmother strikes volume 9 of the collected works of an author who is not only the best known and most influential representative of German literature but whose values, as expressed in his literary works, the Jewish couple shares. Thus, the attack on them is also an attack on Goethe—and on the Germany that Goethe represents. Moreover, since the leather-bound edition of Goethe belongs to the grandfather, and since it was given to him as a present by his parents, there is strong sense in which, after his death, it enables his wife to remember and honor her late husband. This is part of the reason she carries the edition with her to different places for as long as she can possibly manage. Goethe's *Collected Works* becomes a leitmotif in *Aller Tage Abend*, expressing and representing humanist values radically opposed to those of antisemitism and Nazism.[14] The significance of the combination of Goethe's name and his *Collected Works* is further strengthened by the quotation from the poem "Meeresstille" ("Calm Sea" or "Flat Calm") that follows the reference to his works. As I know this poem, one of Goethe's most famous and most widely read (and taught in German schools), I register that Erpenbeck quotes the poem's last four lines. I consider these lines an integral part of *Aller Tage Abend*, and my interpretation is influenced by my focus on the novel's narrative presentation of the Holocaust; I therefore regard the calmness and silence of the sea as a sign of something ominous, perhaps a storm, looming on the horizon. Could this storm be the Holocaust, and could the poem also suggest that the Holocaust was surrounded by a "deathly silence"?[15] Of course, Goethe was no prophet; yet, as Hans-Georg Gadamer observes, "the meaning of a text goes beyond its author" (1960/2013, p. 307). Since I read and interpret the poem from my own perspective, a post-Holocaust perspective that in addition to its interpretive limitations also has interpretive possibilities, the poem's meaning can move beyond the meaning that Goethe was conscious of at the time of writing.

Vienna

Thinking of her murdered husband after the attack, the grandmother reflects, "A day on which a life comes to an end is still far from being the end of days" (p. 15).[16] Suggesting a combination of memory and mourning, on the one hand, and stamina and hope, on the other, the reflection is coupled with the novel's title in a way that augments the importance of the grandmother as a character in the narrative and also hints at its continuation. This is what happens in book 2, and to explain how it could happen, Erpenbeck inserts an "Intermezzo" between the two books—and indeed between all five books that her novel consists of. Erpenbeck does not need to "explain" this narrative strategy: as a writer of fiction, she can design her narrative any way she wants, and in *Aller Tage Abend* she takes advantage of this privilege. Creating not just one fictional world but several, she explores the possibilities of narrative fiction. This kind of exploration is not just an aesthetic innovation; it is a notable instance of an aesthetic narrative structure that shapes and gradually intensifies the novel's thematic concerns by combining a plot centered on the main character and those around her with forms of repetition and historical references.[17] As the novel's implied author, Erpenbeck makes her third-person narrator reflect that

> if, for example, the child's mother or father had . . . put [some snow] under the baby's shirt, perhaps the child would suddenly have started breathing again, possibly cried again as well, in any case its heart might have gone back to beating. (p. 57)[18]

The function of the four intermezzi is essentially twofold: first, they explain to me as a reader how the narrative can continue; second, illustrating the possibility of making one and the same character experience different yet connected fictional worlds, they shape my interpretation of the novel by inviting me to wonder about the range and possibilities of fiction—and thus perhaps also of my own life. At the same time, these elements suggest how easily these possibilities can be reduced, even eliminated, by historical processes—particularly those involving violence and war—that the characters cannot escape.

In a key passage that takes place in the family's apartment in Vienna in the aftermath of the First World War, the narrator describes the child's father sitting down beside his wife's bed when she is asleep, making

> one further attempt to get to the bottom of what has seemed to him the greatest riddle in all the history of mankind: how processes, circumstances, or events of a general nature—such as war, famine, or even a civil servant's salary . . . can infiltrate a private face. Here they turn a few hairs grey, there devour a pair of lovely cheeks until the skin is stretched taut across angular jawbones. . . . In other words, there is a constant translation between far outside and deep within. (p. 73)[19]

Not just giving her narrator access to one of the character's thoughts, Erpenbeck makes the protagonist's father—who, she is convinced, "died of the war" (p. 135)[20] a few years later—reflect on a key aspect of her novel's thematics: the connections between different dimensions of existence, the "constant translation between far outside and deep within." The ethical dimension of this complex thematics is reflected on his wife's face. I have noted that Emmanuel Levinas highlights the importance of the human face, stressing the ethical challenge and responsibility represented by my encounter with the face of the Other. Although Levinas's notion of the Other is characterized by an irreducible alterity that makes it difficult to understand, I suggest that, in this passage, aspects or manifestations of the Other are perceived by the wife's husband as he is looking at her face. "The Other," writes Davis,

> makes me realize that I share the world, that it is not my unique possession, and I do not like this realization. My power and freedom are put into question. Such a situation is ethical because a lot depends upon how I respond. (2007b, p. 48)

When, using narrative fiction, Erpenbeck activates this radical challenge, she directs it not just at the husband; she also suggests that the challenge is relevant for the other characters, for her narrator, and for me as a reader. One salient aspect of the passage is that, much as he loves his wife, the husband is so traumatized by the First World War that his ability to support her is severely limited. His mind has been infiltrated by historical events and processes, and it is precisely his own experience that enables him to reflect on the connections between the marks left on the face of an individual, his wife, and the difficult circumstances under which this individual has lived. His reflections are furthered by his inability to respond to Levinas's ethical demand.

One variant of the demand is that the family members need to help each other to survive. The grandmother—who has come to Vienna too, taking her Goethe edition with her—continues to care for her daughter and her family. In common with her father, the novel's protagonist also comes to hate the war. Book 2 shows that while the characters' experiences of their time in Vienna are by no means identical, there is a gap between the values of the Jewish family and the antisemitic attitudes they encounter. The mother learns that "*Fire, locusts, leeches, plague, bears, foxes, snakes, insects, lice* were names that had often been given to Jews here in Vienna, but she hadn't known that" (p. 67, original emphasis).[21] That this list of insulting words is repeated twice (on pp. 75 and 109) suggests that the family was repeatedly subjected to variants of antisemitism from many people they met in Vienna, individuals as well as groups. The mother is particularly exposed as she needs to stay in line at the market. The hostile attitude affects her, leaving a mark on her face.

Erpenbeck's incorporation of antisemitic attitudes and expressions into the narrative of book 2 contextualizes and historicizes European antisemitism in the interwar period, while at the same time inviting the reader to relate it to the violent attack by Andrei and his friends on the grandmother and grandfather in book 1. While the Holocaust is not alluded to until the last scene of the second book, the two first books are a pertinent reminder of the connection between the Nazis' mass murder of Jews and the widespread antisemitism in early 20th-century Europe. The Holocaust, Erpenbeck's narrative suggests, is the most extreme manifestation of antisemitism. What are the values of the Viennese inhabitants who make the antisemitic comments that hurt the protagonist's mother?

Although they must have seen her face, they do not respond to the ethical obligation signaled or represented by that face. Although antisemitic words and actions harm the individual, those who utter the words and execute the actions tend to avoid direct contact, including eye contact, with the human being whose values they do not respect, thus paradoxically and ironically questioning their own values. Since the narration is associated with the perspectives of the Jewish characters, as a reader I do not learn much about the characters responsible for the antisemitic action. That the third-person narrator also does not know them well suggests that her perspective is affiliated with a Jewish perspective. However, the grandmother, who is almost killed by the stone that hits volume 9 of Goethe's *Collected Works*, and her husband, whose death is caused by a different weapon, know Andrei sufficiently well to be shocked by his violence. This kind of shock and utter disbelief may be the main reason Andrei's name is mentioned many times: it signals their painful realization that their neighbor in Brody and, they thought, their friend has values that prove lethal when transformed into action.

From my interpretive perspective, part 32 of book 2 plays a key role in *Aller Tage Abend*—structurally, thematically, and ethically. As a reader I am no longer in Vienna in this last scene of the novel's Vienna section. In fact, I do not know where I am:

> In 1944 in a small forest of birch trees, a notebook filled with handwritten diary entries will fall to the ground when a sentry uses his rifle butt to push a young woman forward, and she tries to protect herself with arms she had previously been using to clutch the notebook to her chest. The book will fall in the mud, and the woman will not be able to return to pick it up again. For a while the book will remain lying there, wind and rain will turn its pages, footsteps will pass over it, until all the secrets written there are the same color as the mud. (p. 110)[22]

Trying to remember my response to this passage when I first read it, I think it was one of bewilderment. Who is this young woman? Where is she, and why is she being pushed forward by an armed sentry? What is the meaning of the notebook? The temporal reference to "1944" does not tell me much, but since I know that part of the industrial Holocaust occurred in that year it could perhaps provide an interpretive hint or signal. Yet there is a great difference between "a small forest of birch trees" and a gas chamber, and the "young woman" cannot be the protagonist because she has killed herself in Vienna, thus dying once more before being resurrected again in the next intermezzo. Could the "young woman" perhaps be her younger sister?

The passage demonstrates why the narrative analyses presented in this book are based on a second reading. When I reread part 32 of book 2, I know that it is related to, and in large part explained by, an equally significant passage at the end of the novel, in part 3 of book 5. Since these two passages are closely connected in a way that advances my interpretation, and since that connection is important with a view to Erpenbeck's narrative ethics, I will incorporate my comments on them into my discussion of the novel's ending. Yet I want to make two observations on the passage as it presents itself to the reader here. First, Erpenbeck's choice of not identifying the young woman makes me wonder not just about the woman's identity but also what she has done to be punished in this way. Thus, Erpenbeck invites me to relate my uncertainty about what is happening to the woman to the precariousness and confusion that European Jews must have felt in the years leading up to the Holocaust. This does not mean that I can understand their uncertainty— of course I cannot. But it means that I can perhaps grasp a little more by becoming cognizant of how little I understand. Then I also see more clearly how, and to what extent, my questions are ethical questions. Moreover, the fact that the young woman is not identified helps to make her a representative of all European Jews.

Second, I have mentioned that there is a great difference between "a small forest of birch trees" and a gas chamber. Susan Bernofsky, whose translation from the German is excellent, uses six words to render the German noun *Birkenwäldchen*. Rereading this word in the original text, I add the letters *a* and *u* to the noun's first six letters, thus creating the word *Birkenau*. I am not arguing that all readers of the novel will associate the word with the extermination camp Birkenau at Auschwitz. Nor am I claiming that this association necessarily makes my interpretation of the passage more persuasive; as I have suggested, the sense of uncertainty and confusion it creates is an essential reason it is important, especially by stirring ethical questions. And yet once I have made the connection between the two words, the Holocaust is suddenly there, hidden and yet forcing its way into the narrative's center.[23]

Moscow

The protagonist's realization of the need for documentation of what occurs in history—and particularly historical events and processes that involve destruction, violence, and suffering—is a main reason she thinks highly of her father's work as a meteorologist. The end of the intermezzo between book 2 and book 3 tells the reader that if she survives and her life goes on—thus providing a contrast to the life of her father, who "died of the war"—"[s]he would have taken possession of her father's excerpts from *Notes on Earthquakes in Styria* and, weeping as she wrote, used them for her very first article: 'May the earth gape open once more and swallow up the war profiteers!'" (p. 116).[24] The ethical impetus of this sentence is evident in and becomes a motivating factor for the protagonist's work in Moscow, where, as a member of the Communist Party, she attempts to use "her writing to write her way back into life" (p. 119).[25] Her writing takes a variety of forms and involves various genres, including poetry translations, the *Sisyphus* manuscript that later becomes her first novel, and three different accounts of her life. Although she emerges more clearly as the novel's protagonist in book 3, the other family members, though absent, are present in her thoughts and memories. The Holocaust is also a looming presence, forcing its way into the narrative via her worries about her mother in Vienna.

Two aspects of book 3 are particularly relevant to my critical concerns: the protagonist's accounts of her life and her unanswered letter to her mother. Exploiting the elasticity of her main narrative instrument, Erpenbeck makes her third-person narrator relay fragments of the protagonist's accounts to the reader while at the same time adding elements of the protagonist's thoughts about her situation and her future. While all three accounts have biographical, political, and ethical elements, they show me how difficult it is, or can be, to account for my past, including my actions and relations to others, without thinking of the purpose of the account. What, asks the protagonist, "are the right words? Would a truth take her farther than a lie?" (p. 120).[26] In her first account she writes, "*I was born in 1902 in Brody to a civil servant and his wife, in other words I had a bourgeois background*" (p. 120, original emphasis).[27] The first part of this biographical sentence is a statement of fact; the second part is an interpretation of that fact from a communist perspective. She writes this because she wants to be honest, knowing that, in the Soviet Union's Communist Party, her background will be considered bourgeois because her father was not a factory worker but a clerk. Yet she remembers that, in Brody as in Vienna, the family was poor. "And what exactly made this background bourgeois? Perhaps the fact that when her Jewish grandmother fled from Galicia to Vienna more than twenty years ago, she dragged along an edition of Goethe's *Collected Works*?" (p. 120).[28] If, as the discourse indicates, the protagonist decides not to include this information in her account, that decision, though understandable, presents her with an ethical challenge since her memory of her grandmother is precious to her, and since the grandmother's books by Goethe have proved, and continue to prove, inspirational for her granddaughter's work as writer—also as a communist writer.

Recapitulating the narrative's main events and processes of her life, the three accounts reveal that there is no neutral version of these events and processes. The protagonist's only access to them is through her own experiences and memories that, though invaluable, are malleable and incomplete: "And so the past moved through the movements taking place in the present. But could looking at things in a certain way really change the things themselves?" (p. 135).[29] The question becomes pressing for the protagonist after her husband is arrested and, trying to support him, she fears she too may be arrested. This climate of uncertainty and fear motivates and underlies her three accounts—fragments of her life that, though similar, are not identical. For example, when applying for membership in the Communist Party "[s]he is required to list those who vouched for her, even though U.—who has since been expelled from the Party and condemned to death in absentia for high treason by the Soviet courts—now lives in Paris" (p. 134).[30] Thus, while in her first account she refers to U. as "*a respected functionary of the Communist International*," in her third she apologizes for having been "*influenced by U., an enemy of the people*" (pp. 134, 135, original emphasis).[31]

The question of the protagonist's different accounts or narrative versions of her life in book 3 is connected with family members' diverging memories of her father in book 2. As already indicated, she thinks that, though he was not physically wounded, he died of the war. Her younger sister, however, does not think so, and their mother has yet another explanation of her husband's death in 1920:

And so each of them—she herself, her mother, and her sister, too—described their father's death in quite different terms, even though the fact of his death confronted all of them in equal measure; each of them assigned it a different cause and meaning, as though it could be spoken of only in terms of this or that story, as a sort of dead stub that in some form or other had fused with each of their lives. (p. 136)[32]

In this passage the third-person narrator performs two narrative functions simultaneously: giving linguistic shape to and passing on the protagonist's reflections to the reader, the narrator links her perspective closely to that of the protagonist. Erpenbeck uses this narrative method throughout the novel, but here the method's narrative ethics is particularly striking because it not only indicates respect for the protagonist's challenges when she is remembering her father but also reveals her memories' narrative dimension. This effect is strengthened by the way in which Erpenbeck incorporates the protagonist's first-person accounts of her life into the third-person narrative. As a reader I am invited to agree with the protagonist's reflections, and as I am inclined to do so I am reminded of the narrative aspects of my own memories (Brockmeier, 2015; Freeman, 2010).

The combination of the protagonist's different accounts of her life and her family's conflicting memories of her father establishes a connection with the second feature of book 3 that I want to consider. This aspect concerns her mother. When, not long after her arrival in the Soviet Union, she sends her mother a package, the mother writes back from Vienna to thank her daughter for the food it contains. However, a later letter to her mother is not answered. As a reader I sense that something is wrong, but I have to wait until the next intermezzo to learn why the mother has been unable to reply: "Her letter to her mother had long since come back to her stamped *Evacuated to the East*, so she had no family left in Vienna, and probably nowhere else either" (p. 173, original emphasis).[33] Repeated in part 4 of book 4, this phrase, *Evakuiert nach dem Osten*, is a euphemism for being deported to a Nazi concentration camp. One reason I know this is that I remember reading in Sebald's *Austerlitz* that Austerlitz's mother "was sent east in September 1944."

Why does not Erpenbeck make her narrator give the reader this information about the protagonist's mother in book 3? One interpretive possibility is that it is unavailable to the narrator because the protagonist is unable to even think about it while fearing the death of her husband, who has been arrested, and probably also dreading her own death. Toward the end of book 3, she asks herself a series of questions that, stirred by her experience of multiple identities and her uncertainty about her own situation as well as those of her husband and her mother, connect the narrative's ethics to issues of power, violence, and human suffering:

> Was she ever even the same person? Were there any two moments in her life when she was comparable to herself? Was the whole not the truth? Or was everything treason? If the person who is to read this account remains faceless to her, what face should she be showing him? Which is the right blank face for a blank mirror? (p. 147)[34]

These questions keep haunting the protagonist until—in common with her husband, but separated from him—she dies in one of Stalin's Gulag camps, the violence of which could almost match that of the Nazis' concentration camps.[35] For me, the questions in the passage above, and the last three in particular, constitute elements of an ethical core or center in *Aller Tage Abend*. I will therefore return to them by way of concluding the chapter. But here I want to emphasize, in addition to underlining the importance of the questions' ethical dimension, the way the protagonist relates the two last questions to a reader who may be "faceless." As I am also reading versions or fragments of her account, there is a sense in which my interpretive activity approximates that of the reader whose face the protagonist cannot see but who has the power to decide whether she will live or die.

Although Erpenbeck gives the protagonist yet another life in the next intermezzo, there is an important connection between the information about her mother's death in that intermezzo and her own death in part 7 of book 3. It opens by recording that "[l]ast summer, when she was still alive," she and the other women in the Gulag camp had to dig trenches outside the camp, "so when winter came and the ground froze, they would have somewhere to be buried" (p. 161).[36] Before the Holocaust turned into industrial mass murder by poison gas, the Nazis' *Einsatzgruppen* in Russia would often order the Jews they were going to murder to dig their own graves.[37] I do not want to make these two facts—one fictional and one historical—more similar than they are, but in addition to the historical accuracy of Erpenbeck's reference to the brutality of the Gulag system there is a noticeable proximity in time and place.

The resemblance between the deaths of the protagonist and her mother at the end of book 3 is strengthened in its last paragraph. The narrator's perspective is still related to that of the protagonist, but as she is now dying and no longer able (or allowed) to write, there is a growing distance between narrator and main character. At the same time, there is a link, however covert, between what the protagonist has said and written in Moscow and the desperate situation she is in now, in the Gulag camp:

> It's a shame that no one can see the boundary where words made of air and words made of ink are transformed into something real: as real as a bag of flour, a crowd in which revolt is stirring, just as real as the sound with which the frozen bones of Comrade H. slid down into a pit in the winter of '41, sounding like someone tossing wooden domino tiles back into their box. (pp. 161–162)[38]

Comparing the sound of the protagonist's burial to that of someone tossing domino tiles into a box is an arresting image that makes me think the narrator has been a silent witness to the killing of a person who has tried to use words to account for herself, but whose words and written accounts may have led to her death. Who had the power to decide that she no longer deserved to live? Who decided that her mother was to be *Evakuiert nach dem Osten*? The protagonist does not know, and neither do I as a reader. What I do know, or think I know, is that it has proved difficult to hold individuals responsible for crimes of this kind. Those accused—for example, the guards at Bergen-Belsen filmed by Alain Resnais at the end of *Night and Fog*—typically place responsibility elsewhere, claiming that they were just following orders. While the passage highlights the connection between (oral or written) words on the one hand and the consequences of those words on the other, it also draws attention to the contingency and repetitive pattern of violent actions. Its accentuation of the violence of Stalin's Gulag system does not reduce the novel's emphasis on that of Nazi camps, however. Rather than comparing two different systems, Erpenbeck makes her characters experience, and her reader realize, that systematic violence was a constituent element of both.

Berlin

The intermezzi in *Aller Tage Abend* do not eliminate the sense of resignation, hopelessness, and even despair that pervades the novel. Demonstrating that fictional narrative is a powerful mode of exploration, Erpenbeck constructs a narrative discourse that, remembering the dead, approximates to

an act of mourning. Yet embedded in this mourning is a creative energy furthered by the implied author's exploration of possibilities manifested in the
book's intermezzi. They perform an essential structural and narrative function by relating the protagonist's different lives to each other and establishing
a kind of narrative progression from one book to the next. Additionally, the
intermezzi invest the narrative with an element of human resistance, stubbornness, strength, and hope that counteracts the forces of violence, death,
and destruction. Although I need to qualify this point by noting that the protagonist is the only character to be granted several lives, it does not follow
that it is unimportant.

In her two last lives the protagonist is in Berlin—first in East Berlin, the
capital of the German Democratic Republic in the 1970s, and then, resurrected after yet another death, in Berlin, the capital of a reunited Germany
around 1990. Starting to read book 4, I was first confused because I connected the death of a woman who falls down the stairs in her Berlin home
both to the lethal fall of her grandmother in book 2 and to the death of the
woman who fell into the pit in a Gulag camp in Russia at the end of book 3.
On a second reading, I consider this kind of interpretive confusion a gain of
the narrative: aspects of falling, literally as well as metaphorically, are essential thematic components in this novel in which kinds of falling are joined
with each other: the protagonist repeatedly falls when she dies, soldiers fall
in the war, and Jews fall when they are shot by the *Einsatzgruppen* or gassed
in the extermination camps. Moreover, it is

> as if memory, too, were a form of falling. Now she really is a "fallen woman"
> for the first time in her life, and if it weren't less a laughing matter than a
> dying one, she'd have to laugh. Did her mother think of her in her final
> moments? *Is* this her final moment? (p. 178)[39]

Inserting humor into a rather bleak narrative, the sentence shows how easily
the protagonist associates her own falling with that of her mother. In part 4
of book 4, I read that toward the end of the war the protagonist "learned
through her work at the radio station what had been happening to the Jews
in countries defeated by Germany" (p. 179).[40] This information is combined
with a repetition of the euphemism that I have already mentioned: "The
letter had come back to her stamped *Evacuated to the East*" (p. 180).[41] "In
a novel," writes J. Hillis Miller in *Fiction and Repetition*, "what is said two
or more times may not be true, but the reader is fairly safe in assuming that

it is significant" (1982, p. 2). In this case the repeated euphemism is both significant and true, but its information value for the protagonist is limited. Restricted or no knowledge about the Holocaust becomes a major feature of the narrative ethics of the last two books and, by implication, the whole novel.

At one level, this lack of knowledge is associated with the metaphor of memory as a form of falling. At a different yet related level, it is linked to the narrative and thematic function of the protagonist's son. In the letter to her mother that is returned to her Moscow address stamped *Evakuiert nach dem Osten*, the protagonist writes, "*I have a son now, he is three years old and is named Sasha*" (p. 180, original emphasis).[42] Sasha's father turns out to be a Russian poet, but the protagonist seems to wish that he should, or could, have been her husband—had he not been arrested. That they are both named "Comrade H." (p. 162) accentuates the problem of different identities that becomes pressing in the protagonist's three accounts of herself in book 3. I am forcibly reminded of these accounts, and of the protagonist's identity struggle, when the beginning of book 4 presents me with several italicized sentences that are apparently parts of an obituary of the protagonist:

> *Born in Brody, the daughter of an Austrian civil servant, she grew up in Vienna and in 1920 became a member of the Communist Party. In 1933 she emigrated to Moscow by way of Prague. There she contributed to the understanding between peoples as a translator of Soviet poetry for the journal* Internationale Literatur *and immediately after Hitler's treacherous attack on the Soviet Union began her active antifascist work for the underground radio station operated by Radio Moscow. . . . After returning from exile, she moved to Berlin and here, in her tireless efforts on behalf of world peace and Socialism, she began to publish her first autonomous literary works.* (p. 177, original emphasis)[43]

Presumably published in a Berlin newspaper and celebrating the deceased as a major author of socialist literature, the obituary presents the protagonist as a representative of the values of the GDR. This is apparently how the author of the obituary, as well as the newspaper, wants the nation's inhabitants to remember her. When I compare this variant of collective memory with the memory of the protagonist that I have formed by reading the narrative discourse, I agree with several points. However, there are omissions that make me pause. While the protagonist's opposition to the values of

Nazism was strong and consistent, she was probably less sure about the values of Soviet communism—particularly the variant of communism she experienced when struggling to write the different accounts of her life, and also the version of communist rule that led to her death in a Gulag camp.

This observation is affiliated with another, though related difference between the obituary and the accounts of herself the protagonist writes in communist Russia: whereas the obituary aims to present an authoritative, official picture of an important person who, contributing to the socialist values of the GDR, becomes, or should become, part of the nation's collective memory, the protagonist's own accounts are less stable and more exploratory, groping for the right phrases and attempting to decide which parts of her story to include and which parts to exclude. In contrast to an obituary, the predominant generic features of the protagonist's accounts are those of autobiography and testimony. Whether or not these two genres assume the form of an independent story (as do the testimonies discussed in Chapter 1) or are integrated into the narrative fiction of a novel, they lead the reader to expect that the information provided is true, or at least not false. But true or false for whom, and how does the reader/recipient of the protagonist's accounts understand truth? What is the reader's version or conception of a truth the protagonist may not know? When her husband, "Comrade H.," is arrested, he is interrogated by a party official who asks, "*What does 'not at that time' mean? I have to say I don't have the impression that this testimony is completely truthful*" (p. 153, original emphasis).[44] Does the official know something H. does not? Since the interrogating official knows that H. lives in Moscow with his wife, also named "Comrade H.," does he suspect H. of lying to protect his wife? Moreover, does the protagonist think, or suspect, that H. has been withholding information to protect her, thus failing to make his testimony "*completely truthful*"? Is his false, or incomplete, testimony one reason he has disappeared?

Discussing Holocaust testimonies in Chapter 1, I referred to Derrida's observation that although

> the testimonial is by law irreducible to the fictional, there is no testimony that does not structurally imply in itself the possibility of fiction, simulacra, dissimulation, lie, and perjury—that is to say, the possibility of literature, of the innocent or perverse literature that innocently plays at perverting all of these distinctions. (2000, pp. 29–30)

My discussion of the protagonist's accounts of her life in book 3 suggests that, in addition to identifying the basic constituent elements of the genre, Derrida's remarks on testimony also indicate the possible effects or consequences that characters' (forced or optional) use of aspects of testimony can have in a fictional narrative.[45] Both versions of Comrade H.—that is, husband and wife—appeal to the faith of the other. I have noted that since the protagonist experiences the other as "faceless," she feels she does not know to whom she is addressing her accounts. This uncertainty, she realizes, may make her testimony less convincing; it may reduce the faith of the other. The passage that records the official's questions and H.'s answers includes no reference to the interrogating official's face—it is as though he represents the authorities who have ordered H.'s arrest.

The complexity of the novel's narrative ethics is enhanced by the ways in which the third-person narrative incorporates textual segments of first-person narrative, such as the protagonist's accounts of her life in book 3 and her obituary at the beginning of book 4. As the protagonist's accounts are written by her, the identity of that first-person narrator seems clear—although, as I have indicated, she is unsure about her identity. In other cases, however, references or quotations—often presented in italics in the text—are not related to an identifiable narrator. I have already mentioned an example of this narrative variant in book 2: "*Fire, locusts, leeches, plague, bears, foxes, snakes, insects, lice.*" As the inhabitants of Vienna gave such insulting names to Jews, the narrative discourse presents them as collective rather than individual utterances—and thus also as parts of a collective memory of those utterances and attitudes. A further variant on the novel's narrative presentation of speech, thoughts, and writing is references to and quotations from literary works—some, though by no means all, of which are clearly identified.

These variants complicate the novel's narrative ethics by inviting the reader to ask questions; their ethical dimension is stronger and more insistent on a second reading than on a first. This effect, which it not just aesthetic and ethical but also interpretive, is strengthened by the way Erpenbeck makes her narrator combine the narrative presentation of speech, thoughts, and writing with perspectival variation. The element of interpretation becomes conspicuous in passages or textual segments that I find confusing and difficult to understand. The italicized segment in which H. is interrogated is an illustrative example. Neither the third-person narrator nor the protagonist introduces the passage, which opens thus: "*I understand that Comrade H. has been living for approximately three years together with his wife, Comrade H., in Moscow*" (p. 153, original emphasis).[46] I have suggested that the "I" who is speaking here is probably a party official who, perhaps partly because of that function, is skeptical about H.'s testimony. But who is he exactly? Does the protagonist know the textual segment, or has the third-person narrator inserted it to show the reader how ignorant the protagonist is of her own situation? As my inability to answer these questions aligns my perspective with the protagonist's perspective, I find that my questions may also be her questions—and vice versa. The questions' self-interpretive signs further my own interpretation by inciting me to ask more questions, including: How would I have acted if I were forced to account for myself or testify under these circumstances? Can I be sure I would not have lied to protect a person I love? If I did, would that lie be unethical? Would I have been able to trust my own memory, including the memory of somebody or something I had tried to forget?

While my own experience—including my memories, perspective, actions, and thoughts—affects my interpretation of *Aller Tage Abend*, it is also influenced, and in one sense aided, by the novel's self-interpretive elements, a number of which, as I have suggested, assume the form of questions. One reason these questions become ethical is that, rereading the novel, those that are distinctly, even insistently ethical color my understanding of *all* the questions—especially those asked by the protagonist. Moreover, when I reread the novel I tend, more often than I did when I first read it, to relate the protagonist's questions to the narrator's reflections, many of which also address ethical issues and challenges. Although both these interpretive processes are initiated by Erpenbeck as implied author, my interpretation of the narrator's questions and reflections is uniquely my own. Variants of this interpretive pattern underlie all the points about *Aller Tage Abend* made in this chapter—and indeed all the texts discussed in this book. I write "variants" because my interpretation aims, and needs, to respond to variations of the narrative discourse. One such modulation is that since the protagonist is an old woman in her last two lives, she asks fewer questions in books 4 and 5. The reason for this change may be that she is starting to suffer from dementia—her cognitive abilities are reduced. Toward the end of book 4, her son, who plays a key role in the last two chapters, reflects on the challenge of remembering his mother after her passing:

Will he have to pick up her glasses to remember her eyes, her wallet to remember her fingers, a pair of shoes to see her feet eternally in their shoes, and her woolen blanket to remember until the end of days how her body looked when she was napping after lunch? How many objects and coverings will be needed if she is to retain at least a life of memory inside him? (p. 198)[47]

It is as though, reflecting on these questions, Sasha admits to himself that it will prove almost impossible to keep his mother in mind as she was and as he would have liked to remember her. Rereading the passage, I register a touch of irony here: when Sasha has the opportunity to acquire his great-grandmother's Goethe edition in Vienna in book 5, one reason he does not do so is that volume 9 is damaged. That it was damaged in Brody at the beginning of the 20th century by a stone thrown by pogromists, and that it is perhaps the single most important physical object the family may still possess, he does not know. Although he now "tries to see himself through his mother's eyes, from the outside, as it were," he recognizes that "this is difficult" (p. 199).[48] It is hard, the narrative suggests, to adopt another's perspective, and it is even more demanding if the person is gone—whether he or she is dead or absent.

The word "difficult" therefore applies not just to the problem of remembering his mother but also to not forgetting his father. That this is also a great challenge becomes evident when the father, who has been absent all of Sasha's life, suddenly appears out of nowhere, has a short conversation with his son in his deceased wife's study, and then disappears again, leaving Sasha entirely alone. What is the significance of this strange scene at the very end of book 4? I am inclined to think that the father leaves his son not because he wants to but because, for some reason he does not explain, he has to. Whatever the motive or the reason, the father will be alone, and it will be difficult for him to remember both his son and his wife. As regards Sasha, the narrative reveals a memory trajectory that is different yet perhaps just as painful—provided Sasha had known what happened to his family in the Holocaust.

This last point anticipates my discussion of the second of two ethical concerns of the narrative of book 5: the violent intrusion of the Holocaust into the protagonist's family. Importantly, however, I read about this intrusion— the Nazis' murder of three members of her family—*after* I have read about the process of forgetting and the difficulty of remembering that, in my interpretation, constitute the first ethical concern of book 5. Since the narrative's order (Genette, 1980) is crucial here, I first comment on the processes of forgetting and remembering presented at the beginning of book 5. For the first time, just before she dies, the protagonist has a name: "The week Frau Hoffmann is going to die, the day after her ninetieth birthday, Sister Renate has the early shift" (p. 209).[49] Presumably, then, "Frau Hoffmann" is "Comrade H." It is mildly ironic that when the protagonist is given a name, she is no longer sure who she is nor where she is nor what time it is. There is also a touch of irony in the excerpts of dialogue that reveal fragments of Frau Hoffmann's memory of her time in Moscow. When breakfast is served at the nursing home, she claims that thousands of people have been invited: "But Frau Hoffmann, there really aren't thousands of us here. Yes—thousands! And I don't know why these people have assembled here, I cannot determine the cause, the purpose of this meeting—but it must have a purpose!" (p. 210)[50] Yet the combination of irony and humor in this passage does not imply that the protagonist is being ridiculed in any way. Although, as an old woman suffering from dementia, Frau Hoffmann has problems with her short-term memory, she still remembers fragments of her political activities in Moscow, including key words such as "cause," "purpose," and "meeting." Why does she remember these fragments? Perhaps one reason is that, no longer recalling which day of the week it is in the present, she remembers perfectly well the anxiety and fear she experienced after her husband had been arrested in Moscow: "Beside Frau Millner, Frau Hoffmann sits with her eyes shut, counting the seconds, because she knows that the executions start at eight o'clock. Every minute a group of ten prisoners is shot" (p. 218).[51] By making her narrator present Frau Hoffmann's fragment of memory in this way, Erpenbeck indicates that when the protagonist is counting "One. Two. Three." (p. 218) she is remembering some of the most frightening and painful moments of her life.[52] The counting, which makes no sense to those around her, illustrates the relevance as well as the truth of the narrator's comment: "The day room is full of stories not being told" (p. 219).[53]

The ethics of the early part of book 5 is shaped, and gradually strengthened, by the interaction of three narrative elements. First, signaling the narrator's respect for the protagonist's pacifist conviction and her hatred of war, it reveals her care for and anxiety about her husband, Comrade H., or, as I gather at this stage of the narrative, Herr Hoffmann. Second, I read this part of the novel as a contribution to and defense of an ethics of caring not limited to Frau Hoffmann and the other patients at the nursing home in Berlin. The strongest contributing factor to such an ethics of care, or caring, is the work patiently and respectfully carried out by Sister Renate and her colleagues at the home. The ethics of this work has an intrinsic value; that value is extended to include care for other individuals or groups of people who are weak or vulnerable.[54] Concomitantly, I am being invited to consider an alternative ethics of *not* caring for, perhaps even despising and in the last instance murdering such individuals or groups. This interpretive invitation illustrates the way in which the narrative makes me think of the ethics of Nazism—and of the Holocaust as a mass murder of Jews consonant with that ethics. Third, the early part of book 5 portrays the processes of memory and forgetting that establish a basis for the narrative presentation of Sasha as the only survivor of the family.

The combination of these three narrative details shapes and highlights a key ethical aspect of book 5. Sasha is in Vienna, looking for information about this family and for family items. However, Sasha "knows neither who his great-grandmother was, nor where she lived.... As far as this descendent of a Viennese resident is concerned, ... it took less than a human lifetime for the city to lose all connection to him" (p. 224).[55] Even though, here as in virtually the whole narrative, Erpenbeck is using her third-person narrator as her main narrative instrument, in this case I am not sure who is speaking. Is the narrator perhaps making a more categorical statement here than the implied author does, or would have done? As noted above, I understand the third-person narrator as part of the fictional world (though not a character in the plot), while the implied author is the idea or image of the author that I form when reading and rereading the narrative text. However, if, as I am inclined to think, there is an attitudinal difference here between the narrator's unqualified statement and the implied author's assessment and reflections, that kind of tension does not impair or discourage my interpretive effort. Rather, it is related to and intensifies the questions I ask when reading the following passage:

> The son can make his home anywhere in the world, in Berlin for example. If he knew what questions to ask, knew what, where, and to whom, then an official of the Jewish Community of Vienna would surely be able to dig up one or the other list and inform him that his great-grandmother was brought to Opole in the district of Lublin with the first transport of

February '41, that his grandmother moved six times within Vienna and then was sent via Minsk to Maly Trostenets in July '42, and that his aunt spent many months hiding in a friend's apartment and then was sent in '44 to Auschwitz. But given what he knows, he finds Vienna just as dusty as any other metropolis. (pp. 224–225)[56]

I have already coupled this key passage with the last paragraph of book 3. Taken together, these two textual segments of *Aller Tage Abend* place the Holocaust, a word not used once in the novel, at the center of its narrative ethics. The passage is shocking in two ways that mutually reinforce each other: while I am shaken to learn that so many members of the protagonist's family perished in the Holocaust, I also find it shocking—and deeply worrying—that Sasha, the only survivor, is ignorant of what happened to his great-grandmother, his grandmother, and his aunt. Having commented on the information that could be provided about each of these members of Sasha's family, I return to the ethical challenge that his lack of knowledge about them poses to me as a reader.

Although it could have been a coincidence in historical reality, in Erpenbeck's fictional universe it is not coincidental that the three family members murdered in the Holocaust belong to and represent three different generations. One implication of this generational range is that, had the protagonist and her son lived in Vienna at the end of the war and not in Moscow, they might both have been deported to Auschwitz together with Sasha's aunt. That the great-grandmother is the first family member to be murdered in the Holocaust affirms her Jewish identity while at the same time strengthening the narrative connection between this passage at the end of the novel and the attack on her and her husband at the narrative's beginning. As a constituent element of the novel's structure, this narrative connection is literary; as it highlights the contest of values and the use of violence, it is also ethical. While Sasha's great-grandfather is killed in an unprovoked attack stirred by antisemitism, she,

[t]he owner of the Goethe edition and the clock is already nearly eighty when she has to leave everything behind, and in February '41, leaning on her cousin's arm, she begins her journey to the Jewish Home for the Aged on Malzgasse, which, for the sake of convenience, has been designated the first collection point for deportations to the East. (p. 226)[57]

Presented at the beginning of the next chapter of book 5, this sentence introduces an analepsis that gives me a little more information about the background for the great-grandmother's deportation. There is a lot I do not understand, however. How did the Nazis find her in Vienna? Is her cousin not Jewish, since he apparently could move around freely in the city? What I think I understand, though, is that her Jewish identity is the sole reason she is arrested and that it is painful for her to leave the Goethe edition and the clock behind. The twofold importance of the edition of Goethe's *Collected Works* is thus reinforced: not only does Goethe, and by implication the humanism and tolerance of the literature he created, represent an opposition and a positive alternative to the values of Nazism; for the great-grandmother, the edition is also a precious memory of her husband, who was its first owner. Forced to leave the edition behind, she can no longer remember him the way these volumes, that is, literature, have enabled her to do. The vulnerability or fragility of memory is further explored by the way in which the narrator associated the great-grandmother's experience of losing the Goethe edition with Sasha's thoughts about the same edition 50 years later. Looking for a present to take back from Vienna to his mother in Berlin, he comes across the edition in a secondhand bookshop. Pulling out "Volume 9, the spine of which is a bit scraped . . . [he] puts the book back in its place. How can he carry an entire Goethe edition on the train to Berlin?" (p. 226).[58] There is dramatic irony in this question: had he known the edition's familial history he would certainly have bought it, but as he is ignorant of that history he does not. What is a practical question for him becomes an ethical question in the narrative discourse. The narrator's ability to move between different temporal layers creates a thought-provoking interlinking of memory and knowledge as well as, correspondingly, lack of knowledge and loss of memory. The relevance of this interlinking to the challenge of remembering the Holocaust is strong. How can I remember an event about which I know little, perhaps almost nothing? Moreover, given my limited knowledge, how can I then reflect on the Nazis' motives for their crime and on the contest of values involved?

My questions as a reader are inspired by questions that Sasha could have asked himself, but the narrative discourse makes me unsure whether he does. The loss associated with his inability to recognize the value of his great-grandmother's edition is accentuated when the narrator returns to and extends the analepsis that provides a partial explanation of how and when the deportations in the family happened. After the great-grandmother's cousin has taken her to the Jewish Home for the Aged, he takes her Goethe edition and her clock to different addresses in Vienna, trying to locate the person he can give the objects to. Finally, he finds the woman to whom the "objects speak without speaking, and the woman now knows something she didn't want to know: that there is a moment when it is forever too late" (p. 227).[59] The woman is the great-grandmother's daughter, who later receives orders to move to a different location in Vienna: "Although the woman finds these moves quite burdensome, she nonetheless lugs the *Complete Works* of Goethe along with her, as well as the clock, these last two remaining possessions of her mother, who has long since been deported" (p. 228).[60] While the great-grandmother carries the Goethe edition with her as a memory of her husband, her daughter does so to remember her mother. If the clock measures the process of remembering, it also, as Sasha's ignorance of the murdered members of his family reveals, indicates the process of forgetting. Both processes accentuate the narrative dimension of remembering as well as of forgetting (Brockmeier, 2015; Ricoeur, 2000/2006). Moreover, the clock can measure the "moment when it is forever too late." For Sasha's grandmother, the act of receiving the clock from her mother's cousin is one such moment; she knows that the clock will never show the time when mother and daughter can meet again. There is a suggestive connection between the phrase "forever too late" and the last sentence of the following passage:

> But no forest has grown as of August 13, 1942, when she boards the train at the Aspang Station in Vienna that will take her to Minsk. Forcing the doors, clearing out the shared apartment that served as a transit station for Jews at Hammer-Purgstall-Gasse 3/12, and making an inventory takes the Gestapo's Division for the Processing of Jewish Personal Effects two and a half days. The clock has meanwhile come to a stop. (p. 228)[61]

Before joining the German word for "forest," *Wald*, with that for a small forest, *Wäldchen*, I note that this passage gives the reader more details about the way the deportation system worked than does the sentence that refers to the deportation of the great-grandmother. As Raul Hilberg tells Lanzmann (and the viewer) in *Shoah*, the Nazis developed an elaborate system of transporting Jews "to the East," and the passage informs me about parts of this system. That the clock has stopped suggests that the grandmother's life will come to an end very soon. There was also a system of distributing and selling Jews' possessions, including, in this case, the clock and the Goethe edition. Opening the heavy suitcase and discovering that it contains books, the Gestapo officer is dismissive of its value: "nothing but books, just look what's on the back of them: nothing but Goethe; he slams the suitcase shut again. *To be or not to be*, he says, grinning, as he gets to his feet" (p. 229, original emphasis).[62]

The quotation's last sentence indicates a very considerable attitudinal distance between the narrator and the Gestapo officer. Erpenbeck as the implied author distances herself from the Nazis' values, including those revealed by their attitude to literature. As I also feel a need to distance myself from the officer, I recognize that the only way of doing so is by reading, rereading, and interpreting the novel. My interpretation of its narrative discourse stresses two aspects of the passage's narrative ethics.[63] First, when the Gestapo officer refers to the suitcase's content as "nothing but books . . . nothing but Goethe," he not only inadvertently reveals his ignorance of the value of literature as an integral part of European civilization but also shows that he is contributing to the destruction of that civilization. I write "European" rather than German civilization because his quotation of the most famous line from Shakespeare's *Hamlet* extends its realm both spatially and temporally. My attitudinal distance from the officer is strengthened and confirmed by the irony to which he is subjected by the narrative discourse.

Second, I am forced to realize that, important as it is for me to stress that my values are opposed to those of the officer, that attempt may disclose an interpretive impasse. The officer's "grinning, as he gets to his feet" incites the sense of hopelessness that becomes part of my experience of reading and interpreting this passage. While I find the officer's attitude to and words about Goethe and Shakespeare uncivilized and vulgar, I realize that he does exactly what is required of him as a contributor to the Holocaust. That its implementation was uncivilized made it more effective. The Gestapo officer's combined ignorance of and disrespect for literature is extended to include contempt for different kinds of writing, including notebooks and diaries. Thus, there is a connection between the part of the chapter that describes the Gestapo officer's dismissal of the Goethe edition and the notebooks referred to in the closing paragraph of book 2.

That the connection is unclear does not make it less significant; on the contrary, from my perspective it may be the most important link established in and through the narrative discourse. It is condensed into a constellation of two words, *Wald* and *Birkenwäldchen*. The word *Wald* occurs at the beginning of the passage just discussed: "But no forest has grown as of August

13, 1942, when she boards the train at the Aspang Station in Vienna that will take her to Minsk." The "but" refers back to the preceding sentence, in which the narrator asks herself—and me as a reader—why the clock and the Goethe edition are so valuable, even indispensable, for the grandmother: "Perhaps there's secretly something magical about these inherited belongings, just like in the fairy tale, where, in time of need, a comb thrown over your shoulder can grow into a forest" (p. 228).[64] There is both a contrast and a connection between "a forest" (*ein Wald*) and "no forest" (*kein Wald*), and this combination of contrast and connection is coupled with the word *Birkenwäldchen* at the end of book 2. As I relate that word to the extermination camp Birkenau, I also associate the combination of *ein Wald* and *kein Wald* with Sasha's aunt, who, as the key paragraph quoted above informs me, "was sent in '44 to Auschwitz." Why does the narrative not give me more information about the deportation of the protagonist's younger sister? One reason could be that all the information the narrator can give me has already been provided in the paragraph that includes the word *Birkenwäldchen*. This word is a self-interpretive element that influences my interpretation, particularly when, rereading the novel, I connect it with the repetition of *Wald*. *Birkenwäldchen* is as close as Erpenbeck wants or is able to take me to the site of the Holocaust. In *Aller Tage Abend* as in *Austerlitz*, the narrative's emphasis is on the deportations—on the forced movement *nach dem Osten*. Without making these two novels more similar than they are, they both gravitate toward the Holocaust, a word that neither of them includes. The Holocaust thus becomes a blank in the narrative, an ellipsis that approximates to a paralipsis—something so decisive, definite, and painful that it becomes unmentionable.

That said, there is a very considerable difference between the protagonist and first-person narrator Austerlitz's search for his parents and, in Erpenbeck's novel, the third-person narrator's brief reference to the woman, later identified as Sasha's aunt, who is murdered at Auschwitz-Birkenau. What the paragraph at the end of book 2 does, in addition to reporting that a Jewish woman is being murdered, is highlight the notebooks the woman is carrying. The way these *Tagebuchaufzeichnungen* are related to *Birkenwäldchen*, on the one hand, and to the later information about the deportations of the great-grandmother and the grandmother, on the other, constitutes the center of the novel's narrative ethics. The possibility that the woman may be carrying her sister's diary suggests that memory, including the value of a good memory as well as the challenge of a traumatic one, plays a key role in this ethics. If the notebook is invaluable to the woman because it is a memory of her older sister, then it may mean just as much to her as the Goethe edition does to her grandmother. A different, though related interpretive possibility is that, inspired by her older sister, she has become a writer herself. In any case, the notebook represents values opposed to those of the sentry who forces the woman onward, causing her to drop it. As a result, both she and her diary are destroyed, and the possibility of a full life that includes good memories disappears.

From this perspective, *Birkenwäldchen* is an oxymoron that consists of two contradictory elements: the extermination camp Birkenau-Auschwitz symbolizes murder and death and, more precisely, the mass murder of six million Jews; conversely, "a small forest of birch trees" symbolizes growth and life and, more specifically, the "magical" quality of "inherited belongings, just like in the fairy tale, where, in time of need, a comb thrown over your shoulder can grow into a forest." In my interpretation of *Aller Tage Abend*, the contradiction of this oxymoron is not resolved. But it reinforces the ethical questions I have identified and discussed, especially those related to and revolving around the challenge of not forgetting the Holocaust and the fragility of memory as time passes and new generations' knowledge about the Nazis' crime decreases. Perhaps the most pressing question is this: How can I remember, or not forget, what I do not know? This question leads me to conclude that, as regards the narrative presentation of values in *Aller Tage Abend*, Sasha plays a key role.

Sasha cares for his mother, and he is by no means uninterested in the history of his family. It is also possible that his memory, or lack of memory, is marked by his childhood in Russia and his father's absence. After his mother dies, having fallen down the stairs in book 4, he has many questions he would have asked her, but "[a]long with his mother, the answers to all these questions have died as well" (p. 187).[65] Since I consider Sasha's mother to be a Holocaust survivor, I interpret her silence—including, for example, her inability to answer questions Sasha might have asked her about her grandmother's Goethe edition—as a reflection on the challenge of not forgetting the Holocaust when the last time witnesses are gone. I conclude that there is a twofold reason the thrust of that silence involves a measure of uncertainty (or even pessimism): first, it is associated with the lack of knowledge represented by Sasha; second, it is related to the irrevocable loss of the invaluable authority that the Holocaust survivors possess because of their unique experience.

This concluding point is supported by four observations that also build on and follow from the narrative analysis presented in this chapter. First, Erpenbeck's narrative in *Aller Tage Ende* enables her to create a fictional universe in which the characters' experiences of events are distinctly individual and yet thought-provokingly collective. Reading and rereading the narrative, I find that the protagonist's many lives become believable as constituent elements of the narrative fiction while at the same time being anchored in and providing a fictional interpretation of historical events and processes of 20th-century Europe. Since the historical information is largely correct, as a reader I learn a lot about that history; importantly, I am encouraged, even urged to learn more—particularly about the Holocaust.

Second, Erpenbeck's perspective and speech presentation are constituent elements of that discourse. The third-person narrator plays a key role here, moving from one character to another, adopting different perspectives and relaying their speech as well as their thoughts to the reader. Sometimes the narrator is very close to the character Erpenbeck makes her focus on. The most salient example occurs in chapter 17 of book 2, in which the protagonist's mother becomes a first-person narrator: "Was she crying? I don't think so. I was just surprised when she refused to get up" (p. 87).[66] The mother is worried about her elder daughter, who is mourning her friend's death. Why does Erpenbeck suddenly use a first-person narrator here, and why does she revert to using a third-person narrator again in the following chapter? One possible reason could be to show how closely the third-person narrator is related to the characters, particularly the protagonist. However, as this explanation does not account for the segment in chapter 4 of book 3 where an unidentified "I" interrogates Comrade H. in Moscow, the essential point to make here is that the novel's narrative discourse assumes the form of a third-person narrative that incorporates a number of first-person narratives, including the protagonist's accounts of herself and her notebook that disappears together with her younger sister. As this event demonstrates, the thrust of this remarkably elastic, fragmented, and yet connected narrative is ethical.

Third, the novel's ethics is presented through and represented by all the characters, including those I want or need to distance myself from. Both interpretive processes, those that involve ethical distancing as well as those that further ethical approximation, build on self-interpretive elements that I respond to in my processes of reading and rereading. While the third-person narrator's presentation of the characters gives me an idea of their values, her attitude to them varies from acceptance and endorsement to critical distance. The ethics of Erpenbeck as implied author draws on the narrator's as well as the characters' ethics. Rereading the novel, I am forcibly struck by the way ethical issues and concerns are presented as questions asked by the characters, by the third-person narrator, and sometimes through a narrative discourse in which the narrator's ethics is blended with that of one or more characters. Three questions asked by the protagonist just before she dies in chapter 24 of book 2 provide an example: "Why wasn't she allowed to tell anyone that her grandmother was Jewish? Was there really so little love in the world that it wasn't enough to glue things together? Why were there differences, why this hierarchy of worth?" (p. 101).[67]

Demonstrating the disastrous consequences of such a "hierarchy of worth," Erpenbeck shows how the characters' lives are connected in ways that defy the differences in the world. Whether she does so as historical author, I do not know, as my image of her as implied author is built on my reading and interpretation of the narrative discourse of her novel. And yet, as in the case of Sebald, it is not irrelevant that Erpenbeck is German; born in Berlin in 1967, she spent her childhood in the German Democratic Republic. There is no doubt that her memory of that period, including the Cold War and the reunification of Germany in 1989, has left a mark on her that underlies the narrative of the novel (Hähnel-Mesnard, 2022; Poltermann, 2015). Combined with her postmemory of the Holocaust, the memory of the collapse of the GDR and Germany's reunification also influences the narrative's ethics.[68] Whether, or in what way, this knowledge changes my interpretation of *Aller Tage Abend* I am not sure, however, since it is the narrative discourse, and especially the questions it includes, that makes the ethics of that discourse insistent and thought-provoking, inviting me to ask my own ethical questions. Yet I conclude that some basic knowledge about Erpenbeck as historical author gives an edge to these questions. One of the most difficult and pressing is whether and in what way I am implicated in the matrix of the Holocaust. Can I be certain that my values, especially those of which I may not be conscious and those I unknowingly suppress, are good values in the sense of furthering actions that would oppose the Holocaust? More specifically, would I, in a given situation, have had the moral determination and courage to act in accordance with my values to save the life of somebody who was in danger? These questions take me back to the point of departure constituted by my reflections on the *Donau* in the introduction.

These questions also take me to a concluding comment on the way Erpenbeck's novel presents ethical questions as ethical challenges framed by history and context. I am certainly not implying that, to continue using the example from the novel just quoted, the question of human worth is not a general, ahistorical ethical demand; if it is not, then "a hierarchy of worth" emerges immediately. What the novel suggests, though, is that as human beings we can deal with ethical challenges only in specific situations that are part of a given familial and societal context and that contribute, albeit perhaps in a modest way, to the formation of history from within. The values presented in *Aller Tage Abend* are expressed and represented by the characters and narrators' memories. It is the novel's fabric of narratives that creates the connections between its different parts—temporal and spatial relations and transitions that invest a bleak narrative with a spark of hope for the future.

Notes

1. "Noch im vergangenen Sommer sind wir/von hier nach Marienbad gefahren./Und jetzt, wohin fahren wir jetzt? (W. G. Sebald in 'Austerlitz')" (Erpenbeck, 2012, p. vii). Subsequent citations are given in parentheses in the text.
2. Before the German invasion, the spa of Marienbad (Mariánské Lázně) was a center of international Jewish bath tourism. See *Encyclopedia of Jewish History and Culture*, https://referenceworks.brillonline.com/entries/encyclopedia-of-jewish-history-and-culture/marienbad-COM_0513#d5725068e41
3. This comment also applies to the other narratives interpreted in this book.
4. A helpful collection of essays is Marx and Schöll (2014); a thoughtful monograph that relates Erpenbeck's work to the German authors Lutz Seiler and Julia Schoch is Hähnel-Mesnard (2022). Schubert (2016) discusses *Aller Tage Abend* by linking the novel to German history. Referring mainly to Erpenbeck's *Gehen, ging, gegangen (Go, Went, Gone)* but implicitly also to *Aller Tage Abend*, Meretoja (2021) and Ritivoi (2023) consider variants of memory and translation as a resource for other-oriented empathy in processes of dialogical understanding. Polterman (2015) and Erlanger (2024) have published informative interviews with Erpenbeck.
5. "Der Herr hat's gegeben, der Herr hat's genommen, hatte die Grossmutter am Rand der Grube zu ihr gesagt. Aber das stimmte nicht, denn der Herr hatte viel mehr genommen, als da war—auch alles, was aus dem Kind hätte werden können, lag jetzt da unten und sollte unter die Erde" (2012, p. 11).
6. "Jetzt sitzt sie auf dieser kleinen Fussbank aus Holz, die sie von ihrer Grossmutter zur Hochzeit bekommen hat, sitzt da mit geschlossenen Augen, so wie sie andere in Zeiten der Trauer hat sitzen sehen. . . . Nach jüdischem Brauch haben sie es heute begraben, und nach jüdischem Brauch wird sie nun auf der Fussbank sitzen für sieben Tage, doch der Mann spricht nicht mit ihr" (2012, pp. 14, 16).
7. "Wo kann denn die Seele des Kindes nun hin? Ins Fegefeuer, ins Paradies oder die Hölle? . . . Vielleicht gab es doch jenseits des Lebens einfach nur nichts?" (2012, p. 16).
8. The collective body of Jewish religious laws, based on the written and oral Torah.
9. The Nuremberg race laws, announced by the Nazi regime on September 15, 1935, are often associated with the Nuremberg rallies (cf. the discussion of *Triumph of the Will* in Chapter 2).
10. "Erst damals war ihr klargeworden, dass auch sie selbst eigentlich jüdischer Herkunft war" (2012, p. 107).

11. "Aber Andrej hörte nicht, oder tat so, als ob er nicht hörte, was wahrscheinlicher war, denn er wusste ja, wer in dem Haus lebte, das er. mit Steinen bewarf. Dann flog ein Stein von Andrej durch eine Fensterscheibe, flog nur um Haaresbreite an ihrem Kopf vorbei, krachte hinter ihr in den verglasten Bücherschrank und traf den 9. Band der in Leder gebundenen Gesamtausgabe von Goethe, die ihr Mann von seinen Eltern als Geschenk zum Schulabschluss bekommen hatte. *Keine Luft von keiner Seite!/Todesstille fürchterlich!/In der ungeheuern Weite/Reget keine Welle sich!*" (2012, p. 19). The lines are repeated in chapter 30 of book 2, this time linked to the perspective of the grandmother's daughter, who together with her husband sees Goethe's *Iphigenie auf Tauris* at the Burgtheater in Vienna. *Iphigenie* is the title of her granddaughter's (i.e., the protagonist's) first novel.
12. "Dann ist sie eine jüdische Witwe, die den Tod an der Hand hält" (2012, pp. 21–22).
13. "und von Andrej, den sie von Kindesbeinen an kennt" (2012, p. 21).
14. This observation does not mean that there is no ambivalence in Erpenbeck's use of Goethe and the literature he created as an ethical counterpoint to Nazism. Some readers may even find the references to Goethe ironic: the fact that many Nazis knew his *Collected Works* did not stop the advance of Nazism in Germany.
15. This interpretation is inspired more strongly by the German original than by the English translation. The German words *Todesstille, fürchterlich*, and *ungeheuer* can all be associated with the Holocaust.
16. "Am Ende eines Tages, und dem gestorben wurde, ist längst noch nicht aller Tage Abend" (2012, p. 23).
17. Although the historical references in Erpenbeck's novel do not function in exactly the same way as in Littell's *Les Bienveillantes*, in both novels they insistently relate the fictional work to historical reality. Moreover, as the references are often historically correct, they strengthen the narrator's authority. As regards narrative presentations of the Holocaust, this is crucial.
18. "Hätte aber zum Beispiel die Mutter oder der Vater . . . eine Handvoll Schnee . . . dem Kind unters Hemd gesteckt, dann hätte das Kind vielleicht plötzlich wieder angefangen zu atmen, vielleicht auch zu schreien, jedenfalls hätte sein Herz wieder angefangen zu schlagen" (2012, p. 71). Erpenbeck's use of the hypothetical subjunctive *hätte* enhances the element of play and artistic imagination in this intermezzo, as well as in the following ones, even more strongly than does the English translation.
19. "Wenn sie aber schläft, setzt er sich gern neben ihr Bett und unternimmt einen weiteren Versuch zu ergründen, was ihm seit einiger Zeit als das grosse Rätsel der Menschheitsgeschichte erscheint: wie nämlich Vorgänge, Zustände oder Ereignisse, die allgemeiner Natur sind—zum Beispiel ein Krieg, oder lang andauernder Hunger, oder auch ein Beamtengehalt . . . in ein beliebiges privates Gesicht hineinschlüpfen können. Hier machen ein paar Haare grau, dort fressen sie ein paar liebliche Wangen auf, bis die Haut nur über kantige Kiefernknochen gespannt ist. . . . Von ganz weit aussen nach ganz weit innen wird also fortwährend übersetzt" (2012, p. 88).
20. "dass er am Krieg gestorben war" (2012, p. 160).
21. "*Feuer, Heuschrecken, Blutegel, Pest*, oder *Bären, Füchse, Schlangen, Wanzen* und *Läuse* wurden die Juden hier in Wien immer wieder genannt, aber sie hatte das nicht gewusst" (2012, p. 81).
22. "Im Jahr 1944 wird in einem Birkenwäldchen ein Heft mit handschriftlichen Tagebuchaufzeichnungen auf die Erde fallen, als ein Wachposten eine junge Frau mit seinem Gewehrkolben vorwärts stösst, und sie sich mit den Armen, mit denen sie vorher das Heft gedrückt hat, zu schützen versucht. Das Heft wird in den Dreck fallen, und die Frau wird nicht zurückkommen können, um es aufzuheben, das Heft wird ein Weilchen dort liegen, Wind und Regen werden darin blättern, Schritte werden darüber hinweggehen, bis alle Geheimnisse, die dort aufgeschrieben sind, die gleiche Farbe haben wie der Morast" (2012, p. 132).
23. As Jens Brockmeier has informed me, the English translation also misses the aspect of meaning that comes with the German diminutive *-chen*, *Birkenwäldchen*, which is often used in children's discourse. Thus, a tiny element of fairy tale—and perhaps of hope?—may be embedded in a word whose echo of the Holocaust makes it at once desolate and brutally realistic.
24. "Sie hätte die Exzerpte des Vaters aus dem 'Aufzeichnungen über Erdbeben in der Steiermark' an sich genommen und daraus unter Tränen ihren ersten Artikel gemacht: *Soll die Erde sich doch noch einmal auftun und die Kriegsgewinnler verschlingen!*" (2012, p. 138).
25. "sich durchs Schreiben ins Leben zurückzuschreiben" (2012, pp. 141–142).

26. "Aber was sind die richtigen Worte? Käme sie mit einer Wahrheit weiter als mit einer Lüge?" (2012, p. 142).

27. *"Ich wurde als Tochter eines Beamten 1902 in Brody geboren, hatte also einen bürgerlichen Hintergrund"* (2012, p. 142).

28. "Worin bestand eigentlich ihr bürgerlicher Hintergrund? Darin vielleicht, dass ihre Grossmutter vor über zwanzig Jahren bei der Flucht aus Galizien nach Wien eine Gesamtausgabe von Goethe mitgeschleppt hat?" (2012, p. 142).

29. "Durch die Bewegungen, die in der Gegenwart stattfanden, bewegte sich also auch die Vergangenheit. Aber konnte ein Blick auf die Dinge tatsächlich die Dinge selbst verwandeln?" (2012, p. 160).

30. "Die Bürgen muss sie angeben, auch wenn U. inzwischen aus der Partei ausgeschlossen worden war und nun, von den sowjetischen Gerichten wegen Hochverrats in Abwesenheit zum Tode verurteilt, in Paris lebte" (2012, p. 159).

31. *"verdiente Funktionärin der Kommunistischen Internationale . . . von der Volksfeindin U. beeinflusst"* (2012, p. 160).

32. "Jede von ihnen, sie selbst, ihre Mutter und auch ihre Schwester, hatte damals der Tod des Vaters, der als Tatsache ihnen allen im gleichen Masse entgegentrat, also anders bezeichnet, jede von ihnen ihm eine andere Ursache und Bedeutung gegeben, so als sei nicht anders von ihm zu sprechen, als nur in der Form dieser oder jener Geschichte, als von einem abgestorbenen Ende, das auf die oder jene Weise verwachsen war mit dem Leben einer jenen von ihnen" (2012, pp. 161–162).

33. "ihr Brief an die Mutter schon lange mit dem Stempel *Evakuiert nach dem Osten* an sie zurück, in Wien also keine Familie mehr, wahrscheinlich nirgendwo mehr" (2012, p. 206).

34. "War sie überhaupt jemals dieselbe? Gab es auch nur zwei Momente in ihrem Leben, in denen sie mit sich selbst vergleichbar war? War nicht das Ganze das Wahre? Oder war alles Verrat? Wenn der, für den der den Lebenslauf lesen wird, in sein Gesicht hat, welches soll dann das Gesicht sein, das sie ihm zeigt, welches blinde Gesicht einem blinden Spiegel?" (2012, p. 175).

35. For an incisive discussion of survivors' memories of, as well as fictional narratives about, the Gulag system of forced labor established during Joseph Stalin's reign of the Soviet Union, see Toker (2000).

36. "Als sie noch lebendig war . . . damit sie später im Winter, wenn der Boden gefroren wäre, einen Platz hätten, wo sie sich begraben könnten" (2012, p. 192).

37. Although in Littell's *Les Bienveillantes* Aue tries to distance himself from the *Einsatzgruppen*, his killing of Ibrahim is a chilling example of this brutal practice. See Chapter 4.

38. "Es ist schade, dass man die Grenze nicht sehen kann, an der Worte aus Luft und Worte aus Tinte sich in etwas Wirkliches verwandeln, ebenso wirklich werden wie eine Tüte Mehl, eine Volksmenge, die in Aufruhr gerät, ebenso wirklich wie das Geräusch, mit dem die gefrorenen Knochen der Genossin H. im Winter einundvierzig in eine Grube hinunterrutschen, dieses Geräusch hört sich so an, wie wenn jemand hölzerne Dominosteine in ein Kästchen zurückwirft" (2012, p. 193).

39. "als wäre die Erinnerung auch ein Sturz. Jetzt ist sie zum ersten Mal tatsächlich ein gefallenes Mädchen, und wenn es nicht zum Sterben wäre, müsste sie lachen. Ob ihre Mutter auch an sie gedacht hat in ihrem letzten Moment? Ist das überhaupt der letzte Moment?" (2012, p. 212).

40. "als sie durch ihre Arbeit beim Rundfunk erfuhr, was in den von Deutschland besiegten Ländern mit den Juden geschah" (2012, p. 214).

41. "Der Brief war mit dem Vermerk: *Evakuiert nach dem Osten* zurückgekommen" (2012, p. 214).

42. *"Ich habe inzwischen einen Sohn bekommen, er ist jetzt drei Jahre alt und heisst Sascha"* (2012, p. 214).

43. *"Als Tochter eines österreichischen Beamten in Brody geboren, in Wien aufgewachsen, war sie seit 1920 Mitglied der Kommunistischen Partei. 1933 emigrierte sie über Prag nach Moskau. Dort trug sie zunächst als Übersetzerin für sowjetische Lyrik bei der Zeitschrift* Internationale Literatur *zur Völkerverständigung bei und begann sofort nach dem heimtückischen Überfall Hitlerdeutschlands auf die Sowjetunion ihre aktive antifaschistische Arbeit beim illegalen Sender von Radio Moskau. . . . Nach ihrer Rückkehr aus der Emigration übersiedelte sie nach Berlin und begann hier, in nimmermüdem Einsatz für Frieden und Sozialismus ihre ersten eigenständigen literarischen Werke zu veröffentlichen"* (2012, pp. 211–212)

44. "Was heisst *damals* nicht? Ich muss sagen, ich habe nicht das Gefühl der restlosen Wahrhaftigkeit" (2012, p. 183).

45. Mikhail M. Bakhtin's understanding of the novel as a genre that feeds on and exploits other genres, incorporating them into a complex and evolving narrative structure, provides a partial explanation of Erpenbeck's use of the genre of testimony in *Aller Tage Abend*. See Bakhtin (1982).

46. "Wie ich erfahre, lebt Genosse H. seit ungefähr 3 Jahren mit seiner Frau, der Genossin H., zusammen in Moskau" (2012, p. 182).

47. "Wird er ihre Brille aufheben müssen, um sich an ihre Augen, und ihr Portemonnaie, um sich an ihre Finger zu erinnern, ein Paar Schuhe, um für immer ihre Füsse in den Schuhen zu sehen, und ihre wollene Decke, um sein restliches Leben lang nicht zu vergessen, wie ihr Körper beim Mittagschlaf aussah? Wieviele Hüllen und Dinge wird er brauchen, damit sie wenigstens ihr Erinnerungsleben in seinem Kopf behält?" (2012, p. 236).

48. "Zum ersten Mal versucht er jetzt, sich selbst mit den Augen der Mutter, sozusagen von aussen, zu sehen, aber das fällt ihm schwer" (2012, p. 236).

49. "In der Woche, in der Frau Hoffmann, einen Tag nach ihrem neunzigsten Geburtstag, sterben wird, hat Schwester Renate Frühdienst" (2012, p. 249).

50. "Aber Frau Hoffmann, Tausende sind wir hier wirklich nicht. Doch—Tausende! Und ich weiss nicht, warum diese Menschen zusammengekommen sind, ich kann den Grund, den Sinn dieses Treffens nicht in Erfahrung bringen—aber es muss doch einen Sinn haben!" (2012, p. 250). The German word *Erfahrung* (experience) in the original text indicates even more strongly than the English translation how decisive the years in Moscow were in Frau Hoffmann's life and what a lasting impression her activities in the Communist Party made on her.

51. "Neben Frau Millner sitzt Frau Hoffmann mit geschlossenen Augen und zählt die Sekunden, veil sie weiss, dass seit 8 Uhr mit den Erschiessungen begonnen wurde" (2012, p. 260).

52. Recent research has explored ways in which the identity of a person suffering from dementia can be presented and preserved through storytelling (Hydén & Antelius, 2017).

53. "Eins. Zwei. Drei. . . . Der Aufenthaltsraum ist voll unerzählter Geschichten" (2012, p. 260).

54. The strongest textual indication of this kind of extension of work ethics is the passage at the beginning of part 2 where, after having quoted the first stanza of a popular German song, the narrator comments that while the patients were perhaps five or six years old when they learned it, "[n]ow they sit here singing it with voices that have grown old, locked up in old age as if in a prison" (2014, p. 217). "Jetzt sitzen sie hier und singen es mit ihren altgewordenen Stimmen, ins Alter eingesperrt wie in ein Gefängnis" (2012, p. 259). *A Poetic Language of Ageing* explores the potential of poetry and poetic language as a means of conveying perspectives on later life (Lehmann & Synnes, 2023).

55. "Aber er weiss weder, wer seine Urgrossmutter war, noch, wo sie gewohnt hat. . . . Wien ist, was den Mann angeht, von Geschichten ganz und gar reingewaschen" (2012, p. 266).

56. "Der Sohn kann, wo er will in der Welt, zum Beispiel in Berlin, zu Haus sein. Wenn er wissen würde, welche Fragen er stellen müsste, und das überhaupt und wem, dann hätte ein Beamter der Israelitischen Kultusgemeinde von Wien sicher diese oder jene Liste hervorholen und ihm sagen können, dass seine Urgrossmutter mit dem ersten Transport Februar einundvierzig nach Opole im Distrikt Lublin gebracht wurde, seine Grossmutter nach sechs Umzügen innerhalb Wiens im Juli zweiundvierzig über Minsk nach Maly Trostinez, und die Tante, die sich noch lange bei einer Freundin versteckt gehalten hatte, vierundvierzig nach Auschwitz. So aber ist für den Mann die Stadt Wien so staubig wie jene andere Grosstadt" (2012, p. 267).

57. "An die achtzig Jahre alt ist die Besitzerin der Goethe-Ausgabe und der kleinen Standuhr, als sie alles zurücklassen muss und im Februar einundvierzig, auf den Arm ihres Vetters gestützt, den Weg ins Jüdische Altersheim in der Malzgasse antritt, wo der Einfachheit halber die erste Sammelstelle für Transporte in den Osten eingerichtet worden ist" (2012, p. 269).

58. "den 9. Band, der am Rücken leicht abgeschabt ist . . . stellt den Band dann wieder zurück, denn wie sollte er eine ganze Goethe-Ausgabe im Zug nach Berlin transportieren" (2012, pp. 268–269).

59. "die Dinge sprechen ohne zu sprechen, und die Frau weiss jetzt, was sie nicht wissen wollte, nämlich dass es einen Moment gibt, in dem es für immer zu spät ist" (2012, p. 270).

60. "Obgleich der Frau das Umziehen inzwischen schon schwerfällt, schleppt sie sich beide Male auch mit dem gesamten Goethe ab und mit der Uhr, den zwei Habseligkeiten ihrer bereits deportierten Mutter" (2012, p. 271).

61. "Bis zum 13.8.1942, an dem sie am Aspangbahnhof in Wien den Zug besteigt, der nach Minsk fährt, wächst aber kein Wald. Das Aufbrechen, Inventarisieren und Leerräumen der jüdischen Sammelwohnung in der Hammer-Purgstall-Gasse 3/12 durch die Gestapo-Verwertungsstelle für jüdisches Umzugsgut dauert zweieinhalb Tage. Die kleine Standuhr ist inzwischen zum Stillstand gekommen" (2012, pp. 271–272).

62. "alles nur Bücher, liest, was auf dem Rücken der Bücher steht, sagt: alles nur Goethe, klappt den Koffer wieder zu, *Sein oder Nichtsein*, sagt er im Aufstehen und grinst" (2012, p. 272).

63. As my comments on the narrator and the implied author also depend on my reading of the discourse, they both are, at least in part, interpretive. See Gadamer (1960/2013) and Meretoja (2018a).

64. "Vielleicht hat es mit diesen Hinterlassenschaften ja eine geheime Bewandtnis, so wie im Märchen, wo in grösster Not aus einem Kamm, den man hinter sich wirft, ein Wald wächst" (2012, p. 271).

65. "Mit der Mutter ist auch ihr Blick auf ihn gestorben, und alles, was jenseits seiner eigenen Erinnerung liegt" (2012, p. 223).

66. "Hat sie geweint? Ich glaube nicht. Nur gewundert, dass sie nicht aufstehen wollte" (2012, p. 105).

67. "Warum durfte sie niemandem sagen, dass ihre Grossmutter jüdisch war? War denn so wenig Liebe in der Welt, dass es zum Zusammenleimen nicht reichte? Wozu gab es die Unterschiede, dieses Gefälle?" (2012, pp. 121–122).

68. Interviewed by Steven Erlanger in April 2024, Erpenbeck said that her grandmother's experiences informed *Aller Tage Abend*. Her grandmother Hedda Zinner was Jewish and antifascist. Born in Ukraine circa 1904, Zinner became a communist in 1929 and left Germany for Vienna and Prague after Hitler came to power in 1933. With her husband, Fritz Erpenbeck, she emigrated to the Soviet Union in 1935. Returning to the GDR in 1947, she became a noted writer and an honored East German artist, receiving the Order of Karl Marx in 1980. Her grandmother's idea of the GDR was, Erpenbeck says, "better than the country itself." Hedda Zinner died in Berlin in 1994. See Erlanger (2024).

8

Concluding Reflections

Working on this book, I have found myself repeatedly looking at Georg W. Fossum's photograph of the *Donau*. As I reflect on the photograph, I realize that my understanding of it has changed as I have reread, rewatched, and written about my chosen texts; it is as though aspects of these narrative presentations of the Holocaust are hinted at or suggested by the visual image. At the same time, I sense that my interpretation of the photograph before I began to write the book may have influenced my interpretations of the narratives, perhaps even my selection of them.

Commenting on Fossum's photograph at the beginning of the introduction, I noted that it prompts me to ask demanding questions, including: How can or should I, a Norwegian born after the Second World War, respond to the failure to rescue the Norwegian Jews from being deported to Auschwitz in 1942–1943? I still do not know how to reply to that question, nor have I been able to satisfactorily answer related questions about the Holocaust stirred by Fossum's photograph and by the verbal narratives and film narratives that I discuss. If I sometimes gave partial answers, I have found that they tend to generate new questions. One conclusion I have reached, though, is that the most pressing questions about narrative presentations of the Holocaust are *ethical* questions. Although, and yet also because, it has proved difficult to answer the questions, I can at least ask them and reflect on them by linking them to my own perspective and fragments of my own memory and experience. If ethical questions are constituent elements of my overarching research question about the interplay of memory and narrative ethics in the nine narratives I interpret, they are also an essential part of my conclusion. They are affiliated with and support a key point that Hans-Georg Gadamer makes in *Truth and Method*: "The essence of the *question* is to open up possibilities and keep them open" (1960/2013, p. 310, original emphasis). This is what I have aimed to do in this book.

One of the possibilities opened up by the ethical questions that I have identified and discussed is this: Will we—as individuals and as members of the international community—be able not to forget the Holocaust?

Memory and Narrative Ethics. Jakob Lothe, Oxford University Press. © Oxford University Press (2025).
DOI: 10.1093/9780197579534.003.0009

As I cannot answer this question, I keep it open. Yet I have found that the presentations of the Holocaust narratives interpreted in this book reduce the risk of forgetting the unspeakable crime against humanity committed by Nazi Germany. The interplay of narrative and memory is a key aspect of all these presentations, whether they assume the form of testimony, narrative fiction, or film. The presence of the Holocaust as an external field of reference (Hrushovski, 1984; Toker, 2010) contributes decisively to the ethical questions engendered and shaped by the texts' narrative discourse.

An important reason I wanted to begin this study by discussing four of the testimonies presented in *Time's Witnesses* is signaled by the temporal dimension of the book's title: as the four Holocaust survivors narrate after a long period of silence, they communicate their stories while approaching the demarcation line that will be drawn by their own passing. I conclude that this form of time concentration—between the ending of the silence and the ending of the possibility of narrating—gives an edge to the testimonies' narrative ethics by investing them with a sense of urgency that is not just personal but also societal. Although the memories narrated by Maria Gabrielsen, Ella Blumenthal, Edith Notowicz, and Olga Horak are individual, they are socially mediated. One striking instance of the interplay of individual and collective memory that emerges from my interpretations is the provocation that the survivors experience when confronted with attempts to misrepresent, or even deny, the Holocaust. The testimonies' unique combination of individual and collective memory makes them an invaluable contribution to our cultural memory of the Holocaust. They thus become manifestations of "the interplay of present and past in socio-cultural contexts" (Erll, 2010a, p. 2). At the same time, the women's voices from the Holocaust confirm that "testimony is a crucial source for history" (LaCapra, 1998, p. 11). Their voices also remind me that testimony "poses special challenges to history. For it raises the issue of the way in which the historian or other analyst becomes a secondary witness" (p. 11; cf. LaCapra, 2016). As a listener to and then as an editor and co-author of the women's testimonies I was such an "analyst." As a "secondary witness" I interpreted what the women told me, and, although I accurately recorded and then presented their narratives as written text, my interpretation inevitably colored the process of editing—and thus it also colors the 10 testimonies of *Time's Witnesses*. Moreover, although the witness can claim, with unique authority, "I was there" (Ricoeur, 2000/2006, p. 163), her testimony is also an interpretation of a complex set of traumatic memories. This interpretive aspect of the witness's experience enhances its ethical import. Concomitantly, my interpretation of the witness's interpretation can be valuable, for both me and other readers of *Time's Witnesses*. The combination of my limited perspective and temporal distance from the Holocaust can further an interpretation that is uniquely my own, while at the same time contributing to an "open-ended dialectical societal discourse [that] should not seek to 'do' the Holocaust and then move on, but should avoid closure by encouraging or posing further questions" (Smith, 2001, p. 444; cf. Gadamer, 1960/2013). This concluding point concurs with Roger Frie's observation, "We cannot ultimately separate our personal memory from collective remembering" (2017, p. 177). That the questions will inevitably change when the last Holocaust survivors are gone makes it more rather than less important to continue to ask them.

In spite of the great difference between the media of verbal narrative and film narrative, several of these concluding reflections also apply to and follow from my narrative analyses of Leni Riefenstahl's *Triumph of the Will*, Alain Resnais's *Night and Fog*, and Claude Lanzmann's *Shoah*. The issue of interpretation is an important connecting point between these three films too. Lanzmann is a keen interpreter of the fragments of narrative imparted to him, and thus to the viewer, by his interviewees, and this point applies not just to the testimonies of Holocaust survivors such as Simon Srebnik and Abraham Bomba but also to the comments made by a perpetrator such as Franz Suchomel and by Polish bystanders. Resnais makes Cayrol serve as a narrator in *Night and Fog*, but Cayrol's rhetorically effective narration is also an interpretation that I find ethically problematic. The problem of interpretation also looms large in *Triumph of the Will*. Asked about her film, Riefenstahl claimed that, focusing on film aesthetics, she just documented the Nuremberg rally in 1934. Yet the physical reality of the rally was carefully staged, not least by her. The film's aesthetics blends into the narrative ethics that it generates. Highlighting and deftly exploiting Germany's collective memory of defeat in the First World War, Riefenstahl's film narrative is an interpretation that accords with Nazi ideology and supports Hitler's will. I conclude that, even though Riefenstahl directed the film before the Holocaust and the word "Jew" is never mentioned in it, there is a revealing connection between the Nazi propaganda of *Triumph of the Will* and the propaganda film *Theresienstadt: Ein Dokumentarfilm* that the Nazis forced the Jewish director Kurt Gerron to make in Theresienstadt in 1944—a film in which Austerlitz, the main character of W. G. Sebald's novel *Austerlitz*, thinks he can see his mother, Agáta, who saved his life before she was murdered in Auschwitz.

Rewatching and writing about *Triumph of the Will*, *Night and Fog*, and *Shoah*, I tend to interpret these nonfiction films as responses to each other. As I rewatch *Night and Fog*, I continue to be struck by Resnais's use of Riefenstahl's image of Hitler and Himmler as they are greeting the marching soldiers in *Triumph of the Will*. In my interpretive experience as a viewer of both films, I relate this image to Resnais's presentation of dead bodies in the Nazi concentration and extermination camps. The constellation of the images makes me ask: Who is responsible? While the question concerns perpetrators, including Hitler and Himmler, it is also relevant for me as an implicated subject since I am one of those beyond perpetrators, bystanders, and victims who are not innocent when it comes to historical violence and the abuse of stories to justify that violence (Rothberg, 2019). Rewatching *Shoah*, I am reminded of Resnais's visual presentation of dead bodies because Lanzmann does *not* incorporate documentary footage from the camps into his film. I have noted that the self-interpretive signs embedded in the visual images of the dead in *Night and Fog* not only support but also contradict Cayrol's voice-over by revealing a contrast between his interpretive comments on the visual images and my own interpretation of those images: although Cayrol does not mention the word "Jew," I conclude that since most of the dead bodies I see on the screen are victims of the Holocaust, in one important sense *Night and Fog* is a Holocaust film. Yet I also conclude that the film is flawed because it fails to identify the victims as Jews, thus making that crucial identification dependent on the viewer's extratextual knowledge about the Holocaust.

What are the ethical gains of Resnais's narrative presentation of murdered Jews as "strangely fragile, physically present, inviting a haptic gaze despite the abject untouchability of the corpse" (Wilson, 2011, p. 135)? Could Lanzmann's skepticism about inviting such a gaze be one of the reasons he consistently avoids using documentary footage from the camps in *Shoah*? The director's avoidance of such footage enables him to focus on and sustain his exploration of witnessing, including the need to bear witness as well as the challenge and pain of doing so. My interpretation of Lanzmann's film concludes by emphasizing the significance of silence as well as temporal, spatial, and attitudinal distance; these phenomena indicate the most important constituent elements of the film's narrative presentation of the Holocaust, and thus also of its narrative ethics. Hindsight is a precondition for narration in *Shoah*; Lanzmann relies completely on his interviewees' readiness and ability to narrate fragments of their memories to him—and to the viewer. While Suchomel and some of the Polish bystanders are reluctant to speak because of what they did or did not do, Srebnik, Bomba, and Müller manage to communicate aspects of their traumatic memories as fragmented narratives while at the same time interpreting those memories. In one sense, the dead are absent from *Shoah* since, in contrast to Resnais, Lanzmann does not show me a single image, whether photographic or filmic, of a dead human body. In a different sense, the dead permeate the whole film: the incalculable loss of six million murdered Jews infiltrates all levels and aspects of the film narrative, making the dead insistently present as the survivors attempt to remember those who are lost. This kind of absent presence is more powerful and more haunting than the images of dead bodies in *Night and Fog*. It calls the film's epigraph from *Isaiah* strikingly to mind. Even though *Shoah* may not give the murdered Jews an everlasting name, the survivors' testimonies cumulatively form a united testimony that becomes an act of mourning and a tribute to the victims of the Holocaust.

The narrative discourse of *Shoah* illustrates three of the main tenets of narrative hermeneutics: first, the film narrative is characterized by and is in a way premised on variants of distance and hindsight (Freeman, 2010; Gadamer, 1960/2013); second, it demonstrates that "the intricacies of autobiographical meaning-making are not just represented or expressed by narrative, they only come into being through and in narrative" (Brockmeier, 2015, p. 119); third, it supports the notion of narrative as "not only an *object* of interpretation [but also] *a mode of interpretation*" (Meretoja, 2018a, p. 44, original emphasis). Aspects of all three tenets are observable in all the narratives I discuss. In *Shoah*, they are operative even at those points or stages of the film narrative where the process of autobiographical meaning-making, a process that is an integral part of the task of bearing witness, grinds to a halt. Bomba's long silence is the most compelling example of this kind of narrative ellipsis—a gap that simultaneously constitutes and reveals a narrative crisis sparked by a crisis of memory.

If there is a thought-provoking connection between the silence at the center of Bomba's testimony and other segments of silence throughout *Shoah*, there is also a linkage between the film's silences. They become meaningful because of the way they are framed in the narrative discourse and because of the silence that will ensue when, very soon, the last Holocaust survivors will have passed away. Even though the consequences of the disappearance of the last witness are yet unknown to us, narrative fiction and the fiction film are a great resource when it comes to the task of remembering the Nazis' fanatical attempt to destroy all the European Jews. The four novels discussed in this book present the reader with very different approaches to and negotiations of the Holocaust—a word hardly used by any of the novel's authors. Yet I have found that in all of them—Jonathan Littell's *Les Bienveillantes*, Kazuo Ishiguro's *The Remains of the Day*, W. G. Sebald's *Austerlitz*, and Jenny Erpenbeck's *Aller Tage Abend*—the Holocaust is a looming presence, and even more on a second reading than on a first. I conclude, I hope not too optimistically, that, both considered in isolation and as a group of novels, these fictional narratives will continue to enable readers to learn about, ask questions about, and reflect on the Holocaust, thus strengthening the possibility of remembering and reducing the risk of forgetting it. Literature and arts can indeed contribute to and enrich our cultural memory.

One reason *Les Bienveillantes* illustrates narrative fiction's contribution to the collective task and responsibility of remembering the Holocaust is Littell's use of a Nazi perpetrator, Maximilian Aue, as the novel's protagonist and sole narrator. Few perpetrators have spoken or written about their involvement in the Holocaust; in *Shoah*, Lanzmann lies to Suchomel to make him talk about his work as a guard at Treblinka. By contrast, drawing on the resources of narrative fiction, Littell invents a complex text in which he makes Aue tell about his life as a Nazi perpetrator in an effective and brutally honest way, describing his killings and giving a detailed account of his contribution to "the Holocaust by bullets" (Desbois, 2008) and to the industrial Holocaust. It is a wrenching experience to gradually realize, particularly on my second reading, that although Aue may be some kind of monster, he is an individual character and not just a general representative of Holocaust perpetrators. This realization augments the challenge of reading the novel since it strengthens my need to ethically distance myself from Aue while at the same time complicating that process of distanciation. In my interpretive experience, this aspect of the ethics of reading *Les Bienveillantes* is correlated with the concluding point I make about the novel's narrative discourse: its most salient aesthetic *and* ethical feature is the increasing attitudinal distance between Aue's quasi-causal narrative presentation of his story and his experience of other, suspended, and perhaps half-forgotten elements of that same story. Although Aue continues his violent pattern of action until the end, the fragments of dream and hallucination establish a counterdiscourse that undermines and questions the values of Aue's quasi-causal account. As I have found that this variant of textual dynamics plays a key role in the formation of the novel's narrative ethics, I conclude that Aue's memories and incomplete account of his experiences at Stalingrad constitute a turning point in his discourse. The interplay of the ethics of the telling and the ethics of the told is particularly thought-provoking at this stage of the narrative: Stalingrad was also the turning point in Nazi Germany's war against the Soviet Union (Beevor, 1999).

The greatest interpretive challenge posed by the novel's narrative discourse is perhaps that of attributing a set of values to Littell as implied author that is sufficiently different from Aue's values to enable the reader to come to terms with the novel's narrative ethics. Although one of the conclusions reached in my chapter on *Les Bienveillantes* is that as the novel's only narrative medium may not only support but also damagingly infiltrate the implied author's purposes, I want to extend, and in one sense qualify, that conclusion by suggesting that the values that emerge through Aue's dreams and hallucinations constitute an alternative ethics that I can relate to that of the implied author. From the perspective of narrative hermeneutics, whatever knowledge I can gain about the implied author's purposes and the novel's intrinsic intentionality follows from my own interpretation of the narrative discourse. Thus, I consider the textual dynamics between Aue's quasi-causal narrative on the one hand and the fragments of an alternative narrative ethics hidden in and emerging from his dreams and hallucinations on the other as the most original and most rewarding constituent element of an ethically challenging novel.

This kind of challenge is different from that of distinguishing between Stevens's values and the implied author's values in *The Remains of the Day* since Ishiguro not only criticizes but also endorses several of Stevens's values. Such an endorsement, which partly revolves around the key word "serve," is absent from Littell's portrayal of Aue. Yet I stress that, as an SS officer in Nazi Germany, Aue serves too; while Stevens serves Lord Darlington, Aue serves Hitler. Moreover, although Littell does not endorse Aue's service in the SS, he invites me to reflect on the difference between the consequences of serving or not serving in a democracy and a totalitarian regime. In the context of the narratives interpreted in this book, my reflections on this difference are colored by those of the protagonist in Erpenbeck's *Aller Tage Abend* when, writing her autobiographical accounts in Moscow, she is wondering whether she is serving the Soviet communist regime in a way that those in positions of power will find acceptable.

If the issue of the Holocaust enters Ishiguro's novel indirectly via the dismissal of Ruth and Sarah, allusions to the Holocaust are stronger in Ivory's presentation of Elsa and Irma. Rather than highlighting this difference, however, I conclude by emphasizing the significance, as well as the interpretive thrust, of the Holocaust as an underlying presence in Ishiguro's literary narrative as well as Ivory's film narrative. In both fictional narratives, the external field of reference constituted by the Holocaust furthers the texts' narrative ethics by revealing how, through the mnemonic search movements of the novel and the film's discourses, Stevens reflects on the ways in which, in concert with his work ethic of serving Lord Darlington, he became complicit in antisemitism and its consequences. Although the media of verbal narrative and film narrative use different techniques to indicate Stevens's complicity in the Holocaust, in both these forms of narrative communication Stevens's journey westward to meet Miss Kenton functions as a catalyst for the emergence of memories that he has attempted to repress or ignore. When he is forced, first by Miss Kenton and then by Lord Darlington, to reflect on his active role in the dismissal of the Jewish girls, those reflections are stirred not only by his individual memory but also by the collective memory of the Second World War and the Holocaust. While the interplay of these two dimensions of memory is a characteristic feature of the narrative ethics of Ishiguro's novel as well as Ivory's adaptation, I conclude that both the literary narrative and the film narrative present individual and collective memory as expressions of a complex cultural memory in which, to appropriate a key point made by Paul Ricoeur in *Oneself as Another*, "[m]oral judgment has not been abolished; it is rather itself subjected to the imaginative variations proper to fiction" (1990/1994, p. 164). These "imaginative variations" are integral parts of the narratives' negotiations of values. They contribute to the relational ethics presented and shaped through the narrative discourse of Ishiguro's novel as well as Ivory's film.

Toward the end of my discussion of *The Remains of the Day*, I ask whether—and if so, how and to what extent—the author's Japanese biographical background plays a role in his narrative presentation of ethical issues. I conclude that while Ishiguro's memory, via his parents, includes Japan's participation and defeat in the Second World War, his understanding of the challenges of Europeans' memory of the Holocaust, an event that occurred in the same war, is remarkable. His memory is truly multidirectional (Rothberg, 2009). So is the memory of Sebald, who, born in Germany in 1944, emigrated to Britain in the 1960s and thus wrote *Auster-litz* in voluntary exile. As I have attempted to show in the chapter on Sebald's novel, it is an extraordinary example of how, in a work of narrative fiction, the two main characters are engaged in a search for a kind of truth that provides a contrast, as well as an alternative, to the lies and abuse of story in the propaganda film about Theresienstadt that Austerlitz sees when he is searching for his mother. This search for truth includes not only acknowledging that the Holocaust happened and realizing its colossal dimensions but also asking why and reflecting on how it *could* happen, how it is remembered, and the contest of values involved. Although Sebald as implied author has invented the novel's plot, there is a sense in which he too is engaged in the search, and so am I as a reader. There is even a sense in which, as the number "18.5.44" (Sebald, 2002, p. 415) at the end of the novel suggests to the reader who knows that this was Sebald's birthdate, Sebald as historical author writes himself into the implied author's discourse by inserting an autobiographical element that links him closely both to the German frame narrator and to the Jews who were being murdered in Kaunas until May 1944.[1]

Yet I have noted that if "18.5.44" is a trace of Sebald, that self-interpretive autobiographical sign not only furthers but also complicates my interpretation of *Austerlitz* since I read the numbers in two different ways. If I interpret the date as the German frame narrator's attempt to associate himself with the murdered Jews in Kaunas, the date expresses a mnemonic act distinguished by mourning and a painful sense of loss, while also including a reflection of the fragility of memory. If, on the other hand, I relate the date to the Nazis who kept murdering Jews in Kaunas until the month in which Sebald was born, then I highlight the frame narrator's, and Sebald's, sense of being an implicated subject. This reading draws attention to my own responsibility as a reader, leaving open the possibility that I am also implicated in the Holocaust. The concluding point I want to make here is that these two interpretations do not cancel each other out. Rather, they exist in parallel, demonstrating the interpretive potential of narrative fiction as Sebald presents it to the reader.

Significantly, both interpretations of "18.5.44" are influenced by my response to and interpretation of the visual images that form an integral part of *Austerlitz*'s narrative discourse. As I reread and interpret the date, two visual images come to mind: the map of Theresienstadt that covers two pages of the novel (Figure 6.4) and that of Breendonk much earlier in the narrative (Figure 6.3). How, and how strongly, these visual images influence my reading of the date I am not sure. I conclude, though, that the combination of written text and visual image prompts demanding questions that, precisely because I find them difficult to reply to, I have an ethical obligation to keep open. Gravitating toward the Holocaust, the questions, which are generated by and inseparable from the novel's narrative discourse, signal that a "complete" narrative of the Holocaust can never be constructed. But they suggest that, aided by a fictional narrative such as *Austerlitz*, I can and should continue to learn about, interpret, and reflect on the narrative fragments that, pointing to a lost whole, make me remember the irreplaceable quality and uniqueness of the lives and experiences lost in the Holocaust.

If the demanding questions that emerge from the narrative discourse of *Aller Tage Abend* are associated with those of all the texts I have discussed, they bear a particularly strong relation to ethical and interpretive questions raised by *Austerlitz*. In common with Sebald's novel, *Aller Tage Abend* is a fictional narrative. Yet both present and explore the consequences of the violent intrusion of the Holocaust into the protagonists' families. Marked by the violence of the 20th century, the characters of both novels are confronted with conflicting values and value systems. So too are the novels' narrators and implied authors. While Sebald primarily focuses on male characters and narrators (although Agáta is a key character and Věra an important narrator), Erpenbeck's narrative discourse presents the various lives of one female character. It is also important that whereas Sebald is a German British author who died in 2001, Erpenbeck is a German writer of fiction who belongs to the generation after Sebald—and who, as the epigraph in *Aller Tage Abend* indicates, is inspired by him. Chapters 6 and 7 show that, as representatives of two generations of German authors, Sebald and Erpenbeck have written novels that testify to an ongoing attempt to negotiate the painful memory—and legacy—of the Holocaust. Arguing that the narrative ethics of *Aller Tage Abend* revolves around the German word *Birkenwäldchen*, I regard this word as an oxymoron that consists of two contradictory elements: Auschwitz-Birkenau symbolizes the Holocaust; conversely, "a small forest of birch trees" (Erpenbeck, 2014, p. 110) symbolizes growth and life. I want to take this interpretation one step further by suggesting that while the first element of the oxymoron is associated with the values of Nazism, the second represents those, including the protagonist's mother and sister, who embrace and defend values opposed to Nazism. If one value of the first element is the evil action (Vetlesen, 2005) represented by the soldier's violence against the unnamed woman in *Birkenwäldchen*, one of the values of the second is the woman's care (Løgstrup, 1956/1997) for the manuscript she is carrying. There is a connection between her care for the manuscript that may belong to her sister (the novel's protagonist) and Chavah's preserving the memento of her murdered baby in Meisel's testimony.

Although the contradiction of this oxymoron is not resolved, it reinforces and gives an edge to the ethical questions I have discussed—questions asked in and through the narrative discourse. As I have found that several of these questions are related to and revolve around the challenge of not forgetting the Holocaust and the fragility of memory as time passes and new generations' knowledge about the Holocaust decreases, I conclude that one pressing question is this: How can I remember, or forget, what I do not know? The question follows from my interpretation of Erpenbeck's characterization of Sasha, the protagonist's son. Sasha has an honest wish to remember his mother, and by implication also his grandmother and great-grandmother. And yet, when Erpenbeck, exploiting the resources of narrative fiction, gives Sasha the opportunity to acquire his great-grandmother's Goethe edition in Vienna in book 5, he does not do so because it is too heavy to take back to Berlin and volume 9 is damaged. That it was damaged in Brody at the beginning of the 20th century in an antisemitic attack on his own family, and that it is perhaps the most important physical object the family still has access to he does not know. Neither does he realize that the values represented by the Goethe edition are German values opposed to those of Nazism. Sasha's failure to buy Goethe's collected works does not just reveal how fragile his memory of his family's history, and thus of the Holocaust, is; it also invites me to reflect on the vicissitudes of collective memory.

Throughout the narrative discourse of *Aller Tage Abend*, the interplay of memory and mourning—or more precisely, the way in which fragments of memory include and often seem to be constituted by traits of mourning—furthers the novel's narrative ethics. I make a similar concluding point about *Austerlitz*, and I also conclude that aspects of mourning the lost and the dead are integral parts of the mnemonic processes communicated in and through all the Holocaust narratives I have interpreted. While my focus throughout has been on the texts' narrative discourse, I have aimed to show how the implied author or film director designs, shapes, and presents the discourse as narrative communication. That this communication is demanding does not mean that it is unimportant. Rather, the ethical challenges that the characters and narrators face as they try to translate their memories, including their traumatic memories, into verbal narrative or film narrative contribute decisively to the narratives' impact, suggestiveness, and continuing relevance not only for me as an individual reader or viewer but also for the society in which I live and even, beyond that, for the international community. Two persons and characters (both of whom are also narrators) who illustrate this aspect of Holocaust narrative are Abraham Bomba in *Shoah* and the German who becomes Austerlitz's friend in *Austerlitz*.

As this example shows, both historical persons and narrators and fictional characters and narrators perform key functions in the formation of the narrative ethics of the texts I have interpreted. Sometimes the values of one person or one character can be so pronounced, and so strongly opposed to different values, that they approximate to the values endorsed by the author or director, and thus by the narrative discourse. Although some of the characters' values cannot be expressed through language because the character has been murdered, their action, of lack of action, makes an impression on the narrator, the implied author, and me as a reader. Two examples of this facet of the novels' narrative ethics are Agáta, who saves her son Austerlitz's life by sending him on the *Kindertransport* to Great Britain, and the young Jewish woman who, hanged by the Nazis in Ukraine, keeps haunting Aue in his dreams and hallucinations. Most of the persons, characters, and narrators occupy intermediate positions in that they represent different, even conflicting values; a notable example, in Ishiguro's novel as well as in Ivory's adaptation, is Stevens in *The Remains of the Day*. In common with these narratives, Littell's *Les Bienveillantes*, Sebald's *Austerlitz*, and Erpenbeck's *Aller Tage Abend* are "thought experiments . . . in the great laboratory of the imaginary"; they are also "explorations in the realm of good and evil" (Ricoeur, 1990/1994, p. 164). As readers and viewers, we participate in these explorations.

Noting that the narrative ethics of the texts I have interpreted is particularly significant and interpretively suggestive when the historical person or fictional narrator experiences a crisis of narration, I conclude that such a crisis tends to be created by a failure or inability or unwillingness to remember—or by an experience of remembering something that cannot or should not be narrated. This pattern is conspicuous in the Holocaust testimonies I have discussed. As the witness attempts to transform his or her painful memory into an autobiographical narrative, that narrative is bound to be fragmented and incomplete. Sometimes, as in the testimonies of Olga Horak and Abraham Bomba, it breaks down. The silence that follows reveals and emphasizes two of the most fundamental dimensions of Holocaust narrative. The first dimension is related to and follows from my interpretation of the silence—the narrative ellipsis or gap—that constitutes an empty core of Bomba's testimony. Although narrative is a powerful mode of exploration, it cannot reach this lacuna. Bomba's most traumatic memory may be the most important one to impart to Lanzmann as his listener, and to me as a viewer, but it cannot be communicated. This uncommunicated memory is part of Bomba's experience, but not of his autobiographical narrative. What gives the memory a partial meaning, though, is the way the silence is framed by the film narrative. Thus, paradoxically, the significance of narrative is accentuated just at the point when the narrative fails. What is the narrative ethics of Bomba's silence? I cannot know, but his facial expression as he continues to cut his client's hair in the barbershop in Tel Aviv suggests both a silent act of mourning his dead relatives and his utter incomprehension when remembering, and in one sense reconfronting, the Nazis' evil actions in Treblinka.

The second dimension of silence that I want to highlight is the silence that will follow the passing of the last Holocaust survivors. At the time of writing, Olga Horak is still alive, and so are Maria Gabrielsen, Ella Blumenthal, and Edith Notowicz. But they are old women, and the time of the passing of the last time's witness is fast approaching. Will future generations experience the same lack of knowledge about the Holocaust as Sasha does in *Aller Tage Abend*? I hope not, but I do not know. What I do know is that the challenge of not forgetting the Holocaust will become even greater when there is no longer a survivor who can say "I was there" (Ricoeur, 2000/2006, p. 163). Entering the phase of "post memory," to appropriate a concept coined by Aleida Assmann, "[w]e will, rather, must, rely solely on external and material forms, frames and genres of mediation" (2018, p. 213; cf. Assmann, 1999). As Astrid Erll points out:

> These media of cultural memory . . . are rarely uncontroversial. Their memory-making effect lies not in the unity, coherence, and ideological unambiguousness of the images they convey, but instead in the fact that they serve as cues for the discussion of those images, thus centering a memory culture on certain medial representations and sets of questions connected with them. (2010b, p. 396; cf. Erll, 2011)

It is to be hoped that this "memory culture" will be concerned with and recognize the importance of preserving the memory of the Holocaust. We need, and will continue to need, to read, watch, and interpret all the variants of Holocaust narrative that I have discussed—and more variants too. I hope that Holocaust narratives will inculcate in the next generation a sense of shared experience, responsibility, and obligation not to forget. But I cannot be sure they will have this effect. "Memory of the Holocaust is never shaped in a vacuum, and the motives for such memory are never pure" (Young, 2010, p. 357; cf. Young, 1993). Fortunately, many Holocaust testimonies have been recorded, either as written narratives, as documentary film, or as video testimonies inscribed into cultural memory. The importance of continuing historical research on the Holocaust is perhaps greater than ever; there is a need to compare references or allusions to the Holocaust in testimonies, documentaries, narrative fiction, and film with historians' fact-oriented accounts of the genocide. If such references or allusions are wrong or misleading, the use of stories becomes abuse of stories. The danger of such abuse is illustrated, for example, by allusions to Nazism and the Holocaust in Russian propaganda about the current war in Ukraine.

In their introduction to *The Use and Abuse of Stories*, Hanna Meretoja and Mark Freeman endorse Gadamer's emphasis on the centrality of dialogue for the project of narrative hermeneutics, "the dialogue that exists between interpreter and text and, equally important . . . the dialogue that exists, or that might exist, between those *different* interpreters who come to the task of interpretation" (2023, p. 9, original emphasis). Rereading and rewatching my chosen texts, I have attempted to establish a dialogue with them, not least by trying to identify the texts' self-interpretive elements and making these aspects influence my own interpretation. At the same time, I have repeatedly reminded myself of the limitations, yet also the interpretive possibilities, of writing about Holocaust narrative from the perspective of a Norwegian born after the Second World War. Reflecting on Fossum's photograph of the *Donau*, I conclude that, in combination with my temporal distance from the deportation of Norwegian Jews in 1942–1943, my limited perspective and my limited knowledge about the Holocaust influence my interpretations of my chosen texts. Yet I also conclude that, as Gadamer argues, this kind of influence is not necessarily an interpretive weakness. An example is the smoke from the chimney of the *Donau*—for me, it becomes a *punctum* that establishes an affective link to the Holocaust.

Serving as a leitmotif throughout, Fossum's photograph of the *Donau* has also helped me to develop my approach. The narrative analyses of values presented in and through the narrative discourse of the texts I interpret represent a key feature of this approach. Seen thus, my book is oriented toward and aims to contribute to narrative analysis rather than narrative theory. As I also hope to have demonstrated, I understand and practice "narrative analysis" as a concept sufficiently inclusive to enable me to study the interplay of aesthetics and ethics in different narratives, including the fragments of narrative in the testimonies discussed in Chapter 2 and the narrative breakdown in Bomba's testimony in *Shoah*. Focusing on narrative ethics, each analysis presents and discusses a variant or textual manifestation of possible ways in which historical/collective and individual/autobiographical memory are connected.

Combined with and because of my insistence on the need for analysis of narrative discourse, I hope to have made a theoretical contribution as well. I briefly indicate three features. First, in order to conduct the narrative analyses the way I do, I have found it helpful, even necessary to integrate in one approach the insights and concepts of a range of disciplines, including (in addition to classical and rhetorical narrative theory), Holocaust studies, memory studies, narrative hermeneutics, narrative psychology, and narrative ethics. Second, although I employ, and thus combine and appropriate, parts of research done in all the disciplines just mentioned, I allow the narrative that I analyze to influence my combination and use of these components. This methodological flexibility impacts my interpretations, which are consistently based on a second reading or viewing. The nexus between rereading or rewatching and interpretation is a distinctive feature of the narrative analyses presented in this book. I consider memory and narrative closely related, and I argue that narrative ethics and aesthetics are intertwined in the narrative discourse. While I conclude that, as approached and interpreted in this book, narrative ethics is a relational system, I also conclude that the relational dimension of ethics informs and strengthens the negotiations of values in verbal narratives' and film narratives' presentations of individual and collective memory. Third, narrative hermeneutics, particularly as developed by Gadamer and Meretoja, underlies all my analyses of narrative presentations of the Holocaust. The influence of narrative hermeneutics has made me reluctant to use the pronoun "we" when making points and observations that, as Gadamer has shown, are in fact my own—that is, based on and delimited by my own experience, perspective, and knowledge (or lack of knowledge). Illustrated by my inclination to use "I" rather than "we," my awareness of this kind of interpretive delimitation does not necessarily make my contribution less important. But it invests, I hope, the interpretations of my chosen narratives

Figure 8.1 Mother's diary

with a measure of humility that, in addition to its intrinsic value in analyses of narrative presentations of the Holocaust, can hopefully establish a dialogue with interpretations of the same texts conducted by other readers and viewers.

As readers and viewers of Holocaust narratives, we relate them to aspects of our own autobiographical narratives in different ways. Rereading and rewatching the texts I have interpreted, I associate them not just with Fossum's photograph of the *Donau* but also with a diary that my mother, Eldfrid Lothe, kept when she was in Cambridge, England, in 1939. On September 1, she writes that, after the announcement of Germany's invasion of Poland, there is an ominous atmosphere in the city. When she was an old woman, my mother developed dementia. Her cognitive abilities, including those of reading and remembering, declined. Yet in this last phase of her life, the small, black diary she had kept in Cambridge in her youth became a remarkably precious physical object for her (Figure 8.1).

Although, or because, she could no longer read what she had written in it, she would carry the diary with her around the house, repeatedly forgetting it in her bedroom or the bathroom or the kitchen. It seemed to me that, for her, the diary had become the physical manifestation of a broken narrative (Hydén & Brockmeier, 2011). My mother had forgotten what she did in Cambridge and why she was there, but the way she held on to her diary was a token of the importance that, even in a state of dementia, she attached to 1939, a year that marked a crucial moment in her autobiographical narrative—and in European history too (Carrard, 2008). I could have taken the diary from my mother, putting it in a safe place to make sure that she did not lose it or inadvertently destroy it. But that would have been the wrong thing to do. Instead, over and over again, I found the diary she was looking for and gave it back to her.

I hesitate to call this act a manifestation of care, as Knud E. Løgstrup (1956/1997) understands this concept. These were small acts of kindness, and most sons and daughters would probably have done the same to a parent suffering from dementia. Still, for Løgstrup, even small caring acts— including, not least, those I am not conscious of performing—are significant. Moreover, although, as I have noted, Løgstrup's idea of care is different from Emmanuel Levinas's notion of the ethical demand of the Other, that notion also became surprisingly relevant to the fragmented, nonverbal communication I had with my mother about her diary. For Levinas, my "responsibility for the other . . . is not a question of receiving an order by first perceiving it and then obeying it in a decision, an act of the will" (1995/1999, pp. 32, 33). Rather, as Mark Freeman puts it, "this responsibility is called forth, primordially, by the very 'face' of the other person" (2021, p. 24). There was something strange about my mother's facial features as she was carrying her diary from room to room in her home—it was as though her attention was directed toward 1939 rather than the present moment with her son. For me, the weight that my mother attached to her diary came to epitomize the peculiar combination of memory's fragility and memory's importance. The diary became especially precious for my mother at a stage of her life when she could no longer explain why.

As a first-person narrative of fragments of a person's life, a diary is necessarily selective—and thus interpretive. While my mother's diary entry for September 1, 1939, is an instance of individual memory, it also includes aspects of collective memory. Reading her interpretive diary entry, I build on and extend her interpretation by associating it with the topic of this book.[2] Nazi Germany's invasion of Poland on September 1, 1939, enabled the Nazi state to control the territory of Eastern Europe in which the greatest part of the Holocaust occurred a few years later. The ominous atmosphere that my mother noticed in Cambridge in September 1939 prevailed in Europe until 1945. More specifically, I relate my mother's act of carrying her diary to Frau Hoffmann, the protagonist in *Aller Tage Abend*, who, suffering from dementia in the nursing home in Berlin, utters words that make no sense to those around her. Yet the nurses continue to care for her. Although these acts of care constitute an element of hope in Erpenbeck's novel, an aspect of uncertainty, or even resignation, is suggested by the inability of those who care for Frau Hoffmann to understand that, in her state of dementia, she is recalling the critical moments of her life when she was subjected to Stalinist terror in Moscow. That not even her son Sasha has this knowledge, and that he is also ignorant of his own family's losses in the Holocaust, suggests that the question of whether the world will prove able not to forget the Holocaust remains open.

Notes

1. In Geoffrey Hill's (1994) poem "September Song," the birthdate of the murdered girl ("*born 19.6.32—deported 24.9.42*") is the same as Hill's own.
2. The diary entry also makes me think of and reflect on W. H. Auden's (1940) poem "September 1, 1939."

References

Aaron, M. (2016). Ethics and digital film. *Film Criticism, 40*(1). https://quod.lib.umich.edu/f/fc/13761232.0040.101/—ethics-and-digital-film?rgn=main;view=fulltext

Abbott, H. P. (2020). *The Cambridge introduction to narrative* (3rd ed.). Cambridge University Press.

Achebe, C. (2006). An image of Africa: Racism in Conrad's *Heart of Darkness*. In P. Armstrong (Ed.), Joseph Conrad, *Heart of darkness* (pp. 336–349) (4th ed.). Norton.

Adams, J., & Vice, S. (Eds.). (2015). *Representing the perpetrator in Holocaust literature and film*. Vallentine Mitchell.

Adorno, T. W. (2019). Titles: Paraphrases on Lessing. In R. Tiedemann (Ed.) & S. Weber Nicholsen (Trans.), *Notes to literature* (pp. 283–290). Columbia University Press.

Agamben, G. (2012). *Remnants of Auschwitz: The witness and the archive* (D. Heller-Roazen, Trans.). Zone Books. (Original work published 1986)

Alphen, E. van (1999). Symptoms of discursivity: Experience, memory, and trauma. In M. Bal, J. Crewe, & L. Spitzer (Eds.), *Acts of memory: Cultural recall in the present* (pp. 24–38). University Press of New England.

Alphen, E. van (2018). The decline of narrative and the rise of the archive. In H. Meretoja & C. Davis (Eds.), *Storytelling and ethics: Literature, visual arts and the power of narrative* (pp. 68–83). Routledge.

Altes, L. K. (2008). Ehical turn. In D. Herman, M. Jahn, & M.-L. Ryan (Eds.), *Routledge encyclopedia to narrative theory* (pp. 142–146). Routledge.

Altes, L. K. (2014). *Ethos and narrative interpretation: The negotiation of values in fiction*. University of Nebraska Press.

Ambrosewicz-Jacobs, J. (Ed.). (2009). *The Holocaust: Vocies of scholars*. Austeria Publishing House.

Andrew, D. (1999). Adaptation. In L. Braudy & M. Cohen (Eds.), *Film theory and criticism: Introductory readings* (pp. 452–460). Oxford University Press.

Andrews, M. (2014). *Narrative imagination and everyday life*. Oxford University Press.

Arendt, H. (1948). The concentration camps. *Partisan Review, 15*, 743–763.

Arendt, H. (1963). *Eichmann in Jerusalem: A report on the banality of evil*. Viking Press.

Arendt, H. (2003). Collective responsibility. In H. Arendt, *Responsibility and judgment* (J. Kohn, Ed.) (pp. 147–159). Schocken.

Arendt, H. (2017). *The origins of totalitarianism*. Penguin. (Original work published 1951)

Arendt, H. (2018). *The human condition* (2nd ed.). University of Chicago Press. (Original work published 1958)

Aristotle. (1995). *Poetics* (Stephen Halliwell, Ed. & Trans.). Harvard University Press.

Armstrong, P. (2013). *How literature plays with the brain*. Johns Hopkins University Press.

Assmann, A. (1999). *Erinnerungsräume: Formen und Wandlungen des kulturellen Gedächtnisses*. C. H. Beck.

Assmann, A. (2015). Impact and resonance. In S.-A. Naguib & T. Stordalen (Eds.), *The formative past and the formation of the future: Collective remembering and identity formation* (pp. 41–69). Novus Press.

Assmann, A. (2018). The empathetic listener and the ethics of storytelling. In H. Meretoja & C. Davis (Eds.), *Storytelling and ethics: Literature, visual arts and the power of narrative* (pp. 203–218). Routledge.

Auden, W. H. (1940). *Another time*. Random House.

Auerbach, E. (2003). *Mimesis: The representation of reality in Western literature* (Willard Trask, Trans.). Princeton University Press. (Original work published 1947)

Avisar, I. (1988). *Screening the Holocaust: Cinema's images of the unimaginable*. Indiana University Press.

Bachelard, G. (1994). *The poetics of space* (M. Jolas, Trans.). Beacon Press. (Original work published 1958)

Bakhtin, M. M. (1982). Forms of time and chronotope in the novel. In M. Holquist (Ed.), *The dialogic imagination: Four essays* (pp. 243–250). University of Texas Press.

Bal, M. (1991). *Reading "Rembrandt": Beyond the word-image opposition*. Cambridge University Press.

Bal, M. (1999). Introduction. In M. Bal, J. Crewe, & L. Spitzer (Eds.), *Acts of memory: Cultural recall in the present* (pp. vii–xvii). University Press of New England.

Bal, M. (2002). *Travelling concepts in the humanities: A rough guide*. University of Toronto Press.

Bal, M. (2017). *Narratology: Introduction to the theory of narrative* (4th ed.). Toronto University Press.

Bal, M. (2018). Is there an ethics to story-telling? In H. Meretoja & C. Davis (Eds.), *Storytelling and ethics: Literature, visual arts and the power of narrative* (pp. 37–54). Routledge.

Barjonet, A., & Razinsky, L. (Eds.). (2012). *Writing the Holocaust today: Critical perspectives on Jonathan Littell's* The kindly ones. Rodopi.

Barthes, R. (1982). *Camera lucida: Reflections on photography* (Richard Howard, Trans.). Jonathan Cape.

Bauman, Z. (2001). *Modernity and the Holocaust*. Cornell University Press.

Baumel-Shwartz, J. T. & Laqueur, W. (Eds). (2001). *The Holocaust encyclopedia*. Yale University Press.

Bazin, A. (1967). The ontology of the photographic image. In *What is cinema?*, vol. 1 (H. Gray, Trans.) (pp. 9–16). University of California Press.

Beauvoir, S. de. (1995). Preface. In C. Lanzmann, Shoah: *The complete text of the acclaimed Holocaust film* (pp. iii–vi). Da Capo Press.

Beauvoir, S. de. (2001). La mémoire de l'horreur. In C. Lanzmann, *Shoah* (pp. 9–14). Gallimard.

Beedham, M. (2010). *The novels of Kazuo Ishiguro*. Bloomsbury.

Beevor, A. (1999). *Stalingrad*. Viking Press.

Belgaux, C. (2020). Georg W. Fossum's photograph. *Morgenbladet, 201*(48), 16–18.

Benjamin, W. (1979). The storyteller. In H. Arendt (Ed.) & H. Zohn (Trans.), *Illumina-tions* (pp. 83–109). London: Fontana. (Original work published 1936)

Bennett, A. (2023). Introduction. In A. Bennett (Ed.), *The Cambridge companion to Kazuo Ishiguro* (pp. 1–10). Cambridge University Press.

Benz, W. (Ed.). (2002). *Lexikon des Holocaust.* C. H. Beck.

Berenbaum, M., & Peck, A. J. (Eds.). (2002). *The Holocaust and history: The known, the unknown, the disputed, and the re-examined.* Indiana University Press.

Bergo, B. (2014). Emmanuel Levinas. In E. N. Zalta & U. Nodelman (Eds.), *The Stanford encyclopedia of philosophy* (Fall 2024 ed.). Stanford University. https://plato.stanford.edu/archives/fall2024/entries/levinas/

Bergson, H. (1988). *Matter and memory: Essay on the relation of body and spirit* (N. M. Paul & W. S. Palmer, Trans.). Zone Books. (Original work published 1896)

Betz, A. (1982). *Hanss Eisler: Political musician.* Cambridge University Press.

Borowski, T. (1967). *This way for the gas, ladies and gentlemen.* Viking Penguin. (Original work published 1946)

Bond, L., & Craps, S. (Eds.). (2020). *Trauma.* Routledge.

Booth, W. C. (1983). *The rhetoric of fiction* (2nd ed.). University of Chicago Press.

Booth, W. C. (1988). *The company we keep: An ethics of fiction.* University of California Press.

Breitman, R. (1991). *The architect of genocide: Himmler and the final solution.* University Press of New England.

Brockmeier, J. (2009). Reaching for meaning: Human agency and the narrative imagination. *Theory and Psychology, 19*(2), 213–233.

Brockmeier, J. (2013). Fact and fiction: Exploring the narrative mind. In M. Hyvärinen, M. Hatavara, & L.-C. Hydén (Eds.), *The travelling concepts of narrative* (pp. 121–140). John Benjamins.

Brockmeier, J. (2015). *Beyond the archive: Narrative, memory, and the autobiographical process.* Oxford University Press.

Brockmeier, J. (2022). *Erzählen als Lebensform.* Psychosozial-Verlag.

Brockmeier, J. (2023). Verstehen and narrative. In H. Meretoja & M. Freeman (Eds.), *The use and abuse of stories: New directions in narrative hermeneutics* (pp. 89–122). Oxford University Press.

Brockmeier, J., & Harré, R. (2001). Narrative: Problems and promises of an alternative paradigm. In J. Brockmeier & D. Carbaugh (Eds.), *Narrative and identity: Studies in autobiography, self and culture* (pp. 39–58). John Benjamins.

Brockmeier, J., & Meretoja, H. (2014). Understanding narrative hermeneutics. *Story-worlds, 6*(2), 1–27.

Broszat, M. (Ed.). (1998). *Kommandant in Auschwitz: Autobiographische Aufzeichnun-gen des Rudolf Höss.* Deutscher Taschenbuch Verlag.

Bruland, B. (2012). Norway's role in the Holocaust. In J. C. Friedman (Ed.), *The Routledge history of the Holocaust* (pp. 232–247). Routledge.

Bruner, J. (1986). *Actual minds, possible worlds.* Harvard University Press.

Bruner, J. (1987). Life as narrative. *Social Research, 54*(1), 11–32.

Bruner, J. (1990). *Acts of meaning.* Harvard University Press.

Bruner, J. (2001). Self-making and world-making. In J. Brockmeier & D. Carbaugh (Eds.), *Narrative and identity: Studies in autobiography, self and culture* (pp. 86–93). John Benjamins.

Buchholtz, S., & Jahn, M. (2005). Space in narrative. In D. Herman, M. Jahn, & M.-L. Ryan (Eds.), *Routledge encyclopedia of narrative theory* (pp. 551–555). Routledge.

Buelens, G., Durrant, S., & Eaglestone, R. (Eds.). (2014). *The future of trauma theory.* Routledge.

Bullock, A. (1991). *Hitler: A study in tyranny* (abridged ed.).HarperCollins. (Original work published 1952)

Butler, J. (1990). *Gender trouble: Feminism and the subversion of identity.* Routledge.

Butler, J. (2005). *Giving an account of oneself.* Fordham University Press.

Camper, F. (2007). *Shoah's* absence. In S. Liebman (Ed.), *Claude Lanzmann's* Shoah: *Key essays* (pp. 103–111). Oxford University Press.

Carr, D. (1986). *Time, narrative, and history.* Indiana University Press.

Carrard, P. (2008). September 1939: Beginnings, historical narrative, and the outbreak of World War II. In B. Richardson (Ed.), *Narrative beginnings: Theories and practices* (pp. 63–82). University of Nebraska Press.

Caruth, C. (Ed.). (1995). *Trauma: Explorations in memory.* Johns Hopkins University Press.

Caruth, C. (2016). *Unclaimed experience: Trauma, narrative, and history.* Johns Hopkins University Press. (Original work published 1996)

Cavell, S. (1979). *The world viewed: Reflections on the ontology of film.* Harvard University Press.

Cayrol, J. (1946). *Poèmes de la nuit et du brouillard.* Éditions Pierre Seghers.

Cesarani, D. (2006). *Becoming Eichmann: Rethinking the life, crimes, and trial of a "desk murderer."* Da Capo Press.

Cesare, D. D. (2023). *If Auschwitz is nothing: Against denialism* (D. Broder, Trans.). Polity.

Chamberlain, H. S. (1912). *The foundations of the nineteenth century.* John Lane Company.

Chambers, R. (1984). *Story and situation: Narrative seduction and the power of fiction.* Manchester University Press.

Charon, R. (2006). *Narrative medicine: Honoring the stories of illness.* Oxford University Press.

Charon, R. (2017). Introduction. In R. Charon, S. DasGupta, N. Hermann, C. Irvine, E. R. Marcus, E. R. Colsn, D. Spencer, and M. Spiegel (Eds.), *The principles and practice of narrative medicine* (pp. 1–12). Oxford University Press.

Cherry, M. (2023). *Failures of forgiveness: What we get wrong and how to do better.* Princeton University Press.

Clendinnen, I. (2002). *Reading the Holocaust.* Cambridge University Press.

Cohen, Albert (1972). *Ô vous, frères humain.* Gallimard.

Cohn, D. (1999). *The distinction of fiction.* Johns Hopkins University Press.

Cole, T. (2016). *Holocaust landscapes.* Bloomsbury.

Coupechoux, P. (Ed.). (2003). *Mémoires de déportés: Histoires singulières de la déportation.* La Découverte.

Coury, David N. (2002). "Auch ruhiges Land . . .": Remembrance and testimony in Paul Celan's *Nuit et Brouillard* translation. *Prooftexts, 22*(1&2), 55–76.

Craps, S. (2012). *Postcolonial witnessing: Trauma out of bounds.* Palgrave Macmillan.

Cresswell, Tim (2004). *Place: A short introduction.* Oxford: Blackwell.

Culler, J. (2011). *A very short introduction to literary theory* (2nd ed.). Oxford University Press.

Davis, C. (2007a). *Haunted subjects: Deconstruction, psychoanalysis and the return of the dead.* Palgrave Macmillan.

Davis, C. (2007b). *Levinas: An introduction.* Polity Press.

Davis, C. (2018a). *Traces of war: Interpreting ethics and trauma in French twentieth-century writing.* Liverpool University Press.

Davis, C. (2018b.) Truth, ethics, fiction: Responding to Plato's challenge. In H. Meretoja & C. Davis (Eds.), *Storytelling and ethics: Literature, visual arts and the power of narrative* (pp. 23–36). Routledge.

Davis, C. (2023). Truth, lies, and the hermeneutics of suspicion. In H. Meretoja & M. Freeman (Eds.), *The use and abuse of stories: New directions in narrative hermeneutics* (pp. 36–54). Oxford University Press.

Davis, C., & Meretoja, H. (Eds.). (2020). *The Routledge companion to literature and trauma.* Routledge.

Delage, C. (2005). *Nuit et Brouillard*: A turning point in the history and memory of the Holocaust. In T. Haggith & J. Newman (Eds.), *Holocaust and the moving image: Representations in film and television since 1933* (pp. 127–139). Wallflower Press.

Delbo, C. (1990). *Days and memory* (R. Lamont, Trans.). Marlboro.

Deleuze, G. (1969). *Logique du sens.* Paris: Éditions de Minuit.

Deleuze, G. (1985). *Cinéma 1: L'Image-temps.* Éditions de Minuit.

Deleuze, G. (1989). *Cinéma 2: The time-image* (H. Tomlinson & R. Galeta, Trans.). Athlone Press.

Delfour, J.-J. (2000). La pellicule maudite: Sur la figuration du réel de la Shoah. *L'Arche, 508*, 14–15.

Derrida, J. (1989). *Mémoires: For Paul de Man* (C. Lindsay et al., Trans.). Columbia University Press.

Derrida, J. (2000). *Demeure: Fiction and testimony* (E. Rottenberg, Trans.). Stanford University Press.

Derrida, J., & Stiegler, B. (2002). *Echographies of télévison: Filmed interviews* (J. Bajorek, Trans.). Polity Press.

Desbois, P. (2008). *The Holocaust by bullets.* Palgrave Macmillan.

Devereaux, M. (1998). Beauty and evil: The case of Leni Riefenstahl's *Triumph of the will.* In J. Levinson (Ed.), *Aesthetics and ethics: Essays at the intersection* (pp. 227–256). Cambridge University Press.

Didi-Huberman, G. (2007). The site, despite everything. In S. Liebman (Ed.), *Claude Lanzmann's "Shoah": Key essays* (pp. 113–123). Oxford University Press.

Downing, L., & Saxton, L. (2010). *Film and ethics: Foreclosed encounters.* Routledge.

Duttlinger, C. (2004). Traumatic experience: Remembrance and the technical media in W. G. Sebald's *Austerlitz*. In J. J. Long & A. Whitehead (Eds.), *W. G. Sebald: A critical companion* (pp. 155–171). Edinburgh University Press.

Eaglestone, R. (2023). Ethics and agency in Ishiguro's novels. In A. Bennett (Ed.), *The Cambridge companion to Kazuo Ishiguro* (pp. 187–199). Cambridge University Press.

Eikhenbaum, B. (1973). Literature and cinema. In S. Bann & J. Bowlt (Eds.), *Russian formalism: A collection of articles and texts in translation* (pp. 122–127). Edinburgh University Press. (Original work published 1926)

Eisler, H. (2014). Film music to "Nuit et brouillard." In Breyer, K. & Dahin, O. (Eds.), *Hanns Eisler Complete Edition*, VI, Film Music, vol. 23. Breitkopf & Härtel.

Erdinast-Vulcan, D. (2013). *Between philosophy and literature: Bakhtin and the question of the subject*. Stanford University Press.

Erlanger, S. (2024). A novelist who finds inspiration in Germany's tortured history. *The New York Times*, April 26. https://www.nytimes.com/2024/04/26/world/europe/jenny-erpenbeck-east-germany-kairos.html

Erll, A. (2010a). Cultural memory studies: An introduction. In A. Erll & A. Nünning (Eds.), *A companion to cultural memory* studies (pp. 1–15). De Gruyter.

Erll, A. (2010b). Literature, film and the mediality of cultural memory. In A. Erll & A. Nünning (Eds.), *A companion to cultural memory studies* (pp. 389–398). De Gruyter.

Erll, A. (2011). *Memory in culture* (S. B. Young, Trans.). Palgrave.

Erll, A. (2019). Homer, Turko, Little Harry: Cultural memory and the ethics of premediation in James Joyce's *Ulysses. Partial Answers, 17*(2), 227–253.

Erll, A., & Nünning, A. (Eds.). (2010). *A companion to cultural memory studies*. De Gruyter.

Erpenbeck, J. (2012). *Aller Tage Abend*. Penguin.

Erpenbeck, J. (2014). *The end of days* (S. Bernofsky, Trans.). Portobello Books.

Falke, C. (2017). *The phenomenology of love and reading*. Bloomsbury Academic.

Felman, S., & Laub, D. (1992). *Testimony: Crises of witnessing in literature, psychoanalysis, and history*. Routledge.

Felski, R. (2015). *The limits of critique*. University of Chicago Press.

Fink, H., & MacIntyre, A. (1997). Introduction. In K. E. Løgstrup, *The ethical demand* (pp. xv–xxxviii). University of Notre Dame Press.

Fludernik, M. (2009). *An introduction to narratology*. Routledge.

Foucault, M. (1979). *The history of sexuality* (Vol. 1). London: Allen Lane.

Freeman, M. (2010). *Hindsight: The promise and peril of looking backward*. Oxford University Press.

Freeman, M. (2015). Narrative hermeneutics. In J. Martin, J. Sugarman, & K. L. Slaney (Eds.), *The Wiley handbook of theoretical and philosophical psychology: Methods, approaches, and new directions for social sciences* (pp. 234–247). John Wiley & Sons.

Freeman, M. (2017). Narrative at the limits (or: What is "life" really like?). In B. Schiff, A. E. McKim, & S. Patron (Eds.), *Life and narrative: The risks and responsibilities of storying experience* (pp. 11–27). Oxford University Press.

Freeman, M. (2021). *Do I look at you with love? Reimagining the story of dementia*. Brill Sense.

Freeman, M. (2023). The inevitability, and danger, of narrative. In H. Mertoja & M. Freeman (Eds.), *The use and abuse of stories: New directions in narrative hermeneutics* (pp. 15–35). Oxford University Press.

Frie, R. (2017). *Not in my family: German memory and responsibility after the Holocaust.* Oxford University Press.

Friedländer, S. (1997). *Nazi Germany and the Jews: The years of persecution, 1933–1939.* HarperCollins.

Friedländer, S. (2003). "The final solution": On the unease in historical interpretation. In N. Levi & M. Rothberg (Eds.), *The Holocaust: Theoretical readings* (pp. 69–74). Edinburgh University Press.

Friedländer, S. (2007), *Nazi Germany and the Jews: The years of extermination, 1939–1945.* Harper Collins.

Friedman, J. C. (Ed.). 2012. *The Routledge history of the Holocaust.* London: Routledge.

Frow, J. (2014). *Character and person.* Oxford University Press.

Fulbrook, M. (2023). *Bystander society: Conformity and complicity in Nazi Germany and the Holocaust.* Oxford University Press.

Furst, L. R. (2007). Memory's fragile power in Kazuo Ishiguro's *Remains of the day* and W. G. Sebald's "Max Ferber." *Contemporary Literature, 48*(4), 530–553.

Gadamer, H.-G. (1975). *Wahrheit und Methode: Grundzüge einer philosophischen Hermeneutik.* Erweiterte Auflage. J. C. G. Mohr/Paul Siebeck. (Original work published 1960)

Gadamer, H.-G. (2013). *Truth and method* (J. Weinsheimer & D. G. Marshall, Trans.). Bloomsbury. (Original work published 1960)

Genette, G. (1980). *Narrative discourse: An essay in method* (J. E. Lewin, Trans.). Blackwell. First published as *Discours du récit* (1972). Éditions des Seuil.

Genette, G. (1997). *Paratexts: Thresholds of interpretation* (J. E. Lewin, Trans.). Cambridge University Press. First published as *Seuils* (1987). Éditions des Seuil.

Gerron, K. (Writer & Director). (1944). *Theresienstadt: Ein Dokumentarfilm aus dem jüdischen Siedlungsgebiet* [Theresienstadt: A documentary film from the Jewish settlement area]. [Film]. Produced by Karel Pečený (Aktualita Prag).

Gilbert, M. (1987). *The Holocaust.* HarperCollins.

Gilmore, L. (2001). *The limits of autobiography: Trauma and testimony.* Cornell University Press.

Goldenberg, M. (2012). Double jeopardy: Being Jewish and female in the Holocaust. In J. C. Friedman (Ed.), *The Routledge history of the Holocaust* (pp. 389–411). Routledge.

Gompertz, W. (2017). Kazuo Ishiguro keeps calm amid Nobel Prize frenzy. BBC, October 5. https://www.bbc.com/news/entertainment-arts-41517882

Gorman, D. (2008). Theories of fiction. In D. Herman, M. Jahn, & M.-L. Ryan (Eds.), *Routledge encyclopedia of narrative theory* (pp. 163–167). Routledge.

Görner, R. (Ed.) (2003). *The anatomist of melancholy: Essays in memory of W. G. Sebald.* Iudicium Verlag.

Griswold, C. (2007). *Forgiveness: A philosophical exploration.* Cambridge University Press.

Grønstad, A. (2016). *Film and the ethical imagination.* Palgrave Macmillan.

Grønstad, A. S. (2020). *Rethinking art and visual culture: The poetics of opacity*. Palgrave Macmillan.

Gustafsson, H., & Grønstad, A. (Eds.). (2015). *Cinema and Agamben: Ethics, biopolitics and the moving image*. Bloomsbury.

Habermas, J. (1994). *Justification and application*. MIT Press.

Haggith, T., & Newman, J. (Eds.). (2005). *Holocaust and the moving image: Representations in film and television since 1933*. Wallflower Press.

Hähnel-Mesnard, C. (2022). *Zeiterfahrung und gesellschaftlicher Umbruch in Fiktionen der Post-DDR-Literatur: Literarische Figurationen von Zeitwahrnehmung im Werk von Lutz Seiler, Julia Schoch und Jenny Erpenbeck*. V&R unipress.

Hain, H.-J. (2004). Leerstellen in der deutschen Gedenkkultur: Die Schreitschriften von W. G. Sebald und Klaus Briegleb. *German Life and Letters, 57*(4), 357–371.

Halbwachs, M. (1925). *Les cadres sociaux de la mémoire*. Libraire Félix Alcan.

Halbwachs, M. (1992). *On collective memory* (L. Coser, Trans.). University of Chicago Press.

Hawthorn, J. (Ed.). (1987). *Propaganda, persuasion and polemic*. Edward Arnold.

Hawthorn, J. (2019). History, fiction, and the Holocaust: Narrative perspective and ethical responsibility. *Partial Answers, 17*(2), 279–298.

Hawthorn, J. (2023). *Studying the novel* (8th ed.). Bloomsbury.

Hawthorn, J., & Lothe, J. (2013). Introduction. In J. Lothe & J. Hawthorn (Eds.), *Narrative ethics* (pp. 1–10). Rodopi.

Hebard, A. (2011). Disruptive histories: Toward a radical politics of remembrance in Alain Resnais's *Night and fog*. In G. Pollock & M. Silverman (Eds.), *Concentrationary cinema: Aesthetics as political resistance in Alain Resnais's* Night and fog (pp. 214–237). Berghahn Books. First published in *New German Critique 71* (Spring–Summer 1997), 87–113.

Herman, D. (2008). Narrative theory and the intentional stance. *Partial Answers, 6*(2), 233–260.

Herman, D., Jahn, M., & Ryans, M.-L. (Eds.) (2007). *Routledge encyclopedia of narrative theory*. Routledge.

Hermans, T. (1996). *Translation's other: An inaugural lecture delivered at University College London on Tuesday 19 March 1996*. University College London.

Hermans, T. (2022). *Translation and history: A textbook*. Routledge.

Hilberg, R. (1992). *Perpetrators victims bystanders: The Jewish catastrophe 1933–1945*. HarperCollins.

Hilberg, R. (1996). *The politics of memory: The journey of a Holocaust historian*. Evan R. Dee.

Hilberg, R. (2003). *The destruction of the European Jews* (Vols. 1–3) (3rd ed.). Yale University Press. (Original work published 1961)

Hilberg, R., Staron, S., & Kermisz, J. (Eds.). (1999). *The Warsaw diary of Adam Czerniakow: Prelude to doom*. Elephant Paperbacks.

Hill, G. (1994). *New and collected poems, 1952–1992*. Houghton Mifflin Harcourt.

Hirsch, J. (2004). *Afterimage: Film, trauma, and the Holocaust*. Temple University Press.

Hirsch, M. (1997). *Family frames: Photography, narrative, and postmemory*. Harvard University Press.

Hirsch, M. (2012). *The generation of postmemory: Writing and visual culture after the Holocaust*. Columbia University Press.

Hirsch, M. (2012). An Interview with Marianne Hirsch. Columbia University. https://cup.columbia.edu/author-interviews/hirsch-generation-postmemory

Hirsch, M., & Kacandes, I. (Eds.). (2004). *Teaching the representation of the Holocaust*. Modern Language Association of America.

Hoffmann, E. (2004). *After such knowledge: Memory, history, and the legacy of the Holocaust*. Public Affairs.

Holocaust Encyclopedia (2024). United States Holocaust Memorial Museum, Washington, DC. https://encyclopedia.ushmm.org/en

Holte, S. (2015). *Meaning and melancholy in the thought of Emmanuel Levinas*. Vandenhoeck & Ruprecht.

Horstkotte, S. (2008). Photo-text topographies: Photography and representation of space in W. G. Sebald and Monkia Maron. *Poetics Today, 29*(1), 49–78.

Hrushovski, B. (1984). Fictionality and fields of reference: Remarks on a theoretical framework in the construction of reality in fiction. *Poetics Today, 5*(2), 227–251.

Hühn, P., Meiser, J. C., Pier, J. & Schmid, W. (Eds.) (2021). *The living handbook of narratology*. Center for narratology, University of Hamburg. https://www-archiv.fdm.uni-hamburg.de/lhn/node/11.html

Hutcheon, L. (2013). *A theory of adaptation* (2nd ed.). Routledge.

Hydén, L.-C., & Antelius, E. (Eds.). (2017). *Living with dementia*. Red Globe Press.

Hydén, L.-C., & Brockmeier, J. (Eds.). (2011). *Health, illness, and culture: Broken narratives*. Routledge.

Hyvärinen, M. (2017). Foreword: Life meets narrative. In B. Schiff, A. E. McKim, & S. Patron (Eds.), *Life and narrative: The risks and responsibilities of storying experience* (pp. ix–xxv). Oxford University Press.

Insdorf, A. (2017). *Cinematic overtures: How to read opening scenes*. Columbia University Press.

Ishiguro, K. (2005). *The remains of the day*. Faber and Faber. (Original work published 1989)

Iser, W. (1972). *Der implizite Leser: Kommunikationsformen des Romans von Bunyan bis Beckett*. Fink.

Iser, W. (1978). *The act of reading: A theory of aesthetic response*. Johns Hopkins University Press.

Ivory, J. (Director) (1993). *The remains of the day* [Film]. Columbia Pictures. https://www.netflix.com

Jäckel, E. (2019). On the purpose of the Wannsee conference. In J. S. Pacy & A. Wertheimer (Eds.), *Perspectives on the Holocaust: Essays in honor of Raul Hilberg* (pp. 39–50). Routledge.

Jaggi, M. (2001). The last word. Interview with W. G. Sebald, *The Guardian*, December 21.

Jameson, F. (1992). *Signatures of the visible*. Routledge.

Keen, S. (2007). *Empathy and the novel.* Oxford University Press.

Kempinski, A. (2007). "Quel roman!" Sebald, Barthes, and the pursuit of the mother-image. In L. Patt (Ed.), *Searching for Sebald: Photography after Sebald* (pp. 456–471). Institute of Cultural Inquiry.

Kenaan, H. (2013). *The ethics of visuality: Levinas and the contemporary gaze.* I. B. Tauris.

Kerner, A. (2011). *Film and the Holocaust: New perspectives on dramas, documentaries, and experimental films.* Continuum.

Kershaw, I. (1998). *Hitler 1889–1936: Hubris.* Allen Lane.

Kershaw, I. (2000). *Hitler 1936–1945: Nemesis.* Allen Lane.

Kershaw, I. (2008). *Hitler, the Germans, and the final solution.* Yale University Press.

Kertész, I. (2004). *Fatelessness: A novel* (T. Wilkinson, Trans.). Vintage Books. (Original work published 1975)

Kilbourn, R. J. A. (2004). Architecture and cinema: The representation of memory in W. G. Sebald's *Austerlitz*. In J. J. Long & A. Whitehead (Eds.), *W. G. Sebald: A critical companion* (pp. 140–154). Edinburgh University Press.

King James Bible. Oxford University Press.

Kozloff. S. (1988). *Invisible storytellers: Voice-over narration in the American fiction film.* University of California Press.

Kracauer, S. (1965). *Theory of film: The redemption of physical reality.* Oxford University Press.

Kracauer, S. (2004). *From Caligari to Hitler: A psychological history of the German film* (revised & expanded ed.). Princeton University Press. (Original work published 1947)

Laanes, E., & Meretoja, H. (2021). Editorial: Cultural memorial forms. *Memory Studies, 14*(1), 3–9.

LaCapra, D. (1996). *Representing the Holocaust: History, theory, trauma.* Cornell University Press.

LaCapra, D. (1998). *History and memory after Auschwitz.* Cornell University Press.

LaCapra, D. (2007). Lanzmann's *Shoah*: "Here there is no why." In S. Liebmann (Ed.), *Claude Lanzmann's "Shoah": Key essays* (pp. 191–229). Oxford University Press. First published in *Critical Inquiry* 23 (Winter 1997), 231–269.

LaCapra, D. (2016) Trauma, history, memory, identity: What remains? *History and Theory, 55,* 375–400.

Lackey, M. (2012). *The modernist God state: A literary study of the Nazis' Christian reich.* Continuum.

Landsberg, A. (2004). *Prosthetic memory: The transformation of American remembrance in the age of mass culture.* Columbia University Press.

Langer, L. (1975). *The Holocaust and the literary imagination.* Yale University Press.

Langer, L. (1991). *Holocaust testimonies: The ruins of memory.* Yale University Press.

Lanser, S. (1992). *Fictions of authority: Women writers and narrative voice.* Cornell University Press.

Lanzmann, C. (Director). (1985). *Shoah* [Film]. New Yorker Films. YouTube – SvkH Archives, Part 1: https://www.youtube.com/watch?v=eNcvwHgyXcg, Part 2: https://www.youtube.com/watch?v=C-XyfftYSP0

Lanzmann, C. (1990). Le lieu et la parole. In Michel Deguy (Ed.), *Au sujet de "Shoah": Le Film de Claude Lanzmann*. Belin.

Lanzmann, C. (1991). Seminar with Claude Lanzmann, April 11, 1990. *Yale French Studies, 79,* 82–99.

Lanzmann, C. (1995). Shoah: *The complete text of the acclaimed Holocaust film*. Da Capo Press.

Lanzmann, C. (2001). *Shoah*. Gallimard.

Lanzmann, C. (2009). *Le lièvre de Patagonie: Mémoires*. Gallimard.

Lefebvre, H. (1991). *The production of space* (D. Nicholson-Smith, Trans.). Blackwell. (Original work published 1974)

Lehmann, O. V., & Synnes, O. (Eds.). (2023). *A poetic language of ageing*. Bloomsbury.

Leitch, T. (2020). *The Oxford handbook of adaptation studies*. Oxford University Press.

Levi, N., & Rothberg. M. (Eds.). (2003). *The Holocaust: Theoretical readings*. Edinburgh University Press.

Levi, P. (2005). *If this is a man* (S. Woolf, Trans.). Abacus. (Original work published 1958)

Levin, I. (2013). The social phenomenon of silence. In M. L. Seeberg, I. Levin, & C. Lenz (Eds.), *The Holocaust as active memory: The past in the present* (pp.187–197). Ashgate.

Levinas, E. (1969). *Totality and infinity: An essay on exteriority* (A. Lingis, Trans.). Duquesne University Press. (Original work published 1961)

Levinas, E. (1982). *Éthique et infini: Dialogues avec Philippe Nemo*. Fayard.

Levinas, E. (1990). Reflections on the philosophy of Hitlerism. *Critical Inquiry, 17*(1), 62–71. (Original work published 1934)

Levinas, E. (1999). *Alterity and transcendence* (M. B. Smith, Trans.). Columbia University Press. (Original work published 1995)

Leys, R. (2000). *Trauma: A genealogy*. University of Chicago Press.

Liebman, S. (Ed.). (2007a). *Claude Lanzmann's "Shoah": Key essays*. Oxford University Press.

Liebman, S. (2007b). Introduction. In S. Liebman (Ed.), *Claude Lanzmann's "Shoah": Key essays* (pp. 3–24). Oxford University Press.

Lindeperg, S. (2014). *Night and fog: A film in history* (T. Mes, Trans.). University of Minnesota Press. (Original work published 2007)

Littell, J. (2010). *The kindly ones* (C. Mandell, Trans.). Vintage. (Original work published 2006)

Littell, J. (2021). *Les bienveillantes*. Gallimard. (Original work published 2006)

Long, J. J. (2007). *W. G. Sebald: Image, archive, modernity*. Edinburgh University Press.

Long, J. J., & Whitehead, A. (Eds.). (2004). *W. G. Sebald: A critical companion*. Edinburgh University Press.

Long, R. E., & Ivory, J. (2005). *James Ivory in conversation: How Merchant Ivory makes its movies*. University of California Press.

Lothe, J. (2000). *Narrative in fiction and film: An introduction*. Oxford University Press.

Lothe, J. (2008). The title of W. G. Sebald's novel *Austerlitz*. In M. Jansson, J. Kantola, J. Lothe & H. K. Riikonen (Eds.), *Comparative approaches to European and Nordic modernisms* (pp. 109–126). Helsinki University Press.

Lothe, J. (2011). Forgiveness, history, narrative: W. G. Sebald's *Austerlitz*. In C. Fricke (Ed.), *The ethics of forgiveness: A collection of essays* (pp. 179–196). Routledge.

Lothe, J. (2012). Narrative, memory, and visual image: W. G. Sebald's *Luftkrieg und Literatur* and *Austerlitz*. In J. Lothe, S. R. Suleiman, & J. Phelan (Eds.), *After testimony: The ethics and aesthetics of Holocaust narrative for the future* (pp. 221–246). Ohio State University Press.

Lothe, J. & Hawthorn, J. (2013a). *Narrative ethics*. Rodopi.

Lothe, J. (2013b). Authority, reliability, and the challenge of reading: Jonathan Littell's *The kindly ones*. In J. Lothe & J. Hawthorn (Eds.), *Narrative ethics* (pp. 103–118). Rodopi.

Lothe, J. (2016). Narrative, testimony, fiction: The challenge of not forgetting the Holocaust. In L. Brozgal & S. Kippur (Eds.), *Being contemporary: French literature, culture, and politics today* (pp. 162–176). Liverpool University Press.

Lothe, J. (Ed.). (2017a). *Time's witnesses: Women's voices from the Holocaust*. Fledgling Press.

Lothe, J. (2017b). Introduction. In J. Lothe (Ed.), *Time's witnesses: Women's voices from the Holocaust* (pp. 1–23). Fledgling Press.

Lothe, J. (2017c). Narrative beginnings and expectations in testimony and fiction: Primo Levi compared to Samuel Steinmann and W. G. Sebald. In S. S. Grumsen, P. K. Hansen, R. A. Kraglund & H. S. Nielsen (Eds.), *Expectations: Reader assumptions and author intentions in narrative discourse* (pp. 98–116). Medusa.

Lothe, J. (2017d). Introduction. In J. Lothe (Ed.), *The future of literary studies* (pp. 9–36). Novus Press.

Lothe, J. (2018). The author's ethical responsibility and the ethics of reading. *CounterText*, 4(1), 57–77.

Lothe, J. (2019). Narrative communication as a rhetorical act: James Phelan's poetics of narrative. *Poetics Today*, 40(1), 355–365.

Lothe, J. (2020a). Aspects of evil and ethical challenges in Claude Lanzmann's *Shoah*. In O. Lysaker (Ed.), *Between closeness and evil: A Festschrift for Arne Johan Vetlesen* (pp. 333–356). Scandinavian Academic Press.

Lothe, J. (2020b). Narrative. In H. Meretoja & C. Davis (Eds.), *Trauma and literature* (pp. 152–161). Routledge.

Lothe, J. (2022). Ethics. In L. Gammelgaard et al. (Eds.), *Fictionality and literature: Core concepts revisited* (pp. 265–283). Ohio State University Press.

Lothe, J. (2023a). Literary and film narratives. In H. Meretoja & M. Freeman (Eds.), *The use and abuse of stories: New directions in narrative hermeneutics* (pp. 265–285). Oxford University Press.

Lothe, J. (2023b). Variants and consequences of violence in Iris Murdoch's *The sacred and profane love machine*. In C. Falke, V. Fareld, & H. Meretoja (Eds.), *Interpreting violence: Narrative, ethics and hermeneutics* (pp. 59–71). Routledge.

Løgstrup, K. E. (1997). *The ethical demand*. University of Notre Dame Press. (Original work published 1956)

MacIntyre, A. (1997). *After virtue: A study in moral theory*. Duckworth. (Original work published 1981)

MacIntyre, A. (1998). *A short history of ethics* (2nd ed.). University of Notre Dame Press.

Marcus, A. (2006). Kazuo Ishiguro's *The remains of the day*: The discourse of self-deception. *Partial Answers, 4*(1), 129–149.

Marrus, M., & Paxton, R. O. (2019). *Vichy France and the Jews* (2nd ed.). Stanford University Press.

Marx, F., & Schöll, J. (Eds.). (2014). *Wahrheit und Täuschung: Beiträge zum Werk Jenny Erpenbecks*. Wallstein Verlag.

McCulloh, M. R. (2003). *Understanding W. G. Sebald*. University of South Carolina Press.

McGlothlin, E. (2016). Empathetic identification and the mind of the Holocaust perpetrator in fiction: A proposed taxonomy of response. *Narrative, 24*(3), 251–276.

McGlothlin, E. (2021). *The mind of the Holocaust perpetrator in fiction and nonfiction*. Wayne State University Press.

McHale, B. (2011). Speech representation. In P. Hühn. J. C. Meister, J. Pier & W. Schmid (Eds.), *The living handbook of narratology*. Interdisciplinary center for narratology, University of Hamburg. https://www-archiv.fdm.uni-hamburg.de/lhn/node/47.html

Megaree, G. P. (Ed.) (2009–). *Encyclopedia of camps and ghettos 1933–1945* (7 vols.). Indiana University Press.

Meretoja, H. (2017). Narrative hermeneutics and the ethical potential of literature. In J. Lothe (Ed.), *The future of literary studies* (pp. 135–147). Novus Press.

Meretoja, H. (2018a). *The ethics of storytelling: Narrative hermeneutics, history, and the possible*. Oxford University Press.

Meretoja, H. (2018b). From appropriation to dialogic exploration: A non-subsumptive model of storytelling. In H. Meretoja & C. Davis (Eds.), *Storytelling and ethics: Literature, visual arts and the power of narrative* (pp. 101–121). Routledge.

Meretoja, H. (2021). Non-subsumptive memory and narrative empathy. *Memory Studies, 14*(1), 24–40.

Meretoja, H., & Davis, C. (Eds.). (2018). *Storytelling and ethics: Literature, visual arts and the power of narrative*. Routledge.

Meretoja, H., & Freeman, M. (2023). Introduction: Challenges and prospects of narrative hermeneutics in tumultuous times. In H. Meretoja & M. Freeman (Eds.), *The use and abuse of stories: New directions in narrative hermeneutics* (pp. 1–12). Oxford University Press.

Michael, R. (1981). The terrible flaw of *Night and fog. Martyrdom & Resistance, 7*(1), 13.

Miller, J. H. (1982). *Fiction and repetition: Seven English novels*. Blackwell.

Miller, J. H. (1987). *The ethics of reading: Kant, de Man, Eliot, Trollope, James, and Benjamin*. Columbia University Press.

Miller J. H. (1995). *Topographies*. Stanford University Press.

Miller, J. H. (1998). *On narrative*. University of Oklahoma Press.

Miller, J. H. (2011). *The conflagration of community: Fiction before and after Auschwitz*. University of Chicago Press.

Miller, J. H. (2015). *Communities of fiction*. Fordham University Press.

Mitchell, J. W. T. (1994). *Picture theory: Essays on verbal and visual interpretation*. University of Chicago Press.

Mondzain, M.-J. (2007/2010). La Shoah comme question de cinéma. In J.-M. Frodon (Ed.), *Le cinéma et la Shoah: Un art à l'épreuve de la tragédie du 20e siècle* (pp. 29–36). Cahiers de Cinéma. English version (2010): The Shoah as a question of cinema. In *Cinema and the Shoah: An art confronts the tragedy of the twentieh century* (A. Harrison & T. Mes, Trans.). SUNY Press.

Mosse, G. L. (1994). *Fallen soldiers: Reshaping the memory of the world wars*. Oxford University Press.

Mueller, A. C. (2014). Die jüdische Mutter in Jenny Erpenbecks Roman *Aller Tage Abend*. In F. Marx & J. Schöll (Eds.), *Wahrheit und Täuschung: Beiträge zum Werk Jenny Erpenbecks* (pp. 157–167). Wallstein Verlag.

Müller, F. (1979). *Eyewitness Auschwitz: Three years in the gas chambers*. Stein and Day.

Naguib, S.-A., & Stordalen, T. (Eds.). (2015). *The formative past and the formation of the future: Collective remembering and identity formation*. Novus Press.

Newton, A. Z. (1995). *Narrative ethics*. Harvard University Press.

Nichols, B. (1991). *Representing reality: Issues and concepts in documentary*. Indiana University Press.

Nichols, B. (2010). *Introduction to documentary* (2nd ed.). Indiana University Press.

Nora, P., & Littell, J. (2007). Conversation sur l'histoire et le roman. *Le Débat*, 2(144), 25–44.

Nussbaum, M. (1992). *Love's knowledge: Essays on philosophy and literature*. Oxford University Press.

Olick, J. K., Vinitzky-Seroussi, V., & Levy, D. (Eds.). (2011). *The collective memory reader*. Oxford University Press.

Osborn, P. (2012). Minding the gap: Mourning in the work of Murdoch and Derrida. In A. Rowe & A. Horner (Eds.), *Iris Murdoch: Texts and contexts* (pp. 110–125). Palgrave Macmillan.

Pahaut, C., & Maerten, F. (2006). *Le fort de Brendoonk: Le camp de la terreur nazi en Belgique pendant la Seconde Guerre Mondiale* (3rd ed.). Éditions Racine.

Patt, L. (2007a). Introduction. In L. Patt (Ed.), *Searching for Sebald: Photography after Sebald* (pp. 16–101). Institute of Cultural Inquiry.

Patt, L. (2007b). (Ed.) *Searching for Sebald: Photography after Sebald*. Institute of Cultural Inquiry.

Patterson, D., Berger, A. L., & Cargas, S. (Eds.). (2002). *Encyclopedia of Holocaust literature*. Oryx Press.

Pavel, T. C. (1986). *Fictional worlds*. Harvard University Press.

Pederson, J. (2018). Trauma and narrative. In J. R. Kurtz (Ed.), *Trauma and literature* (pp. 97–109). Cambridge University Press.

Pellauer, P. & Dauenhauer, B. (2022), "Paul Ricoeur." *Stanford Encyclopedia of Philosophy*. Stanford University. https://plato.stanford.edu/archives/sum2024/entries/ricoeur/

Phelan, J. (2005). *Living to tell about it: A rhetoric and ethics of character narration*. Cornell University Press.

Phelan, J. (2007). *Experiencing fiction: Judgments, progressions, and the rhetorical theory of narrative*. Ohio State University Press.

Phelan, J. (2014). Narrative ethics. In P. Hühn, J. C. Meister, J. Pier, & W. Schmid (Eds.), *The living handbook of narratology*. Interdisciplinary Center for Narratology, University of Hamburg. https://www-archiv.fdm.uni-hamburg.de/lhn/node/108.html

Phelan, J. (2017). *Somebody telling somebody else: A rhetorical poetics of narrative*. Ohio State University Press.

Phelan, J., & Martin, M. P. (1999). The lessons of "Weymouth": Homodiegesis, unreliability, ethics, and *The remains of the day*. In D. Herman (Ed.), *Narratologies: New perspectives on narrative analysis* (pp. 88–109). Ohio State University Press.

Phelan, J., & Rabinowitz, P. J. (Eds.) (2005). *A companion to narrative theory*. Blackwell.

Pollock, G. (2007). *Encounters in the virtual feminist museum: Time, space and the archive*. Routledge.

Pollock, G., & Silverman, M. (Eds.). (2011). *Concentrationary cinema: Aesthetics as political resistance in Alain Resnais's* Night and fog (1955). Berghahn Books.

Poltermann, P. (2015). Jenny Erpenbeck: "People in the west were much more easily manipulated." *The Guardian*, June 6.

Prince, G. (1991). *A dictionary of narratology*. Scholar Press.

Rancière, J. (1996). *Film fables*. Berg.

Rasson, L. (2012). How Nazis undermine their own point of view: Irony and reliability in *The kindly ones*. In A. Barjonet & L. Razinsky (Eds.), *Writing the Holocaust today: Critical perspectives on Jonathan Littell's* The kindly ones (pp. 97–110). Rodopi.

Razinsky, L. (2012). The similarity of perpetrators. In A. Barjonet & L. Razinsky (Eds.), *Writing the Holocaust today: Critical perspectives on Jonathan Littell's* The kindly ones (pp. 47–60). Rodopi.

Reiter, A. (2000). *Narrating the Holocaust*. Continuum.

Rentschler, E. (1996). *The ministry of illusion: Nazi cinema and its afterlife*. Harvard University Press.

Resnais, A. (Director). (1956). *Night and fog (Nuit et brouillard)* [Film]. Argos Films. https://vimeo.com/189672641

Richardson, B. (Ed.). (2008). *Narrative beginnings: Theories and practices*. University of Nebraska Press.

Ricoeur, P. (1984). *Time and narrative* (Vol. 1) (K. McLaughlin & D. Pellauer, Trans.). University of Chicago Press.

Ricoeur, P. (1985). *Time and narrative* (Vol. 2) (K. McLaughlin & D. Pellauer, Trans.). University of Chicago Press.

Ricoeur, P. (1988). *Time and narrative* (Vol. 3) (K. McLaughlin & D. Pellauer, Trans.). University of Chicago Press.

Ricoeur, P. (1994). *Oneself as another* (K. Blamey, Trans.). University of Chicago Press. (Original work published 1990)

Ricoeur, P. (2006). *Memory, history, forgetting* (K. Blamey & D. Pellauer, Trans.). University of Chicago Press. (Original work published 2000)

Riefenstahl, L. (Director) (1935). *Triumph of the will (Triumph des Willens)* [Film]. UFA. https://www.youtube.com/watch?v=Qgzm2Vhhq28

Rimmon-Kenan, S. (2002). *Narrative fiction: Contemporary poetics* (2nd ed.). Routledge.

Ritivoi, A. D. (2006). *Paul Ricoeur: Tradition and innovation in rhetorical theory.* State University of New York Press.

Ritivoi, A. D. (2023). Found in translation: Solicitude and linguistic hospitality in storytelling. In H. Meretoja & M. Freeman (Eds.), *The use and abuse of stories: New directions in narrative hermeneutics* (pp. 202–223). Oxford University Press.

Roth, J. K. (2005). *Ethics during and after the Holocaust: In the shadow of Birkenau.* Palgrave Macmillan.

Roth, J. K. (2009). Gray zones: The Holocaust and the failure(s) of ethics. In J. Ambrosewicz-Jacobs (Ed.), *The Holocaust: Vocies of scholars* (pp. 32–40). Austeria Publishing House.

Roth, J. K., Maxwell, E., Levy, M., & Whitworth, W. (Eds.). (2001). *Remembering for the future: The Holocaust in an age of genocide* (3 vols.). Palgrave.

Rothberg, M. (2000). *Traumatic realism: The demands of Holocaust representation.* University of Minnesota Press.

Rothberg, M. (2009). *Multidirectional memory: Remembering the Holocaust in the age of decolonization.* Stanford University Press.

Rothberg, M. (2019). *The implicated subject: Beyond victims and perpetrators.* Stanford University Press.

Rothberg, M. (2020). Trauma and the implicated subject. In C. Davis & H. Meretoja (Eds.), *The Routledge companion to literature and trauma* (pp. 201–210). Routledge.

Rothman, W. (1988). *The "I" of the camera: Essays in film criticism, history, and aesthetics.* Cambridge University Press.

Rothman, W. (1997). *Documentary film classics.* Cambridge University Press.

Rousset, D. (1946). *L'Univers concentrationnaire.* Editions de Pavois.

Said, E. W. (1975). *Beginnings: Intention and method.* Johns Hopkins University Press.

Sarkar, B., & Walker, J. (Eds.). (2010). *Documentary testimonies: Global archives of suffering.* Routledge.

Sanyal, D. (2015). *Memory and complicity: Migrations of Holocaust remembrance.* Fordham University Press.

Sarbin, T. (Ed.). (1986). *Narrative psychology: The storied nature of human conduct.* Praeger.

Sarris, A. (Ed.). (1967). *Interviews with film directors.* Avon Books.

Saxton, L. (2011). *Night and fog* and the concentrationary gaze. In G. Pollock & M. Silverman (Eds.), *Concentrationary cinema: Aesthetics as political resistance in Alain Resnais's Night and fog* (pp. 140–151). Berghahn Books.

Schacter, D. (1996). *Searching for memory: The brain, the mind, and the past.* Basic Books.

Schaffer, B. W. (1998). *Understanding Kazuo Ishiguro.* University of South Carolina Press.

Scheffel, M., Weixler, A., & Werner, L. (2014). Time. In P. Hühn, J. C. Meister, J. Pier & W. Schmid. *The living handbook of narratology.* Interdisciplinary center for narratology, University of Hamburg. https://www-archiv.fdm.uni-hamburg.de/lhn/node/106.html

Schiff, B., McKim, A. E., & Patron, S. (Eds.). (2017). *Life and narrative: The risks and responsibilities of storytelling experience.* Oxford University Press.

Schubert, K. (2016). Kein Zivilisationsbruch. Wahrscheinliche Geschichte: *Heimsuchung* (2007) und *Aller Tage Abend* (2012) von Jenny Erpenbeck. In C. Hähnel- Mesnaard &

K. Schubert (Eds.), *Störfall? Auschwitz und die ostdeutsche Literatur nach 1989* (pp. 91–108). Frank & Timme.

Sebald, W. G. (1999). *Luftkrieg und Literatur*. Carl Hanser Verlag.

Sebald, W. G. (2001). *After nature* (M. Hamburger, Trans.). Random House. (Original work published 1998)

Sebald, W. G. (2002). *Austerlitz* (A. Bell, Trans.) Vintage. (Original work published 2001)

Sebald, W. G. (2003). *Austerlitz*. Fischer. (Original work published 2001)

Sebald, W. G. (2004). *On the natural history of destruction* (A. Bell, Trans.). Modern Library. (Original work published 1999)

Seeberg, M. L., Levin, I., & Lenz, C. (Eds.) (2013). *The Holocaust as active memory: The past in the present*. Ashgate.

Sereny, G. (2006). Questioning the perpetrators: To give and to take. In H. Kramer (Ed.), *NS-Täter aus interdisziplinärer Perspektive* (pp. 121–134). Martin Meidenbauer Verlagsbuchhandlung.

Shen, D. (2011a). Unreliability. In P. Hühn, J. C. Meister, J. Pier, & W. Schmid (Eds.), *The living handbook of narratology*. Interdisciplinary center for narratology, University of Hamburg. http://lhn.sub.uni-hamburg.de/index.php/Unreliability.html

Shen, D. (2011b). What is the implied author? *Style, 45*(1), 80–98.

Shen, D. (2021). "Covert progression" and dual narrative dynamics. *Style, 55*(1), 1–28.

Silverman, K. (1996). *The threshold of the visible world*. Routledge.

Silverman, M. (2006). Horror and the everyday in post-Holocaust France: *Nuit et brouillard* and concentrationary art. *French Cultural Studies, 17*, 5–18.

Silverman, M. (2011). Fearful imagination: *Night and fog* and concentrationary memory. In G. Pollock & M. Silverman (Eds.), *Concentrationary cinema: Aesthetics as political resistance in Alain Resnais's* Night and fog (pp. 199–213). Berghahn Books.

Smith, B. L. (2024). Propaganda. In *Encyclopedia Britannica*. https://www.britannica.com/topic/propaganda

Smith, S. (2001). The trajectory of memory: Transgeneration and the pitfalls of narrative closure. In J. K. Roth, E. Maxwell, & M. Levy (Eds.), *Remembering for the future: The Holocaust in an age of genocide*, vol. 3: *Memory* (pp. 437–451). Palgrave.

Spencer, D. (2023). Narrative medicine: The book at the gates of biomedicine. In H. Meretoja & M. Freeman (Eds.), *The use and abuse of stories: New directions in narrative hermeneutics* (pp. 305–339). Oxford University Press.

Spiessens, A. (2022). Translating the perpetrator's testimony: *Kommandant in Auschwitz* (Holocaust) and *Une saison de machettes* (Rwanda). In S. Deane-Cox & A. Spiessens (Eds.), *The Routledge handbook of translation and memory* (pp. 22–41). Routledge.

Spitzer, L. (2004). "You wanted history, I give you history": Claude Lanzmann's *Shoah*. In M. Hirsch & I. Kacandes (Eds.), *Teaching the representation of the Holocaust* (pp. 412–421). Modern Language Association of America.

Stackelberg, R., & Winkle, S. A. (Eds.). (2002). *The Nazi Germany sourcebook: An anthology of texts*. Routledge.

Stam, R. (2005). *Literature through film: Realism, magic, and the art of adaptation*. Blackwell.

Storeide, A. H. (2012). *Which* narrative of Auschwitz? A narrative analysis of Laurence Rees's documentary *Auschwitz: The Nazis and "the Final Solution."* In J. Lothe, S. R. Suleiman & J. Phelan (Eds.), *After testimony: The ethics and aesthetics of Holocaust narrative for the future* (pp. 247–268). Ohio State University Press.

Suleiman, S. R. (2004). The 1.5 generation: Georges Perec's *W* or the memory of childhood. In M. Hirsch & I. Kacandes (Eds.), *Teaching the representation of the Holocaust* (pp. 372–385). Modern Language Association of America.

Suleiman, S. R. (2006). *Crises of memory and the Second World War.* Harvard University Press.

Suleiman, S. R. (2012). Performing a perpetrator as witness: Jonathan Littell's *Les Bienveillantes.* In J. Lothe, S. R. Suleiman, & J. Phelan (Eds.), *After testimony: The ethics and aesthetics of Holocaust narrative for the future* (pp. 99–119). Ohio State University Press.

Sætre, L., Lombardo, P., & Linkis, S. T. (Eds.). (2017). *Exploring text, media, and memory.* Aarhus University Press.

Taylor, C. (2009). *The culture of confession from Augustine to Foucault.* Routledge.

Teo, Y. (2014). *Ishiguro and memory.* Palgrave Macmillan.

Terdiman, R. (1993). *Present past: Modernity and the memory crisis.* Cornell University Press.

Toker, L. (2000). *Return from the archipelago: Narratives of gulag survivors.* Indiana University Press.

Toker, L. (2010). *Towards the ethics of form in fiction: Narratives of cultural remission.* Ohio State University Press.

Toker, L. (2012). *The kindly ones* and the "scorched earth" principle. In A. Barjonet & L. Razinsky (Eds.), *Writing the Holocaust today: Critical perspectives on Jonathan Littell's* The kindly ones (pp. 153–163). Rodopi.

Toker, L. (2013). The Holocaust in Russian literature. In A. Rosen (Ed.), *The literature of the Holocaust* (pp. 118–130). Cambridge University Press.

Toker, L. (2019). *Gulag literature and the literature of Nazi camps: An intercontextual reading.* Indiana University Press.

Toker, L. (2022). Paralipsis and intention(ality). *Neohelicon, 49,* 13–23. https://doi.org/10.1007/s11059-021-00588-9

Troupin, O. Y. (2020). *Cancrizans:* The quest for origin and the assault on alterity in Jonathan Littell's *The kindly ones. Partial Answers, 18*(2), 315–334.

Trevor-Roper, H. (2013). *The last days of Hitler* (5th ed.). Pan Macmillan. (Original work published 1947)

Ursano, Robert T., Fullerton, C. S., Weisaeth, L., & Raphael, B. (Eds.). (2017). *Textbook of disaster psychiatry* (2nd ed.). Cambridge University Press.

Vetlesen, A. J. (2005). *Evil and human agency: Understanding collective evildoing.* Cambridge University Press.

Vice, S. (2000). *Holocaust fiction.* Routledge.

Vice, S. (2011). *Shoah.* Palgrave Macmillan.

Walker, J. (2005). *Trauma cinema: Documenting incest and the Holocaust.* University of California Press.

Walkowitz, R. (2001). Ishiguro's floating worlds. *ELH, 68*(4), 1049–1076.

"Wannsee Conference and the 'Final Solution.'" (2024). *Holocaust Encyclopedia*, https://encyclopedia.ushmm.org/content/en/article/wannsee-conference-and-the-final-solution

Watts, C. (1977). *Conrad's* Heart of darkness: *A critical and contextual discussion*. Mursia International.

Weber, M. R. (2003). Die fantastische befragt die pedantische Genauigkeit: Zu den Abbildungen in W. G. Sebalds Werken. *Text+Kritik: Zeitschrift für Literatur, 158*, 63–74.

Welsh, D. (1983). *Propaganda and the German cinema, 1933–1945*. Oxford University Press.

Wiesel, E. (1978). Trivializing the Holocaust: Semi-fact and semi-fiction. *The New York Times*, April 16.

Wiesel, E. (2004). *Night; Day; The accident: A trilogy*. Hill and Wang.

Wilson, E. (2011). Resnais and the dead. In G. Pollock & M. Silverman (Eds.), *Concentrationary cinema: Aesthetics as political resistance in Alain Resnais's* Night and fog (pp. 126–139). Berghahn Books.

Wolfe, A. (2011). *Political evil: What it is and how to combat it*. Vintage.

Woolf, Virginia (1998). *Orlando: A biography* (R. Bowlby, Ed.). Oxford University Press. (Original work published 1928)

Young, J. E. (1988). *Writing and rewriting the Holocaust: Narrative and the consequences of interpretation*. Indiana University Press.

Young, J. E. (1993). *The texture of memory: Holocaust memorials and meaning*. Yale University Press.

Young, J. E. (2010). The texture of memory: Holocaust memorials in history. In A. Erll & A. Nünning (Eds.), *A companion to cultural memory studies* (pp. 357–365). De Gruyter.

Zetterberg Gjerlevsen, S. (2016). Fictionality. In P. Hühn, J. C. Meister, J. Pier, & W. Schmid (Eds.), *The living handbook of narratology*. Interdisciplinary center for narratology, University of Hamburg. https://www-archiv.fdm.uni-hamburg.de/lhn/node/138.html

Index